CUBANS

Cubans

Voices of Change

Lynn Geldof

St. Martin's Press
New York

Library of Congress Cataloging-in-Publication Data

Geldof, Lynn.
    Cubans : voices of change / Lynn Geldof.
      p.   cm.
    ISBN 0-312-07689-4 (pbk.)
    1. Cuba—Politics and government—1959-   2. Cuba—Social
conditions—1959-   3. Oral history. I. Title.
F1788.G36   1992
972.9106′4—dc20   92-3627
                                                                    CIP

First published in Great Britain as *Cubans* by Bloomsbury Publishing Ltd.

First U.S. Edition: June 1992
10 9 8 7 6 5 4 3 2 1

For my father, Bob Geldof

A NOTE ON CUBAN CURRENCY

1 peso = 1 dollar approximately. The black market rate is 7 pesos.

Acknowledgments

I would especially like to thank Marge Zimmerman, Martine Hernández and Pata Aguilar who were there in the bad times, always, and without whose support this book would not have materialised.

My sister, Cléo McFarland, was also a rock throughout.

Corinna Chute brought light and balm.

A warm thank you must go to my Cuban friends who provided entertainment and often resolved seemingly intractable problems usually to do with my car.

Then there are the many good folk who supplied logistical back-up in Cuba, the United States and Ireland: Meic and Lila Haines and family, Monica Melamid and Rafael Andreu, Stieg Forsberg and Nitza Kakossaios, Roy and Aisling Foster and family, Judy Appelbaum and Betsy Cohn, Johnny Fox and friends, Michèle Clear and Robert Navan.

In New York, Sandra Levinson pointed me in useful directions.

Bob Hobby cheerily developed my photographs.

Gary MacEoin was a tremendous source of inspiration as was the late Phyllis McGee.

My housemate, Paddy Woodworth, has been a stoic. The solitary condition of this kind of work makes for bad company. He has borne the long winter graciously.

Jeananne Crowley did tremendous PR work.

Of course, without Colm Tóibín's insistence and instructions,

ACKNOWLEDGEMENTS

his continuous remote control of progress and final imprimatur, I would never have moved to do anything.

To him and my brother, Bob Geldof, who undertook the major task of placing the idea of this book with my publishers, I am eternally grateful.

Finally, I would like to warmly thank Liz Calder at Bloomsbury who commissioned *Cubans*; Mary Tomlinson and Alison Mansbridge who saw it through the press; and Alexa de Ferranti of the publicity department.

Contents

Introduction xi
Chronology xix
Abbreviations xxiii

IN CUBA

1   Fichu Menocal 3
2   Cipriano Chinea Palero 25
3   Carmen Comella 34
4   May FitzGerald 42
5   Arcadio Suárez Rodríguez 49
6   Pablo Blanche 55
7   Maribel Santos Ferro 59
8   Carlos Fundora 70
9   Ramón Fernández Larrea 92
10   Arturo Cuenca 109
11   Raimundo Sánchez 116
12   Marta Beatriz Bartelemy 125
13   Tania Escalante 133
14   Damián Martínez 146
15   Raúl Ygarza Bracho 150
16   Juan Carlos Aliaga 155
17   Vilma Garzón 161
18   Charlot Mesa 164
19   Alfonso López 171

CONTENTS

IN THE US

20 Carlos García   189
21 María Cristina Herrera   204
22 César Luaices   217
23 Msgr Brian Walsh   225
24 Andrés Gómez   239
25 Carlos Alberto Montaner   258
26 René José Silva   266
27 Elba and Jorge   280
28 Mirta Ojito   297
29 Andrés Santana   307

THE ACADEMICS

30 Rafael Hernández   319
31 Wayne Smith   334
32 Jorge Domínguez   345

Further Reading   357

Introduction

My earliest association with Cuba came about when, as an adolescent, I contemplated the possibility of apocalypse from beneath my classroom desk while reciting the Sorrowful Mysteries of the Rosary. One of the nuns had just advised us that we might never see our families again, and the sky had darkened. It was the Cuban Missile Crisis of 1962.

In sharp contrast to this memory was the period of three and a half years that I spent in the country, in 1985–9, which were among the most exhilarating (and frustrating) of my life.

During that time I would occasionally take a holiday back home, where the question invariably asked was, 'What's it like?' People wanted to know what life there was about, how people saw their country, who the Cubans were. I commented on this to my writer friend Colm Tóibín, and he suggested a book. We thought it should be Cubans on their own terms: Cubans talking – about their lives, about Cuba.

It seemed obvious that a large part of the book should be given over to the present generations, the first of which is the generation of the Revolution itself. A major part of Cuban history will die out with them, and it seemed extremely important to hear their voices. The second generation were children at the time of the Revolution and are now in their thirties and forties. The last generation, the young people, are the products of the Revolution, the fulfilment (or not) of the dream.

Part II is given over to the circumstances and relationship to the island of the approximately 1 million Cubans who live in the US, mostly in Miami but also in New York.

In the final section I let the academics speak on the direction Cuba, and the Cuban Revolution, is taking.

Only three of the subjects are non-Cubans: two Irish people and one American. They were included for their particular connections with Cuba and I think they contribute significantly to an overview of the past thirty-odd years.

On my own initiative and as a precaution against possible reprisal, I changed the identity of one person only.

So far as possible I stayed out of the conversation with the men and women in this book. I would simply ask them to tell me about their lives or an aspect of them. Often it was difficult not to contest some issue. I also found younger people were disappointingly brief in their responses. I was deeply moved by many of the people I spoke to and found others hilarious. One facet of Cuban conversational skills I enjoyed – apart from a distinct verbal facility – was a tendency to use direct speech when recounting an event involving other people, and to employ a variety of voices to cover the different characters. At times it was difficult to keep up with and pitiful to transcribe – theatre without the visual back-up. And then there was the rhetorical 'why?' and the Hispanic tag 'no?' both of which I love. The latter is particularly hard to accommodate in English.

I decided to leave the word *compañero/a* in the original because it has a multitude of meanings from pal to comrade, long-time lover to companion. It is also the correct form of address in Cuba, covering Sir, Madam, Mr, Mrs, Ms. It is how you attract someone's attention. In Miami, of course, it must be used with the utmost discretion to avoid offence and contumely.

Inevitably, and as anticipated, a pattern emerged in the conversations. A number of the older people bring oral history of nationhood finally achieved.

In this my own background helped me perhaps appreciate aspects of Cuban life and thought that others might not so readily identify with. The similarities, in broad strokes, between the history and geo-political location of my country, Ireland, and that of Cuba are important. We are both tiny islands in the shadow of a major world power and have both had to fight, bloodily, for the right to assert national identity and sovereignty. Even in this last aspect there is a common thread in that both, at the point of independence, had to cede a portion of territory to the powerful neighbour: Ireland, the six counties of Northern Ireland; Cuba, the Guantánamo Naval Base (see p.49).

When towards the end of my stay in Havana I finally saw *Memories of Underdevelopment** by Tomás Gutiérrez Alea, one of Cuba's foremost film directors, I was struck. The hero, a son of the upper middle classes, opts to stay on after the 1959 Revolution, having seen his family off to Miami. Remote from events taking place around him, he reflects at one point on the nature of underdevelopment and the chaos of survival living: life as a series of reflexes to random events where there is no planning and no interrelation between things.

Though Cuba was never the poorest or most illiterate country of the Americas, as a virtual protectorate of the US the distribution of wealth and land followed the neo-colonial pattern, with most of the economy concentrated in the hands of the few and much of the profits reverting to US patrons. The majority of Cuban people depended on that structure for survival, but beyond survival there was nothing. The Revolution, then, was the vehicle by which Cuba might emerge from that violent state.

Some of Cuba's older generation can testify to the insecurity of the dispossessed before Fidel Castro came to power. The divisions in society are set in relief by Fichu Menocal's description of the good life: 'And we forgot absolutely what was below. We drifted so high on that cloud of golden prosperity . . .' (See p.5.)

In many respects my own perceptions of Cuba over the period of my stay parallel the changes which emerge between the generations in this collection of voices. As Jean Stubbs noted in the preface to her splendid book *Cuba: The Test of Time:* 'Havana looks very different flying in from Paris, London or New York than from Mexico City, Kingston or Managua.' I flew in from

---

* Based on the book of the same title, *Memorias del subdesarollo*, by Edmundo Desnoes.

Central America on Christmas Day 1985, and the sight of Cuban children, after the poverty and desolation I had witnessed, was a thrill. Here the bellies were full and the hair shiny. There were no rubbish-dump scavengers.

As time progressed, like the younger people, I took this comparative prosperity and security as given and could become more objectively critical of, and less apologetic for, day-to-day problems – bad management; bad policies, often; dysfunctional democratic centralism. An article in the Communist Youth newspaper *Juventud rebelde* in October 1988 addressed the issue:

> [The problem is] the decision-making process, the trouble and effort that goes into finding solutions to the country's problems is conducted in such silence that it makes people think: those up there don't have a clue about what's going on, or they aren't doing anything about it.

The young generation is confident and impatient, and a sizeable sector of it wants access to consumer goods. Their concerns are more appropriate to young people of the developed world but are none the less real. Miami, not Managua, is their reference point. They want cars and videos and foreign travel and fancy gear. It is a paradox of the Revolution that this should be so: by providing youth with a guaranteed base-line of security, it has allowed them to want more worldly things. As Professor Jorge Domínguez, in the final section of the book, notes: 'in many ways what is interesting, I think, is that the alienation of the young is made possible by the successes of the Revolution'. (See p.345.) No underdeveloped country can meet that demand.

The notion of Cuba as a monolithic state has gone. These interviews were mainly recorded in the year before the climate in Eastern Europe was so radically to change. As such, they are testimony to the divergence and openness of opinion then prevalent. Rather than the pressured response to a dramatically evolving situation, they are a reflection of and on a particular reality at a particular time: a freeze-frame of Cuban society as the elements for change come into focus, anticipating to some extent the events of the winter of 1989.

Of course, the main opposition lives in exile on the other side of the Straits of Florida, though a number of illegal human-rights organisations have sprung up in Cuba in the last four years. The configuration of these has shifted and changed as leaders have left the country, been imprisoned or have fallen into feuding among themselves.

Opinion in Miami is not monolithic either. There have been three major waves of migration to the US from Cuba in the latter half of this century. Prior to the Revolution, there was the inevitable magnetic draw of the rich metropolis promising a better life. Those that left after it, in the 1960s, were also economic refugees, but they fled to protect their interests, bringing their wealth with them. This group became what is the motor of political opposition to Fidel Castro. And finally, there are the 125,000 who left the island in the Mariel boat lift of 1980. Again, the motive then was mainly the quest for a better life.

The seeds of the civil war that never happened, thanks to geography (though pockets of resistance to the Revolution held out in the Escambray Mountains until 1965, with the help of US arms drops), are now beginning to stir again with the collapse of the socialist bloc. The chairman of the Cuban American National Foundation (see p.272), Jorge Mas Canosa, one of the strongest lobbyists in Washington and the brains behind Radio and TV Martí, has set himself up as president of a government in exile, and the paramilitary organisation Alpha 66 are in training again.

All this is musical accompaniment to the continuing *danse macabre* the US has locked itself into with Cuba in response to its daring to challenge the recycled, but effectively unchanging, Monroe Doctrine of 1823, whereby the US arrogates the right to interfere in the countries of the hemisphere to protect American interests and lives. Indeed, in that same year, the then Secretary of State, John Quincy Adams, described Cuba in terms of an apple whose gravitational pull would naturally let it fall into the lap of the US. The US did, of course, enjoy the fruit for over half a century, only to have it taken away in 1959. For this there is no forgiveness or accommodation. As Dr Wayne Smith says: 'Cuba has the same effect on US administrations that the full moon used to have on werewolves: they just lose their rationality at the mention of Castro or Cuba.' (See p.340)

So, Cuba's geo-strategic location has been a determining factor in modern Cuban history. José Martí called it 'geographic fatalism' and noted in May 1895:

The Antilles lie at a pivotal point in America. If enslaved, they would be nothing more than a bridge for an imperialist republic's war against the suspicious and superior world already preparing to deny it power; nothing more than a fortress for an American Rome.

The Cuban Revolutionary Party founded by Martí in 1892 to fight the Second War of Independence was the first politically organised independence movement in Latin America. Martí emphasised unity and the single party as the main weapons against the oppressor. These remain an axiom of present-day Cuban politics.

US intervention frustrated the emergence of a true nation state after independence from Spain. Some eighteen months after the 1959 Revolution it imposed a crippling economic embargo still in force thirty-one years later. (See p.351.) It exerts pressure on international financial institutions to deny Cuba credit. Nor did it eschew military intervention in the abortive Bay of Pigs invasion.

One of the characteristics of Cuba and Cubans which I hope comes across here is the intriguing way it and they defy neat classification. Cuba is an anomaly, really, neither fish nor fowl in terms of political models, where certain (and, indeed, uncertain) political forces are historically fused and embodied in the persona of Fidel Castro.

The epic quality of the Revolution itself; the often quixotic deeds of daring and valour that it inspired; and the youth, charisma and commitment of its leaders became legend and religion. Cuban nationhood was born on 1 January 1959, and by 1961 socialism had become its safeguard.

This is, crucially, the opposite to the situation obtaining in Eastern Europe until 1989.

Despite a $5 billion annual subsidy from the Soviet Union, it is too simple to label Cuba a satellite. The marriage has always been one of convenience, with Cuba acting independently in most areas of foreign policy. To give just one example, the Soviet Union has, in the past (I am thinking here of the invasion of Czechoslovakia), had to pull Cuba into line by threatening to cut oil supplies.

But what is to happen to Cuba, in Cuba now? Before the collapse of Eastern Europe the question was, how would Cuba survive the death of Fidel Castro? Today, of course, the question has become, how will Cuba and Castro survive this shift in world politics? Until now, Cuba's extreme vulnerability to the US has been offset by its relations with Eastern Europe and the Soviet Union. As the US journalist Marc Cooper writing in the *New Statesman & Society* (11 May 1990) put it:

> Thinking about Cuba's future puts to the test not only the Cubans' capacity for self-examination and criticism, but also raises the question of what political choices America is willing to permit the third world. If it automatically discounts the possibility of a revolution reforming itself and surviving, then the only alternatives it offers an underdeveloped nation like Cuba is to be an Albania or a Panama, if not an El Salvador.

I returned to Cuba for three weeks in June 1990 after a year's absence and was surprised to find the country in the throes of just such an examination, with practically all the issues raised here under nationwide discussion.

Much, of course, will depend on the willingness or ability of the Soviet Union to maintain its support. And while short-term assurances have been received, everything, firstly, depends on the survival of that union. Of Cuba's trade, 69 per cent is with the USSR.

The ball, essentially, always lands back in the US court. Can an accommodation be found and Cuba given the political space to breathe or will the vengeful empire squeeze the life breath out of it?

Cuba compelled me to examine new avenues of thought and to be more respectful in judgment. I hope this book goes some way to answering the questions I was originally asked. And, further, that it stimulates honest debate.

Lynn Geldof
Dublin, March 1991

Chronology

1868–78 First War of Independence against the Spanish led by Carlos Manuel de Céspedes.

1895–8 Second War of Independence led by José Martí, Antonio Maceo and Máximo Gómez. Martí, poet, essayist, philosopher and National Hero, is killed in battle. The US joins in when victory is at hand and then occupies the island for four years (1899–1902).

1901 In return for withdrawal of US troops, among other pressures, Cuba accepts the Platt Amendment which is appended to the new Cuban constitution granting the US rights of intervention. It remains in effect until 1934.

1902 20 May: Cuba becomes a republic.

1903 Under continuing pressure, Cuba agrees a lease, in perpetuity, with the US for the 117 sq. mile area that is now the Guantánamo Naval Base.

1920 'Danza de los Millones' (Dance of the Millions). A short-lived period of prosperity as a result of high world market prices for sugar.

1924–33 Dictatorship of Gerardo Machado.

1934 After less than one year as president, Dr Ramón Grau San Martín is forced out of office by Fulgencio Batista at the head of the military. First Batista regime lasts until 1944.

1952 10 March: in a coup d'état Batista overthrows the government of Carlos Prío Socarrás.

1953	26 July: the Moncada Barracks attack marks the beginning of the insurrection against Batista from which the 26 July Movement (M-26-7) took its name.
1956	Fidel Castro, Raúl Castro, Che Guevara and seventy-nine others set out from Mexico in the yacht *Granma* to take Cuba. Arrangements go badly wrong and only twelve survive the landing. They take to the *sierra* to launch the guerrilla campaign against Batista. The Rebel Army (Ejército Rebelde) and Radio Rebelde, inaugurated by Che Guevara, come into being.
1959	The Cuban Revolution. On New Year's Eve 1958, Batista flees the country and the Rebel Army under Che Guevara enters Havana on 1 January.
1960	The US imposes economic embargo in October.
1961	The US breaks diplomatic relations with Cuba on 3 January. The Literacy Campaign is launched in the same month and illiteracy is brought down from 24 per cent to 4 per cent in that year.
	16 April: Castro declares socialist nature of Revolution.
	17–19 April: Bay of Pigs (Playa Girón) invasion defeated.
1965	The Communist Party of Cuba is formed.
1967	Che Guevara is killed in Bolivia.
1968	Nationalisation of last private businesses.
1970	Failure of 10 million tonne sugar harvest.
1972	Cuba becomes a member of the Council for Mutual Economic Assistance (CMEA or Comecon).
1975	Cuban troops sent to Angola.
1977	Ban on travel to Cuba by US citizens lifted by President Jimmy Carter and the two countries open Interests Sections with own diplomatic staff.
1978	*El diálogo*: a group of Cuban Americans found the Committee of Seventy-five with the aim of establishing a dialogue between the exile community and the island authorities.
1979	Cuban Americans are permitted to visit their families in Cuba.

Chronology

1980	1 April: using a minibus, twelve people seeking asylum crash through Peruvian Embassy gates.
	Cuba announces anyone wishing to leave can be picked up at the port of Mariel. Some 125,000 people leave the country.
1984	In December, Cuba and the US sign Immigration Accord whereby Cuba agrees to take back 2,746 Mariel 'excludables' and the US accepts an annual quota of 20,000 Cubans.
1985	Radio Martí, the anti-Castro station broadcast to Cuba, is launched in Miami and Cuba suspends Immigration Accord.
1986	Third Congress of the Cuban Communist Party initiates 'rectification' campaign.
	The Cuban Catholic Church holds ENEC conference on the role and function of the Church in Cuba.
1987	November: the 1984 Immigration Accord is restored.
1988	Angola and Cuba win the battle of Cuito Cuanavale which brings South Africa to the negotiating table.
	In December two peace treaties governing the withdrawal of South African and Cuban troops from Angola, and setting a timetable for the independence of Namibia, are signed by Angola, South Africa and Cuba.
1989	April: President Gorbachev visits Cuba.
	Four senior army and state security officers are tried and executed on drug-trafficking charges including a Hero of the Republic of Cuba, General Arnaldo Ochoa Sánchez. Ten others are jailed in the same connection. Later, the Minister of the Interior, General José Abrantes, and others are imprisoned on related charges including corruption and abuse of power.
1990	TV Martí starts up trial transmissions via a balloon anchored off the Florida Keys.

Abbreviations

CDR	Comité de Defensa de la Revolucíon (Committee for the Defence of the Revolution)
DAAFAR	Defensa Antiaérea y Fuerza Aérea Revolucionaria (Anti-aircraft Defence and Revolutionary Airforce)
FAPLA	Forças Armadas Populares para a Libertação de Angola (People's Armed Forces for the Liberation of Angola)
FAR or MINFAR	Fuerzas Armadas Revolucionarias, or Ministerio de (Revolutionary Armed Forces, or Ministry of)
FMC	Federación de Mujeres Cubanas (Federation of Cuban Women)
FMLN	Frente Farabundo Martí de Liberacíon Nacional (Farabundo Martí National Liberation Front)
ICAIC	Instituto Cubano del Arte e Industria Cinemategráficos (Cuban Film Institute)
ICRT	Instituto Cubano de Radio y Televisión (Cuban Institute of Radio and Television)
ISA	Instituto Superior de Arte (Higher Institute of Art)
MINAL	Ministerio de Alimentación (Ministry of Food)
MININT	Ministerio del Interior (Ministry of the Interior)
MPLA	Movimento Popular para a Libertação de Angola (Popular Movement for the Liberation of Angola)
PCC	Partido Comunista de Cuba (Communist Party of Cuba)
UJC	Unión de Jovenes Comunistas (Young Communist Union)

ABBREVIATIONS

UNEAC   Unión de Escritores y Artistas de Cuba (Union of Writers and Artists of Cuba)

UNITA   União Nacional para a Independencia Total de Angola (National Union for the Total Independence of Angola)

In Cuba

1

Fichu Menocal

Feliciana Menocal — Fichu — lives in the converted coach-house of the family residence built by her grandfather in the Vedado district of Havana. She is the grandniece of Mario G. Menocal, the US-approved President of Cuba from 1912 to 1920. The open living and kitchen area of the house gives on to a patio full of tropical vegetation, some planted in old toilet bowls. The rooms are filled with objets d'art, ceramics, some of which she makes herself, and family portraits and paintings. She is keeping an eye on one of her grandchildren. Her daughter, Alicia, is in the bedroom. Fichu is fifty-eight. Our conversation is in English.

24 January 1989

Well, my family – from both sides, mother and father – they were Cuban for 300 years, maybe 400. I don't know, but both sides of the family are in a genealogical book written on the history of Cuban families by the Conde de Santacruz [called] *Historia de las familias cubanas* . . . Really, an extremely interesting study. Very, very well done. At a time when very few people did this kind of very serious research, this man did. And, well, that's something important from the point of view of a lot of people. Because not every family was included in it, only the families that this fellow decided that were important enough. And *eh,* my family was rich. Not so rich as to be millionaires, but they were very well-to-do. And they were very well accepted. And they had been accepted for generations.

3

Of course, after what we call '*Danza de los Millones*',* after the First World War, a new lot of very rich people came. And also after the *Guerra de Independencia* [the second Independence War], the real Cubans, the land-rich, became very poor, or they felt very much the pinch. Because they had to give a lot for the Independence War. Although Cubans won their independence, they lost their prosperity as families, and the new rich were the Spanish that stayed in the cities and profited from this upset, *eh*, very upset situation, and also they had some cash to start business with the Americans.

But anyway, my family still was very well recognised and well-to-do. Very well, my parents, my grandparents, although I also could notice from the early times that my parents were more cultured than others. And I could realise that [from] the way they chose to decorate their houses and how they chose better quality pictures and not just normal reproductions that you can buy from any museums. But, well, that I just took for granted, that was the normal medium. I didn't realise, I wasn't aware of the difference of the stratas in society . . . I remember, for example, I never knew what discrimination was and I thought we didn't have any discrimination in Cuba. I really felt the horrors of discrimination when I first went to the States and travelled. I was fourteen when I first went to Miami, [and] from that moment I realised what discrimination was. We didn't have that discrimination in Cuba to that size, up to that depth and horror, but yet we did have, there was.

I remember when I was twelve, in 1944, Grau [Dr Ramón Grau San Martín] came into power by very popular, democratic elections. Very highly celebrated in the States as being very popular, very democratic. Those years, well, it was a second wave of prosperity again by a war, when sugar reached a very high price and everybody became rich in Cuba. Well, everybody had money, so it was very easy for anyone to be a president. But then he proved how dishonest a president can be, and all the evils – not all the evils, even more evils – came to Cuba . . . I realised my father was very much against all this *bandillismo, gangsterismo*, all this *eh* . . . *robo*,

* Dance of the Millions – a short-lived period of prosperity in 1920 as a result of high world market prices for sugar.

4

terrible theft and corruption, horrible corruption . . . but still, well, socially life went on like in a fairy tale, we drifted on clouds of prosperity . . . we adorned ourselves in golden lace, and no matter where we drifted, everybody was happy, we were the happiest, we were the richest, everybody was fine, everybody was lovely. And families just . . . there was a rivalry – who was going to have a more fantastic party. Parties that could cost $50,000. At that time that was an incredible amount. And these parties were thrown, and to be selected, to be invited to one of those parties was really the most . . . Well, I don't know.

I practically went to all those parties. And we forgot absolutely what was below. We drifted so high on that cloud of golden prosperity, nobody could remember, everybody just went to Paris and bought their frocks. Summer frocks, winter things . . . it was a lovely but such an unreal situation. When everybody decided, who cares? You know, that sort of society. Who cares very much whether the President is just so-and-so . . . well, he's just a politician, we are not politicians, we are above politics. We are the ruling class, the economic class, and we are the most important people because we are the richest and we come from the better class. And who cares whether Grau or Prío [Carlos Prío Socarrás] . . . well, after all, somebody has to be there and nobody wants to dirty their hands. We just left politics for politicians, we are just the most, the better, the fantastic people . . . Everybody, they either had a Florentine château or a Versailles-like château and everybody was rolling in millions. I remember I went to see a friend of mine – she was having a fantastic party: the first birthday of her first-born. And she had a copy, I think it [her house] was a copy of the Malmaison. And in her bathroom, all covered with mirrors, her dressing-room, there was, for example, a shell just full of strings of real pearls. A beautiful silver shell and her strings of pearls, real pearls, of course, were there, and all her jewels were presented . . . and when I look back on that display of wealth, who could think at the time that anybody in Cuba was really miserable? Who could think at that time that anybody in Cuba was hungry, when rich people had so much?

We were so wealthy. I mean, it's not that my family, my immediate family, was so wealthy, but we were wealthy enough, and anyway we were completely accepted in that medium. There were families that had much more. Though extremely wealthy families were the ones that came into wealth after Independence. But anyway, everybody was wealthy enough. We were all accepted.

And how were you groomed as a young woman? What was your education?

Oh (*laughs*) we were groomed to speak perfect English. And also possibly perfect French. To be perfect hostesses. To enjoy and admire everything that came from mainly the States or France. And we were groomed to accept rich Americans . . . not exactly as our equals, but we had to show them that we actually were better than them. But in a very delicate and diplomatic way we had to show them that they were just upstarts in such a delicate way, just showing them how cultured and how wealthy we were and how luxurious life could be in this little paradise.

Meanwhile, well, events were brewing in the underground, I mean really in the basement, there wasn't really an organised movement [but] below our sights, things were brewing and we were so happy as, well, I suppose as Louis XVI was on the day of the Bastille when he wrote (*laughs*) on that fatalic day, he wrote in his diary: '*Rien*'. To him that day was empty, nothing happened on 14 July 1789. For us nothing was happening except who is getting married and which Paris couturier is going to prepare her wedding gown and where are they going for their honeymoon. Is it Venice or is it just Paris or who is going to have the most fantastic wedding? I remember a wedding when they brought from Paris the pastries, the pastry men, and they stayed here and they made a fantastic business afterwards, even after the Revolution. I remember this fantastic wedding. You had to go and see the wedding presents. There was a silver room; there was the coral room; there was the jewels room; and eventually you came from one room where everything was on display with a card, of course, of who sent it, and eventually you reach to the golden room. I don't know whether there was a diamond room, I can't remember, but I still remember the golden room and then another display with cards that said, say, 'Mumsy will give me my house.' Popsy was giving her all the furniture. And an uncle, Uncle So-and-so, well, every member of the family was giving her an amount of money so that whatever. I suppose it was a blank cheque. Just buy furniture, just buy decoration so that they would build this Malmaison château. They did eventually. That is where I found this shell, this enormous shell (*laughs*) full of, *eh,* this array of real strings of pearls.

Well, and meanwhile, practically unknown to most of us, mainly also unknown by me, all this, the poor section of the country was brewing . . . And things came to happen when Bastista [Fulgencio Batista] took over and kicked out Prío Socarrás in 1952. Ah, and then, just one year later, the Moncada.* And the Cuban people could not really believe there was a democracy because officially they had the right to vote, but they couldn't, they didn't have the least idea how to vote, and vote for what? Vote for the rich egoistic people that were having $50,000 fiestas; that were travelling every year to Europe; that were having a grand time? Or voting for the corrupt politicians, the gangsters, voting for the business people that were selling our country to the Americans to be the prostitution centre? That was the right they had. There was no other right. It was a fake. And why should they defend Prío? Why should they defend the rich? They had no part of that. Of course they were very glad when things started to brew up, when they heard that something was happening in the Moncada. It was just a rumour. It was squashed, like the elephant can squash a little ant. And the rumour, even the news, nobody knew who Fidel Castro was or what he was. But anyway, it came slowly, the idea seeped that somebody was fighting for something and there was hope. And it really was a very completely *sui generis* and original movement. And we started hearing news that we could hardly believe. I had never heard the words of hope for a different world until I started hearing news on the radio, on Radio Rebelde, that we were being persecuted . . . it was the first time that I became really socially aware and things that I had sometimes

---

* The Moncada Barracks attack, marking the beginning of the insurrection against Batista, on 26 July 1953; this is the event from which the 26 July Movement took its name.

accepted, that people were born rich or were born poor but that they were condemned always to be poor or always to be rich . . . oh, so many things started to brew and I began to question everything that I used to believe in. (*Sighs*)

During the two or three last years when Fidel Castro managed to come, that was at the highest point of the frivolity of the high society in Cuba; the highest point of corruption at a political level; and the highest point of persecution against every single person. The levels were incredible. And for the first time in these thirty or forty years, people started believing that there could be a change. Nobody was really very sure of what this change could mean, but it was a change. Then, well, everybody knows what happened. How incredible it was when Batista simply deserted. It was sort of . . . it was incredible really because at the time that he deserted he had practically 50,000, even 100,000 men completely armed. And he was in full control of practically every single garrison. And he had the complete support of the Americans. And he had the support of the economic class. But of course, to be on the safe side, they [the economic class] were also giving some money to the rebels, thinking that they were going to buy security. The truth, maybe you can understand if you go to Santa Clara, and you realise that the rebels at the time that Batista left, they were practically going to cut off the island in two at the Santa Clara point.

But, thank God, well, he was wiser than Somoza,* and maybe that's why he died in bed of cancer and he wasn't blown off. Just going there he saved Cuba of another 100,000 deaths. In the end he would have been thrown out, because by that time there was such a consciousness of what it meant and such a hate for Batista that it was just a question of maybe one or two more years of extremely blood-filled, bloody, very bloody struggle, but they would have won anyway. So we were saved of those two bloody years.

He left and there was the apotheosis of triumph. I had never heard Fidel until he spoke from Santiago de Cuba and it was nationally broadcasted.† Because whenever he was able to talk from Radio Rebelde, well, the broadcast received was very bad

---

* Anastasio Somoza of Nicaragua, who held on to power until the end, when the Sandinistas finally overthrew him, in 1979.
† Castro's inaugural address, on 2 January 1959.

and generally it was short messages or very short speeches and it was very difficult reception. But that was the first time I heard Fidel. Frankly I was so moved, so deeply moved, and from then on . . . I think he really is a political genius. He sent his two best commanders – Che [Guevara] and Camilo [Cienfuegos] – immediately, to take control of the two most important military garrisons in Havana, but he took his time, because actually he was not well known. His picture had never been published. He was a legendary hero. But how could they, the press here, publish his picture? And besides, if anybody had managed to see his photograph, it was the photograph of a very young man in his very early twenties, not the real Fidel that came down from the mountains, also a very young man, but with a beard and in his thirties, his early thirties. In fact I remember that he had been here in this house because he was, yes, he studied law together with my two brothers. And he came many times here to share his studies with my brothers, and even at that time he was famous for being a political leader.

At that time we . . . *eh (breaks into Spanish)* student leaders had stature, no? Like political leaders but at university level. Even then you could tell he was anxious to be a leader and he had charisma. He was someone who stood out, and I remember perfectly when he came here the first few times to discuss things with my brothers or to talk about the forthcoming exams – he came two or three times – and then my mother realised that he was armed, that he had a pistol on him, which wasn't at all unusual. In those days anyone would carry a pistol. Besides, it was perfectly logical since there were shoot-outs. I'm talking about before 1952.

(In English again) But anyway I remember well that he used to come. He used to come here to study sometimes or to check about exam dates etcetera.

Did you suddenly realise it was he who was involved in the Moncada attack?

Oh yes, yes, yes, yes, of course. I knew it was the same person that used to study law with my brothers, but we, at least I, my sister and I, never really met him, he just came occasionally. He was already engaged to the girl that eventually was his wife. And he always came with his wife's brother. His brother-in-law was his sort of henchman, his comrade, they were always together and, well, my brothers always had their study room full of friends and he was one more of them. Of course, one that we knew that was very active in university politics.

Was your family involved?

Oh, my father was very badly affected. He was one of the few that disagreed completely with the Batista coup. He had hopes that eventually, democratically, by evolution, we would become a better nation. And he was absolutely opposed to the coup of Batista and immediately presented his resignation from the national bank where he was working in a very high position. And because of the very delicate position that he held, they agreed that his resignation would be accepted in a question of months and as soon as he was able. But he wrote a letter saying that he would not be under Batista's payroll or anything. So, as soon as he could, he resigned in a question of some months. And, well, he took a sabbatical year, travelled for a while, and as soon as he came back from this sabbatical year he started to meet with a group of friends that were called Sociedad de los Amigos de la República [Society of Friends of the Republic: SAR], a group of idealistic people, all very well-known people, very well-intentioned people, people that were very well accepted by the American embassy, that would not go into a revolution, but would simply be very democratically engaged. But things did not turn like that. I think, actually, they were laughed at both by Batista and by the real people of Cuba. And, of course, Batista wouldn't ever think of giving up to them anything. They didn't win, they didn't gain anything. But anyway, it was an elegant stand. At least they did not accept Batista's dictatorship. It was a question of principles.

What about your mother?

Oh, well, her life continued placidly. She was not a frivolous person, her concerns were art and she was quite bohemian for her upbringing and she accepted quite easily the new life that came with 1959. We were six, four brothers and two sisters, and the funny thing is that practically all my brothers, at least two or three of them, were extremely active politically during what we call the insurrection. At the time I had two or three children. I was too busy having and raising my children and I sympathised enormously but I wasn't really active. But my brothers, mainly the twin brothers, were really active. So active that eventually they were caught. They were taken prisoner and they had to go, yes, they were caught, they were imprisoned, my two brothers and the wife of one of them, and we managed, barely, to take them out by using a lot of influence. It was very painful and difficult, but eventually they were released after some days. And of course, during that time, during those days in the 1950s, I think it was late 1957 or early 1958 when they were taken and imprisoned by Batista's forces. They managed to seek refuge in the Brazilian embassy as political refugees and they went out of the country, they went to the States and lived in the States and continued in the States to be very active in this 26 July Movement.

Of course, we supported them totally. By that time my father was active not only in the SAR, but also he had started to be very sympathetic towards the 26 July Movement, and my brothers were very active. They were completely involved in the *clandestinidad*.

Yet my brother and sister-in-law had to go into exile in the States. There they continued to be very active, returning immediately after Batista's departure and the taking over by the revolutionary movement, and they returned in less than three or four days. They were back here.

There was the euphoria. The incredible euphoria of that first month. Incredible euphoria, I had never seen before and I don't think I have ever seen afterwards. Such movement (*cries softly*) – a total complete *entrega*, commitment, such complete happiness at Batista's departure and the revolutionary people taking over. And, of course, it was an *incógnita*, it was a complete *incógnita*. Nobody was really sure, not even the rebels knew what they were really for, what they stood for, what they believed in. They believed in overthrowing Batista, for human rights, for the well-being of everybody, against injustices. But they were all, we now realise, too general. But anyway, they were beautiful, beautiful days.

Everybody believed in the best, the ideal. Everybody was Sir Galahad, everybody was against corruption, against badly done things. Everybody was for a new tendency, for well-being, for justice, for liberty. Well, I suppose, in the end, I believe I have been very, very, very lucky to have been *una testigo a veces,* sometimes a witness, sometimes a participant of a revolution that I think is only second to the French, to the French Revolution. And through the very bad moments that we have passed as participants, I never thought I could be moved to such extreme moments of emotion – of desperation, like for example when we had to accept that Camilo had been swallowed by the sea.* The horrible desperation that everybody felt, seven to eight million people were just crying (*cries*) because Camilo had disappeared. Yes, I am still surprised how the whole of the people, all of us, now without classes – that is also something that is really unbelievable, how we have become a society without classes, really, there are no economic classes in Cuba, practically. You can go from one to the other and find people with more or less the same culture, and dress the same, with the same habits. There's no underground classes, no, that has disappeared, thank God. And we have been witnesses of moments of joy, moments of desperation. We have shared such *eh* weariness, or such despair, or such joy, like for example when the invasion in Girón, in Playa Girón [Bay of Pigs], everybody was concerned. Deeply concerned. And everybody was moved. Like for example in 1970 when we were supposed to make ten million [tonnes] of sugar and we couldn't do it. Everybody during a whole year was absolutely concerned and devoted to making ten million tonnes of sugar. And when it wasn't done we were deeply concerned. So many moments that we have, the whole country, the whole nation, we have felt deeply with joy, with sadness.

When Grenada was taken over by the Americans, how everybody wept. How everybody wept. I don't think that could ever have happened before. [Before] people were concerned because of

---

* Comandante Camilo Cienfuegos disappeared in an aircraft accident in late October 1959. As neither the body nor the aircraft was ever recovered, it is believed he crashed into a swamp or the sea. His anniversary is commemorated on 28 October by people throwing flowers into the sea.

the party or the wedding of So-and-so. And the low people, they were concerned about whether they were able to put ten cents on the lottery and win a little prize. No. How we were concerned by something that happened in a place where practically no Cuban had ever been except a small group that had been there to construct a bridge or to construct an airport. How we care about so many things, about sometimes crazy projects. Sometimes we care more deeply about them than about having more consumer goods. And we can understand about having less consumer goods. But building an extremely important industrial complex in Moa* and being industrially developed, we believe in that, and that is something that we never believed before, because Cuba belonged to a very small group of persons who were the possessors, the rest were possessed. Cuba belonged to a very small group of people, and the others did not possess even themselves, not even their dreams. That was not democracy.

I really believe that this society may have its defects – which society hasn't? – but it's a much fairer society in all. We don't need more respect for human rights. We are very rightly respected as human beings in general. And we have, maybe we need a little bit more consumer goods here and there, and, of course, every society and every human being and everything needs to be improved. Nothing is perfect. We can be improved. There is room for improvement here or there or anywhere else. But I think it's a very fair society.

Your family split up.

Oh, that was the most painful thing. The families – everybody, everybody. One hundred per cent of the Cubans were absolutely for Fidel Castro and the revolution and whatever he stood for . . . but during the first year, the first months, then slowly people lost this or things were nationalised or they were confiscated. Sometimes it was a fair thing, sometimes it was unfair, but we called it *La Revolución del Callo* – you know what is a *callo*? It is a thorn in the feet, the toes.

* Cuba's main nickel-mining area.

Corn.

Horn, no? A corn, corn, corn. That was a *callo*. Because one day you had a business, and it was nationalised. Up to that moment you were all for the well-being of humanity and for all these poetic things, but then somebody stepped on your corns, and you started shouting: *ahhhhhhhh*! And (*laughs*) you started screaming, 'Unfair, those people are communists,' and, well, out goes idealism and then of course you had to rush to the States, and from the other side of the bull-ring, they would watch what was happening in Cuba. After all, the Americans could not stand there and see what was happening here. So they would come and they would fix things and then the Cubans in Miami would return very happily to recover what was taken from them and, oooh, imagine, they had been exiles. Oh-ho, they had gone to Miami so they would come back full of medals and honours and after all, so it was fantastic. People just went in droves to Miami. Their idea was, oh, we will stay several months and, *eh*, the children will go to a nice American school and everyone will practise their English and it will be a very good experience and we'll wait there while things settle back in Cuba.

They had never been politically persecuted. The great emigration was simply because Cubans did not accept a real change in their life, their way of life. Of course, they never thought it was a forever thing. They always thought, we'll be back in three months after the Americans or the Marines have put everything back in order and we can return to our normal way of life. They had absolutely no idea of fighting for whatever they believed in, either here in Cuba or over there. And besides, they had no real political feeling, they just wanted life to continue as always. And that's all. And they didn't want any real economic change, any social change, any real change. They thought that elections would be called immediately and another set of corrupt or demagogic politicians would come over and everybody would take over and it would be business as usual, and that's that.

(*Sighs*) Well, that wasn't it. It was a forever thing. These thirty years have passed and they haven't come back. They had to stay there. It has been very miserable. It has been so cruel, this disruption, this fracture, this separation of the families. Cubans have been always very loving families, no matter how different you could think, still everybody loved their brother and we couldn't stand living apart. That was the most painful thing. Now I have been to Spain and have talked to people, to all of them.

Your brothers?

My family. We don't mind so much having to start another life somewhere else, having lost this or that. But what we are always sad about is the loss of togetherness, the way of Cuban families – what a nephew used to call the Cuban diaspora. How we were separated. Anyway, life went on here or there, but the disruption, being apart, was really most painful.

All your family went?

Everybody went out. On my side, everybody went out. No, my mother stayed. Some old people decided to remain as long as they had one child here, somebody to cling to, and they preferred to remain in their own houses as my mother did and my mother-in-law. They stayed and they lived quite comfortably. They still, even after they lost a lot, they still had a very good income and their own houses with all their comforts and the things they were used to, like an old rocking-chair or their own beds. Things that they were used to. And their memories and their picture books and their photographs, all that.

And why did your brothers leave having been involved?

That was the thing. Ah, there was a sort of joke that, well, it was all right with revolution, it was all right with communism, but not so much. There was a point, you could accept this but not that much else. They left, they said, well, we thought there would be an election and we thought it would be just a question of justice, social justice. But it would be a democracy. We never thought it would be communism or this . . . Actually, those that really had been deeply involved, very closely involved with Batista, were the ones that left early, because they really had a very dirty background. Well, my family had not been involved in that way, but eventually, after a year and a half, I remember my father died in March 1959, and everybody was here. It was such a fantastic, incredible demonstration . . . the amount of thousands of people who came to the funeral. One year later, in March 1960, all we six brothers and sisters, we went together with my mother to a Mass. In March 1961, it was only my mother, myself, one brother. In 1962, only my mother and myself.

So did your family lose a lot of property?

Yes, I suppose they did lose, yet they would not have been badly off. For example, still my mother and my mother-in-law, both were able to live as very wealthy matrons. My mother-in-law died as she had always lived, in her own beautiful, three-storey house, a sort of small palace in the very centre of Vedado, which is the most important part of Havana. And she died in 1968 or 1969 with a chauffeur, a cook, with a helper and three maids that lived there. Three live-in maids. She died as she had always lived, as a grand lady. My mother also, she had her house here in Havana. She had a beach house in Varadero and she kept always two maids. She died in 1984 with the two maids and practically every comfort that you could have, because they had very good pensions and they had also income and it was respected. Of course, that income was not inheritable. I did not inherit my mother's income.

This income came from investments abroad?

No, from investments in Cuba. As Cuba and the States had broken relations, and practically everybody broke relations with Cuba, Cubans that stayed here in Cuba could not enjoy their interests on their money abroad.* But they had, for example, pensions, as

---

* Money from investments abroad could not legally be transferred to Cuban accounts because of the trade embargo imposed by the United States in October 1960. Compensation for nationalised lands or properties was paid out in monthly instalments, which in this case they called pensions.

my mother had, or rents, because they had rents from either, say, farmland that had been bought by the state, or apartment houses that had been also bought by the state and sold to the people that lived in them. But your children could not inherit it. It was for the old people to enjoy as long as they lived.

I did not inherit my mother's rent, but I was quite capable of earning my own living. Why should I receive any more rent? I think it was a fair resolution.

Had you, as a young girl, expected to work?

No. I was not really trained to work. I was trained to be a very nice hostess. I was a cultured girl with a lot of social trimmings that would come in very handy anywhere else but in revolutionary Cuba. (*Laughs*) I was very surprised when after the Revolution I found that I had to work. Well, I had been educated for another society, not for the one that I had to live in. And I had to, *eh* . . . I had to start working at a very low level. Let's say, thank God I knew how to type. Not too well, maybe with four fingers. So I was very lucky to get a typing job at the National Library and as soon as I could I went to university at night. I worked during the whole day and went at night. I studied librarianship. And, *eh*, I enjoyed myself enormously, working and earning my living, and I discovered that I was a very able and intelligent person. I could never believe it. I thought I was just a well-trained hostess and I learned how to earn my living. And I'm very proud of it.

I don't think it was unfair. Why should I live off anything that was not produced by my mind or my hands? Why should I live off something that I inherited when I can earn it? I think my children have been very well trained in this society. Of course, I think I helped. But they are all university trained, and no matter where they have to live, they will always be very well trained to earn their living and to help their society. That's good enough. I remember when Che [Guevara] wrote his farewell letter, he wrote, 'I leave nothing to my children, because I trust, I believe that the state will endow them with all their real needs and so they will be able to provide for themselves.'

Well, what else can you need if you are able to provide for

yourself? That's all. You don't have to . . . well, as some Spanish poet said, 'Podemos viajar ligero de equipaje' [We can travel light]. So, I worked at the National Library. I started at the National Library as a typist, and because I went to university at night, had my fifth child practically at the university, I was promoted. I think I was thirty-two. Yes, I was thirty-two when my last child was born. And I was very proud of that achievement.

I was promoted, I wrote a book, I did researches and I . . oh yes, yes, yes, yes, I had a child, I wrote a book and I planted a tree. But I don't intend to die so soon. That's a Cuban saying, that to have a complete life you must have a child, write a book and plant a tree. I have done the three things. But I don't think that still my life is full. My cycle has not reached its zenith. I must now see my grandchildren grow.

You haven't said yet why you decided to stay.

Well, I thought . . . I still think a person has a duty towards their country. Especially when your country is in such a difficult position as ours is. We have been attacked mercilessly by other countries which are so much more wealthy and powerful and old and civilised, and everything that we aren't. But for the first time we are trying honestly to do something, to come out of the bottom of the pit where we were. We were just the dumping ground of the Americans. Where they could come here for prostitution and gambling and dope and horse-racing. Why not stay here and give your best to your country where you belong? And after all, we were the privileged ones, the ones that really got a good education. Why not stay here and give all our best to this country? This nation needed us. They needed me. I still think I am needed here.

I think the people that left the island left because they loved their way of life better than their country. And they went to the States because there they would continue to live in the same way and they were not willing to do any sacrifice for their country. Here it has been very difficult. Everything has not been perfect, but I still believe that we have tried honestly, sometimes mistakenly but honestly, to improve our position, our economy, our industry, and I think we have improved. Even the poorest person in Cuba is better off than a poor person in any country in Latin America. Any poor Guatemalan would consider himself rich to be in the place of the poorest Cuban now.

I think it was my duty to stay, as it was the duty of my two grandfathers to go at great sacrifice to war against Spain.

What was it like having young children in those early years of the Revolution when there was very little about?

Oh, it was tremendously difficult, extremely difficult, extremely difficult. Now we are prepared for everything, we are seasoned veterans. I think I can survive anywhere, anywhere. And I can make use of anything. I don't like to throw away even a bottle. Everything can be useful. But, well, the first few years, nobody thought it was going to be so harsh, because, well, we were used to having everything and during the 1960s things disappeared completely and absolutely and there was nothing, nothing. Well, I had to make use of anything to make practically even shoes for my children. I had to knit, I had to sew, I had to do everything for them. Even knit socks. Knit underwear for the girls, like pants for example. If we managed to obtain thread, we would put two together, two or three threads together, we would join two or three spools of thread, because one is too thin to make a little pants and also stockings. Because there was nothing. Nothing, nothing, nothing, nothing. We were not really producers . . . it was cheaper and easier to import from the States. When the blockade was imposed [in October 1960], there was nothing available besides whatever raw materials that were left. And besides, even the plans, the industrial plans, simply broke . . . so the scarcity was enormous. Not only in goods like, for example, shoes or clothes or towels, not only that, food was so scarce. During all the 1960s, there was no butter available. Maybe once a year, maybe we would be given a very small amount. The only thing that could be assured for children and for pregnant women was milk. Fresh milk for children up to seven, a quart a day. It was extremely difficult looking for food. We would go to the countryside with things. Let's say a flower vase or an old long dress or maybe a necklace, and exchange it, barter . . . if we could make friends with a *campesino*, with a

19

farmer, so we could buy things from them like some chickens or eggs. It was terrible until the 1970s when things started to improve slowly, we were saved because, thank God, or thank whoever you want to thank, the egg problem was solved. And it has been like that ever since. And we know that with eggs there is no problem, and in 1974 or 1975 milk was for the first time available, milk and butter, at the free market, it was not rationed any more, and you can buy milk and yoghurt and butter and many kinds of cheese, they are freely available. Well, that was a tremendous victory.

At present, very little is rationed. And it's very important, because the things that are rationed are extremely cheap: it's a way to ensure that everybody has the right to buy the really important things, I mean things to eat, edible things like beans, rice, milk, sugar, milk for the children at an extremely low price. Those things can also be bought, in whatever amount you want, at the normal price, not subsidised. But of course, those very low prices are subsidised, and I think it's fair that everybody can have at this extremely low price, everything that is necessary.

Butter is not subsidised any more or regulated, it's alway on the free market. Free, not because you get it free, free because it's not regulated. But during those years, practically until 1975, we were willing to pay 15 pesos for each pack of cigarettes. And rum, well, rum was not available at all. But then people used to brew in their houses alcohol that was *horrible*. *(The dog barks at the pained emphasis)* You could smell two blocks away who was brewing, there was no way of hiding it, the horrible smell. And anyway we did it here and it was sold at astronomical prices. And anybody could die of hepatitis or cirrhosis if you drank a lot. Thank God, *(laughs)* things started to be available at a higher price.

Sometimes people tell me that Cuba is the only country in the world that has a quota system or this ration card. It's not true. I found in Mexico, and I found in Costa Rica, and I found in many places that there is a sort of a rationing, because what they call the *canasta básica*, the basic things, are provided at special state stores at very low prices for the poor people that are registered in the vicinity. And even in the States, what are the milk coupons? It's

the same idea. And what about the food coupons for the poor?*
So, if you look at it from that point of view . . . I think it's
very fair to ensure that every child till seven has the possibility
to buy at an extremely cheap price a bottle of milk. I think it's
very fair. I have nothing against that. For example, I go and buy
milk at 1 peso whenever I want, all the milk I want. But then my
grandchildren are assured to have their quart of milk for only 25
cents.

What's your lifestyle like now?

Well, I'm retired. I have so many things to do, so many occupa-
tions. Very active, lots of activities, for example, dog-breeding,
and I do ceramics and I go a lot to my beach house.

I breed dachshunds. And we have a [National Kennel] club.
And I don't know why they made me president of the club. But
I enjoy it enormously. Well, it's an opportunity to start again a
social life with a different set of people. And I enjoy it, and we
organise exhibitions here in Havana, in Santa Clara, in Holguín,
and we are 200, maybe 300, people making all the trip with all the
dogs in a train to Holguín. Sometimes I (*hoots*) . . . the last time
I went to Santa Clara there were 200 people in three carriages of
the train. Well, the cosmonauts don't know anything about travel
problems! But I enjoyed it enormously.

What about young people today, the younger generation?

Well, the new generations, that's a problem. They don't remember
the harsh times. Harsh times before or after the Revolution. And
whatever good they have, which is plenty, they take it for granted.
They believe that in all countries in the world, they would be given
such good medical attention. They are sure. They have grown up
being so secure in this sense, that they take it for granted. My
children accept from me when I tell them that no, in Spain, for
example, medical attention to the poor is terrible or non-existent.

---

* She is referring to the US federal stamps programme for people living on
public assistance.

But when they see a film they see only the people driving around in big, flashy, new cars, and living comfortably, and how free they are to buy a ticket and go from one country to the other and travel freely.* Well, they can travel freely, all those that have money to buy the ticket. The ones that don't have money to buy the ticket, they don't go anywhere. And even all the normal means of transport are extremely expensive. Like even the metro. Nothing can be cheaper and more humble and popular than the metro. The metro in Spain costs about 60 cents or a dollar approximately, compared in Cuba, where the bus fare is only 10 cents. And the transport, inter-provincial transport, still has the same price as thirty years ago.

When I want to go to Varadero† I still pay 1.55 pesos a ticket. That was exactly what I used to pay thirty years ago. And, I have seen people begging around stations [abroad] for money to complete a fare. But the young people sometimes tend to think that is not true. That maybe it's just government propaganda when they are told those things. And they think that if they manage to go to a capitalist country, by the second day they will own a car and live in a flashy apartment and have a fantastic job. It's not like that. Very few succeed.

Well, I won't deny that the States is the biggest and most powerful and the richest country in the world. That's right. The only problem is I, and the rest of the ten million Cubans, we are not Americans, we are not citizens of the USA. We are Cubans, and I still believe that we have to stay here and make Cuba better. Improve Cuba. Improve our system. There's plenty to improve. Plenty to work with.

The young, well, sometimes they tend to think they want more consumer goods, and everybody wants to have a tape-recorder or

* The 1984 Immigration Accord between Cuba and the US allows for 20,000 Cubans to emigrate to the US every year. These quotas, however, are not nearly being fulfilled. Women over forty and men over forty-five are eligible for travel visas. Intellectuals, musicians and sportspeople get to travel relatively easily.

† Varadero is a magnificent beach resort where Fichu has a house built by her father. Those who remained in Cuba were allowed to keep two houses, the second of which had to be out of town, in the country or at the beach.

a video. Those things are produced in Japan and we have to pay dearly for them. In hard currency. And instead of buying videos for the people, we buy milk. Powdered milk so that every child in Cuba has assured a quart of milk a day at a very cheap price. And that is very important. And, for example, the *círculos infantiles,* state kindergartens, they are fantastic. My five grandchildren are in them, and they are so luxurious, it's incredible – the food they eat, the attention they receive. There's nothing like that, absolutely nothing in Spain or in all the countries where I have been. Well, maybe some nations like Sweden, or France maybe, they can offer social security, they can offer those things. But why should we, a very poor and underdeveloped country struggling to come out of all our problems, and facing at our doorstep the most powerful and the richest country in the world that happens to be our bitterest enemy, that for thirty years has thought of nothing but to squash Cuba – well, frankly, I think it's a very unfair comparison. But if you compare Cuba with another country with ten million inhabitants of Latin America, the comparison . . . we come out winning.

Why do you think the United States is an implacable . . .

Enemy of Cuba?
    Who else has told them the truth that we have told them? And who else has managed to survive? I'm still surprised that we haven't been squashed. We are so little compared to them, and so poor, and we depended so much. I had here a book that was called *Our Cuban Colony. Our Cuban Colony.* Really. Well, they lost money. They lost some properties. I think it's fair that they lost them. Why not? And they say, pay us some compensation. I don't think it's needed. They invested, say, $5,000 at the beginning of the century, and by 1959 or 1960 they had taken out in profits about a thousand times whatever they invested. They compensated themselves. And I think it's more important to progress economically and industrially and socially. And we had to do all the more important things like, first, to survive, which was quite difficult, and to develop economically, industrially, everything. And roads had to be built, and so many good things, but it was very hard. So far, I

think only the Mexicans during their revolution were able to . . . and they were hated for that, the Mexicans.

Anyway, you remember that the first country Fidel insisted on visiting after the winning of the Revolution was the States. And he was not received, and he wanted to be received. And he wanted to be accepted. And he wanted to talk. And neither Eisenhower nor Nixon received him. He received only kicks. Well, I don't wonder that they hate us, but anyway, just this year, I have seen that Yasser Arafat . . . that now they are talking, so anything can happen. Anything can happen.

2

Cipriano Chinea Palero

Chinea, as he is called, has a fine, chiselled face and a gravelly voice to match. He is from Las Villas province and, unusually in Cuba, is a bachelor. He is forty-seven. He works in the Sierra Maestra restaurant in the Habana Libre Hotel, formerly the Hilton, where he would often stop and have a chat with me. This interview takes place in the echoing disco-bar on the top floor of the hotel.

29 September 1988

I started as a cleaning boy. I had to clean all the doors of the hotel, clean the first lobby, the second lobby and some other areas. And often, when, for example, Sra Carmen Coll or La Fresneda came into the lobby and didn't see their faces reflected in the floor, I had to clean it all over again. And so I did.

They paid me 118 pesos and I had to pay for my lunch out of that. I paid 50 centavos for my meal, so I was left with a total of 74 pesos.

But I always wanted to get on in life, and I became what is known as a *mochila*. *Mochila* is what you call in English a busboy, someone who does the heavy work. He has to put the water and bread and butter out on the tables, carry the dirty tray-loads, carry the plates – all the dirty work. In those days, he was the one who worked most and earned least. Then I became a waiter, which is up a scale in the hierarchy, better wages, I got around 148 pesos. But I still had to pay for my lunch and whatever else I ate or drank. Then I moved up to the cabaret. The casino was beside this Cabaret Caribe, and what is today called the Solidarity Room was the old casino.

While I was there I saw and met a lot of the Mafia. They used to go to cabarets as a rule. In those days the Caribe, the Sans Souci, the Riviera, the Capri, the Nacional were all top-class cabarets and that's where those gents used to go. I know that their boss was a guy by the name of Charlie White. An American name but he wasn't American. He was Italian. This was 1961.

So, although the Revolution had been won, there were still casinos and the Mafia?

Oh yes. Run by the Mafia. They controlled them. The casinos remained after the Revolution until one day in the Plaza [Revolution Square] the Comandante en Jefe [Fidel Castro] said that from that day, in 1962 if my memory serves me correct, the casinos would be closed. That's when they nationalised, or rather they got rid of, the casinos. But until that time, the Mafia operated them.

That Charlie White guy lived in an apartment in the Focsa building, and he had a number two who controlled the Capri, a character by the name of Niceo Constanze. And another of them I knew was Santo Traficante, and he controlled the Sans Souci and the Hotel Habana Libre, that's the casino here. They had a lyrical or classical singer called René Cabell – a Cuban, of Cuban origin – who collaborated with them. Charlie White's body was covered in scars according to those who looked after him, and he had to have a daily fix of drugs – morphine or cocaine or whatever – to function at all. His assistant injected him. He was short, thick-set, with a ruddy complexion. About fifty years old. Niceo Constanze was big and tall and as fat as a fool. He was also about fifty. And Santo Traficante was tall, thin and white. They simply didn't get involved. They had their *palas,* their front women or their dealers. The *pala* is the woman who sells you your chips and does the rigging. She rigs it up and then hides whatever cheating might be going on. Do you follow? So what they did then was, when the casino closed, they would come along, collect the loot and head for their offices. I don't know who it was told me, a few years back, that the same Charlie White and Niceo Constanze killed Santo Traficante in Las Vegas for something he did to them here. I don't know how they did their dirty deals, I only overheard ordinary conversations.

They were silent types. But always working out ways of getting the biggest cut. Extorting from others. How can I get rid of you so I can have it all? Do you follow me? They smoked marijuana in all the casinos in those days. There was coke, all kinds of drugs. They often worked while under the influence of drugs, drugged up to the eyes. They worked, they cruised around, but drugged. I never saw them with their wives because they always had someone different on their arm. Today they'd appear with one and tomorrow another and you couldn't tell if this woman was this fella's or the other fella's.

They'd arrive and say, 'Bring me a Pernod,' or, 'Bring me a Johnny Walker on the rocks.' And my job was to serve them. I would bring them the Johnny Walker on the rocks but I'd be listening as well. I overheard a conversation between Charlie and Santo Traficante – 'I rented an apartment on the top floors of Las Cibeles, 21 and N Streets.' 'I got one in the Focsa.' 'How do you think the night will turn out?' 'Well, we'll see, let's see how things go.' That sort of thing. And me bringing my gin and orange juice or my Johnny Walker on the rocks.

But these guys would circulate. And they would never let you take their photograph. They didn't like having their picture taken. They would circulate around their casino, check it out and disappear. They might first come here to the Habana Libre casino, into the cabaret and then on to the Capri, the Riviera, always on the move, keeping an eye on their business. I can't honestly say I had any relationship with them, they would just ask me for a Pernod and I'd bring them the Pernod.

They didn't leave many tips because they were only passing through. They'd order their drink, have it and go. They might leave 40 cents, a dollar . . . not much. They would have a whisky, pay for it and leave the rest, 20 or 40 cents. They were about their business, on the move all the time.

It's somewhat difficult for Cubans to get into the hotel nowadays.

It is not difficult. If we go now to the Antillas or anywhere else we'll see a huge number of Cubans, it'll be full of Cubans. Let's go now and you'll see. Our problem is the safety of tourists. For example, we have restaurants like the Barracón, which is dollars only. El Patio is the same, and there are a few other facilities confined to dollar-paying guests. Why? Because the hard currency that tourists leave is what we, the Cuban state, use to invest . . . For example, you can come here tonight and see that it is full of Cubans, full of Cubans, visiting guests or who have made a reservation and then come along like anyone else. Now, what we cannot do is fill our facilities with Cubans so that when a group of tourists arrives we have nowhere to put them. Because we need that hard currency to buy surgical instruments, to buy factories which we have to purchase abroad, to provide health-care facilities for which the people do not pay. You don't have to pay to have a kidney-stone destroyed or to have an operation, nothing at all. And there are some sections of the population who do not understand this. I can close my restaurant today because a man wants to hire it – 'I am going to give you $2,000 to hire out your restaurant.' I cannot say to that man, 'No. This is for the people, not for you.' No, no, no, no, no. I close my restaurant and I give it to that man because he is paying for it all in hard currency, because, as I said before, this is the way, the means by which hard currency comes in, with which we then buy factories, surgical instruments, agricultural machinery *for the people*. Because we don't charge people anything for these things. What costs us in dollars, we give them free. We give it to them free.

There are those who don't understand that what they want isn't possible. But they want – some, not a large section – to go to the restaurant and also have free health-care. And that's not on. It's not possible. Because in the old days a visit to the doctor would cost you 20 pesos, and where were those 20 pesos if you couldn't afford to buy a bit of iodine, let alone tetracycline?

And who paid your wages?

The Cuban state. I started working after the Revolution. The Revolution paid me. The Mafia still had their concessions. The hotel had still not been nationalised, and even after its nationalisation the casinos were left alone. They left here when they got rid of the casinos. If they hadn't they might still be here. And they had a major plan to build all along the Havana seafront, the whole shoreline including what is today Habana del Este. Casinos and brothels the whole way, that's what they had in mind. They even had the sketches drawn up. And now thousands of families live in Habana del Este and there are secondary schools, polyclinics,* a hospital . . . And they [the Mafia] wanted to set up thousands of prostitutes and bring in millions-worth of marijuana, morphine, cocaine, heroin and what have you. But they fled. What else could they do? They had nothing left. And that den of *mafiosi*, of drug-addicts, of degenerates in every sense, is now a functions room for the people.

How much do you earn now?

Now that I am head waiter I earn 191 [pesos] on top of which I get a bonus for having a language – I learnt English on the job – I get an ordinary bonus, and they pay me extra for working nights, and I get a certain percentage commission which comes to about 300 pesos a month. I can live fine on that. Everyone has to adapt, because the poor man can't live like the rich man. And if you earn 200 pesos you have to get used to living with 200 pesos. You can't spend 500. Because if you earn 200 and they pay you your 200 today and you spend 300, tomorrow you haven't a bean. No, no, no, no, no.

And you also find those who don't want to get on in life, and they remain stuck in the same place for ever. Not me, no, no. You have to get on. To know how to read is to know how to walk. To know how to write is to know how to get ahead. That's what the teacher said. For if you settle for earning 20 pesos and you don't want to earn 40, then you will stay earning 20. But if you try to improve your circumstances and earn 40, you will want to go on to earn 80, because it's better.

My childhood was one of poverty. My parents were very poor peasants who worked in the fields in Las Villas province and had

---

* Small general hospitals responsible for health-care in the community.

nothing. There were six of us and my parents, and they cultivated a patch of ground. First we had to give half of what we grew to the landlord, so if we grew four pumpkins we would have to give him two and keep two for ourselves. That later changed and we had to give him a quarter of our produce. But he always got his share. Like we grew tobacco, corn, beans and the rest, and we had to give him a quarter of it all. And if by chance, as happened on one occasion, the weather ruined the tobacco, he would lend us money, but you would have to pay him back with interest. That was the way it was in the past all right. A desperate situation, with people living in alleys, in houses made of tin and palm-leaves.

We lived in a palm-thatched hut made of planks of palm-tree. You could make planks from the tree and the roof from the leaves and you had a dirt floor. That was our house. That's where myself and my brothers and sisters were raised. Towards the end of 1959, the beginning of 1960, a brother-in-law of mine began working here in the Habana Hilton Hotel and so I just packed my bags and came up here out of the blue. I was seventeen. I appeared out of the blue and went to look for him, and he then got me the job.

The service in Cuba is very bad.

Yes, I know. It could be bad management. The level of education of the person serving could also have a lot to do with it. And I also think a lot has to do with the sector itself. If a doctor doesn't have a vocation to be a doctor, he cannot be a doctor. And if a teacher hasn't the vocation to be a teacher or doesn't like teaching, he should not be a teacher. And if someone doesn't like this, doesn't have a vocation for it or doesn't love their work – because you have to love your work, it's your livelihood – if they don't like it, I would prefer them to tell me, 'I want to be a carpenter, a plumber, a brickie,' or, I don't know, 'a fisherman'. But the number of people who have come into the sector with this notion, this idea of tips, is really shocking. And when they see that the reality is different, they say, 'It isn't what they said it was like.'

Management is fairly good here. As I said, there are a few who don't do their work because they don't like it or because they couldn't care less about it, which is another thing. But they are expected to work. The problem is, most of them working here had no experience of the past. If they had lived under the other system they would have been thrown out. Then there was more discipline and more responsibility. Why? Because if you didn't do your job you were out. You were thrown out automatically. (*Brings his hands smartly together*) You lost your card, you went to the personnel officer and they gave you three, or four or five days' pay and that was it. But that's the capitalist system. The capitalist always wants to have money in his pockets. And when some business is no longer paying, he gets rid of it. Because he wants to have his pockets full, as I said. Socialism is different. Socialism is about education, the making of the new man, about a different series of values and concepts, not that sort of repression. I remember a case here of an employee who once arrived five minutes late, and the boss said to him, 'You're five minutes late.' And he said, 'Yes, sir. Please, my mother is in hospital and my father is in the asylum and I am their only son and I had to go and see her. That's why I'm late.' And he said, 'As you are a man with a lot of problems, I don't want you. When you sort them out, come back.' That's not socialism. Socialism gives that man the chance to resolve his problems and it guarantees him a job. That man couldn't go back any more.

Had it been a girl, she would have gone to a brothel. There can be no prostitutes in brothels here.* There are no brothels here. A lad would have had to sell tickets – we don't have any of those here – or become a shoeshine. No. That's capitalism. Socialism is about educating that person, not throwing them on to the streets without work. Without work they'd have to steal, thereby turning the prisons into storerooms of men who have no work because they were fired. Prisons aren't for storing men and women. It's a question of educating them gradually.

And has this new man been born?

Oh yes. Because although we see some bad young people, that's not to say they are all like that. No, no. There are a few who are

---

* Prostitution is illegal in Cuba but has resurfaced in recent years.

not great, but it would be as well to consider their background and see who their parents were. You would have to analyse a whole series of factors. But I can tell you that the new man is amongst us. You can see it in the training of the *camilitos*, for example, or the pupils of the Lenin School.* Youngsters come in here to the restaurant, like the other day, two couples arrived in and the young men pulled out the chairs for the young ladies.

But that's not new.

But it is correct. I said they were kids. Youngsters. So I asked them where they were studying and they said, 'We are at teacher-training college.' And I noticed their manners. That's the new man for you. The person who is aware of their manners. Not those kids who go around throwing stones and don't want to go to school because their parents can't handle them or because the granny is soft on them or whatever.

There is a certain lack of respect, though, because in all these social changes, in the transition from the system through which the parents lived to the one in which they are bringing up their children, the parents have often been unable to communicate to their children what they went through, what it all cost. And the kids have had it all easy with the Revolution. And what comes easy, you don't appreciate properly. You cherish what has been hard come by, what has involved sacrifice and struggle. But you don't cherish what has come easy.

So, how do you resolve that contradiction?

No. I don't think there is a contradiction there. Little by little it will sort itself out. They will get a better understanding. Because the grandchildren of the Camilitos and the children of the Lenin School students will receive a different education. And the new generations, successively. It's like a tree that you plant. You have

---

* The *camilitos* are children aged thirteen and over who attend a military academy named after Comandante Camilo Cienfuegos. The Lenin School is a specialist secondary school for gifted pupils with scientific and technical talents.

to water it every day and it grows and grows until one day it bears fruit. If you don't tend it, if you don't water it, it will not bear fruit.

What will happen when Fidel dies?

No, nothing. He has to die. That's the law of life. But we have the Party. It's not just Fidel now, there's the Party which is strong. And the people are resolute. By the law of nature nobody is eternal. Because what happened when Lenin died? What happened? Nothing. What happened when Brezhnev died? What will happen when Gorbachev's number is up? Nothing. The Party is indestructible. And get this clear: new regimes rise up and the succeeding one is always better than the one that went before. That is plain. Capitalism is now in decline, and by the law of life socialism is on the rise, and after that will come communism, and after that an even better phase than communism – that is inexorable. Nobody can avoid it. Just like when Jules Verne spoke about submarines and space travel, they said he was mad. And then so many years after he wrote that, we see that submarines exist and that space travel is a reality, and any moment now we'll be living up there who the hell knows where.

And do you believe in an afterlife?

After death? We are simply matter. Good fertiliser for those plants there. (*Laughs*) Nothing else. Nothing else. Now our deeds, our ideas and our principles, for which we are capable of dying, they remain on. I believe that. They remain alive. The rest, no, the rest is only matter. But what we did, for example, Che's work is still alive. His example. Physically he is dead but his ideas, his principles, the beautiful pages he wrote won't die. Nobody can kill those off . . . nobody.

3

Carmen Comella

Carmen Comella is a Sacred Heart nun. She left Cuba in 1959 to work abroad and returned in 1983. Today she lives in a convent in Havana where she does mainly pastoral work. We meet at the convent. Carmen is wearing civilian clothes. She is fifty-four.

30 May 1989

When schools were nationalised the nuns of our congregation who were here on the island decided to leave. They were afraid and they left. Perhaps they thought there was nothing for them to do. That was in 1961. Vatican II had still not happened and the Church changed a lot after Vatican II. I think that if the Revolution had happened in 1970, we wouldn't have left. We would have thought, 'We'll stay and be creative in what we do.' Like we are doing now. We are not teaching and yet we are here. But I don't pass judgment. You have to take into account the times when events happened.

They all left the country?

Some sisters came back in 1971. One came back to see her mother and she stayed. Then another came, and so gradually the numbers built up. There are six of us. We might be starting a novitiate now with one or two young women who began their training in the religious life here. And these are youngsters who were born after the Revolution, so they are products of it. I think that is great.

They have a perspective which I believe will be very useful for the congregation. This is a new generation, young people who have a commitment to this society. This is a serious commitment and they want to work for their people, for their growth, and they like our line of teaching which is educating others, the whole person, and they believe we can do that in this society. Even without actually teaching. Because a classroom is not a prerequisite of education. Education takes place everywhere. If I had time, I would like to go to a park and play with the children – baseball, whatever. By that I don't mean proselytism, because, generally, the Catholic Church is not proselytist, simply to show them that instead of fighting they could play with a different spirit. That's education.

In the morning I go to do exercises with the old folk, which I love, and I keep it up mainly because it does me good.* I'm pretty agile, I cycle and all the rest of it. I could do exercises here, but I believe the contact with people in my area is valuable. These aren't people who come to the church, but nevertheless we have a lovely relationship. They come when they need something. And when I also need something, I ask them and we do each other favours. We're great pals . . . I go to their parties, they sometimes come here, though not for religious feasts, but they like it and, 'Oh, I heard you had a feast day yesterday. Great. Ah, let's go in and see the crib,' things like that. I think we've a fine relationship. So, firstly, I'm in contact with the forty or fifty people in my group, and then when they have bigger parties I meet the two or three hundred old folk from around here.

I left Cuba in 1959 after finishing my novitiate. It was normal practice in my congregation to go abroad to finish training, and I went to Puerto Rico. I stayed there for twenty-four years, almost the most important years of my life. I studied literature, Hispanic Studies, in the University of Puerto Rico. I got my BA and I worked in the Sacred Heart University for eighteen, nineteen years. And there you have it.

I came back to Cuba again in 1983, in February of 1983. I came

---

* There is a nationwide keep-fit programme for senior citizens or whoever wants to join in, usually conducted in open green areas from 8.30 to 9 a.m.

back because I myself asked for the transfer. It seemed to me that the time was right, that I had given many years of my life to Puerto Rico and its people and had worked also, of course, in the congregation, and I just thought that with the congregation in Cuba short of personnel, that this was my place. And I don't regret that decision. I have rediscovered my roots and I feel very happy about working for my people and with my people. And I work with everybody – believers and non-believers – because my aim is the general good and the human development of all. And, of course, my most direct work is with those who have the faith. That's my special mission, but I don't exclude my neighbours or anyone who approaches me.

I do what we call pastoral work here. What does that involve? Well, working on the global education of everyone, but more specifically in the area of the faith. This can perhaps be very systematic work. I don't have many fixed areas of work but I do have many different ones which imply a lot of work. Besides, pastoral work involves human relations, and I believe human relations take up a lot of time; talking to people, listening to them, helping them, visiting them, all takes a lot of time and it's the sort of work that never ends. So really, I don't, perhaps, have enough time. I wish the day had forty-four hours instead of twenty-four, to do more, and especially to have more opportunity to be with people. I see that that is very important here in our country. Well, everywhere, isn't it? In Puerto Rico my experience with young people, old folk, middle-aged people was the same – everybody needs to talk and be listened to. And they also need to be given direction in their life even from the human point of view, and, of course, from a religious point of view. That's why you have to talk and chat to people so much.

I also work here in the parish church. Here there is steady pastoral work to be done, such as going to Mass every day; seeing the people who come; giving catechism classes to young people at all levels – children, adolescents, youngsters; looking after married couples; taking children on outings – simple things like that. There's always that work.

Perhaps on account of my training I also work at national level or at diocesan level helping to develop leaders among the young people in seminars. That isn't a constant but it would appear to be becoming more frequent, this holding of seminars or workshops. Then during summer there are the young people's retreats. We take advantage of the holidays to bring them together and they spend a few days – divided in groups according to age – considering subjects we give them to think about. Subjects on their faith, but also on their life as citizens. And, of course, there's a festive spirit about it all and we have outings.

As I spent the first five years on my return in Santiago de Cuba, I have two work centres – Santiago and Havana. I have been in Havana for years now so I have doubled the number of my relationships. I haven't abandoned people in Santiago, I go there from time to time, and relationships here are increasing all the time. That's my main work, what you might call my daily work. Besides, there's community life which makes demands on time, it's like organising a family. We have to cook, talk and pray together. We also conduct prayer meetings with young people and we have meetings with other Christian denominations. I also have a lot of schoolfriends who are not exactly practising Catholics now. They were at some point, because we went to the same Catholic school. Anyway, I see them and their children, and even their grandchildren now.

My work in Puerto Rico was very different. It's both difficult and easy to compare the two. There I was a university professor. I was Dean of the Humanities School for many years. It was a very administrative job, eight hours a day – a lot of work. It was a different kind of work, let's say, with greater responsibilities, perhaps. Not that what I do now does not carry responsibilities. It creates tensions as well. It certainly does. But it was different. A different world. An academic world, which you don't get here . . . Maybe before I reach retirement age I will be able to teach. I think that's a goal that the Party and the state as much as ourselves would like to attain. I always held on to a literature class [in Puerto Rico], because I wanted to keep in direct touch with the students and not just be an administrator. So it was the exact opposite of what I do now.

Here I also have a lot of work. Perhaps not having a very organised pastoral system yet – we are getting there – and perhaps the usual difficulties, more in the past than in the present, caused by tension between the Church and the state, has created problems. In this sense work has perhaps been more difficult here. Small things, you might say, that cause problems, but that's the way humanity is, isn't it. You have to analyse why this happens. So, you see, it's quite different here. There I had a very systematised and organised job, and here it's very asystematic, but it also involves a lot of work. And, you know, here you have to be more creative. I notice that my creativity has grown. I have discovered that things I have never done, nor felt capable of doing, well, here I am doing them. And they turn out more or less fine.

Also, it is one thing to work in a capitalist world and another matter altogether to work in a socialist world. You don't want for anything in a capitalist world. You have no shortage of X and sometimes there is waste on that account. Here, for example, I don't have a video, I don't have computers, I don't have a lot of things. It's a limitation, it must be said. A computer saves a lot of time. But, as I mentioned, that has made me be more creative and made me live without technology. It has made me get on without technology. And when one can do that, humanism has room to grow. So, it has helped me weigh things up. Perhaps with all the technology I had before, my humanism, that human part of me that also helps others grow, was diminished. Now that I have less technology at my disposal, I need more people to help me, and perhaps I also believe that man's humanity can be impoverished when there is too much technology. This has to be given a lot of consideration. But I do undoubtedly stress that it is also a limitation. The fact is, it has made me be more creative. But life is more austere, more austere in every sense, naturally. And that can be a virtue, just like poverty.

What sort of people come to you?

The children of Catholic parents who were baptised when they were small and who have been coming to catechism lessons for a long time. But we have an increasing number of youngsters coming to our groups who have not been baptised and who have never received instruction. They are searching. They all come looking for something. They are looking for something different. They have doubts. Usually a grandmother or an aunt or their mother will have told them at some stage that they were baptised, and will have spoken to them about the faith, about God, about Our Lady. Some come saying, 'You see, my aunt has a picture on her wall and she prays and says that it's important in life to believe in something.' That sort of thing.

There is a lot of religous syncretism as well. It's a belief. That they have a syncretic religion or syncretic beliefs means they believe there is something else, and usually they believe in God. Perhaps they don't believe . . . or, rather, they believe in beings that can solve their problems, who listen to them. They believe that there is something else after this life. So, the young people who come here have had some experience of religious faith and they come for different reasons. They just come in off the street. Youngsters with existential problems or philosophical doubts. They can be eighteen or nineteen. Sometimes they arrive with no intention of talking about faith. We respect that. Sometimes they talk amazingly about existentialism, about Sartre and Camus, they've read *The Plague* and so they begin to ask you about things, they express doubts, and you can spend months talking to them about philosophy and literature. Others come with literary-artistic ideas, and along the line they almost all express a concern about faith. What is it? Who is God? And they're off. Some only make it half-way, they get lost and don't come back. But others persevere and continue. We take it very slowly and we don't push them. They are the ones who have to choose: for example, to take the first step, to receive baptism. We push no one and it is all very calm. But people are coming in increasing numbers. People of all ages. And infants. More adults are bringing their babies to be baptised. Of course, the babies aren't making the choice, it's the parents who afterwards don't come to the church but they think they can now have their children baptised and they're bringing them. The numbers have tripled or more in the last year. The ratio is something like seven to one. We do about twenty-one christenings to about two or three before.

What about the Pope's visit?★

★ Scheduled for 1991.

The Pope has not visited many socialist countries. Really, I think that besides Poland, his own country, he has not officially visited a socialist country. He went to Nicaragua, but of course Nicaragua still has a very different kind of socialism to ours, and that was a few years ago now. But I really think it will be very interesting. And very positive. Positive for the country, very positive for the Church, very positive for the state, for everybody. The people I do exercises with, who don't go to church, are delighted. 'We'll go along. You let us know.' 'Do you think we could invite him to the park?' And I say, 'Well, I don't think he'll be able to come to the park, but wherever he goes I'm sure he'll invite the old folks.' So there is a lot of excitement. He is an international figure, a man of great prestige and charisma, and I think that charisma flows out. Everybody is influenced by a person's charisma.

There have been changes taking place in Cuba . . .

Well, of course, these started some time ago, and through this 'rectification' period* I have hopes that we can really make changes that will improve our situation in many ways. People, undoubtedly, are getting tired, tired of this same hard life. I said that austerity has its great virtues, but perhaps continuous austerity can tire out our people. And sometimes you pick up on that depression.

I believe in the Revolution's achievements, and above all else I love my people a lot and I seek their well-being, as I am sure does the Party and those who direct it. The problem is that, mixed up in all this, is the sin we all have within us – limitations and sin. Sin in the sense communists understand it too, omission and a lack of values – theft, lies, injustice. All that is sin, all sin. And that, neither we Christians nor good communists want. Can't want. So I hope whatever change there is in Cuba reduces the incidence of sin, and that things become more easy for the people; that truly we might

---

* The 1986 'rectification' campaign was implemented to root out corruption, privilege and economic inefficiency in the bureaucracy; to reinstate moral over material incentives in the workplace; and to curb market controls by increasing centralised planning.

all feel happy in building socialism, a socialism in which we can all feel good, and that relations between the Church and the state continue to improve . . . Often in the past you would hear of the intolerance there was in religious matters. Well, really, I think that is diminishing . . . I say that quite calmly, since Fidel and other leading government personalities have often defended the rights of believers and their right to worship without fear of disrespect or abuse. I would be prepared to defend that any time. I haven't come up against it, but should a child I know or an adult be put down for his or her faith – and you hear of these things but there are other reasons – I would follow it through to the end. And not just for the good of the Church and the person, but also for the good of Cuba and society. I would do it any time, and with no fear at all. I would be prepared to do so because I believe that only in this way can we attain our goals and many other things. I think fear has sometimes paralysed us . . . Sometimes people conjure up fear, and when you get to the bottom of it there is nothing. But, of course, often they say to me, 'Well, you're all right, you've nothing to lose. You have a lot of security,' and that's true. We have a lot of security and I acknowledge that. We have a lot of support. But I say to them, 'Well, if you feel someone is being done down, bring them to me and I will put myself in their place.' And up to now this has not happened.

4

May FitzGerald

May Wickstead FitzGerald, from Ireland, lives in the Santovenia Old Folks Home in Havana, which is run by a religious order. She proudly shows me all over the lovely, if decaying, colonial-style building, with its columns and tiles, lush gardens and shrieking tropical birds, which at times make conversation very difficult. She walks with a frame but with tremendous energy. Miss May has a clear and beautiful Kerry accent. She first came to Cuba in 1920 and was ninety-four at the time of this interview.

15 September 1987

I like Vedado. I had a nice little open house there, you know. I had two rooms and I had my little doggie and all the people there, they all liked me, and I came here because I fell one evening.

I was watering my plants and the pail of water went on one side and I on the other. And so I couldn't get up. But fortunately I'd a maid who had just come in, and she heard me calling, and my little doggie was barking out on the roof, so she took me and called up the Red Cross and they took me to a hospital, the Calixto García, and there I was for a month.

And the doctors were all in love with me and did everything, but they had no hopes of curing me, and I was praying very hard and I made a novena and they believe I was saved by my novena. They said, 'We didn't cure you. We had no hopes.'

This leg is a little shorter than the other, and this hand, look, on account of my fall. But I have no pain, thank God.

Then I came here. They recommended me here. The lady counsel [British consul] came here with Cathy [a friend], and they were saying, 'This is an English teacher and she would like a room to herself.' And she [the director of the home] said, 'What's her name?' 'Miss May. We call her Miss May.' 'Miss May! She was my teacher for three years. I remember her little penthouse and I know all her pupils. Dr Pérez Estrada was a very good pupil of hers. Well, all right, I'll give her a room.'

So, but I had to pay very much. I had to pay high. I sold my apartment. I had the right to sell the apartment. The owner of the building was my pupil, too. So, she went to Miami and she died and I had my apartment and I could sell it. I sold it for $5,000, and that's the money I'm spending here. And that's going to finish in no time, Cathy has it for me. And the sister said, 'That doesn't matter, you can always stay here.' 'She's welcome. They all like her.' So here I am, a foreigner. I have to speak my bad Spanish to all these old people. But, you know, they think that I, being a foreigner, am very rich. I have a room to myself and they envy me, more or less.

I got no pension because I was teaching in the Sacred Heart convent and the [convent of the] French Dominicans and I knew French very well. I spoke French better than Spanish. I was five years in France. I love France. I went all over France. My Spanish isn't as good as my French because I had many rich pupils, you know, and their parents all spoke English. The people were very pretentious and very well educated and very nice and very refined and they were very friendly.

There I was, then, when Fidel became important. All the nuns had to leave and, naturally, as I was in a convent school, I got no pension. And there are two teachers here from the government schools. I don't understand them. They taught English so badly and they have a good pension. But if I made a claim and wrote to Fidel Castro I might get a pension. But I don't want Fidel to know that I am here.

He might want you to teach him English again.

I remember he was in a boarding house where we were four girls, where I lived for two years, and I like those girls very much because they were much younger. He came after, and then he heard those girls who spoke English. They loved to speak English, and then one day he said, 'Where have you learnt English? In what college have you learnt English?' And they said (*posh voice*), 'We didn't learn English in a college, we learnt English with Miss May. She lived here for four years [sic] and we were always in her room.' He said, 'Congratulations. You speak better than I do and I went to Belén College. I need to improve my pronunciation.' It's true. He doesn't pronounce very well . . . I like his Spanish, he speaks very good Spanish, but his English is not perfect.

And then some time after, a lot of Americans came here, and they couldn't speak Spanish, so this young boy used to interpret for them, Julio Suárez, and Fidel heard him speaking English with the Americans, and he said, 'Come here, young fellow, in what college did you learn English like that? You speak better than the Americans.' And Julio said, 'I didn't learn in a college, I learnt with Miss May. She had a lovely little penthouse in Vedado and a lovely little chihuahua dog and tropical plants, and I went to her place very often.' He [Castro] said, 'What? Miss May? I know that name.' And then he said, 'I need to practise my pronunciation. I haven't the time now, but I may have time later.' And then Julio said to me, 'Do you want me to tell Fidel where you live and give him your address?' I said, 'Oooh, Fidel is very handsome.' He had a very nice face when he was young. 'Mmmmm, but no, I don't want to teach him. I wouldn't want to teach Fidel, he might put me in jail for something I'd say.' And then he says, 'He might give you a medal because he says I pronounce very well.' I said, 'Oh no, Julio, don't tell him anything about me.' And especially here. He couldn't come here, you know. It's a convent.

But these nuns here are very good. Oh, they are wonderful how they take care of those people, and you know they take all sorts of people here. You know they are completely crazy and they are so good to them you can't imagine. Here we get everything. Fidel is good to them because they are very good to the poor people and they take in all those poor helpless people that don't pay. They pay nothing, some of those people, and they give them clothes and everything. You can't imagine how good they are to them, and special attention and special chairs, they're pushed along in a chair.

It's lovely here. There are about 400 people here – 200 men, 200 women. And they are all very good, you know. They're so religious, they go every morning to the church. So do I. In the morning we get a little coffee, and then we go there, and then we come back and we have our breakfast.

We have four cinemas, they're very nice. Very often we have movie pictures but I don't understand them very well. We have a lovely theatre, too. We have a drug store, and what else have we? We have an infirmary for the sick people. They have everything. For the men and for the women separately. And this lovely little park here. Most of the men come here, you know. And then we have another park all around, immense, with a whole lot of poultry and animals, so we have meat.

It's very lonely for me here though. It's lonely for me here. Nobody of my own. We had a home. The British had a home, you know, in Miramar, for the English, and I stayed there for three months. Well, there were only a few. There were three Irish girls – Miss O'Connor and Miss O'Kelly. They were English teachers. They were retired and we had a swimming pool by the sea. This was before Fidel became popular. Well, it was washed away by a wave, by a storm. The home is gone now. And they also had a hospital for the English. They haven't got that any more. They've no colony here now, I think I'm the only one. There's Miss Reed. Miss Reed was born here, but the father and mother were consul in Camagüey. And she's very nice. She's the only one that resides here. She and I both go to the parties [at the British embassy].

I'd die without Cathy. She's very good, she does everything for me. Her father too. We were good friends, although he was from the North of Ireland and I was from the South. And Cathy has to come with my tea because here they don't believe in tea. No tea. The ambassador's wife gave the Reverend Mother a box of tea. But she never gave me any. And now the nun that serves at our table, Sor Gloria, says, 'Miss May, I would like some tea.' And I said, 'I haven't any. You have to get it from the embassy.' They have tea at the ambassador's, you know. They are very nice all those at the embassy, aren't they? I like them better than those that were there before. Those who were there before were very pretentious.

What about the Cubans?

Oh, they're very uneducated, very changed, you know. They are very mixed, the blacks and whites. On the television we see more black people than white. They're very changed. They're not so refined. They were more refined in years gone by. (*Laughs*) But they're friendly with me. Sometimes they take me for an *americana*. They think I'm a rich *americana*. They come to my door. 'Give me this, give me that.' I've to lend them something else . . .

I like Fidel because I understand his Spanish. He speaks very distinctly and he's good to the working people. He gives work to many people and he helps them. But, em, I don't like his English, he doesn't speak it so well. But his Spanish, yes. And he's very occupied all the time, very busy. He helps the workers and he's good to these people here in this home. He's pleased with the nuns . . . the nuns they have plenty to eat and we have always on Sunday a wonderful lunch and very tender meat. I don't know where they get it. I've never had such tender meat as I get here.

We have many cooks and the principal cook, he sings in English. He sings in a beautiful voice, but he wants to practise his English and he comes and sings for me. What a lovely voice. All over the dining room everybody hears him. I don't like the *guajiro* [country] songs they're singing on Sunday night, I don't like it.

I have a nurse who comes one day a week to help me. It's very hard at my age, you know. They don't believe I'm so old and they don't help me enough. They can't believe I'm ninety-four, they can't believe that. And I get no sympathy because I look younger than I am. But I feel my age. I have to take my own shower in the morning and that's not easy.

Do you have proof of your age?

I have my recommendations from the convent that I was teaching in for eight years. And they were so delighted with me they wanted me to enter the convent. In the Sacred Heart and in the French

Dominicans. But I hadn't the vocation. I wanted to go back to dear old Ireland again. So I lost my pension and they had to go away when Fidel became important because there's no religion taught in the schools now. And they only taught religion. There are other nuns in Vedado, but they take care of the sick like the nuns here. They are allowed to stay to take care of the sick and the old people, but not to teach. No teaching.

Here I have only two pupils who come. I have no time. One is a little one, she is about seventeen years old. She is so pretty, a friend of Cathy's. She doesn't believe in anything. No religion. But she's very intelligent. In no time she's learnt so much – the present, the past, the future, the negative, the interrogative – everything she knows. Her father and mother are divorced, you know, and her father is delighted with her classes. She comes here and I don't charge her for her classes. Only she has to bring me my tea (*said with glee*). And Cathy gives her the tea. So she brings me my tea when she comes. And she has an hour's lesson. And she's quite intelligent, you know. When there's something she doesn't understand, she says, 'Why do you have to put that in the negative?' and I explain to her. And then she adds, 'That's plenty.' And then she goes home.

I was born in Castlegregory, outside Tralee, near the sea, in my grandmother's home. Well, I was born there, and then after, my father was an officer in the Royal Irish Constabulary. My grandmother didn't like it because she was very Irish and, of course, he got a good pension from the English. But then we went from Tralee to County Cork. He was sent to County Cork and I went to college in the Sisters of Charity. They had a very nice convent in Dunmanway. And there they were very good to me and they liked me very much. They thought they wanted to make me a teacher of their school, but I didn't want to be a teacher, I wanted to be a nurse, but not a teacher. So then I went to London to be a nurse, but I was too young. I was in love with the little children there, you know, and I almost fainted at two operations, so I couldn't continue. And I came back again. (*Laughs*)

I like French very much and I like France. Oh, I'd a lovely time there. I went to Deauville. And there I was with the English boys and the officers who couldn't speak French and I helped them to buy their things. They were all so nice and friendly, you can't imagine. But I'd one Scotch friend in kilts, you know. He was very handsome but he liked me very much. But he said after the war that he thought he would go to South Africa. So I said, 'Huh, goodbye. I'm not going to marry anybody who's going to South Africa.' (*Laughs*) I liked the Australians best of all. Oh, they were very nice, the Australian boys. Handsome, nice, and I liked how they spoke, too. And the New Zealanders were a little more pretentious, but I liked them too.

I came back to Ireland, and then they said, 'Well, you're going to teach in the North of Ireland. So then they sent me to Belfast, near to where Cathy's father lived. I was teaching there and they were very nice to me, those people in the North of Ireland where I was teaching. Then the children got grown up and they had to go to college and I came back home. And when I got home, I got an offer to teach in Cuba.

An Irish teacher. She had to go home because her mother died. Her father needed her. So I took her place with the richest family in Cuba – the Gómez Mena's. And when I arrived there I had two young girls. They didn't go to school, I had to teach them everything in English and then the mother said to me before the month was up, 'Listen, if we are not pleased with you, we're going to send you back to Paris.' I didn't want to go back to Paris because after the war it was horrible. And then I said, 'Well, all right.' And then when the month was finished she said, 'Come here, I want to pay you. We're very pleased. We are delighted with you. You are a good teacher and the children love you.' I left them after one year. I went home on my holidays and then I went to Mexico to teach. But I went with another English teacher and she was a good friend of mine from Dublin.

Well, the pupils there, I liked them better than here. They were very nice, but the climate didn't agree with her and with me, yes. So, I had to come back, I had to leave Mexico on account of her and come back again to Cuba. I was thinking of going to New York to teach but we stayed in Cuba to give private lessons, and here I am ever since giving private lessons.

5

Arcadio Suárez Rodríguez

Arcadio and his compañera, *an old black woman who is virtually blind, live in the worst 'house' I saw in all my time in Cuba. Lopsided and precarious, it would hardly qualify as a shack now, though once it must have been considered adequate, one of a typical row in the poor area of Guantánamo city, close by the railway line. There are gaps between the planks which make up the structure, and the floorboards are worn away to the earth below. A flimsy wooden partition divides the space in two. There is no electric light and no running water.*

Arcadio is a mulatto, of mixed black and white descent. He is seventy-four. He raised a family with his wife, from whom he is separated. For many years, he worked at the US Guantánamo Naval Base* and paid into a pension scheme. He does not receive the pension to which he is entitled.†

4 June 1989

I began to work on the base on 2 February 1946. I was let go on 20 February 1964 – 20 February 1964. (*Repeated with deliberation*) They

* The Guantánamo Naval Base, an area of 117 square miles, was leased under pressure and in perpetuity to the US in 1903.
† Some of his former workmates do receive the pension. I discussed the matter with the then Head of Mission of the US Interests Section in Havana, John Taylor. He said he would look into it but that at present Arcadio would have to live in the US to qualify for it. Given the small sum concerned, however, it would be worthless there. He could not explain why some should have received it and others not.

had some problem there and so they got rid of a lot of workers and I was in the third group to go. They gave us the option of staying, but as a Cuban and a veteran who liberated these parts, I came home to be with my *compañera*. Do you know what I mean? I came home.

I had been working there a fair few years until all that happened. And here we are waiting for our pension and it hasn't arrived. We paid into a scheme for years but it hasn't arrived. Some have got it, but many haven't. That's what we are waiting for . . . I hear they paid some, but not others. They haven't paid us. It's over there and they haven't sent it. It's there.

You had to get a pass to work on the base, so as a worker and with the unemployment there was around here we asked for a pass. So then they brought the passes to us and I went over. And I spent all that time working until they got this idea when they said to us, 'Whoever wants to may stay, because we're going to close this [border] off once and for all.' And as a Cuban and a veteran I said, 'No, I'm going back to my Cuba.' My father was a veteran. Do you know who that is there? (*Pointing to a picture on the wall*)

Maceo?

Right. My father fought in Maceo's column. My father. This is the machete my father used in the war to liberate Cuba in 1895, this sabre here. It had a hilt but the veterans' army cut it off afterwards because as civilians they couldn't use it. I have to rub it with grease to get it out and use it. It must be a metre long. That was in 1895. He fought with Maceo.* When he died, I collected it from Maceo's Fort. I unbuckled it. Maceo was the Bronze Titan.†

I worked at different things at the base. I was a painter. I did gardening. Really, you had to work in whatever they gave you. I worked everywhere so I know the base well. From Puerto Escondido to La Piedra. The work was good. All the workers there worked well. They paid us, let's say, accordingly. The only thing is, we had a lot of travel expenses to-ing and fro-ing. But,

---

* Antonio Maceo, in the second War of Independence.
† Bronze refers to the colour of Maceo's skin, and Titan to his stature as a hero.

really, they paid well. If you worked over the eight hours you got time and a half. Or if you worked on Saturdays and Sundays.

When the Revolution happened we were inside. And when we were going home we found that they had taken Caimanera and we saw the lines were all down. And we passed them and we came to this place, and the rebels told us to turn back as there were still places closed off to civilians. They overran Caimanera that day we came out. Then on the Saturday a frigate called the *Maceo* bombarded Caimanera. We hid up in the hills. Then the frigate fired cannon at us. Batista's government pounded Caimanera. So we just stayed in the holes we'd dug out until orders came from the base to cease firing.

The Revolution won and we continued working as before, coming and going. There was no problem. There we'd work, arriving in the morning and going back at night. Some actually slept there. Some came and went every day and others stayed and went home on Fridays.

There was a customs officer who searched you to see if you were smuggling. No more than that. There we were. Now, what I would like is for them to send me my dough. That's what I'd like. I really need it. And I sweated enough for it. Slaved enough. Catching boats and trains and getting up at the crack of dawn depending on what transport you took. Let's see, from here to Caimanera is about three-quarters of an hour, and then twenty-five more minutes to get to the base. Some of us would get the train to the boat and others would go by taxi.

There were a lot of us – men and women. A fair number. At one stage there were about six thousand of us workers. Six thousand Cuban workers. They never treated anyone badly. We never got rough treatment there. You just went to your work and you returned home. Because if someone treats me badly, I'll work that day but you won't see me tomorrow. I'm off. And wherever I go I speak the truth, because the truth has no boundaries, I say. Treat me rough and I don't come back.

After a year working on the base we began to pay into a pension fund. We paid for our retirement, which is what I am waiting for, because that is mine and I earned it by the sweat of my brow. If they sent it it would help because it would change our circumstances. I worked long years for that. I have lived in this house now since 1946.

Could you not have done something more with the money you earned over the years?

The money I earned was for getting by on, because there was the constant drain of travel expenses. At that time, most of our money stayed there.

And then they said to us that there was a problem and that they were going to close it off. And those that felt like us came back here. Because this is my native land which I will not leave, and when they have to throw the earth over me I don't want it to be from any country, I want it to be from mine. Do you understand? And that wasn't easy because there had been many years of unemployment. Because if you have a job it's to support your family decently. So back I came. The Comandante en Jefe said we had to be given work, so I continued working here until I retired on sickness benefit. I was taken on a building site. I was taken on. I worked for about twelve years and I have been getting by with what the government gave me, still hoping that some day they [the US] will send me what is mine. They don't want to part with it, I don't know. It's odd, because some have got it and others . . . haven't.

My pension here is 69 [pesos]. Minuscule. On account of having had the misfortune of getting sick. The medical commission at the site called in the older men for a check-up. They got us to do some exercises there and when they examined me they took me aside and the doctor told me that I couldn't continue working. So I had to leave. And I couldn't work anywhere else. I was destroyed. Work for me was a point of honour, a matter of self-respect. And I had to face a family, and all this time I have had to face her. Do you understand? On account of all those things that happened.

But all those that were thrown out [of the base] were given work by Fidel. Like everyone else, same wages and all. So I am very grateful to the Revolution and here I am present and happy. But I would like to be fifty years younger for whatever might happen in this country. That would make me thirty or twenty-something. If my father hadn't used this machete in 1895, Fidel wouldn't have been able to do this, would he? So you have to get on with it. And Cuba before all else. First, Cuba. I am proud of being Cuban and a veteran fighter here and we will fight whatever we have to for this. And when we shortly die, let it be Cuban soil they throw over us. I never dreamt of living anywhere else although they said we could stay. That's fine if you don't think of family, of homeland; of mother or father, of grandchild; of anything, only living parasitically for yourself. Well, those of us who knew how to think realised that we worked to support our families in a respectable way, and we came home. And here we are.

But then when they saw that a lot of people were leaving and that they would be left without workers, they gave up the idea and the people continued to come and go. But we had been told that the gate would be closed for ever. They gave us talks and I said, no chance. I collected my belongings and left. And I haven't died. That was 20 February 1964, and here I am still . . . The Comandante en Jefe took us into his bosom and said work had to be found for us. And we *all* began to work. And our families continued eating. So they threw us out and the Revolution took us into its bosom. And that's it.

That base belongs to us. That's ours. It belongs to our country. That contract they have must be up. That's what I hear, that it belongs to Cuba. And we are Cubans. Let's see what happens. We don't know if they are going to hand it over or if they are not. They've had enough time to hand it over . . .

In my day there weren't the education facilities the Prime Minister has given young people today. Now they all study. I didn't have the chance. All I ever did was work – weeding, minding animals, that was my situation. That's the way it was because we lived in the country. In those days in the country you had to work a lot. When night fell you were worn out and it was straight to bed. (*Chuckles*) When dawn broke it was up and out to work. And it was hard work. That was my life.

I learnt to read and write, badly, when I was an adult. I can manage it a little. I never sat at a desk. It's not like Fidel now who has given everyone the chance to learn. You cannot learn too much for the simple reason that knowledge doesn't take up any room.

The Revolution gives them [youth] everything. It educates them, clothes them, puts shoes on their feet. For that reason the Revolution is benevolent. We have to love it and try not to lose it because I think if we lose the Revolution, we lose the world. You have to go out and walk the length and breadth of Cuba to see what this benevolent Revolution has done. For that reason. Yes, for that reason I speak as I do.

(*His* compañera *interrupts, laughing, but not without some derision*) Do you want your soapbox now?

Well, I have to say it. I know what I am saying. There are many who don't see things the same way. But this is − since I was born, and look how old I am − the best government there has been. We didn't own our own land. It was all landlords with big farms and that. You had to be a *colono* [tenant farmer]. You worked and you grew coffee and they gave you a patch of land and you paid them and you kept their farm for them for life. But when they wanted to throw you off their land they could because the laws almost never favoured the small person. That's why I'm happy with this Revolution, which is even-handed. The minister here, Fidel Castro, gave us all a ration card so we could all have a little. Because we all have a right to live. We are all human and we should be able to live.

6

Pablo Blanche

This is a chance encounter in the Guantánamo hinterland. Pablo, who is black, was walking with his bag of newspapers and letters over his shoulder. We sit down and talk in the shade of a tree. Schoolchildren hang around to gawk at the unusual sight of a foreigner in their tiny village. Pablo is seventy.

5 June 1989

My surname is French. I live here, well, I was born and bred here as they say. I am my mother's only child. An only child. I never had anyone else in the world except myself. But I do have my own children, fourteen of them: eight girls and six boys. By different women. Some by one and others by another. By three. I am now living with my daughters and my wife. I have nine of my children currently living in the house. Some are students and others are working. And me here delivering letters and papers. They work in agriculture. My wife can't work because she suffers from varicose veins. That's dangerous. The doctor said she can't work, she has to rest as much as possible.

You must have a big house?

The house is a bit of a problem. A bit of a problem. We haven't had any help in that department yet. Dreadful conditions. It lets in water all over. All over. (*Low, sad voice*) The rain gets in everywhere. We'll see. Everything has its time.

I get 108 pesos pension and a further 40 to 50 for helping out with this. Better than doing nothing. I don't do it so much for the money as for the people; that they get their messages, their letters on time and that.

I spent all my life here – cutting cane, picking coffee, I've just about done everything here. I have repaired roads, this and that, until I became a driver within this process [the Revolution]. I spent twenty-seven years transporting sugar-cane by lorry all around this whole region. I spent nine transporting people. That was before the Revolution.

After the Revolution was won . . . they nationalised this farm. I was driving a cane-cutter. That was in 1959. And I continued working on the cane-cutter when it belonged to the state, to the government. Then things got pretty bad here and it didn't suit me to continue working as the wages weren't worth it and there wasn't anything else. So I went to Guantánamo to work with MICONS, in the Ministry of Construction. And that's where I was for thirteen years, working on a cement-mixer, until my retirement. Then after that, through my work centre, I went cane-cutting as a volunteer for one or two months or the whole year if necessary. And now, as you see, here I am with the newspapers serving the people, and there you have it.

Cane-cutting was a desperate business before. We were cutting cane for 15 centavos a tonne during the Machado crisis period . . . Our lives were very bad. Our families lived very badly. We had no choice but to work either in sugar or coffee. There was no other type of work in Cuba. Cut cane and wait for the coffee harvest. They paid you 5 centavos the tin [a specific measure]. You had to get up at dawn and work all day till 4 or 5 in the afternoon, and you'd end up with 1.50 pesos at the end of the day. Which is not the situation now. Today you work in a brigade. You go to the coffee plantation at 5 in the morning and at 11 a.m. you bring your coffee along and you have already earned 5 or 6 pesos. You get your meals, your clothing. Life on the plantations was really awful before. Today they even pick you up in a truck and bring you back afterwards. You had to go on foot before. There wasn't even a road. It was a mule-track. Now you have a hostel with all the conditions – meals, clothes. It's very different, very different.

Something else that isn't the same is the fact that before we had nothing to do and we wanted to have fun the whole week, but today you have to work, you have to produce. On Saturdays, we have fun, we meet up. The carnival we have here is really great. We can't ask for more. We don't want what we had before, then we didn't produce, because before people had fun for weeks on end but they didn't work. They didn't have work. Today we produce and we have parties and we go to the carnival. We don't have any problems there. We're delighted with that side of things.

It was wild after the Revolution. Everyone lived it up, not a bother in the world. We never would have dreamt of what we have now. We never would have dreamt of how well we live.

I, really, I am overcome when I think of our situation before. For example, family life, education, everything, we didn't have that before because there was even racial discrimination in the schools. They separated us blacks from the whites. What the whites learnt was not what we learnt. I lived through that because I got up to fifth grade. My head was fairly bright in those days but it wasn't because the teachers tried to teach us. It's not like that today. Everyone's equal. In the old days we couldn't just go into any classroom. Blacks couldn't do that. Yet today, it's all one big school, one society.

There were five strata in society before. Here in Cuba. In Guantánamo you had the Club Catalán, El Siglo, El Liceo, La Nueva Era and La Colonia Española. That's the way it was in Cuba. We were only allowed go to La Nueva Era. You are talking to someone with experience of the past. Mulattos danced their legs off in El Siglo. El Liceo was for those who had a slight tinge of colour and whites went to the Club Catalán and La Colonia Española. Today there is no more racial discrimination, we are all the one people.

Listen, what they did here with us poor people, the exploitation they subjected us to, wouldn't be believed. We really lived badly. We always lived here in this area. We had nothing at all. Nothing. We had no work, nothing. We got up in the morning and ran to the shops to see if they'd give us something on tick even without work. There were some really decent shopkeepers like Abelardito Suárez and Alsiño Guerra, and the tears would come to their eyes because they were humanitarians, humanists. They saw people were hungry and they would serve them saying, 'Go on, go on.' And they would give them a little bit of rice and a little bit of this and that. We went through all that in those days. And today we all have work. Overall we are doing well. If somebody isn't working it's because they don't want to. Our schools and hospitals are free. We have what a fellow would have died for the want of before. If he didn't have the money to go to a doctor, the child would have died. You had to pay for a burial. Which you wouldn't have the money for. Today we have health-care. You can take the child to the doctor or to the hospital and you get the medicine free. You have everything, I'm telling you. We are simply delighted here to have what we have.

What's going to happen when Fidel dies?

No, he's never going to die. Nah. Well, if he dies, there are the others who can fulfil the same role as he does. There's only one line to follow. Fidel might die but the line continues, the march goes on. That's for sure. Sure as sure can be, I'm telling you. No deviating from the line here. Nobody wants that. I'm an old man of seventy and I am still ready to do anything to defend this.

7

Maribel Santos Ferro

Maribel is a personal assistant to the editor of a magazine and enjoys her work. As a child she volunteered to go on the Literacy Campaign. Now forty, and married with two children, she recalls those early days and reflects upon the situation in Cuba today.

11 October 1988

When I joined the campaign I was twelve years old. It was an extraordinary experience for me, working with the peasants, because I taught in the country, in the Oriente region, in Contramestre. It was great. Besides, it wasn't too difficult for me as I lived in the country, well, not exactly in the country, I'm from San Cristóbal in Pinar del Río province. That's where I was born and that's where I lived until I was fifteen or sixteen, when I came here to Havana. Being with peasants wasn't something strange to me, as most of my family on my mother's side lived in the country. And I used to go to the country on my holidays. So it wasn't a very difficult situation for me living without electricity, without conveniences . . . and besides, we were so pleased to see how the peasants appreciated the fact that townspeople left their homes – young people, because we were all very young – their homes, their parents, to go and live with them and try and teach them how to read and write. It was very moving, really very moving.

There had been a meeting. Well, it was put to the people . . . Fidel proposed it, so those of us who were interested went to the local office of the Ministry of Education where we filled out the forms. If you were a minor your parents had to sign the form authorising it. They gave us some clothes, ready made-up, a uniform, they gave us all that in the local office of the Ministry. And so we came to Havana in a train. From there we went to Varadero. They had made up a course with some notions of how to teach people to read quickly. So they gave us these pages, a sort of manual, a guide, and they gave us lessons on how to conduct a class . . . because you had to have reached a certain level of education, you know.

I was the youngest in my family and the only girl. The others were all working or studying at the time, so they couldn't join up. They weren't working in the Ministry of Education, but if they had been, they would have had the chance to go. You got your normal salary and everything.

I was away three months. It was my first time away from my family, the first time I was ever away from them. I was only there three months because I got sick. I had an accident, I fell on a mountain. Then I started to get pains in the spine. It was a bruising. But they were very fussy about the health of the children on the campaign – the slightest thing and they'd have you off to the doctor and home . . . I didn't stop teaching because when the doctor saw me and said it wasn't a problem, that it was a bruising, I continued with the campaign in my home village. Because they sent me home to my parents.

I wanted to work and help the peasants on the land, harvesting fruit or whatever. If I didn't do that I'd help in the house, cleaning, cooking – housework, or help in the field. I liked picking fruit. Off I would go and work for three, four or five hours. Then we'd come back to the house. We'd wash, eat and we'd always give our classes to the peasants at night. Always at night. In their free time. I gave classes in a house, not in a school. Sometimes if there was a sugar-mill community, lots of people for one literacy campaigner, several peasants would meet up. That wasn't my situation. I had my classes in a house with the people who lived there, who were a couple, and their three children.

We would eat what they ate. They gave us lots of boiled root vegetables, rice . . . meat from their ration. Every fifteen days they would go down to buy the meat at the community where there was a butcher's and shops. And so they would share what they had from the ration with us. And the milk from their cows, they had cows. They had livestock, so from time to time they would kill a pig and we had meat, lard . . . whatever they ate in their homes, we ate. Exactly the same. We did not transfer our ration to where we were.

The man was sixty and the woman fifty or thereabouts, his wife. The children – one was twenty-seven or twenty-eight. The youngest were beginning to go to school and knew a little bit. A school that was miles away, but anyway, a school, built after the Revolution. A house turned into a school . . . but it was very far away and if it rained they couldn't go. So they barely knew more than the parents. The parents didn't know a thing. Didn't know how to write at all. Not even their names. Incredible. Not even their names. So when we finished . . . they were delighted because they could read, not very well . . . but they could read a story, the newspaper . . . in three months. (*Laughs*) It was very difficult, but they really put a lot into it. A lot. Not like children. You know that children take longer, but they were very eager to learn. Especially the younger ones, they really tried.

When I left they immediately sent someone else, another literacy campaigner. We were all very young with little experience but really that campaign was lovely, really lovely. They wrote to me. They wrote to me for a long time, but you know the way it is. We stopped writing to each other . . . I don't know anything about them, whether or not they are still living in the province of Santiago de Cuba. His name was Jesús Hernández. He was Spanish. He came as a youngster to Cuba and he had a fairly big coffee farm there. It wasn't great but he did make money, he had coffee, he had bananas. Bananas and coffee. He retained his Spanish citizenship at least up until the time I met them. The land was his, it wasn't nationalised. And he, his wife and the children all worked on it. They all worked on the land. They sold the coffee to the state. I don't really know how much they were paid.

And did these people know you were going to arrive?

Yes, they had been told because they had carried out a sort of census all over Cuba, in the most remote parts, before the campaign began. They conducted a survey to find out who wanted to learn to read and write, because there were people who were reluctant to learn. There were people who didn't want to become literate and would not allow it, and so they tried to convince these people when the campaign got going. So they took a census and found out who was willing to have campaigners in their house. My granny, for example, had two teachers in her house throughout the whole campaign, and she gave them breakfast, dinner and tea, my granny.

I always wanted to travel outside my province. To get to know other people, other ways. When my friends and I signed up we agreed, 'Let's ask to be sent to Oriente.' We weren't at all afraid. I was never afraid. I didn't think about it. My parents and my aunts and uncles talked about the counter-revolutionaries, the *alzados*, but I never thought anything would happen to me, nor that I would come up against them. Never. Despite the fact that one night we had stones thrown at us and we thought it was them or that it was boys doing it to frighten us. Because we were in bed and then we suddenly heard a lot of stones being thrown. We got up and we heard footsteps running away. We were surrounded by mountains, and that was the only house. A little house made of palm-trees alone there surrounded by mountains. That was the house. And you cooked with wood. Let me tell you it wasn't easy. Not at all. Because it isn't the same as your own house, with electricity, with proper flooring, with all the conveniences, with your bed. We slept in hammocks there. And to leave all that, to leave that, well, you know what it's like when you're twelve or thirteen – you don't feel any aches or pains and you're afraid of nothing.

Then two years later, in 1962, I went on another campaign, there was a call to young people. I was in the Young Rebels section of what was then called the Young Communists' Union. So they put out a call for the coffee harvest. People with or without experience, young people. So I joined up and off I went again. And I picked coffee. I was away for forty-five days. It was fierce but I must say a very good experience. Very good. Sometimes I recall all those hard times and I feel so strong, so secure, you can't imagine. Although I was always very independent. Since I was a child.

You know, I began to work because I saw my parents had such

a tough life. My father earned 100 pesos and there were five of us children. He earned 100 pesos and my mother never worked outside the home. So I always wanted to help them and I always wanted to work, and they would say, 'No. You have to study, you have to study.' So when I was seventeen I was legally entitled to work, and I did.

My dad worked in a furniture factory which belonged to his brother. The owner was his brother. And he was just another employee. They sold furniture to the people in the village. So, I felt that he . . . I saw that he was exploited by his brother. He had to get up earlier than the brother, and he didn't have a lunch-break and the brother did. Sometimes he did the run to Havana, which is almost 100 kilometres, and sometimes he had to do it twice, taking a lorry-load of furniture to sell there. I felt very sorry for him and I started to work to help out at home. I was very independent. And then I came to Havana and began to work here. I got a place in a school in Havana and I began to study. Then . . . as they only gave me a pass for a few hours, there wasn't enough time to go home to my village in Pinar del Río, so I came to live in an aunt's house here. But this aunt was going to the United States and she started getting at me for studying. 'Why are you studying if it'll be of no use to you anyway?' She left in 1966. That was a bit of a problem. Then the school where I studied agronomy was moved far away and I didn't want to go so far away. And there were a lot of problems – staff shortages, posts unfilled, classes with no teachers – so I became disillusioned and I left it and began to work. That's how I come to be living in Havana now.

I began to work and then, since my aunt was going to the United States, which she finally did, I stayed on in the house. I had the right as she lived there and then the state granted me the right to stay on there paying the rent on the building. The property was transferred into my name and I am now living in that house. It's mine. Well, not yet. I still have a few years to pay on it. A few years. It's not yet mine. I pay 10.50 pesos a month for it because that's 10 per cent of what I earned at the time the contract was drawn up. Now, as I earn more, if I want I can go and have the mortgage raised. But, well, within seven years more or less, it will be my property. I will have paid it off.

Do you think there is still the same feeling for the Revolution as there was in the beginning?

Honestly, I can say that despite all the years gone by I am still motivated by the Revolution. I feel that emotion although now, if they had a campaign now, I couldn't go on it because I am forty. I have two children to look after. My children first, at the present moment, because they need me.

But young people today, I don't know, it's not the same. It's not the way it was then. I don't know if it's because they have got it all. They haven't had the experience I had under capitalism. And I lived it and felt it in my blood. But young people nowadays didn't experience that. Because I have a son of sixteen. They don't know how it was. If they want a pair of trousers, they get them. They see that I work and if I get sick I am paid; that they're not going to throw me out of work. I think they don't appreciate that, they don't appreciate it the way we do . . . I do remind them of it, the years of discrimination against women and all those things. I tell them so they might learn, but I don't think it's the same. As I say, I think that's why. That they didn't live it and that they have everything. While it's true that we sometimes have shortages, there is no real poverty, no hunger, they don't throw you out of a house because you haven't paid the rent that month. You have job security. You don't have to pay for schooling. My son was a day boarder throughout his primary years and I didn't have to pay for dinner or supper. And now that he's at senior cycle secondary level it's the same. He doesn't have to pay for his books. Nothing. All free. But they don't value that. The real merit of what they have they do not appreciate. They don't know how to appreciate it. And now it's time again for the school in the country and he says, 'Hey, great,' and he's delighted and he goes because he wants to.* If you don't want to go, you don't go. He has allergies, he has a few problems, but he goes anyway. And sometimes I visit

* A system whereby secondary-school children in the cities spend forty-five days working in the country to familiarise themselves with production. The numbers involved in this have been reduced in recent years because of the cost involved.

him and I ask, 'Do you feel all right? Do you have any problems? Do you want to come home?' No, no, no, never. Wouldn't hear of it. Home, no.

But as regards helping the Revolution in every way, I don't think there's the same feeling as we had. I haven't lost the desire to help the Revolution. That hasn't gone, despite the years and being older and more tired. Because it really deserves our help, whatever we do for it. I try . . . well, now I don't because my sons do. I am always on top of the eldest to do his guard duty for the Committee [for the Defence of the Revolution: the CDR]; to be responsible; to do his three hours' guard duty; to work at school. But nobody had to tell me those things. (*Laughs*) My parents usually objected to these things because I was very young and it was very far away. I was leaving them. But, as I say, it was my idea, nobody got me going.

What is the Revolution?

The Revolution is something very big. The Revolution got rid of so much injustice, so much unhappiness, because whenever I think of the Revolution or I have my doubts, I always try to make comparisons with what went before and what came afterwards. Always. And I haven't been through schools, I haven't been through political schools, ever. Which help a lot, help you understand. We suffered a lot in the past, the poor people, we suffered discrimination. My village, despite the fact that it was very small, had no rich people. There was a middle class, more or less, but they were not rich and didn't have extensive lands . . . landlords and that, but we poor people were discriminated against. I suffered a lot. And my little friends who were black couldn't go to the same club as I went to. Often we didn't go. Often I didn't go so as to be with them and so we went to a black society which did allow whites. I had a lot of black friends, boys and girls. So, since I suffered these things so much – discrimination against women like my mother who couldn't go out to work because there was no work in the town, barely for the men – when the Revolution happened and there were all these changes – that women worked, that women did all types of work – even my father changed and he was also a bit *machista* – the woman's place was in the home cleaning – and even he changed and let my mother go out and participate in all the activities of the Federation, go to meetings at night, that sort of thing.

Machismo is on the way out. It's a huge task we women have. A huge task, because when I was first married, my husband didn't do anything and didn't want to help me in any way and now, however, I notice that, gradually, with my daily effort – because I can tell you it wasn't easy – he cleans, does the cooking. Just today I told him I would be late and he has to get the supper, and he said fine, all right. (*Laughs*) Things are changing a lot, but it's a huge struggle. They're not all like that, I assure you, but the majority are changing. I notice among my friends, those that work outside the home, that their husbands are helping them more. I can't say the same for those who work in the home. The women who still work in the home, the housewives, still haven't got their husbands to help them like I have. There are still a lot of *machistas*, an awful lot, but we women are to blame. I say that because of my children. When my eldest boy was seven, at an age when he could help me, when he could get the shopping, I didn't let him for fear of what they might say to me, that he was doing women's jobs, notions like that. Yes, indeed. So for fear of that I didn't get him to help me. Now, however, my youngest boy goes to the shop, puts out the rubbish for me, fetches me things and does jobs in the house. Because I went through that with the eldest so they wouldn't call him a girl for putting out the rubbish or getting the messages. So I see that I have made some progress too. I know that I myself have overcome these things and I have helped my husband to get rid of his macho ideas a little bit. I have helped him there.

So what are Cuba's main problems?

For example, I don't have a car. In my house we have neither a private nor a state car. We get around by bus. In the *proletaria,* as we call it. It's the *proletaria* for work, to come home, to go out, and for that same reason we don't go out very often. I suffer an awful lot with that bus. That's the honest truth. I put up with a lot, because sometimes I have to wait an hour and a half for a bus which then doesn't stop. I can only catch one bus for work. And that bus never, ever stops. At rush-hour, from 7 a.m. to 9 a.m., it never stops. Sometimes I have to walk twelve blocks to catch another bus, which is also bad, but slightly better than the other one because I can get it at the stop. I queue and get on and that's it. Coming home is worse. Sometimes I have wanted to die at a stop because I see it's 5.30, 6, 6.30 and I still can't get home . . .

There are debt problems, a huge foreign debt and no money. There is no hard currency to buy buses, everyone knows that, it's no mystery. Imagine, there's also a problem with oil, all these things. Do you know what it's like to run a city like this with so many inhabitants? I think, I don't know, but this has to be solved fast, right now. By December or January this problem has got to be solved, because it really does seriously affect the people. It really does. For example, you have to get to a hospital for an appointment and you have to be there for a certain time and you can't get a taxi and the bus doesn't come or doesn't stop – that's really maddening. And we don't go out at all. We don't go out, so as not to have to get a bus, so as not to have to be squashed, so as not to have to wait so many hours at the bus-stop. I don't know any other country, but it seems to me that the Cuban people put up with a lot and are very revolutionary, because to go to work in the conditions we have to isn't easy. I was hanging out of the bus with my bag waving about in the air and my skirt blowing up (*hoots with laughter*) and I going to work. First trying to get it and then hanging on to it for dear life, all to get to work on time. That isn't easy.

I do have free time, not much, but I do have some. Very little, because I arrive home worn out, as I said, from all the acrobatics in the bus (*laughs*), doing all you can to get home alive. When I get in, well, I get the dinner, I see to my children, help with the homework, and afterwards I wash up and see to the house. I tidy up and quickly do the housework and then I sit down to watch television or I read. I relax for a while and then I go to bed.

I don't know if it's just my life but I feel we are living very fast and I don't think that's just here. There's a vast difference between the sort of lives my father and mother led and what we lead today. But then, the situation isn't the same as twenty and thirty years ago.

Sometimes you have to give up your free time to see to the children, the house, the housework, your husband. But I look after the children myself. I can tell you I am a good mother to my children. They are always clean going to school and they have all their meals. They eat every day. They have breakfast, they don't have their midday meal here because they have theirs at school. But I look after them. I go to parent–teacher meetings at the school. If I don't go, their father does. We always go. We co-operate with the teachers in the school in whatever way we can. And we always do the shopping on Saturdays or Sundays. Sometimes, if there's a chance, we do it during lunch-hour or after work. On the way home we might go into a minimarket and buy things that are off . . . that are not on the ration, that are on the open market, because you have thirty days in which to buy your ration from the local store and I can buy those things any day after 5 p.m. But either my husband or I get a chance to buy things on the open market between 5 and 8 p.m.

I have a fairly stable home. I have quite a lot of stability because . . . well, I like my home. I like housework. I do my work and I look after my home and children. I spend a lot of time on my children and on doing social duties as well, such as guard duty, which is once a month. The MTT,* when I am called up. A few days ago they called me up at 10 at night. And I had just got in because the bus had been dreadful that day and I got home at about 7.30 – 7.30 at night! My husband had got the supper and the kids were washed because, as I said, I have stability with the children, they have their routine.

---

* The MTT (Territorial Troops Militia) was created in 1981 and in 1986 totalled a (voluntary) membership of 1.5 million. Members receive periodic training against the possibility of invasion, the idea being that the defence of the country is a matter not just for the armed forces but for everybody. This is summed up in the concept: 'The war of all the people'. Military Service is three years (two if on active service abroad) and is obligatory for all males between the ages of sixteen and thirty. Students do not have to do military service but may train during their years of study for approximately six months, and after graduating do two years of what is called social service – that is, they work in their specific discipline but in designated areas of the country. They are fully paid. Women may volunteer for military service, but it is not compulsory.

Well, the head of the squad came to tell me of the exercise. It means you have to drop everything in your home – well, if you are sick or have a sick child, you are excused, but at that moment everyone was in the sitting room watching the television, I had no escape. (*Laughs*) Everything was normal – on with the uniform and off to the exercise. You're told to go to a certain place and my husband said, 'Go on, off you go, don't worry.' I put on my uniform and went to the designated place. There we were from 10 at night till 2 in the morning. They gave us a few talks about defence. They distributed some weapons, some *pepechás*,★ that's what they call them, *pepechá*, a machine-gun, they're Soviet with a short barrel and with a disc underneath. They taught us how to assemble and dismantle them, and when we could do that we put them on our shoulder and there we were, wandering about. We walked a good few blocks. I think they do that to see how long it would take to get the troops organised. Well, they congratulated us when the exercise was over. The head of the regiment congratulated us. We grouped fairly quickly and we assembled and dismantled those weapons well. No problem. At 2 in the morning they let us go . . . They gave us a slip for work as we had had to be there during our hours of rest. They gave us a slip of paper so they paid us that day. We didn't have to go to work. I went because I had some work pending. I stayed a while and came home to rest as we had been up all night. I'm not going to tell you that I go every time, because often my husband isn't in Havana, he's down the country, and so I haven't anyone I can leave the children with. So I say, no, I can't go, that I have a certain situation, and there's no problem, they accept the excuse. But I do my social duties. It's a task and I carry it out. I get enough time, just about, by cutting short my hours of sleep or leisure, but I do my duty.

★ P.P.Ch. The initials of the manufacturer.

8

Carlos Fundora

Wandering around Centro Habana I stop at a building site and get chatting to Carlos Fundora. He explains he is working on the first international microbrigade in the country (see p.85). I go around to see him at his home. His sitting room is a corridor in a dilapidated house where his old uncle and disabled young son watch a baseball game on the television. He has two rooms off a yard at the back. Neighbours come in and out all the time as we converse over a bottle of rum. Among other things, Carlos, who is thirty-five, talks of his experiences in Angola as a member of the Cuban troops supporting the Angolan government against South Africa. The mission was successful: tripartite peace accords (Angola, Cuba, South Africa) were finally signed in December 1988 governing the withdrawal of Cuban troops from Angola and the independence of Namibia. A total of 2,016 Cubans died in Angola between 1975 and 1989, the majority in accidents or through sickness; 787 died in combat.

29 January 1989

My family is working class. My father died when I was two, and there were six of us. Our mum brought us all up and we were poor. Poor from the outset because before the triumph of the Revolution it was more difficult . . . We always got some help from my father's family. But it was pretty difficult for a woman to cope with that situation. Then with the Revolution come other aspirations. There are boarding schools, boarding schools for children, and I was a day boarder which meant I got my dinner and we ate again at home. So we would just have our supper at home. My mum started to work and, well, life was quite austere. We played with other people's toys. Sometimes they would give us a present of something, but really I had great admiration for my mother. She was a heroine at bringing up her children . . . Morally we are all good *compañeros*, good sons and daughters and good workers. We are good workers, none of us has been arrested, nobody has broken the law. Three of us are still living with Mum and the six of us are married. And, well, we get along well, we are a fairly united family. Everyone visits each other from time to time and is concerned for the other. And I am proud of that. I was born into poverty and I have learnt from it, because it wasn't easy, and it still isn't, for a woman coping alone and bringing up six children. I was six at the time of the Revolution and the others were all small too. And we all went to school. One became a coppersmith, another is a welder, I have another one who loves the country and animals. There's another who's an electrician living with my mother and the youngest loves sport but is working as a mechanic now. He loves weight-lifting and that and really he is very disciplined, our youngest. We have that double thing, our youngest is a wonderful person. A very strong person, very well brought up, someone who does sport systematically. Everybody admires and loves him, not just the family.

Afterwards, I came here to live in the capital with an uncle of mine which is where I am living now. I did a year-long course in chemical engineering to work in a thermo-electric plant. I got the course and I started working at the Antonio Maceo thermo-electric plant near Regla. I studied at night in the Worker Farmer Faculty, a school which gives workers the opportunity to study. So, I worked until 3 p.m. and afterwards, at 7 at night, I went to the Worker Farmer Faculty. I finished there, which is like getting a senior cycle secondary grade, so with that equivalence I start a B.Sc. course in chemistry at Havana University. I was working all that time and I got to my fourth year in the course. But then I had a child who was born with encephalitis and had to be operated on. That shook me completely and really I couldn't finish the course with only a year to go. I just stopped studying in that fourth year. That was the upshot of that. I was just going to be content with the qualification

I had as a worker, as a middle technician, and get on with it. I am thirty-five now, that was when I was about thirty. And so, I just do my work.

My mum was of Spanish descent. She's white. And my dad was black. The Spanish and the African races mixed. We are Europeans, Africans, Latins. At that time, imagine, there was the same racism that existed everywhere else. There was discrimination. Before, here in Cuba, to see a white woman married to a black man, it was frowned upon. Society was very critical of it and within the family you wouldn't find acceptance. After the triumph of the Revolution – since everyone has a bit of black and white in them – a black was the same as a white, and when the President said that, a lot of people who loved one another irrespective of colour started going out, and nobody says anything now if they see a white woman with a black man. In the family you might still get rejection because changes like these aren't easy. But now, thirty years on, the general feeling is that people couldn't care less.

Of course, you do find people who are racist. From a legal position racism is punishable, but their racism isn't immediately obvious. A white just can't call a black a pig. The black could break his face and he [the white man] is the one with the problem because the law doesn't accept that. Now, what happens? Nobody goes around with a sign on them saying they're racist. Nobody can show they are racist here. Nobody in a position of leadership, nor anybody, can behave in a racist way. But what can you come across? Someone with petit-bourgeois attitudes who might be in a position of responsibility and might in a very sneaky way – because he can't do it openly, the law won't allow it, nobody would allow it . . . There's a labour exchange which has files on people and, well, they send a woman along, she might be black or white, and he doesn't fancy her. He can say, for example – he has to select from five people, and from those five he chooses the most attractive one and she becomes his secretary. He doesn't select the ugliest. That's the way it is. And this happens in certain factories, and he says, 'I want her to be my secretary.' She does a course in the factory because he fancied her. Nobody is certain that that's why she was chosen. But it's inevitable. There are organisations who don't like that, who are against it, but the boss has the power

to do it or not do it. Afterwards it's discussed. It can be discussed –
if it was because he fancied the woman – and that would be analysed
in another context by the board, by the Communist Youth Union
at the factory, or by the Party. They'd look at the issue and therein
lies another tale.

Sometimes it's a question of education. I'm going to tell you
something I've noticed. Blacks were always very discriminated
against. They were always very submissive towards the whites
because, well, they were practically slaves. In certain times they
were slaves. They don't have that refinement. Now there is
equality, there are no problems, but still you find the whites look
after one another better than the blacks in the sense that they protect
each other. Because I noticed it even outside Cuba. For example,
when I was in the People's Republic of Angola the blacks treated
each other badly while the whites looked after one another. They
have never had a good standard of living, they have never been at
the top, they have always been put down and sometimes they think
they have to behave badly among themselves when the logical thing
is for them to unite and do things as best they can. Just because the
white man says no, the black man has to be always downtrodden?
Blacks can have independence and live well also, but what they
have to know is how to lead not by oppressing the other but by
getting on well among themselves and having the education and
training to give to others who don't have it. They reject each
other, which is not right. And I sometimes said that when I was
there – 'You people are killing each other because you don't see.'
It's not that there aren't individuals who, of course, quite apart
from being black, deserve the highest respect and esteem, and I
am very moved by that here. Here, there are as many eminent
black people as there are white. People who really cut their teeth in
sacrifice, in the struggle, who have studied and have demonstrated
their intelligence by becoming doctors, lawyers, and by assuming
positions of responsibility within the republic, within the nation,
and you see that every day.

A few years ago the Party discussed this and decreed that the
percentage of blacks and of women at top levels of the Party
had to be increased. There should be a greater representation of
blacks both in the Party and in government leadership. And that's

the direction it's going in. And all Cubans agree with that. And women as well. In the Party leadership or in posts of responsibility . . . right from the base. From the top to the bottom. Because this was something that had got out of hand here: there wasn't even one woman in a position of importance. There were some, but you could count them on one hand. They were *compañeras* who had fought in the Sierra Maestra. But anyway, they gave jobs mainly to men, not to women. That's not just a problem in Cuba but everywhere. There have always been fewer women in leadership positions. It's the same with blacks and whites here, irrespective of the fact that, well, Blas Roca – who was head of the Party, he was first secretary, like Fidel Castro – was in the Politburo. Juan Almeida is also in the Politburo and Esteben Lazo is in the Politburo, he's black, but there should be more. And although the legislation here is for everyone, that isn't a problem, it should take that aspect into account. But you don't have laws for blacks and laws for whites. It's one nation. Everyone has to abide by the same rules. But sometimes they don't watch their image. Some people know how to cover up their mistakes and others don't. I mean, the black guy does it once and gets caught; the white guy does it three times and no one sees him – as the saying goes, 'The white man steals and the black man carries the can.' These things happen. They happen everywhere. What can you do? That's life. Things don't always turn out as good as we might like them to.

How was it you went to Angola?

I went to Angola in 1985. I had a brother who went in 1980 and who had a problem with his nerves there and had to come back to Cuba after six months because of it. Really, you have to have a fair amount of courage and heroism. He came back to Cuba with his nerves shot. I have a lot of friends who have also been to the People's Republic of Angola. I was working in the Food Industry Reseach Institute, which is where I am now, and I get a message here at home to go to the municipal military committee as a reservist. I am a worker, I was not on active service with the armed forces, though the reservists play an important role in wartime. When I get the summons and I go to the committee, they ask me if I would be prepared to go on a foreign mission. They didn't say what country, they never tell anyone where they are going, whether it's the People's Republic of Angola, or China, or Japan. And you either say yes or no. Well, I had nothing to lose, nor anything against the idea, and I said yes.

They give you a general medical check-up, and if they said you were fit to go, you went. If you weren't fit, the doctor told you so. Sometimes it might be the dentist, sometimes the psychiatrist. You went to them all. And when you came out of that medical commission, they gave you the all clear. If you were not fit, no matter how much you wanted to go, well, you couldn't. After that, up to the last minute, you had the right to say you weren't going. There was one *compañero* who afterwards said he wasn't going. That happens. In a thousand, you might get thirty, twenty, ten, fifteen. In my case, in the group I was going, there were about 1,200 of us, and there were three *compañeros* who said no. And they didn't go. And on the way, I mean, when we were in the vehicle taking us to where we were going to train, they said to us, 'Think about it well and if you have any difficulty, a family problem, tell us.' One *compañero* who had a family problem spoke up and there was no problem.

When they first asked me if I wanted to go on an internationalist mission I said yes. What were my reasons for saying yes? Well, I have three children. I have one who is ill, as I mentioned earlier, and my wife was six months pregnant. Quite a difficult situation. Difficult from a family point of view, but from a psychological viewpoint, from a human viewpoint, I was in a position to go on a mission. I only had those restrictions. My brother had not finished his mission, as I explained, and other Cubans had done it, had been capable of coping with those two years in the People's Republic of Angola. And I think, although my situation wasn't the best, I decided to accept the proposition. And, well, I let my family know, it was fairly hard to tell my mum, because she knew what it was like to some extent, but, well, I waited until the last minute to tell her. But I did in the end. I told her and she didn't say anything. She remained silent. A bit sad, you know, because she knew that the step I was taking wasn't easy.

As for my wife, in this case it was a unilateral decision on my part. I didn't want to tell her either, well, because the decision had been mine, and in these things . . . well, there was a whole series of family problems, with your wife, with the children as well, it creates certain situations. But I hadn't been the only one, I wasn't the only one in that situation. I couldn't say no because my children were going to be sad and wouldn't see me for a certain length of time, or I'm not going to see my wife, I'm not going to have a home life. And so I said yes. They gave me a medical check-up. We did twenty-odd days training and I passed that test satisfactorily.

Was there any connection between the fact that your brother came home early and your call-up?

No. No connection. Because my brother lives with my mum in Havana Province, and I live here [Ciudad de la Habana province], and that connection doesn't exist. My brother went in 1980 and my case arises in 1985. I mean, if there were any coincidence, I wouldn't accept it. No. In that case I wouldn't go even if they had to tie me down. So, weighing it all up I went. I was there for two years. It's really a fairly hard life. It's not easy to understand. You have to be there to really know how hard it is. We were going to a war, but really we weren't going into direct combat with the enemy. We were holding positions in the event of an attack by South Africa. Really, it's a very circumscribed life. It's hard enough just to get water and food. Because the food didn't come from here, from Cuba. The government of the People's Republic of Angola had to provide us with food and there was no guarantee that the food would be good. Really, it was pretty awful. But, of course, considering their own food problems it could be described as good when you think that the people were much hungrier than us, so it was really admirable. We said it was awful because we . . . we are not used to the kind of diet we had there. I lost an awful lot of weight, and not just me, lots of us lost a lot of weight. It's fairly difficult. All those who went to that country should get a gold medal. Not even giving them a castle, metaphorically speaking, could you repay them. We didn't go there for money or anything . . . for instance, I didn't save one *quilo* [cent] from my salary, I gave it all to my kids, so there was no question of saving money while I was away . . . I gave some of it to my mum and some to my kids. I didn't didn't keep any of it for myself because I wasn't interested in making money . . . As I was born poor, I didn't have any sense of avarice. Money doesn't particularly appeal to me.

When I got to the People's Republic of Angola, what drew my attention was seeing so much poverty, because I really hadn't imagined that life there could be so tough, that such conditions as they lived in really existed. It is unimaginable, really. Look, I'm poor here in Cuba, no? But compared to there, I am rich. And that . . . you cannot conceive of how a human being could live as they do. You have to go there and see it, see how they live, almost like animals. They are not human beings but animals scavenging a living. Human beings eating seeds from the trees, who defecate green like animals . . . The prevalence of disease, a lot of epidemics, parasites, infections, the children there . . . you see a lot of malaria and there are three types of it. There's one which attacks the organs, cerebral malaria, which is fatal – if you get it you go down like a chicken, you fall backwards, and people almost fall down unconscious and very near death – that's cerebral malaria. There are three types depending on where it attacks you, but anyway you get a fever, headaches, and one of our main enemies there as troops was sickness. A fairly powerful enemy, despite the fact that we tried to create the best conditions, because all the troops that went to the People's Republic of Angola, for strategic reasons, live underground. And it isn't easy living underground. Two years underground isn't easy and I did it in the People's Republic of Angola. And under harassment. Not a continuous war but harassment every night. They fired 60 mm. mortars at us, ones of 80 mm. and 120 mm. as well. I mean, the UNITA troops [National Union for the Total Independence of Angola], who most harassed us . . . Then, towards the end of 1987, South African battalions were approaching. Battalions of special troops, one or two would stay, one, at most two, battalions, and at this stage they were causing devastations. I mean, the South African troops tried to select FAPLA [People's Armed Forces for the Liberation of Angola] camps, the camps of the Angolan armed forces, to make their commando raids, because it was easier to penetrate them because they were sometimes careless, very careless on occasions, and they could be more easily penetrated.

I was in the Huambo airport area. I was in the DAAFAR [Anti-Aircraft Defence and Revolutionary Air Force], with 57 mm. cannon, and all I can tell you is there were night raids. Between the months of October to December [1987] UNITA kept up the fighting. They tried to harass the Cuban troops. During the other months they didn't, or rather they were organising themselves because really we didn't go there to fight UNITA. UNITA fought against us because they knew that we were a brake on their activities. We stopped UNITA and South Africa making progress. They knew we were hot stuff and they tried to avoid us, although they would try to attack us by surprise at night. Sometimes the attacks lasted forty-five minutes, an hour at most. They would set up their mortars at night, as the nights there are fairly dark, and they would fire them into our unit. Sometimes they hit, sometimes they didn't, fortunately. We were pretty scared by the fright of it, no? Because sometimes I was asleep. It would be about 2 in the morning and then fourteen or fifteen shells would fall in less than a minute. It was enough to drive you crazy. You didn't know where to run to. But we had all this thought out and immediately, as we were underground, we would run out into the trenches which we had already dug out, and from there we would hold off the attack. Sometimes we would set up a 57 mm. cannon, they are anti-aircraft cannon, and we'd fire it, and when they saw what was coming out were mortar cannon, they scattered fast. The battle was soon over. Imagine, a 57 mm. anti-aircraft cannon. They fired the shells from a position, and sometimes they also had RP-7 rockets. They fired those as well because their job was to destroy the airport, one of the most important airports for supplying the area, Huambo airport. Their goal was to pulverise the runway and thereby prevent supplies for the troops reaching the southern region and where they were camped. The Cuban position and the Angolan government's was always very . . . imagine, you're having a rough time and a whole psychology develops to the point when you hate UNITA as if they were your worst enemy, and we weren't there to fight UNITA, although UNITA harassed us . . . if we had gone there to fight against UNITA, UNITA would not now exist in Angola. We said, right. The enemy is there. We knew where they were. We have the best equipment. We have aviation, we have all the means to finish off UNITA in three months, perhaps. UNITA wouldn't last three months in that situation. It wouldn't now exist as an enemy in Angola, as an enemy of the people, as an enemy of the government, if we had been allowed to fight them. We never fought UNITA because the Cuban government position was that it always considered UNITA an internal problem – as did Angola – and something they would have to solve. Because we wouldn't have solved anything killing people. Killing UNITA people wasn't going to solve Angola's problems. You don't solve anything with bloodshed.

Angola now has a possibility of ending the war. They can sit down and talk to UNITA. If they don't talk, well, Angola will continue to have war unless Jonas Savimbi decides to do something else.* I think UNITA does have a lot of influence in the southern region of Angola, a fairly marked influence. I was there and I spoke to people in the province of Huambo. Of every five families, three belong to UNITA, that's why it isn't logical for us to fight against UNITA there, because we would be killing their children.

It was prohibited to leave the unit, we always had to stay inside the unit. But you'd get hungry. You were hungry. You were starving and sometimes you escaped, and you went to the little market that they call the *kandonga*, which is like a market where they display the things on the ground. And I was capable of eating things there and it wasn't easy. It wasn't easy. I went to those places and they were stinking. They sold bread and you didn't know if they had made it there in the middle of that muck . . . and it was a huge effort to go to that market because you had to hold your nose. You had to buy a drink, which wasn't always available, a drink they had which we looked out for because it was factory produced. But sometimes the drink didn't fill you and what you wanted was bread. They made the bread at home. Imagine how

* Jonas Savimbi, leader of UNITA and formerly a member of the now ruling MPLA (Popular Movement for the Liberation of Angola). The Angolan government and UNITA have still not resolved their differences. The US continues to back and supply UNITA.

they lived. Sure, six or seven of them lived in barely two square metres. I don't know how they lived in those houses they call *kimbos*, which are made of mud. There's no floor, they sort of cover it with leaves, but that's the way their houses are. They make them fairly narrow and they sleep and cook in it . . . They don't wash either, they go for ages without washing. You pass them by and the whiff follows you for 40 metres. Not everyone. No. Those who live in the cities not so much, but certainly those who live in those *barrios*, which is the vast marginalised majority. They have water. They have a fair amount of water in their rivers. But they are not very hygienic. Not all of them. But in those places, that's the way they live. Their clothes are in a terrible state. Very bad, very bad, very bad. Apart from that, the government must be going through a fairly critical time because they have no food. There's no clothes for the children. We think the work the International Red Cross [IRC] is doing is very good, irrespective of the fact that we sometimes hate them because when we have had to carry out some operation they interfered and gave [UNITA] warning of it. So we didn't agree with that. But anyway it's good that they did that sort of work avoiding bloodshed.

But you see, the IRC is very much infiltrated by the CIA, by capitalist countries. Really, well, that's the way it is, sadly. You get different people. At the moment it's infiltrated by the CIA. On some occasions we couldn't do things because they were there. Whatever they found out about – for instance, we had to go in a truck convoy to bring food to certain provinces, and sometimes there'd be a UNITA camp which knew the Cubans were going to pass by with food. And even though the convoy was well armed, they tried to ambush the lorries, they laid mines . . . Sometimes they laid certain mines that the first lorry would go over and nothing happened, but then it exploded around the seventh or eighth lorry, cutting your convoy in two. You'd get fighting then, skirmishes. And the first thing they'd do was get up on top of the vehicles and try and find food, because it's true UNITA supplies didn't arrive easily. And besides it not getting there easily, the way they got food supplies was from the peasants, who were petrified. They threatened the people. They'd go to their houses, attack them and take their food if there was any. Many households just left food out for them because if they got as far as knocking on your door they'd go in and take your money, abuse the women, take whoever, beat you with their weapons and you could have bloodshed. So in many villages, what they'd do was leave food out and they'd come during the night and take it. Sometimes . . . you'll find if you ask Cubans what the Angolans are like, some will tell you that they're very cowardly. But I wouldn't say they were cowards, I'd say that they were rather more . . . I mean, it's their way, their way of living. It's a very religious country and I admire that a lot . . .

I would say the Angolan soldier makes a lot of sacrifices. He puts up with too much. Something I never thought I'd see, but sometimes the soldiers there go about with no shoes. The food is abominable and to have an army under those conditions isn't easy. If half of what happened in that army happened here in Cuba, we wouldn't have an army. Because those people put up with being hit. You can't lay a finger on a Cuban soldier. Everything is discipline here, but no superior officer can hit a soldier. There they hit a soldier about the head and he remains silent and doesn't react. And their food is terrible. And you see them there putting up with it, and there are soldiers who have gone seven, eight or ten years without seeing their families. Living in their own country. I met one of those Angolans who hadn't seen his family in ten years. Because they send them from one province to the other – as Angola is a huge country – from one province to the next, and the risk is always of UNITA getting them along the way. The only way you can travel is by plane. If you go overland you run the almost sure risk of getting killed. So I met soldiers there who hadn't seen their familes for seven or five years. They were having a tougher time than me, in other words. Because, look, I didn't see my family for two years, but they hadn't seen theirs for seven, four, three years, and they are in their own country. And they felt all right, because there isn't that closeness among families there. You might get a son who lives very well and the mother lives in abject poverty like someone from the lowest ranks of society, in rags, and the son doesn't care a damn that his mother's in rags and his own child has nothing to eat. That sometimes got to me there. I'd say to myself, what sort of people are they, can they be right in the head? There are men who have – because they do like to procreate, women there generally like to have a child every year and they start having children very young. And there are women there who have six or seven children and the responsibility is entirely theirs. A man can have all the women he likes. He doesn't care if the children have breakfast, dinner or tea, which they almost don't. They don't have breakfast, they don't have anything because there are no cattle, there's no milk. They have very few animals, no hens or anything, and they cannot raise pigs because you have to feed them food and they haven't even enough for themselves.

It's true that the food at the camp was always the same. The same every day. Lots of sardines, lots of rice. Rice, but every day the same thing. We are not used to eating the same thing. And the food wasn't seasoned. What you ate in the day you ate at night, and sometimes we'd throw it out. Sometimes we could permit ourselves the luxury of raising pigs, which sometimes got sick. They got African swine fever. Sometimes, when they got a chance, the Angolans would send over kids of seven or eight, five or six, who could make it to the unit. Sometimes those kids were sent by UNITA and there was a risk for us. Many *compañeros* got killed that way. Those children could leave a bomb or a mine and you blew away like Matías Pérez.* They would sometimes come and eat rotten food of seven or eight days that not even the pigs ate, and it didn't make them sick. Because they have stomachs of cement, those people. I was completely . . . well, they even eat mice. Have you ever seen anyone in this world eat mice? Well, in Angola the children are sometimes reduced to eating mice, they are so hungry.

What they like best is corn. The Portuguese got them used to eating corn. A very cheap food that's useless. They are quite happy with a plate of cornflour, that's their national dish. The Portuguese gave those people rubbish and they developed a culture around maize, and they have yucca which they call *manioca*. It's *manioca* in Portuguese, their national language, although they speak a lot of dialects. The Angolans have over 200 dialects. Communication

* An intrepid balloonist of the nineteenth century who one day disappeared into the skies in his own device.

is not easy. For instance, they speak Kimbundu. In the area of Huambo, where I was, they speak Umbundu which is one of the majority dialects. Another is Fioti. They have about 215 dialects. We were studying the history of the Angolan people over there.

The MPLA movement was founded in 1956 under the leadership of Agostinho Neto, who was a poet. He was a very eminent person with a lot of qualities and revolutionary plans. Really he is the most important personality the African continent has had, but with his death, almost all the hopes of the people are cut short . . . He was the intellectual head, that man – there were others with ideas, with revolutionary passions, but not as connected to the people as he was. Like, for instance, the President, José Eduardo Dos Santos, doesn't know the dialects. He studied in the Soviet Union, he became an economist, a lawyer. But José Eduardo Dos Santos cannot go to one of those provinces to speak . . . He has 500 translators, well, 215 interpreters to translate in all those areas.

Savimbi is a fairly intelligent person. He's from Cuito Velho. Cuito Velho is a neighbouring province of Huambo. We were in the palace Savimbi had there in Huambo because the houses are very nice in Huambo city. Huambo would have been the capital of Angola if it had had a port. It's a landlocked province which was previously called New Lisbon. After they won . . . in 1975 they changed the name of all the provinces. Not all, some.

The MPLA is a revolutionary movement and Savimbi wanted to join the MPLA. Savimbi studied medicine. He studied in France and in Portugal. And from Portugal he asks the MPLA, Neto, to let him join. Well, they accepted him into their ranks. Afterwards, Savimbi leaves his studies and he goes back to Angola . . . (*Carlos's wife bring us out coffee. 'Mira mi negrita . . .' he says, delighted, putting his arm around her waist*) . . . Anyway, he sees he is capable of creating his own movement and he creates UNITA as a national movement alongside the MPLA. But then, when independence is declared in 1975 and the UN recognises Agostinho Neto as President of Angola, [Savimbi] had ambitions of power and so he declares himself the sworn enemy of President Agostinho Neto. Consequently, he declares war on him when Angola is proclaimed independent on 11 November 1975, and asks for assistance. He immediately asks South Africa for help, and the United States.

South Africa, of course, immediately responds to Savimbi's call and begins to invade Angola around the southern flank held by UNITA. All the UNITA movement speaks the Umbundu dialect. Savimbi knew all those dialects. He knew Umbundu. He knew a whole series of dialects. He becomes a personality there. A myth of invincibility was created around Savimbi because he had even studied in the People's Republic of China. He had come to Cuba, too. He did military courses. And he was a gifted student with a lot of talent. Even Comandante Ernesto Che Guevara once said in conversation that if Savimbi ever got to be a true revolutionary, he would be the hope of Africa – and not just of Angola – Savimbi would be the hope of Africa.

So, when in 1975 South African troops begin to penetrate the southern region, Agostinho Neto is really in a critical situation, because they have practically cornered the MPLA and, as President of Angola, he asks Cuba for help and Cuba agrees to help him retain the presidency of the republic and do something to save the MPLA. So, Cuban troops set out from the Caribbean and go to the People's Republic of Angola. Some went by boat, others by air. They were really Cuba's special troops, I mean specially selected troops . . . I mean, it wasn't the first . . . international contact of our troops abroad, because Cuba had already taken part in Algeria, in the war of Algeria. They had also been to the Congo. Cuban troops had also gone to Vietnam. And so troops were sent to Angola and they immediately put a stop to the advance, to the invincibility of the South African troops. For the first time, [the South Africans] come up against an invincible monster, and the first battles took place in Kifangondo.

Some of my friends died there. Not many in combat, more through sickness. Disease was a fairly powerful enemy – anaemia, lack of food. There were some severe cases of malaria . . . I was in hospital once with malaria. They had to fly me from Huambo by plane to Luanda. I was in hospital for a month and a half. No medicine can protect you from malaria. If you get it you just have to be cured . . . we took quinine tablets twice a week. It's pretty sad to be on a mission only to be killed by a disease instead of a bullet.

For many years, Cuba – it's a question of history, of tradition –

when one of her sons falls defending the freedom of another people, feels a lot of respect . . . Perhaps if someone died here defending Cuba they might not be mentioned, defending a social position, saying that, for instance, we ought to fight for an opposition to the Communist Party, someone of that sort. That isn't important. But if he falls in the defence of another country, that's sacred. That is religion here. You could say that that's always been Cuba's position, and why it always planned to support the People's Republic of Angola . . . Sometimes talking to Angolan patriots there they didn't understand and they thought we went there for money or because we were taking over the country! I even heard conversations about us wanting to take over the country! They said we were better colonisers than the Portuguese, which means they thought we were also colonials! And sometimes said out like that you would get furious. But then you had to sit down and think from whose mouth it came, and the enemy had done a lot of propaganda work against the Cuban troops and they saw it like that – 'No, the Cubans are eating our food.' Since they eat badly and we ate perhaps a little better than they did, because we were in a state of combat-readiness doing this, that and the other. Sure, if they took away the little they gave us it wouldn't have been worth it. We couldn't have fought. They would have taken out corpses. They really thought we were eating their food. But, of course, it's true, Angola's economic situation is critical. And they consider themselves a rich country. 'Well, if you're so rich why are you so hungry?' Well . . . I suppose it's national pride that makes you think your country is the best in the world because it's where you were born. As Martí said, 'Our wine is bitter. Bitter though it may be, it's ours, isn't it?' I loved Cuba more after I went away.

Carlos went on to talk about his work with the microbrigades, a unique system of recruiting construction labour through secondment from the workplace, where the remainder of the workforce guarantees to maintain productivity levels. There are variations on the system involving neighbours or other groupings. Though mainly engaged in building housing, the micros also construct community projects such as hospitals, schools and day-care centres. The system was introduced in 1970 but fell into disrepute as being antithetical to prevailing economic structures. Fidel

Castro revived it in 1986 and it has been increasingly popular and successful.

You met me on the internationalist fighters' microbrigade, which was the first one of its kind at a national level. In each municipality there is a soldiers' club, both for the Rebel Army and for the family of internationalists who have been killed, and that's where they are looked after.

One of the worst problems in the country is the housing situation. In 1970, they created a microbrigade movement and the workers from the various enterprises supported the idea. There was great enthusiasm for it in those years, 1971–2, and then it collapsed. The movement died because some character, who apparently had a nice palace himself, got a notion, and the microbrigade movement died. The hope of many families of having their own home and solving the housing problem went by the board, and really it is a fairly critical situation, especially here in Ciudad de la Habana province. The capital is worse off than anywhere else. Ciudad de la Habana is a problem because it's a small area and it's where most people from the provinces migrate to. They want to come and live in the capital for certain facilities it has, certain resources, shopping and that. So this micro movement collapsed and died around about 1974 until our Comandante en Jefe spoke to us about two years ago saying that he realised what a great mistake it was not to have followed it through. And so it was given a new lease of life. Because there had been great industrial growth, a lot of industry, a lot of factories, very good health care, education, all very good, but the housing issue was the critical point.

So last year, while I was at work, I got a message from the soldiers' club to go there. When I went, it was about a micro they were going to set up with people from the Rebel Army, because there are even *compañeros* from the Rebel Army – and this tells you how austere the Revolution has been – who still don't have a house. And now there's a Rebel Army micro. For instance, the *compañeros* from the Rebel Army in Santiago de Cuba didn't build their own houses. The Revolution gave them to them. And many have houses. But Ciudad de la Habana has the most critical problem. By agreement with the Central Committee the internationalist soldiers' microbrigade was set up in every municipality.

We worked together with people from the Rebel Army and afterwards we split up from them. We left it to them and we got our own plot for the internationalist soldiers. It's the first time it was done like that. And you can't solve the housing problem of all the internationalist soldiers with the micro. You can for the Rebel Army because there are fewer of them. These are now older people, and really the Party is helping out with costs so they can have their houses. But in the case of the internationalist fighters, here, for instance, in my municipality of Centro Habana, there simply isn't enough land. Imagine, Centro Habana has more than 10,000 internationalists, between 8,000 and 10,000 internationalists. You could solve it if you had all Havana, but there isn't enough land in Centro Habana.

The present micros exist with the support of every enterprise. Every enterprise sends its workers. The workers earn the salary they get at the enterprise. The enterprise provides all the means of transport, all the facilities . . . And they give over 50 per cent [of the stock]. It was 50 per cent at the beginning. Now it's 60 per cent to the microbrigade and 40 per cent to the state. Why? Because the state needs a housing pool to give to people living in shelters; people whose houses have fallen down or are in bad shape and who have to go to a shelter where they are put up in reasonable conditions, not the best . . . They live in those shelters until the state can give them a house. With that 40 per cent the state solves really a minimum of the problem. The solution isn't yet 100 per cent because there are a fair number of people living in those hostels. A good number. But there's a lot of building going on now since Fidel spoke about it and said the micro question would have to be speeded up and that we should make Havana as beautiful as Paris or London. Well, of course, we aren't going to see that now. We will have to wait a few years for it, but that's what we want.

I'm a planner at the MINAL Research Institute, which is one of the largest in Latin America. It is quite big and has a lot of prospects. Planning work involves drawing up contracts and investing in resources the enterprise needs – working out statistically what the enterprise needs, the resources, and making contracts for them abroad as well as at home so that the institute has the materials it requires. It's a lot of paperwork, a lot of documentation hither and thither, drawing up contracts so that the resources get to the enterprise and the institute can carry out its research . . . That's my work. And, as I say, they came to my house and saw how badly I needed a house and then, well, they gave me a letter to give to the Party and the administration to see what chance there was of releasing me from my work centre to try and solve my housing problem.

They are also doing houses in my workplace. They are building 300 units for the workers. But what happens with those houses? They belong to the enterprise. That is, they are for the workers and the directors. They have built eighty, which they are going to hand over soon. But as I see it, those houses belong to the enterprise, the enterprise gives them to the people and arrogates the right, at any moment, to take them back and give them to whoever. So, I'm not on for that. I want to build my own house and to have my own title deeds, to be the owner of it. I don't want it to belong to the company.

So, I arrived on the micro. I know a bit about it, I'm a brickie. I know how to lay bricks and I began working with people from the Rebel Army. Then the Vice-President of the government came to see us, because the Rebel Army were saying we should build two buildings, that if we split up it'd be quicker. Everyone just wants to build their houses and get back to their jobs because building-site work is pretty tough and people shy away from construction work because you have to sweat a lot and work to get things done. You really have to work to build a house. It's not like pushing a pen. There's no let-up. We work ten hours. We get most of our materials from the government and so you have to train the microbrigaders in the different construction skills. I came here in August last year, but what happened? As there was this split, and the people of the Rebel Army kept that plot where we were going to build, we have barely started. We hope to finish this fourteen-apartment building in nine or ten months, which won't give us all a home. There are seventeen of us. Normally a microbrigade has thirty-three people. We decided not to have thirty-three people to get it built faster and to avoid the problem and the nastiness of having to distribute . . .

because there aren't enough apartments [for everyone]. After that we have to do another for the *compañeros* . . . we are committed to finishing this building and afterwards to helping those who don't get an apartment in this building to do another one. So, it's not just a question of getting your apartment but of committing yourself to the others so they get theirs. We'll work that out ourselves. In the workplace it's a different system of microbrigade. Ours was the first of its kind. I later found out there's one in Habana del Este. They set up another one there where internationalist soldiers are working together with Rebel Army people.

The other microbrigade system is different, it's according to merit, those units of which 60 per cent goes to the enterprise, well, it's not just the person building it has the right to it but anyone in the office who has more merit points than you. So, you go along to build it and you don't know, because it's by merit, merit at work: your career to date, your attitude, your life history. If you are good, you get your house. If you are bad, even though you've built it from top to bottom, you don't get it. In our case, well, all the *compañeros* had a meeting. We are going to build it ourselves and we are going to distribute it. Because, really, whoever has been willing to give the little he has – his life – to me that seems enough. No need to ask if he is good or bad. That question doesn't enter into it.

Earlier you made passing reference to an opposition party . . .

Look, in relation to that, everybody here has to have their own ideas and principles, no? Because to think this is good because Fidel said so, or that is good because So-and-so said so. Not me. Be it Gorbachev or whoever, what's well done is well done. Well, I think we've had thirty good years of it till now, no? It's gone well with the Party leadership we have. If there was an opposition party perhaps . . . perhaps sometimes the opposition of one thing to another might bring improvements, but it could also do harm. There is that duality. We can't say we're perfect, we are not. The Communist Party can make mistakes like any party. But really, the things that have been done for the poor, how we have fought for the poor, and how the poor have had the chance to live without having to have recourse to crime. If you commit a crime, it's because you're a headcase, because you were born like that, because nobody made you that way. Naturally, Radio Martí* and other stations are listened to and lots of visitors come here to Cuba. I do know that we have to improve; do things better. But if other parties were created that would be a right show. The worst thing about Cubans is their tongue. There'd be one character setting up a party and another having a meeting here and another talking over there – it'd be a cock-fight, as they say. It'd be a right show. And this one against that one, and the other against him, and it'd really be a show, and we are not used to that. Under the old system here there were other parties: the Ortodoxo Party, the Popular Party, the such-and-such party and what have you, and nobody knew which way to go . . . It wouldn't be the moment to create a party, in these circumstances. Besides, the education and training you get here is revolutionary, born of a tradition of fighting. The people are very politicised, a lot of politics, but based on our own history, our own accomplishments which, since 1868, from the time of Carlos Manuel de Céspedes until now, is a lovely history. So, today we teach our children about the sacrifice of their ancestors who made this possible.

Really the Cuban government is trying, and has always tried, to emphasise our history, because it's very rich and very dynamic. I believe there are few like it and I have studied Greek and Roman history. We studied the history of America, of the Incas and the Indians who lived here; medieval history, ancient history, we've studied them all. But we love, Cubans love, their own history. It forms them. And that's what people sometimes don't understand: that we are ready to offer our lives far away from Cuba, no? Because wherever there is injustice, its hurts us. As Martí said, 'A blow to another's cheek must be felt as if it were to one's own.'

And another thing, we don't fear death . . . There's a lot of religion here but we don't blind ourselves, we are not a totally religious country. Something I admired a lot in Angola was this religion question. The Catholic religion was big there and I saw

* The anti-Castro station based in Miami.

how those poor people, and I consider myself poor, went to church every Sunday. Those people are really children of God. The real children of God. And I admire that a lot because the poor have always been the ones who have most adored religion with the state of hunger they live in. And when one doesn't have anything, one has to beg forgiveness. One has to always adore something. And they are really faithful children of God because they practise their religion with their hearts . . . I used to chat to them and there, in poor churches, churches made of earth, there they would go religiously every Sunday. They went to pray. They had a lot of Bibles, and sometimes they could barely read or interpret the Bible. Human beings who didn't know how to interpret the Bible, because they had only got to fourth or third grade, but they were happy to have a Bible under their arm and to go there and profess that religion not being able to internalise the text. And that's the nature of that religion . . . You get religious people here. Some practise on the quiet, others have their own idea of it all. Here in the churches. What lovely churches we have, don't we? I used to sometimes tell them that in conversation. 'In Cuba we have more churches than you have in Angola.' Because they said we didn't have any. (*More coffee is brought out for us*) I told them, 'In Cuba we have more churches than here and they are much nicer,' because their churches are made of mud. But anyway, I admired their attitude, their going to church, no? Because when they heard gunfire during the night what they would do is pray. Naturally. It was logical and admirable.

I am a revolutionary but I am not a communist. I don't have a card and I have gone on missions. And although you might think I have a red card in my pocket, I don't. I'm absolutely a revolutionary and I like to see things objectively. I know what's right and what's wrong.

9

Ramón Fernández Larrea

Ramón Fernández Larrea was born in Bayamo, Granma province, one year to the day before the Revolution. He was thirty-one at the date of interview. He is a published poet and a broadcaster and he has received awards in both areas. We talk at his modest house in Guanabacoa, a colourful suburb of Havana. Elvira, his actress wife, keeps us fuelled with interesting lemon drink concoctions. The atmosphere is definitely bohemian.

25 May 1989

At the moment I do a programme called Ramón's Programme. Not because my name is Ramón; the reason we give is that we wanted to make a programme for intelligent people, i.e. for Ramóns not for Mongos.* And so, since we started we have gathered momentum, because, I think, we had our objectives very clearly set out and we came in at a time of change, of renovation at the station, which is the only youth station in the country. It is really the only station for young people, young people in the capital who have so many needs and requirements that have to be met.

This renewal, of which my programme is a part, is happening at a time when a large group of young people, young producers, are joining the station. It's incredible, but you open a door at the station and you find a poet. These are poets who have won

---

* A familiar form of Ramón which also means a fool.

national awards, young poets who have had books published, people who are also making very interesting programmes. Within this renewal we are beginning, as a group, to raise certain issues for ourselves which have also been put to us by the public, mainly young people, such as musical variety, to broadcast a much wider range than has hitherto been the case in this country. To have a profile including everything that is really good in the world and to avoid, to minimise commercial music which unfortunately is what most goes out. To avoid commercial music, bad music in Spanish, to bring back the best of international rock, which was very little known or sometimes very poorly publicised because of prejudice, a lot of prejudice. For a long time no one knew the Beatles. So we are trying, as a matter of principle, to give young people who listen to the radio today the sort of information we ourselves did not have; the information my generation and the generation before me looked for on international stations or off their own bat through records, cassettes and that . . .

The programme is mainly about humour and has two directions. We wanted it to be a funny programme, a humorous programme which could include the movement of young comics that there is in Cuba. These comics are successfully redrawing the parameters of humour, breaking with the double meaning, breaking with the throwaway line, with racist or risqué jokes, to provide a different kind of humour with a fresher vision dealing with real problems in the country, today, and mainly in the capital. And the musical content, which is the other direction, which sets out firstly to give airplay to the disinherited of the New Song Movement* in Cuba – the youngest people now writing and singing who have no way of recording a record or making a tape in a studio because they don't have pull or because they are sidelined by officials for being so young with all their lives ahead of them – and to record them and distribute them . . . And they really have fans. Because every time we announce that Carlos Varela or Adrián Morales or Fran Delgado or Santiago Feliú are having

---

* The New Song Movement started up in 1970 as a movement of renewal using the traditional Cuban ballad to express ideas on contemporary Cuban society and the world in general.

a session, thousands of young fans come along, and they know their songs, too.

So, on the one hand we have that aspect and on the other we aim to play the best of Latin America and the best of world rock, right up to the present, which isn't the best, but to give them information about Speed Metal and Trash Metal, metal, the sound of metal, but at the same time to play the best of the biggest groups that have made musical history, that have influenced music this century. All that mixture of things.

The first task we set ourselves was not to make a programme like the majority of programmes for young people currently being made here and which are made by teams, but to use the youngsters as the basis for enjoying yourself. When they talked to me about the possibility of doing the programme, I was at the time bored doing programmes to earn a living. It annoyed me having to do them and they offered me an hour daily and said, invent a programme. And when I sat down to outline the programme I said to myself, I am going to write a programme that, in the first place, I want to hear; that I be the first to enjoy. What I don't listen to on other stations I don't want to hear on mine. The idea grew from that and began to take concrete form . . .

I'm not the only one scripting the programme at the moment. It'd be madness. It's one hour a day which has to have a heavy dose of humour throughout and a serious selection of music. A selection which isn't repeated. There are three of us writing it at the moment. We have made up a team. We have almost fifteen people in at recordings. So the job of directing these sessions is more difficult.

It all comes on foot of changes in the management of the station and a more scientific approach to programming. There were five or six of us young producers already working there in the old slots, and then suddenly management realised that to reach the targets they were aiming at they would have to dynamite some old programmes and make way for new ones more in line with what young people in the capital wanted. Why? Because something happened. Well, naturally, it's the same everywhere: television displaced radio and cinema, but video displaced cinema and radio and even television programming to some extent, because the

video allows you to put on whatever you want. The radio became
– although it was never totally displaced – became an option for
old dears, or for before you went to sleep, and the youngest sectors
used not to listen to the radio, especially as it was so bad. And it
was very bad. Although . . . from the time Radio Martí came
on the air, which was a challenge to Cuba's media, there's been a
battle of the airwaves, a battle in which the state itself realises that
it has to respond in some way . . . It is within this framework that
those changes I referred to occur. In which really something has
to be done to draw young people to listen to the radio, which was
something for housewives to listen to as they washed and ironed,
especially national radio . . .

So the management of the station gave me an hour a day and
said, 'Make your own programme.' I said, 'My own programme.
Perfect.' They already knew that I had a certain sense of humour
because on other programmes I did I sometimes went a bit over
the top, my style was funnier, fresher and livelier. In fact it was
a challenge, it was something I had been wanting to do for a long
time. I did a programme on a provincial station called COCO,
a very traditional station with an old-fashioned format, which I
think was the embryo of this one . . . The first thing it did was
offend listeners, attack them and try to grab them somewhere. It
tried to give an hour and a half of different options. Nothing on
it seemed serious, though of course, it all was. And it was critical
humour, touching on burning issues of the day. It tried to give
the listener or the people of the capital a third way of dealing with
situations, a way Cubans have always used, and that is laughter.
When a problem was insoluble . . . Cubans looked for a third
attitude, which was, 'Well, this can't be solved, I'll laugh.' 'It can
be solved, I'll laugh anyway.' So the idea was to bring back that
capacity to laugh even at one's own predicament – which is, of
course, not just Cuban, but Latin in general. We got it from Spain
and also from Africa, the national make-up which is a sort of stew,
and which gave us those special characteristics.

If you look at radio programming over the past three years you
will see that there was only one comic slot, one or two, over the
entire national network. Provincial stations had no comic tradition.
Everything was very serious. Ninety per cent dry news and 10 per

cent music, but awful music. A lot of salsa, a lot of lousy songs by all the shittiest Latin American and Spanish singers, and what they played in terms of international music was the worst, the most commercial rubbish. That forms tastes . . . that's why the majority of young people preferred to listen to FM and some Radio Martí programmes . . . I except Radio Rebelde, which was the first to leave its mark on Cuban broadcasting. In terms of vitality, of freshness, of changing voices, of innovation. So, I said to myself, right, I am going to look for those three things, those three elements, and jumble them up.

We tried to play what no one else played. That did bring us certain problems right from the beginning. Because institutional bureaucracy has nothing to do with artistic creativity. It has never had anything to do with it. But there are things. There are very strict rules which tell you that if you play music not sent you by the ICRT [Cuban Institute of Radio and Television], you are . . . guaranteed a certain percentage of trouble. Trouble because there is, supposedly, a commission of wise men who choose the music to be broadcast. It wasn't just me, there was a whole group of intelligent people, young people, artists, at the station – we were immediately agreed, very united as regards this – who had a lot of meetings at which we demonstrated to the ICRT officials that either there was a CIA agent in the commission selecting the music or they were all a crowd of idiots and fools. Because what we didn't understand was how Julio Iglesias's latest record could arrive at the station in two months and that such an important group as U2, that from [their album] *The Joshua Tree* we would get the worst and most commercial song, one song. We took the risk, and won the battle.

We get letters from all over. From university students, from the medical school where nearly everybody listens to us, from secondary schools, from military units where it's forbidden to have a radio – they write to us and say, 'Look, I have a small radio here to listen to the programme.' From all over, really, and not just from young people. People getting on in years listen to it. The grandparents of people I know say, 'Put it on, put on the programme.' So we don't boast, well, we do boast a little about it. We are aware that this phenomenon is not the result of the production itself but of the tremendous necessity there was for such a programme, for its freshness. There was, and still is, a great need for different programming, of the kind that really not only informs through humour but which also gives information the public needs. And the public does need it. That the problems of the capital be really analysed in a playful way but also in a serious way. For example, how long it takes you to get from here in Guanabacoa to your workplace with the transport problems. The problem of bad service. The problem of the real needs we all have, from the woman who wants to work but hasn't got a day-care centre for her child because they're full, to the shortage of things which make life easier. These are the more serious problems, the economic problems of the country. But there are others which can be solved, and sometimes we ignore them or avoid dealing with them. The problem of the distribution of things that we *do* have. They are badly distributed and this annoys people. So when this person arrives home from work annoyed and switches on the radio and hears a programme where those problems are being sent up, joked about and denounced, that person automatically becomes one of our listeners. Because it also relaxes the person, he or she laughs at what had annoyed them during the day. That's a political mission. You make that guy relax and he's back to being the same old Cuban he always was. Cubans say, 'Let me laugh because that lot are a shower of bastards.' That's what they say. But that critical and forthright humour has brought us problems because there are institutions who don't like having the finger pointed at them . . .

At one stage it was almost a sin to be young. It was assumed that if you were very young you were ideologically unprepared to face . . . well, I didn't attack the Moncada Barracks, I didn't go up into the mountains, I didn't fight in the mountains, I didn't come over in the *Granma*, but my generation has had other responsibilities and has proved itself. It has proved itself. I have long hair. Why? Because I feel like it. I just really feel like it. You can't judge a book by its cover. Look at what I do. Speak to me and . . . I don't know. Don't look at me like that. Don't write me off at a stroke and don't marginalise me. That's what my generation are demanding at the moment. Let's get rid of this mistrust . . . And if I am ideologically unsound it's your fault for never letting me contest things and refine myself in the course of daily life, precisely, in the struggle to sort out my values and temper my character. You want me to respond like a little lamb nicely and in silence, but I am not a little lamb. I am as much a wolf as you. But I can also be a very good dog. But not a sheep. Human beings think, they also rationalise, and just for being young you don't cease to reason. And everybody has been young and everyone in their day has been just as foolish and has liked music and the superficial things of life. But when you face into life, life itself shapes you. So, mistrust existed and still exists in some sectors.

We have an intelligent policy whereby we ourselves maintain close contact with the *compañeros* of the Provincial Committee of the Party who listen to the programme. And we have met and we have had discussions and have set out our position. We play this and we say that. We are not improvising, we are not some *ad hoc* operation. We do this because of A, B and C. Explain to them. And then they realise that the outspokenness of the programme, or of the station, or the controversial aspects of it are in many cases their fault for lack of information at our disposal. So, they have tried to solve issues by approaching us. There is now a greater line of communication for exchanging views which does not always have a happy outcome. But we carry on. The proof of it is that the programme has never come off the air. And there have been many listeners who have said, at crucial times for the programme, that it wouldn't last a month. They'll cancel that programme. And we carry on. We carry on.

Sometimes we put out acerbic jokes that we know certain sectors of our listenership will understand perfectly. Because they're already out at street level. But really when you see them in the script they're all innocent. Very innocent . . .

Look, I think the programme is allowed to take certain liberties for a reason. It's not because one's more intelligent than anyone else, but simply because, and it's no secret, you always have to have certain safety valves in difficult and trying situations to let the pressure out, and at the moment, the programme gets support and approval because it is one of those safety valves.

The majority of people who write to us talk and ask about rock.

There has been a bit of a problem with rock, hasn't there?

Yes, it's all part of that same old-fashioned view, of mistrust, that sees rock as a foreign, diversionist manifestation and secondly – this is a sixties attitude – because they mistrust the musicians who play rock and because rock has become a necessity for young people. There are still people who don't realise they need it as a form of catharsis. They need that music, that violence, in order to scream. To scream in an open space and jump up and down and feel better. They mistrust the youngsters of sixteen with their hair on their shoulders. And they don't trust the guy with the tight, patched, dirty jeans. Why? He's a human being who has family troubles, who hasn't yet found his way in life. But let him find himself. Why make him an outcast?

Here I'm thinking a bit about the *frickies*.* But the problem is that any attitude that does not accord with the norms we adults create is construed as a *frickie* attitude. Why? Why? Rebellion has always been the prerogative of youth. Rebellion. With or without a cause. If you are not able to direct and channel that rebelliousness, you're the one who's mistaken, not the other. The other has it. You're not able to control it in doses, to allow him to really find the reason for this rebelliousness, then the problem is you. As a father or an adult. But don't make an outcast of him. Don't force him to create a world apart from your world. Bring him into your world. Let's make a world between the two of us. That's always happened with rock.

The programme is very connected into young people precisely for that reason, because we don't impose any limitations when it comes to playing rock, both Cuban and foreign. And we have been the first to play Cuban rock groups who have managed to make tapes. Terrible tapes, technically very bad, but so what? The people have to hear them, to give them their space, give them the chance to play, because, really, the first problem rock groups have to contend with is the technical equipment. They do the best they can with the little they have. And there are a lot of interesting groups who with the little they have produce very respectable stuff while not trying to imitate anybody.

* Thought to be a derivation of 'freaks'.

But it all goes back to the fact that there was no tradition [of rock], that there was a culture which did not allow it. To play Led Zeppelin on the radio was bad. It was taboo. And to play Santana. Santana was banned on radio. Somebody decided to say, 'Don't play Santana' for something he said twenty years ago that not even he remembers. I don't remember what he said. Some row in an airport in Peru. Something like that. So, they banned him. Some oaf wiped Santana off the map, the first group to play Latin rock by really going back to Latin roots, giving a whole other connotation to a universal phenomenon. The new generations don't know who he is. We are playing him again. We assume it's authorised. We have managed to make ourselves responsible for what we put on and our judgment has to be respected.

I don't want to call this glasnost. Because, I don't know, any parallel . . . it seems to me that something very sensible is happening in my generation which has had it with covering up awkward questions with any old rag but which tries to understand things, to explain them to themselves and explain them to others or give an opinion on them, and from the discussion, the controversy, the polemic, to arrive at the truth. So, not to be afraid of doing this or of being mistaken, either. Sure, what have we to lose? Nothing. On the contrary, I'm going to continue here until I die in this country. I don't have anything to lose. And sooner or later talent sweeps away mediocrity. Sweeps it away. And breaks all the ridiculous rules. All stupidity falls by its own weight. All restrictive dogmas and ideas fall by their own weight. Or sometimes they have to be brought down. They have to be brought down by demonstrating what is reality and what is truth. So, perhaps for that reason, we have broken many rules. The programme and the station are establishing a basic role in the cultural life of the capital at least. The state invests millions in the mass media, and sometimes those millions are invested for nothing. Because really they are not about communication. They are not communicating . . .

It's ages since I've written poetry. I haven't the time. And it's also the fact that my poetry has always been fed on rage, on disillusionment, I don't know, a whole burden I carried. And it seems that since that rage and the disillusionment are channelled through the humour on the programme, I don't have the desire to write. I don't think the programme will last too long. First, I thought it would run for two years. Now I think it will be three years because by then it will be old and will become a cliché, a habit or even something worse. Worse or better . . .

There are people who think it's the easiest thing in the world to write humour, including some comics. Because it is for them. They just take a certain situation and send it up. No, no. First and foremost, humour has to be literature. And serious. It must be well written. Because Mark Twain wrote well. And when Woody Allen writes, he writes well. It's literature first and foremost. But with a sense of the absurd, a sense which is precisely what gives . . . makes an explosion.

I began writing prose. At eleven or twelve I was very influenced by Latin American novelists like Juan Rulfo and Julio Cortázar. I left poetry aside as the influence at that stage was the novel. Then after that I never wrote a story. I came to poetry because, I don't know, it seemed to me to synthesise more what I wanted to say. Incredibly, I came to poetry through a typewriter, so the typewriter and I have been married for a long time. A machine my mother gave me. I was studying in the Camilo Cienfuegos Military School. I was a *camilito*. And I came home one Saturday and I saw the typewriter and I began to put paper in it and to write some poetry. Dreadful stuff, of course. Sure I burnt them or threw them out. Very much in the heroic style of the seventies, of the epic of the seventies when we had no resources, and besides I had hardly read any poetry. I had read César Vallejo and some Walt Whitman, a little Antonio Machado, but anyway I decided it was to be poetry. I was ashamed to show people what I had written for a long time because I was in a military school where the machismo was terrible, where to write was synonymous with homosexuality. I even wrote with a pseudonym and kept all my things locked away. Well, people saw me reading all the time and that was a bit odd. So I had to get into a fight. Fisticuffs with someone just to show that I too was a little man.

I really took up poetry seriously when I went to the teachers' detachment. I began to study to be a history teacher. And then at sixteen or seventeen I began to take it seriously. I managed to keep my first notebook, which is somewhere over there, very bad, full of childhood poems, and I had the chance to read some of it at one of those very good gatherings organised by the Hermanos Saíz Association of UNEAC on Saturdays.* And I began to attend those meetings without being a member . . . and thanks to that notebook I became the youngest member of the Hermanos Saíz Association. In that contact with other young poets, with young novelists, who were part of a generation, of a movement, I began to take shape.

I left the teacher-training college in the fourth year. I had a child. I had a child of one year. I had no work for a year. I couldn't find work. I had to go to Jagüey Grande in Mantanzas because I did some contract work, filing in an office and that sort of thing. That was for a brief period until I joined a brigade of art instructors in Jagüey Grande, on the citrus project there. That's where I linked up with the student radio they have. And I did an exam for literary advisor with the Ministry of Culture. With that exam I came back to Havana. I had to work in outlying villages of Havana which involved some bloody awful journeys. Until I made it to the radio and I began working on the COCO station. So, poetry never earned me a living but it takes precedence over food.

And you are a member of the Young Communist Union?

No. I was. I was. But I became disillusioned with all the bureaucracy and the dishonesty there was at that time, in 1975–6. And besides . . . it was a time when to be like me, a person who speaks their mind, was to invite remarks to the effect that you were a dangerous character and you had problems and all that. And I didn't accept that anyone should say that I had ideological problems and that I had to shut up and put up, go in for the circus of thinking in one way and acting in another. No, no, no, no. I preferred to say, look, I don't agree with this. And so I left the Young Communist Union [UJC] around 1975 or 1976. Fortunately, I don't know, by the luck of the draw as I never made concessions, they agreed with me, a little anyway, and without being a member of the UJC or anything, I have gained, let's say, certain respect as an artist. And although you have long hair and you live a little differently from

---

* Now independent, the Hermanos Saíz Association began as a junior division of UNEAC (the Union of Writers and Artists of Cuba).

the others and you don't mince your words, and what you think is heard and respected, to some extent you avoid some goon trying to put you down or trying to corner you.

Did you do your military service?

No. It seems they realised that I was always a bit off the wall and they didn't let me go. At the medical check-up it seems they realised that I was different, that I was bonkers, a bit odd, and that was it. Clinically: 'He has problems with his nerves. Don't send him.' I had to be mobilised by the military committee to go to Angola but as I was not suitable for the FAR [Revolutionary Armed Forces] I was excluded from the military register . . . I had to go and see the UJC people at national level. They had to ring the MINFAR [Defence Ministry] to authorise it, to get them to authorise my mobilisation. If not I couldn't go, and I was dying to go. Dying for it because at the time I was working at the COCO station and I was sick to the teeth of what I was doing. I said six months anywhere, on top of a stick, but I can't go on here. I really was dying to go.

I went to Angola as a member of a brigade of young artists set up in 1985 by the UJC. They chose eleven of us – a musical group, two magicians, the painter José Bedia, who is now working in Paris, and myself. Really, we didn't know why we were going. Nor did the UJC. Neither did the MINFAR know why we were going. Supposedly, we were to find out what Angola was really like, in a very paternalistic way. But as artists. We were to go there – it was for six months – we were to go there, see the reality of it, and secondly we were supposed to provide a bit of cultural entertainment spread out over the whole of Angola in units. When we saw that nobody knew why the blazes we were there, nor when we were returning or anything, they decided to send us altogether as one brigade. Nevertheless, the painter and I had other experiences as well. We split up from the group for a while and we wandered about from one unit to the other getting to know Angola a little. And we had some very interesting experiences.

At least we found out what war was about. We weren't fighting or anything though, in fact, we were dressed as soldiers, with weapons and all . . . But afterwards we did meet up with the rest of the group and we began to perform. I am not a musician, I can't sing and I can't do magic. And it wasn't always useful to recite a poem, much less one of mine, which was only going to make the soldiers there more sad. I could get a bit more involved in the show, the artistic end, making – at a very basic level – cards and postcards with the painter for the *compañeros*, for the soldiers, who would say to me, 'Hey, poet, write me a few lines for my mum.' 'Write a poem for my girlfriend.' So I would write a poem, I would write a sonnet, a *décima*, and the painter would draw them a card. And then at another level, in the show, I would tell lots of dirty jokes. Lots of them. They really loved someone to get up there and belt out three or four dirty jokes into the microphone. I tried to act them out a bit, miming and that . . . and then, towards the end, I got into acting even more – Elvira says I'm not an actor, that I'm hopeless – acting with the artistic group from the FAR which arrived in the final month. So we joined in. We got into it and we put on a great show. We took part in the sketches and things like that.

It was a life experience. A very good experience, because in the first place I got to know what war was about. It's something terrible. People think that war is the gunfire, war is the fighting. That's not what war is. You breathe war. You feel war in your pores. You feel the tension, you live under a huge strain. Even though you are in the most peaceful city at the time, there is a huge level of risk. You can't go out at night. If you go out by day, you don't go alone, you go armed and with three or four more *compañeros*. You don't take any old transport. You have to be careful of the road that it isn't mined. You don't drink anything, not even water, anywhere, it might be poisoned. When you are asleep you hear the gunfire – pakata-pakata-pakata! You turn over because they are not firing in your direction. It's about seeing people, their poverty. The terrible poverty. Fortunately I had the chance of seeing in the same year – and I returned in 1986 – the two extremes. I was in Angola and afterwards I went to the GDR. I saw the two extremes – developed socialism and absolute poverty. Homelessness. People, children hungry. I saw the way they lived, the poverty, the despair, the strain of war, the waste, the war-wounded. So, Angola was very good because it confirmed certain ideas I had. It tested me as a man, because at one time I was very afraid. Terrorised. And that was a time of perhaps getting malaria; or of today there's no food; or of eating food that had gone off; of even stealing a goat to eat because something had to be done. Those sort of things. Drinking water. Spending two or three days without water waiting for the rain to come. Then to spread the canvas out and drink the water trapped in it because there is no other.

I came home a different person. I was in a state of nerves for three months afterwards. Someone only had to put on the light and the sound of the switch had me on my feet. That's the sort of strain it is . . . You sleep but you have your ears cocked, always listening out for the dawn assailant. A dreadful tension, really, knowing that you are thousands of miles away from your own country in a foreign land, among people who speak a different language, have a different mentality, in a war situation.

Really, I met a lot of people and I made a lot of friends. A lot of very good people. Others were bastards. They'd be bastards in Cuba and they were bastards there. Low types of people, I don't know, who even in a situation like that, where people become close, were not able to bond. But the large majority were good, supportive people, despite the fact that many had very little education – these are the Cuban soldiers – they were from places like Mayarí, *guajiros* from the hills who had really never studied nor had experience of life, I don't know. A basic education and that was it, from different places, and really when it came to solidarity . . . they were quite wonderful. Marvellous human beings and good *compañeros*. I had the chance of getting to know them; of hearing some very sad tales; of knowing that whole human story. That was the best thing that could have happened to me. Though at the beginning I didn't know what the hell I was going to do there, and nor did anybody else, in the end, at least, we drew our conclusions.

What will happen when Fidel dies?

That's a difficult question. I think it's going to be a difficult time, especially in the first while, because people are conditioned to the persona of Fidel as maximum leader. There's a whole attitude, thirty years of a tradition, of his word, of his guidance etcetera, so that clearly many people, many people in leadership positions will be left orphaned. They will be left not knowing how to think for themselves, because, unfortunately, a lot of people don't know how to act for themselves or they are afraid to act for themselves because they don't want to be responsible for certain things. Because they believe that he is omnipresent and omnipotent and can solve all their problems. What they forget is – and it's what gives me hope and faith that they can go on without Fidel or any legendary figure at any time, because the time will come when they have to – that the country underwent a process of institutionalisation specifically to avoid that situation, so that each institution could function responsibly.

The problem is that, unfortunately, people still don't understand that. If we are going to construct socialism and there are institutions, a minister has to accept responsibility for the failures or successes of his ministry. And the Political Bureau of the Central Committee should be that – the guiding hand of the economic and political life of the country but not the body that solves all the problems that arise.

What worries me – and what I am going to say is brave – part of that mentality worries me because you can ask anyone to name the Minister of Public Health, or the Minister of Light Industry, or of Trade or Foreign Trade, and nobody knows them. People know Armando Hart, the Minister for Culture because, well, he was also a revolutionary figure. They know the Minister of the Interior because Abrantes* was known for a long time, but there are people who don't know who he is. They don't know him. They know the Minister of Education because José Ramón Fernández has been there since the Flood.† But there are many ministers whose names are unknown and they run ministries. They are like shadows. That's what worries me. Those people change at lightning speed. They fail, they are replaced, this one, the next, but none finds resonance although they are carrying out

---

* General José Abrantes died in prison in January 1991. He was serving twenty years for corruption and abuse of power following the drug scandal trials of 1989.

† José Ramón Fernández was replaced in November 1990.

instructions from the Political Bureau. But while they remain in the shadows, and do not assume responsibility for their positions, their office, people think that the problems of the medical service will be solved by Fidel instead of by the Minister of Public Health when they complain. So, when Fidel is no longer with us, well, really, there's going to be chaos. Chaos.

There are people who sooner or later are going to come face to face with it. And then they are going to realise that no human being, whatever their historical importance, no human being on their own can solve the problems. The work of a leader is to bring people together and Fidel has done that. He has brought a people together around an idea. He has shown the path. But really to fancy that the end of the Cuban Revolution, of socialism in Cuba, could come with the death of Fidel, I don't believe it. What I do say is that it will be a difficult time, a time of confrontations, and the only salvation will be, I think, when we bare ourselves and people really assume responsibility for themselves. Not in the name of a man, of a human being, but of an idea. And, well, we are going to miss Fidel and it's going to be painful. It's going to be very painful but he is human and one day he will not be here. Like as a child you think your mother is always going to be there and then she dies and you have to go on living, remembering her from time to time with love and affection and sticking to her teaching. But there will be a time when there will be discussion even about Fidel, internally or externally. There will be disagreement with his ideas and achievements, whether or not he was mistaken in some things . . . People think he's infallible in everything. Fortunately, the stance taken during the Missile Crisis was the correct one. The position adopted on many important issues in Cuba has been the right one. But he has also made mistakes. As human beings do . . . Somebody is going to have to take his place. There's got to be somebody, though hardly the kind of leader who can gather a million people together in the Plaza. But more important, it seems to me, is the idea that socialism, I am convinced of this, socialism is the only system that can solve the problems of a country so poor as this, so small, so under threat, and so much a part of the Third World and part of another economic order. It's the only solution to these problems. Because nobody, I am sure, will want to go back to the insecurity of the other system, which on the one hand does offer thousands of attractive things, but as a human being you lose out.

It's going to be very difficult when Fidel dies. But we've got to accept it. It will be a time of contradictions. It will be a time when many dishonest people who have been in his shadow will have to defend their position; when many ordinary people, poor people, who to some extent see Fidel as the personification of the Revolution, are going to realise that for thirty or fifty years he really was the image of the Revolution. But the Revolution is not just him but an idea and the capacity of each individual for renewal, for improvement, for being honest and for working and thinking and committing themselves to certain causes with love and with everything they've got. With everything they've got.

10

Arturo Cuenca

Arturo Cuenca has a glint in his eye. At thirty-three, he reckons he is no longer in the avant-garde of Cuban artists. He was educated at the best art schools and specialised in printing and engraving at the ISA (Higher Institute of Art). He recently cut off a short pony-tail because the teasing in Havana's conservative streets finally got to him. He is president of the Executive of the Visual Arts section of the Hermanos Saíz Association, which started out as a junior division of UNEAC but is now independent.

23 November 1988

I think that the artist, as an individual, is not entirely appreciated or, let's say, his or her social significance is understood in a general way, in theory – the social function of the artist – but not really in concrete terms.

Artists come up against a lot of inefficiency, a lot of bureaucracy, incomprehension . . . because in the true Hispano-Yorubá* tradition, the artist was really a strange character, someone different, bohemian or even immoral. So, the artist in Cuba should fight – at a legal-institutional level – to gain recognition for his or her specific social function, that most important social function in the Cuba of today. And of tomorrow, of course, especially of tomorrow. Because all these prejudices, all these prejudices which

---

* Spanish–African tradition.

operate at all levels of society, from the highest down – the artist always has this problem, has to fight for his place, consciously and seriously and with a knowledge of the context in which he is working and moving; changing traditions or following them, in some instances carrying them on, in others breaking them and in others again changing them . . . [This applies to] the artist in the vanguard at least, the classical artist, and I use classical here without flinching. People always have complexes about saying an artist is classical or popular. I mean the classical artist in the sense that he or she has been trained; is aware of what he or she is doing; of not being where he or she is by virtue of a tradition, a family tradition, but is someone who really chose to be an artist. That's what I mean by a classical artist, and I put myself in that category.

An artist should also be part of social transformation. He should take an active part in social, political, ideological and scientific developments. I mean, I also believe that our artists should play an active and conscious part in this society. In recent times, artists, especially the youngest ones, have been concerned with the ordinary or economic, political, ideological aspects of life in a way that is much closer to political discourse . . . I think this active role, especially among the youngest artists, those from seventeen to twenty-five, is very interesting. They are concerned in a very open-spirited way with criticising and confronting literally, not metaphorically, the problems of social development in our country. I think they are very important and they should be given space. Not that they become the critical conscience of society, but that they be part of that critical conscience as all members of society should be. And an important critical part. Because an artist may know how to express a problem very literally, in images, and in very concrete and expressive objects, in such a way as they will reach the social conscience in a very direct, attractive and forceful manner. I believe there are limitations on this new spirit, among the new generations, to becoming actively engaged in society, especially at the level of public perception and the institutions involved in promoting and supporting these issues. I think it has to do with what I said earlier on traditional prejudices about the artist, which is now a way to keep him from his own work, not to give him the opportunity for social expression. And I think it has a lot to do with individuals and mechanisms – sometimes it's mechanisms, structures, and other times it's an individual in a particular institution. All these things are problems of arts policy in the country.

In theory, there is an arts policy which addresses the issues – the relationship with tradition, the relationship with our roots, the relationship of the artist with society, with the real transformation of mankind, but in practice, he's under fire. There's no understanding, no acceptance, of what that relationship means in practice. I believe that our platform for the arts is really very profound, very intelligent, all-embracing, because there is clearly an awareness in the programme of the link between the process of establishing the Cuban nation and high art. The intelligentsia, the artists, the great scientists have always been closely allied to the superstructure of politics. It was intellectuals, artists, scientists who really forged the Cuban nation. It was not the work of politicians alone, but of a politician like Martí, who was also possibly the greatest poet, the greatest prose writer in Latin American Spanish, of his time. And cases like Martí create a whole culture, a whole theoretical framework for nationhood as connected to high art . . . I love that idea, but in practice it doesn't work. It doesn't work and I think this can be analysed in many ways. From a political point of view – i.e. the political situation in the country, all the political contradictions in our society; economic – the relationship between the political power and the cultural power, between the power structures. There are many ways of analysing these relations. Is there really sufficient social maturity to implement or construct, in practice, such an ambitious arts policy? I don't have a concrete answer to that.

But I do believe that a socialist revolution must be aware . . . I think it is one of the benefits that socialism should bring: to have a power body of all the forces in society, and within that body [to] have artists, art and intellectuals. And more so in a country like Cuba in which those intellectuals, those artists, those scientists, those educators, were the ones who created the Cuban national identity. That political power was gained in no small measure through the passion, the ideas and even the participation in battle

111

of men of culture. I don't think that is fully understood. I'd even go so far as to say it's something feared.

Cuba becomes independent when a tremendous awareness comes about. It was almost the last to gain independence from Spain, at a great time of awareness. I mean, it wasn't something that just happened. It wasn't, let's say, an irrational process. So, I think as an artist that my big struggle is to incorporate art into a political force, a socio-political force, to a force with strength and power – art for art's sake which, as art, is linked to society, not art as a pamphlet . . . but art as great art politically transforming reality, helping the qualitative transformation of society.

When I say great art, I don't mean elitist art, that's another complex term, because really great art is not understood by the people. The great artist, great art, ought to transform those people, but should do so consciously. And I think, in my own case, that that's a struggle. I know it is a struggle. You come up against the most ignorant, the most negative people . . . It hasn't even been easy for me being an artist in Cuba today. I have had to be very strong, I have had to have a lot of faith, I have had to believe in things, not in the emotional but in the rational sense. I have had to be very strong not to let myself be swept away by ignorant bureaucrats, by, *eh*, opportunists of every class. I could make you out an enormous list of people who have done a lot of harm to young artists, who have done a lot of harm to the Revolution, who have done a lot of harm to our principles, acting, it would seem, with impunity. This is what people do not understand . . .

I believe the easiest way is to judge people by their work, by what they actually do. And that is the big contradiction in which I am embroiled as an artist in the last while: in the analysis of that ancient, profound polemic of the contradiction between ideology and science which is really one of the most brilliant aspects of philosophy in the history of philosophy up to Marx. Because, really, Marx carries on or continues a work: he doesn't discover everything, nor is he some kind of God. Basically, he rounds out and develops aspects which had been analysed and had already been anticipated. Well, this relationship is fundamental for me. And all the last part of my work is about this – what is truth and what is appropriate. What is appropriate in a given situation of an historic process and/or what is really true. I mean, you cannot deny that the truth is the same truth for everyone. It's as true for socialists as it is for capitalists. It's true for people of the Left and of the Right. I mean, learn what is objective and you can never be mistaken . . . And what is ideological, or, rather, what is appropriate at a given moment because of relationships of class, or of power, or of common direction – the correlation of forces with other forces – I think that is very important because it is really the measure of how Marxist we are. The Marxist is the person who is – in my interpretation of Marxism – very clear about what he or she is: what suits you at a given moment, your own interests as a class, as a nation, as a group . . . and what is real.

A lot of our problem springs from not understanding or not paying sufficient attention to this question. Because we are always talking about this juncture in our social development, that it's a difficult time. But we have always been at a difficult cross-roads. Cuba has not stopped having difficult times in all its revolutionary process. Revolution is always a difficult process and it is always on the verge of a crisis, but you have to know how to face it courageously and to accept the challenge of the future. And to face up courageously to what lies ahead, to what the Revolution has forged. There is a new attitude now, this young people's attitude. These artists represent youngsters in general. They are, if you like, the aesthetic, artistic expression of a whole new spirit. These are young people created by the Revolution, educated by the Revolution. They don't know the problems of the past, you cannot say they have hang-ups from the past. These are young people who I do not believe want to return to the past . . . what they want is to change socialism, they want to be revolutionaries in their own time. Just as other youngsters of their age made a revolution at sixteen or seventeen, they made a revolution thirty years ago, now they want to make a revolution in their time. Not a revolution with arms, up in the mountains or whatever, but let's say a social revolution, at the level of ideas, of attitudes, of spirit, of new vitality, of a new vision, of what is socialism. Let's say that in so collective, so difficult, and so critical a political process, we are now beginning to appreciate that individuals are not the same, that everyone has something to contribute . . . The unity of difference. Not a false unity which says everyone thinks the same, but a unity of common interests, of the most universal and constructive interests.

Artists today are anxious to take up their social function. In some cases they have even abandoned the traditional form of artistic expression, the most elegant and formal ways, and have gone in for a sort of confrontational style, of the direct message, the literal message without metaphor or elaboration . . . I am talking about the most revolutionary artists, the people who really want to make critical art, an art which contests but from a revolutionary position. From the position of the Revolution at the moment and in accordance with what they think the Revolution should be, and their role in it. And as I said just now, that is not understood. [That position] has generated a sort of fear that this could create problems, even disturbances. It could take on elements of the human rights group Pro Arte Libre.* It has created a fearfulness about this [critical art] movement which I believe, if analysed deeply, would lead to the conclusion that they [the critical artists and the Pro Arte Libre group] are different phenomena, with different objectives – completely different cultural and political processes. They [the critical artists] are being trained in art schools, their parents are committed, in some cases they hold very important positions. There is a total difference between them and other [human rights] groups that might spring up, and are so doing, for different reasons. To some degree these [critical art] groups emerge because there is a crisis, a social crisis, an economic crisis, a crisis of values – a political crisis, you could even say. But this crisis is dealt with in different ways. The different social groups deal with it in very different ways. And I have emphatically defended these youngsters because I think they are the future of Cuban art and Cuban culture. And they have to be supported, given political support, precisely because they are the most vanguard force. They have nothing to lose. What's of interest to them is what really interests them – devoid

---

* A group of amateurs for the most part, whose objective as told to this writer is to get visas for the US. Several received prison sentences of a few months after a wreath-laying demonstration at the José Martí Monument in Havana on 20 October 1988.

of all material or social advantage. They do it because they feel it. It's really like the voice of our subconscious. It's like the child of the Revolution, and it seems to me that it must be given support and understanding. But in general, there is no comprehension of it.

These are our children. And, well, I'm a wild fan of theirs. I think they are great. And it seems to me that one grows old and one cannot be in the vanguard all one's life. There has to be regeneration. That concept must be understood. It must be loved. The new generation must be stimulated and perceived as a splinter of oneself. I think that's the finest way of seeing it, of understanding socialism, as I see it. I don't believe in somebody just because they carry a card, because they tell me they are revolutionaries. First I ask, 'What have you done? What have you done for the Revolution? What have you produced? What have you forged? What have you created? What have you innovated?' That for me is the essence of a revolutionary. And, well, there comes a time when one has to ask oneself if one is no longer a revolutionary. One can call oneself a revolutionary and have ceased to be one. When one stops being a revolutionary in the literal sense of the word, in the deep meaning of the word, knowing that you are making a revolution, that you are transforming things. When you have stopped changing things, because you have exhausted your energies, you really can no longer do it, that's when you ought to leave it to others, to those coming up, and to support them so that they continue your work. Besides, what you did was only the continuation of what was left to you by others who did everything for you, your grandparents. I think that's the kernel of the issue of Cuban art today. It's an art that desires and seeks a political space for its expression. It asks for a political space, but a political space as art.

11

Raimundo Sánchez

Raimundo, thirty-three, is from Santiago de Cuba though he now lives in Havana. He has a tiny little house of three rooms which he shares with his wife and two children. The house is full of personal touches and plants. They have added a wrought-iron balcony upstairs. They have a colour TV and a record player. Raimundo is black.

17 October 1988

My mother was very over-protective of all her children. She tried to give them all she could, perhaps because she didn't have anything as a child and had to work as a maid in a house. Later, she worked in a clothes factory supposedly for her godmother, who loved her, but who had her there as a maid. She gave her one or two dresses but [my mother] worked there all day in that workshop. She was about eleven. She only went to school up to fourth grade, then after the Revolution she got to sixth grade, but then she didn't want to continue because of all she had to do at home with the children. She didn't want to go on studying.

Every Sunday she went to church and she would take us. All my brothers and sisters were baptised and the eldest made their First Communion. Later, as we became more independent, we no longer went to church. But she would go all Holy Week, Palm Sunday, all that sort of thing.

I began to change in secondary school. I became more independent and then later I joined a movement called the Centenario

Youth Column. I was fifteen and I went to Camagüey. I studied there and I became a sort of nurse at a medical post, the equivalent of a nurse. I worked there in an army unit. I finished junior cycle secondary school there and then went on to study at the Worker Farmer Faculty, and I did it in two years. The Faculty is like senior cycle secondary level for workers. Then I went to university in Camagüey for six years, studying and working. It was a little difficult as I had to travel from Camagüey to Santa Clara to study. They sometimes didn't like that at the army unit. I reached the rank of sergeant-major in the army and that's what I actually am. I have two stars. Next month I'll be mobilised for thirty days – it's an exercise they have every year for officers.

Well, military life was the making of me. I had been very over-protected and spoilt as a child, and there I had to deal with life and learn how to cook, wash, iron and do things for myself as I didn't have my mum and dad to do it for me. I found in it a way of becoming completely independent. I felt a need for that and it was how I managed to break away from home. I always had a strong character. I was never an easy child but always on the go, out in the street, playing, doing sports, and for that reason my mum kept us in, she didn't want us to go out.

Well, in the army I became a psychological assessor, which meant producing psychological reports, working with the whole range of psychological tests there were in the country. I worked in a psychiatric military hospital there in Camagüey, and that had a great influence on me. When I was demobilised I went to Guantánamo, and as my brother-in-law was head of psychiatric services there in Guantánamo they got me a job in a diagnostic assessment centre where they assess children with behaviour problems. That's where I got the idea to continue specialising in behaviour.

I came to Havana in 1978 and began to work in a diagnostic assessment centre in Playa. That first year was a disaster as regards the daily work rate, because I couldn't adapt. It was different to life back there where more was expected of you, where there was more discipline. Here there was no control over whether you arrived late. No punctuality. So I had a row with the doctor, because people were used to easier ways. So, I would arrive early, do my workload and finish early. The rest didn't do their jobs and I was seen as a bogey.

That was my first failure. That was a year of adjustment to Havana and working life there. But that experience was a lesson and later I was singled out as an exemplary worker. I became a member of the Communist Youth and with all those accolades, in 1982, I was appointed Vanguard Worker at provincial level and subsequently at national level. As a reward I got a 21-day trip to Czechoslovakia with my wife.

On my return they offered me the directorship of a school for children with behaviour problems in San Miguel del Padrón. I got a better salary and it was easier to get to. That first year in the school went really well. I got on very well with the children and with colleagues. I always tried to motivate them and I learnt a lot from them. There were 156 children in that first year, most of them abandoned by their families. That was around the time of the Mariel exodus [in 1980]. There were a lot of children who had been left behind by their parents with some family relative or a neighbour. There were lots of those cases. Others were hyperactive, others had been stealing. I had twenty-seven people working in the school that first year. Then they reduced the number to twenty-two. It was a great team.

The school was in the middle of a very deprived area of poor families. For the most part the streets there aren't tarmacked, the houses where those children live are in a dreadful state. It is a socially underprivileged area. There are homes there where they don't read the papers, they don't get magazines. Some houses have a television, others don't, and it's the same for other essentials like fridges, radios – they might have one but they wouldn't have the other. In other homes they might see a meal once a day because the parents couldn't care less. There are a lot of single, unemployed mothers with little education. Others have parents who are in jail, covered in tattoos. Some have lesbian mothers who don't know who the father is, and there are cases of mothers involved in prostitution who haven't the time to give the child. So, the school, fortunately, had to take charge of re-educating the likes of these cases, or at least try to give them a basic minimum.

It wasn't the best equipped school but, well, the effort was made to make sure the pupil felt well, that he or she had lunch and morning and afternoon snacks, and that their education was assured. It was a day-boarding arrangement. They would come along at 8 a.m. and stay until 4.30 p.m. I tried to do arts activities with them. On Fridays I would bring my tape recorder from home and play music for them so they could dance. I tried to organise lots of recreational activities.

There were children from Havana City who had never been to Coppelia [ice-cream parlour] or the centre part of town like the Museum of the Revolution, Revolution Square, because their parents had never taken them. So, I and other teachers would take them along, outside working hours, to these places, to Old Havana; we'd take them on the ferry so that they could see the sea and the boats; we'd take them on board Soviet ships on courtesy calls. We'd do all that to broaden their imagination.

Usually the children identify with the teachers because they give them confidence and help them. The teachers bring them clothes, shoes and often they have to pay for things themselves. When you take them to the funfair at Lenin Park you have to pay for the rides, for the ice-cream – the school doesn't have resources for that. In the beginning, it did. It had 50 pesos a month but that was later cut. Economic difficulties of the country.

They would have other activities as well, of course. They would have a television in the dining room, they had a music teacher and a psychologist to give them group or individual therapy. I took part in the psychotherapy sessions. The trouble was that at 4.30 the pupil went home and back to the same scene: disturbed parents, pot-smoking mothers. In some cases the fathers used tablets such as parquisonil, a pill for psychiatric patients, epileptics or schizophrenics. They would take them with beer and, of course, their minds would go. Others had scams with illegal beer and pork rolls,* all that sort of carry-on. That has a bad influence on the children because generally people who would go to those places then would be antisocial types.

* Involving stolen produce or possibly using meat from illegally (privately, unhygienically) slaughtered animals.

Up to last year there were special education facilities for over 6,000 children with behaviour problems in Havana City province. In total there are places for 12,000 children with special educational requirements.

Raimundo also talked about his work for the CDR (Committee for the Defence of the Revolution). CDR representatives are proposed and elected from the body of the neighbourhood or block assembly to which everybody would be expected to subscribe. Primarily a mass organisation of political vigilance, the CDR also has neighbourhood watch and residents' committee functions and is crucial in such areas as vaccination programmes and the recycling of materials.

Where I live, I am responsible for the night-watch in my block. I am deputy co-ordinator of the CDR and a member of the board of the CDRs at municipal level. Part of that covers the Cerro area, which is also very deprived in terms of the children. You get some delinquency often because there are a lot of slums and tenements. You get all sorts mixed up here. You'd find a professional person, a former prisoner, a revolutionary and a delinquent. So, among them you get some really great people and then there are others who aren't worth the bother. The Revolution does have [an improvement] programme for these places at the moment. It first started in Mantilla and now we have it in Cerro, which is called the Transformation of Atarez Workshop.* With the explosion of the microbrigade movement designed to finally get rid of the slums in Havana, the plan was to start in areas like this where there are such big tenements, with over a hundred rooms, with makeshift mezzanine arrangements and everything. In my block there's a slum with over ninety rooms with four hundred people. Small rooms where you'd get seven or eight families with mezzanines, and that isn't easy. That also negatively affects the child. You would have to be very careful how you run a household like that. There are things you can't say in front of the children, the private life of the parents. In many cases the fathers don't live in the house because the mothers have had several partners. Other mothers give

* Housing project involving the community.

their children away, to an uncle, a neighbour, to whoever. Often they might have six or seven children and they only live with one or two. So they are not proper models.

But now, with the new Transformation of Atarez Workshop, they hope to get rid of all the slums through the microbrigade system, building housing, promoting the cultural roots of the area, because you get a lot of Afro-Cuban stuff there. They play a lot of rumbas, religion is very strong, especially *santería* and spiritism.* They are even planning to have an Afro-Cuban museum. It has one of the oldest and most famous *comparsas* [carnival processions] in Havana, the Marquis and Marchioness of Atarez.

And do they not want to get out of the area?

Yes, in some cases they do, but in others, they don't. Because they like that sort of life. They have lived in tenements from generation to generation. To a certain extent I think a comfortable house with all the essentials wouldn't suit them, because they have got used to the slums, to engaging in illegal activities, to operating.

Some people have spent over fifty or sixty years living in slums. They have water, they've done repairs, installed toilets. Others share a bathroom but some have one inside the house. They have a cooker set up inside. Some people go to the toilet in a bucket and then flush it down the communal toilet. But in there you'll find young people studying to be doctors, technicians or at secondary school.

In some instances I don't see any desire among them to improve their circumstances, to change their life, get involved in a microbrigade. Very few young people have that enthusiasm to work on a microbrigade, to work so that they get a house, to get out of this situation. Very few. They like the easy life, the wheeling and dealing. Where people have got out they leave rooms vacant for those who stay behind, and so you might get families of six or seven living in different rooms and a sort of family community grows up. You get maybe five or six families – the children, the mother, the granny, the nephew – who over the years have got

* *Santería* is an Afro-Cuban religious cult. See pp.125–32.

married and made their own families, who have been taking over rooms and staying on.

They have sociologists working there now with the community. There are lots of sociology students working there, political and mass organisations working to win them over, to get them to change their lifestyles and go into the microbrigades, to help build the school which is under way there, to build day-care centres, to change their way of life. That's what people talk about at local government meetings. Not that everything is expected to disappear, all of Atarez, because there are some houses which are solid. This is all long-term stuff, because it isn't easy. I think there are over 200 tenements in my area.

And there's a problem then when they allocate them a house and it doesn't accommodate all the different families, because the Public Health authorities won't permit it. So they have to get two apartments. Often they get them in the same building, but sometimes they're separate, some in one building and the others in another. You get cases of a mother and her daughter getting housed in the same building because they've requested it.

But many don't want to leave the centre because the houses are in Alamar or in La Lisa and they can't get used to living out that far. But there's a saying in Cuba which goes, 'For an improvement in circumstances, you'd even leave your house.' I think if you are living in bad conditions and they are going to give me a house in Habana del Este, comfortable, with running water, a bathroom, clean and healthy, ventilated, why should I stick it out in some old room?

What are Cuban women like? Are they liberated?

Cuban women have set ideas. After a woman gets married and has children she completely changes her way of life. She tends to stop looking after herself; she doesn't go out any more except at weekends when she goes out with the family to eat, although sometimes there isn't the money because things have gone up so much. But maybe not even to take a breath of air on the Malecón. I don't know if the frightful state of the transport service has anything to do with it, because it isn't easy to go out with children. But I think with a little effort it can be done.

I think women are under pressure from machismo. They have freedom, but they have made their own prison there in the home. It isn't common for a woman to go to a bar alone or with two girlfriends. A man gets the impression that a woman who goes to a bar to have a drink, a beer, is behaving out of the ordinary. Put vulgarly: that she isn't worth a curse.

This attitude stems from our background because, before, women who went to bars were generally prostitutes.

Is there prostitution now?

Prostitution? Yes, there is. It's not legal but there is. I'm not talking about a woman who frequently changes partner. There are some who go with foreigners and Cubans. Cubans as well. It's on a small scale. You usually see them in bars down by the docks or you get some in the bars of the hotels who are with Cubans or more usually foreigners, or with Cubans who have money, who are involved in illegal activities, wheeling and dealing.

So, as a Cuban woman you can't go into a bar. Therefore women don't generally do so. I think that's a received attitude that's gone from generation to generation. It's a sort of sin. As yet women here haven't demanded this right to go to a bar. I've never heard it spoken about. I don't really know why. It has just never arisen that a woman should have the freedom to go to a bar for a drink. It's just not [seen as] normal, and much less so for a young woman.

Psychologically, the Cuban woman does not feel liberated as such. There's always that dependence, that dependence on the man, always. As I said before, I think it's traditional and women have not reached that level of consciousness to free themselves completely from men. A man here can have another woman, yet a woman cannot have another man. It's a mortal sin for both, but in many cases she knows that the man has another woman and she is incapable of having another man because, well, he's a man and women cannot do the same, because they think it's not normal.

It's impossible for a society to be happy with this. There must always be equality. In every sense. Women must have total freedom. We're working towards it but the emphasis here has always been for equal rights to work, to study, to social standing, but the sort of freedom whereby a woman can go to a bar, go out with two or three girlfriends to have a beer, that's not seen as normal. If a woman does that it is considered ugly by her peers. It is seen as something wrong or that they are up to something. They have not wanted to change that. Women themselves have not wished to change those customs. I think it's because they are afraid of what men will think of them. I don't know, I think a man might lose his faith in her. I think that's it. Let's say I don't think it's normal for a woman to leave work and instead of going home, she goes for a few drinks with a girlfriend or to her friend's house. If she did that, when she got home her husband would kill her, I think. He'd kill her!

12

Marta Beatriz Bartelemy

Marta Beatriz lives in the Cerro district of Havana. She has two rooms off an alley of low, crumbling, often makeshift buildings which pass for houses. She is a santera, *a practitioner of the Afro-Cuban religious cult* santería, *and her living area is a shrine to the numerous deities she invokes. She speaks with slow deliberation. Marta Beatriz was forty-five at the time of our interview.*

29 May 1989

My godmother* has been a *santera* for forty-four years. She was two when she received the saint because she was born with a ball [tumour] on the brain which affected her neck. The doctor was going to operate on her, which could be done in the morning, and she received the saint and she's still there in perfect order. She sings in Yorubá, and Yemayá† at least – the saint she took – has been great for her.

I took a saint because I was sick. I've suffered from my nerves all my life but apart from that, they were going to operate on my head because I got a stroke which affected my sight, my hand and my foot. And the neurologist set me up for the hospital but I didn't want to go and I took a saint, and to this day there's nothing wrong

---

* In *santería* a godparent represents an initiate into the religion before the *babalawo*, or high priest.

† A deity; see full list on p.132.

with my head. And things haven't gone badly. I adore Yemayá.
And it's not for problems with the law because I haven't had any.
I did it because I needed to. Despite the fact that my ancestors –
my grandmother was Lucumí,* my mother's mother, who died
in 1970 – because before in religion you didn't have saints in soup
tureens or any of that. Saints were kept in gourds, all this lark
of soup tureens wasn't on. That only came in some years back.
You put the saints in gourds. And you didn't show any of this
to your children either. You did it while they slept. If you had a
cleansing, you did it as they slept. Everything while they slept. If
you were going to have them cleansed, you did it while they were
asleep. And nobody ever knew about it. And I have this garment,
look. (*She shows me a white dress*) It's from the Regla de Palo, it's
Sarabanda's.† I've had it since I was fourteen. Modesto Chacón
Morales, who lives in La Hata, gave it to me. Son of a Haitian.
This, for me, is part of my life, because before I was a *santera* I
had this. Since I was a child. And it has been a great help to me
and I look after it. I have a lot of proof of that. I don't use it but
I do have requests. I do make requests [through the garment]. I
ask [Sarabanda] for health for me, for my children. And also when
people get at me or hurt me, for example, I ask him to help me get
free of them. And Yemayá, the saint I have, has certainly served
me well, despite the fact that people here give out about *santería*
a lot. But the government doesn't object to you being a *santera*.
They don't interfere with us, because we are prepared to give our
blood, to go on missions, to belong to a CDR, a federation, an
MTT. The state never bothered us. At least I know the state has
never bothered me.

I never have a drums ritual. I don't like that. The day I have to,
I will, but while I don't have to, I won't. I don't do that. I keep
[the faith] for myself. Do you understand? And my mother is also
a *santera*. My mother took Obatalá thirty-three years ago. My sister
has Ochún and she also had a terrible trial. Her husband was a
Party member and said he didn't believe in 'all that shit'. My sister

* An ethnic group of the Yorubá culture.
† Regla de Palo or Palo Monte, a religious cult from the Congo; Sarabanda is
one of its deities.

has suffered from lymphangitis of the leg since she was fourteen and my mum said she had to offer two hens to Ochún for her health. And he [the husband] reluctantly bought the two hens. Then someone stole one of the hens from my mum at around 5 in the afternoon and at 5.30 a car mounted the pavement by my house killing my sister's only child, and by the time they reached the car, indeed, Ochún had killed him. The hen that had gone off on her – she had one, the other had gone. When the saint came to my mother, that's what it was, it killed my sister's only son.

And if I remember correctly, here in Cuba, the Virgin of Regla appeared in the sea and whoever tried to shoot her got as far as Fifth Avenue and killed himself in his lorry. My mum saw it. Deep-sea divers went out and all, thinking it was some woman tricking, and when the man fired shots at her she got up a sort of foam, and when he got to Fifth Avenue, he killed himself. Oh, yes. I'm religious because I have reason to believe. I'm not a fanatic but I do believe. I really believe in Yemayá and I believe a lot in spiritism, because that also exists.

The father of my children is a *babalawo*. He lives in Michigan, in the United States. He went off with the scum in 1980 and he has had a lot of trouble because Changó told him not to go. He should have stayed here and he's having the devil's own time of it there. Pretty bad, because he shouldn't have gone and spiritism does exist. Spiritism does exist. Many things are very true. What the *santero* doesn't tell you the spiritist will, which you have to believe in, not for evil purposes but to do something good. And I also think I am a realist. Just because I'm a *santera* doesn't mean I don't have to go to the doctor. Because when you become a *santero*, the first place you are sent is to the doctor.

In my house everyone is a *santero*. My aunts and uncles, my cousins and I lived in a tenement in Indio and Monte Streets, in number 18 Indio Street, where they did a lot of drums and . . . if someone is missing a leg and walks with crutches, Oggún comes, throws away their crutches and they start dancing as if they had the missing leg. There was a man who lived there by the name of Juan de la Cruz who had withered legs. He would get Oggún. On the night of 28–9 June, Oggún would come to him and at midnight he would ask for a candle and he would start walking around the tenement which had thirty-six rooms, a basement and an immense roof-terrace. (*A cock crows loudly in the distance*) And he lived on the top storey and he would come walking down on his withered legs with a candle, and it lasted for [three days] while the saint was with him.

And a lady by the name of Florinda who came from Jovellanos used to throw herself on the roof-terrace, and they would make her a fire down below, and when she got Oyá she would hurl herself over the edge and fall into the fire, and she never even burnt a leg.

And over there in Zequeira between Cruz del Padre and Infanta Streets lives a man called Félix who they call Obbadié, which is the saint's name Changó gave him. And when the saint comes, he has a cauldron of flour on the fire and he does this. (*Raising her hands over her head*) He takes it and puts it on his head and dances with it, then he throws the flour all over his body and he doesn't burn himself. So, there's something to it. And when Yemayá comes, he throws himself in a lake or he throws himself into a well.

I celebrate my anniversary on 30 August, just one specific day of the year. I dedicate that day, when I became a *santera*, to her [Yemayá]. I pay tribute to her. But I don't practise *santería*. I keep it to myself. Why should I practise it? There is a lot of exploitation nowadays. For what's worth 5 centavos they charge you 2 pesos. And for what's worth 2 pesos they charge you 4. And really I don't know if it's because you can't get things, but generally everything is very dear. They charge you a fortune for your initiation floor space, although they say it's worse abroad.* Well, it wasn't like that before. The woman who made me a *santera* didn't exploit me. She charged me 250 pesos to make me a saint.

And let me say that if you want to have a party for the saints, you have to get a licence. I'm not getting one. If that's what it entails, I don't have any parties. I don't see why I should have to go to the police station. And I have Yemayá as my saint. But, anyhow, I don't practise it. I don't live off that. Those who have

---

* Several days of preparation are required before being received into the religion. This involves hiring space to live in the house of the godmother or godfather or of the high priest. The person about to receive a saint must shave his or her head and wear white garments.

godchildren take them on to live off. They live on exploitation. To take Elegguá now costs 450 [pesos] . . . and there are some who ask for 500. To take Changó, they ask for 400 pesos.

So, here I am waiting for 30 August to more or less celebrate the anniversary of my saint. Here in my house. I make her a throne. (*She explains the various icons around the room*) That one up there, the black one, is the Virgin of Regla, and in that earthenware jar there in front of that little deer, that's my Yemayá. Yemayá has a lot of glasses of water. I dedicate each glass to a dead member of my family at that shrine. Water and flowers. When I don't have the money, I don't buy her flowers, when I have, I do. Lilies mainly, they're my favourites. And I wish the state would some day sell jars, there were these Chinese ones here in Cuba before. [I would like] to be able to buy one of those for my Yemayá. One of those Chinese jars they used to sell here before, because now even soup tureens are in short supply. In the religion of the Church she is the Virgin of Regla and in *santería* she's Yemayá of the sea. She is the queen of the seas, and that's the saint I have. Her special features – she has seven bracelets, a boat, a sun, two oars, a buoy . . . there are seven things.

And beside that is Ochún, which in the Church is the Copper Virgin. And that one up there with a lot of colours, that's St Christopher who's in the cathedral. In *santería* it's Aggayú. That one over there is the Church's St Barbara and in the religion of us *santeros* it's Changó. Then those two earthenware jars, they're the twins, and in the Catholic faith they are Cosmos and Damian. And that's Ochosí, the hunter. A lovely saint. And there's Oggún who is St Peter. The one with the hat on.

What's that you have in the glass of water?

That's a crucifix. It means God. Because Jesus Christ exists in all religions. (*There are coffee beans and cigars laid out also*) I put those out because my dad drank coffee and he smoked cigars like Peter Lorre.

My sons are religious like me. One has Changó and the other has Elegguá. They took saints because of a pending court case, they weren't sick . . . To see if, by doing this, at least [the authorities] wouldn't be after them.

The last time was terrible. I had to do some running around to get one of them out, until everything was cleared up. Because they wanted to get him for something he hadn't done, a fairly nasty crime, for a robbery which he had nothing to do with. But anyway, they charged him with attempted armed robbery . . . the issue was they were asking for fifteen years. And I as a mother, every mother knows her children, I always said that if it had been for a fight or whatever I knew that was possible, but for robbery, no! I know they don't steal. But I had to accept the prosecution evidence. He got put away for four months . . . Four months of bitterness and hardship, because he has three children. It's a long time.

Accepting that I am a religious person, I also know that if I commit a crime, neither saint nor the dead, nobody, can relieve me of paying my debt to society. You have to be responsible towards society. It doesn't mean you can commit a crime and not be jailed. You have to go to jail. And if you have cancer and you take a saint, you know you may have to die because that's a disease the body can't tolerate for too many years. You have to be realistic.

My sons work and I've one who's studying. He doesn't believe in this. One is a brickie and another a painter. And the youngest, who's sixteen, is in secondary school finishing ninth grade. He doesn't like religion at all and I don't force it on him. Just because I have my beliefs doesn't mean my son has to. And I don't let him participate if he doesn't want to either. And nobody can take my ideas away because I am baptised and confirmed. I am married. I made my First Communion. I am religious, I am a Catholic. And I was in the French Dominican Convent in Paseo and Twenty-third Streets. That's where I studied, in a nuns' school, until I was fifteen. And there you had to pray every day. You had to go to church, receive communion . . . and the last time Padre Pío came here to Cuba, to the church of San Nicolás, I was confirmed. And I have been married twice, in a registry office. I would have liked it to have been in the church but I didn't have the money for it.

How do you choose your saint?

130

A godmother mediating with Eleggua throws snails or you find out through the Orula board. But I don't like the Orula board because the power of Orula is not received in the head. The *babalawos* receive the power of Orula in the hands. Because once you receive your saint, you can't receive anything but your saint in the head. So, the *babalawos* think they are better than anyone else, than the other *santeros*, and they think working their board is fabulous, but they don't realise that Orula doesn't enter anyone's head, so they're not as clever as they think. Not like using soup tureens, which when one is taking a saint do go to the head, but Orula is in the hands, which means you can't determine who your saint is. It has to be done through Olbá, who reveals whether you can have a saint at all and who it should be. You can't just take on a saint like that, though some people have tried it, people in high positions, and they have been destroyed. Because if you're not destined for it, why should you try it? So people will look up to you?

But certainly, I am a believer. And I think I am going to die the same. Because Cubans always believed in something. If it wasn't the Church, it was *santería*. If it wasn't spiritism, it was card-reading. And as I was born into it, I'm not going to change my mind. Because if you swap one thing for another, you believe in neither. I'm neutral. I love my country very much and never in my life have I or my children thought of leaving here. We know that over there, wherever, we might be better off, but we are not leaving here. As for the rest of it . . . when I don't want to be here [in the house], I go outside and stand in the door or I go out the back to see my grand-daughter, who is gorgeous. I have my three grandsons just here. And so, I'm more or less involved with them and then, as I only have to do the washing once a week, I spend my time cleaning and eating. I can't do any more. And within their means my children help me out a fair bit. And they are very good to me.

I don't work. You see, my husband is in the merchant navy. Fifteen years ago I lived with him and he never let me work outside the home. And my sons are men now and they help me financially. I raised my children so that they would help me at a future date. I live here with my youngest son. We [her husband and she] don't have any contact. I am married to him but he doesn't send me maintenance. That law doesn't exist here, that when you no longer live together you have to send money.* I wouldn't want it either.

I used to work in schools, nine years ago. I don't work now because I have this problem with my nerves. As a school librarian. You know how these things are. I was fed up with my work because they were going to give me a house, and as I wasn't a Party member they gave it to a member. They left me hanging in the air . . . The neighbours beside me had blocked toilets and one of my sons caught a general sepsis, a terrible infection, because the excrement was even seeping through the walls. So the school where I worked was going to give me a house, but then when they restored the school they gave the house to a woman who was a Party member and we were left up in the air. And here we are.

The Deities

Yemayá: Goddess of the sea and of maternity. The Virgin of Regla to Catholics.

Obatalá: God of peace and purity who is attached to Olofí, the supreme godhead, who created the world and peopled it with his *orishas* (saints). Las Mercedes to Catholics.

Ochún: Goddess of love and of fresh water, symbolising femininity and sensuality. The Copper Virgin (Cuba's patron saint) to Catholics.

Changó: God of fire, thunder and drums, symbolising virility. St Barbara to Catholics.

Oggún: God of war, iron and metals. St Peter to Catholics.

Oyá: Goddess of the cemetery, lightning and wind, symbolising justice and revenge. La Candelaria to Catholics.

Elegguá: God who opens and closes roads.

Orula: God of divination.

Olbá: King of religion.

Aggayú: Father of Changó.

* Child maintenance laws in Cuba are similar to those in western countries.

13

Tania Escalante

*Tania Escalante is twenty-one and a single parent. She lives in Havana.
She tells me about her circumstances and her hopes for improving them.*

13 January 1989

At the age of three I went to live with my grandparents and an
aunt, the only paternal aunt I have, who was young at the time.
She was about fifteen or sixteen. I lived with my granny because
my mum had problems. She worked odd shifts and couldn't look
after me properly. My granny said to leave me with her, that
she would look after me and raise me. My granny worked. My
aunt looked after me while she worked. I went to school in the
morning and my aunt picked me up. Granny always gave me a
packed lunch or something the day before. Then in the evening
she looked after me until I grew up and went to boarding school.
She always worked until I finished secondary school, when she
retired.

The house was better than my mum's. Much better. But not
exactly what I would have wanted, because they weren't, they
aren't, very affectionate people. They were very cold with me.
They expected me to do things, I don't know. Maybe they just
didn't want to be blamed for bringing me up badly later on. It
wasn't the best, really.

It was a big house. It's an old house but big, although I never
really had a room there. It had two bedrooms, a living room, a

smaller room, a corridor, a dining room and two bathrooms all for us four who lived there at the time.

I didn't see my father very often because he was with his [army] unit most of the time. He would come and go but he never actually stayed. He wasn't part of our lives. I wasn't really happy because I didn't have anyone to play with. I didn't have any friends. I was always indoors because it was a second-floor apartment. They hardly ever took me out. But there was a neighbour whose balcony was beside ours and I would hide on the balcony and tell her to call me along the corridor so that my granny would let me go and play with her. I would say, 'Maria Elena, call my granny along the corridor and tell her to let me go out to play.' So she would do that and they would often let me go, but sometimes not. Until they got wind of what I was up to and they never let me go out again. And they boxed my ears for me as well because it seems I wasn't . . . they had me there on sufferance. It wasn't great.

There was enough money around because my granny always earned good wages. And my grandad always had a managerial position in the cigar factory where my granny also worked. The La Corona factory, which is there by the *Granma* monument. He always worked there. They both must have earned good money. At least in that respect there was no problem. Good food. The clothes weren't anything out of this world, but I had what I needed. They gave me a small birthday party every three or four years, a simple do, not, for instance, what I want for my child. Not the best, because there was no love. I wasn't with my father, and that's what I always wanted – my mum and dad. I don't know. My mum would come and see me at the weekend and I cried a lot to be let go with her. These are things I still remember and I won't forget. I cried a lot . . . I often recall that scene as a little girl, of my mum wanting to leave and me not wanting her to and crying from the balcony. All that contributed to my unhappiness.

Boarding school was absolute joy for me. I really felt at home, really well, really well. I spent three years at the school and I never wanted it to end. I really loved it. I worked in strawberries for the three years. Weeding, making the trenches, planting the strawberries, picking them. They didn't allow us to eat them but we did when no one was looking. We stored the strawberries in little boxes, in wooden boxes like for carrying milk. You stashed the boxes one on top of the other and then lorries came and collected them. I don't know where they went.

I got good reports, that's why I was chosen to study in Germany. There were five places going and I got one of them.

I learnt Russian when I was [at the school]. I was a boarder all year round but I went home at weekends. At that stage I had gone to live with my mum. When I finished secondary school I went to live with her in the tenement where I was born. A room. I went there for a while at weekends. I would go back to the school on Sunday. When I was finishing, my mum got sick and had to go into hospital for a long time. I missed a good few exams. In the end I did them, but all in one go. I got them but I never went [to Germany] because my mum began to talk to me about us having been separated for a long time; that she wanted me to be with her . . . to understand that she had had a lot of problems when she was alone with me, which was why she had left me at my granny's . . .

We both went to Oriente. To Holguín. That was around 1983. Off we went. We lived in my grandfather's house, all her family are in Oriente. I started studying at senior cycle secondary at night in the Worker Farmer Faculty. I was there for about three months but I fell in love with a much older man, a neighbour. I was going out with him for about seven months when one day he suggested I go and live with him. I told my mum and she approved and so I went to live with him. I was fifteen; he was forty-one.

My mother's support in that affair now seems strange to me. Now that it's over and in view of the fact that it was so awful. When I met that man he worked in catering, in the Holguín catering enterprise. He was my grandfather's neighbour. He started coming to our house. We started going out. Nobody said a word to me and I thought it was normal. I don't know, but now I don't see anything normal about it. But I did then. And Mum also saw it as completely normal and fine. She had also married young, much younger than I. At about thirteen, and also in Oriente. That's often the case here, that young girls marry when they are thirteen or fourteen.* So nobody said a word to me about being young. They did point out that he was an older man, but that's it.

I immediately got pregnant. I had the child and two months later, when the baby was two months old, I separated from him because things weren't going well. As soon as I started living with him, he started going out with other women, and started leaving me alone, and he didn't look after me despite the fact that I was pregnant. He didn't care. He even tried to hit me when I started to complain about my life, saying that I was bored and felt alone; that I never saw anyone; that he kept me away from everyone, from my family. I left him and went back to live with my mum. Things didn't go well for me at my mum's so I left and came back to Havana. Without the child. Without the child. My maternal grandmother looked after him, she and my mother. He stayed with them until such time as I could find work, some stability, and could send for him.

After about three months I got a job. At the Seaman's Club. It's a shop which only sells goods in dollars, in front of the Stock Exchange. I started working in the bar there. I was there for five months and then I started working in the shop where I was for two months. It wasn't a permanent job, only a contract. I earned very little, 118 pesos. I was assistant cleaner in the shop, 118 pesos.

I lived in a rented room for which I paid 80 pesos. I was there for about two and a bit months because I met a schoolfriend of mine whose husband was a sailor, and she said to me, 'Look, Tania . . . since you're having problems and you haven't a penny, I am going to be alone for several months, come and live with me until your circumstances improve.' And I went to live with her in Old Havana. It was near my work, three blocks away from it. So, I stayed with her until I left the Seaman's Club. I went to work in the Julito Díaz, a physical rehabilitation hospital in Boyeros. I was there for a good while also earning 118 pesos helping patients. It wasn't nursing. The majority of the patients were old ladies and it entailed dressing them, bathing them, taking them to the toilet, putting them to bed, helping the nurse give them

---

* In Cuba, anyone aged sixteen or over may marry without parental permission. It is possible to marry with parental permission from the age of fourteen.

medicines, taking them to the dining room . . . helping them in whatever way.

The only work I have liked so far is what I am doing now. When I left the hospital I did a course at the Transport Ministry to become a skilled worker, data control they call it. You work in mechanical repairs at a bus station. I note the number of vehicles broken down, I note when they leave, I give vouchers . . . I'm usually the person who does time and motion. I regulate the workers' time – where they get paid, what they get paid, according to what work they have done to the buses, the nature of the mechanical trouble. I get good money. I earn 180 pesos. There are three rotating shifts. They realised that I had ability and they needed someone to supervise the work, and that's what I'm now doing. I supervise the work and I am also secretary to the workshop boss, and I have a fixed shift of 8 a.m. to 4 p.m.

After the hospital I had no work. I was on the street with the child, who had by now been sent to me. I was living at my grandmother's. She had told me to come along and so I stayed with her for a few months until my mother decided to come back to Havana. She had stayed on in her house [in Holguín] and she also had my house, the house I had when I was with the child's father. The house was mine after I began living with him. So, she had her house and mine. She sold them both and came to live back here and bought a place. She gave me half the money from the sale and that's when I was able to get a small room, which is what I have now and where I live with the child.

I bought it illegally. I have one foot inside the door of the house and one on the street. But what was I to do if I had nowhere to live? Up to then I had been wandering around all over the place with the child. I had to take that risk. It cost me 2,000 pesos. It's a tiny room, without a toilet or anything. There's a communal toilet and I have more or less the basics: a bed for the child, a cooker, a table to eat off. I have to get water up from down below. I use a bucket on a rope because the building is very old and we don't have a pump or anything. It goes into a tank down below and I live on the third floor. I do have electricity. I have a meter which I share with two other rooms and we pay it between the three of us. It costs around 5 or 6 pesos a month. Water is free. I don't pay anything for that. I cook with kerosene so I don't have a gas bill. It's a stove you put fuel into. Besides, you couldn't install gas in those conditions.

So, I can manage with the 180 pesos, but I do without a lot. I don't buy myself a nice dress. I don't go out. I don't buy myself shoes. I do without a lot and that's how I manage. I can't complain of my salary because it's the best I've ever had. But, for instance, I got 117 pesos for the last fortnight because I did overtime. I did three double shifts and that pushed my salary up. Normally I get 90 pesos and a few centavos every fortnight. So that I can manage. So that I can get from the 5th to the 20th of the month, for example, I buy up all my ration at the *bodega*. I get tins of stuff and bits and pieces on the free market, and I have 10 or 15 pesos left which I set aside in case the child gets sick or I have to get something done to the house. But no, I can't allow myself the privilege of saying, I'm going to buy myself a dress every month . . . the best I can do is buy something for the child. His father has never taken responsibility for him. No money or otherwise. I don't claim what's due because I don't want anything to do with him. I would prefer to have to continue as I am than to have anything at all to do with him. I haven't pursued child maintenance rights, my granny told me to because it's all a help even if it's not much. But . . .

You have a boyfriend.

Gonzalo is a boy I met last year, on 13 April. It'll be a year since we met soon. He's twenty. He isn't Cuban, he's Chilean, and it's the best relationship I've ever had. It's everything I never had before, because many of the things I stopped doing when I was younger – like going to the beach, laughing with people like me, having fun, forgetting my worries for a while, relaxing, going to parties, having young friends like me – it's the best thing that's happened to me in a long time, besides my child.

He gets on quite well with him, they get on well, but as he's young there are things about the child . . . the child might want to be all over us and he'll say, 'Leave us in peace,' or he'll want to play while we're watching television and that sort of thing, and he doesn't realise that the child is still very small. But generally it's fine, really. At least I don't have those problems of stepfathers I've heard others talk about. His father is a political refugee and they've been here for some years now. Maybe that's why I haven't had problems. I've got friends in the same situation and it hasn't been the same for them. I think I have been very lucky. I have no complaints in that direction so far.

He's a student. He's studying marine biology. He finishes this year and afterwards . . . we don't know yet. He's going to Chile with his mum. He's going back to his own country. Let's see what happens to me. His mum had a talk with me a while ago and . . . I knew he was going but I didn't know that it was so soon. I knew that some day the time would have to come but I didn't know it was now. It seems he couldn't face telling me, so then his mum went to my workplace (*tears well up in her eyes*) and spoke to me, and explained that they had thought of leaving at the end of this term. And so, here I am getting by until he . . . He is very, very undecided. I really don't want him to go but I have never told him not to, nor have I even asked him not to. On the contrary. (*She is now crying*) I have always told him that I am someone who has been alone and that his family is very good. I really like them, and I told him he can't let his mother down for something he may regret later. Besides, he's dying to get back to his country. He's dying to go back there again. But, I don't know. Perhaps because he's in love with me that ties him a little, but I am sure he's going to go. What'll happen then, I do not know. I honestly don't know how I am going to cope with it.

Can't you go with him?

I don't know. It's not that I haven't thought of the possibility, but I haven't made enquiries about it . . . there's the problem of the child. It's not the fact that the child mightn't be able to go, but of the difficulties we would have there, and he's still a small child. We adults might be able to spend fifteen days sleeping on the floor or skip meals, but not him, he's too small. It's a fairly difficult situation.

I know that perhaps when he goes he will miss me for a while. He'll remember me for a while. But then he'll get over it. Because he's starting out [on life]. He's never been married . . . he's a young lad. It'll be much more difficult for me than for him. Because he's going to leave and I am completely alone. He has filled in a lot of the spaces in my life. It's almost impossible for me to imagine life without him. But I have a young child, so what am I to do?

I have future plans. I want to study. I want to do a middle technician's course, whatever, in September. I just want to better myself. Something to do with my work, my enterprise, whatever. I want to study. I want to join a microbrigade to improve my living conditions. I want all that. I know these are fairly ambitious plans, but I know I am going to get there.

My son still hasn't got a place in a day-care centre. It's a big problem. As I was working rotating shifts my granny looked after him. I sent a form to the Ministry of Education asking for a place for him in January last year . . . They sent me a letter saying there should be something for him this February. Let's wait and see. There are several new day-care centres in my *barrio* . . . I even went and spoke to the director of the centre, and she told me I'd have to apply, that she wasn't in a position to allocate places, to wait a little longer and see if they come up with a place from the ministry. I put in for a place when the child was two. They charge you according to what you earn. It would probably cost me about 30 pesos. Roughly. According to what I earn. You can bring them along from 6 a.m. to 7 p.m. You bring them along, they bathe them and give them dinner. Then they have a sleep and they have a snack in the afternoon. They used to give them supper as well but not now. Then you collect them and that's it. But I haven't managed to get a place yet. Nor a kindergarten, which you have as well. They're not the same thing. There are less children and they're for children over three. They only give them dinner there, which doesn't cost anything. They have a siesta and then you pick them up. They have games and things. They have less facilities than in the day-care centre but they mind your child for you.

I get out of work and I arrive home at 6 in the evening, at which point I have to rush out and find milk so as not to miss the child's quota. I often don't have time. So, what I do is, the day I get paid I try my best to rush out of work and then, whenever I pass [a shop] and see something, I get off the bus and buy all the things I need so that when I get home I don't have to go out and buy anything. That day I go mad buying everything. We have our ration card with which we can buy X amount of things – rice, beans, sugar etcetera, per person. I have no complaints about those things . . . What I'm most interested in is chicken, which comes every nine to fifteen days, or meat, it depends. It's chicken one time and another it's meat. Meat comes never less than nine or ten days. Sometimes it comes by the week. One week on, one off. Sometimes it doesn't come for twenty days. The other days we eat tinned food, eggs. I vary it. I would like to have more scope, I don't know, to improve our food at home, but I'm happy enough with what I have. I don't have a fridge, but I have organised it so that if I have something that will go off I leave it in my granny's, or if not in a neighbour's fridge, if they have room. I boil the milk. I boil it well, as often as I can, and then I give it to him as often as possible so as it doesn't go to waste. Usually, I try to make just enough each day for dinner and supper so I don't have to keep anything. The only thing I have in the house is the television. I didn't buy it, my boyfriend's mother gave me a present of it.

I would like my son to study when he is older. I will help him in every way, I will do all I can to prevent him falling into the situation of many young people today – young boys, mainly – who want to leave home at a very early age, who don't go to school. Very few go because they like it. The majority go because, 'Mum and Dad tell me I have to go and if I don't they'll punish me,' or 'If I don't go the teacher will send for me.' I don't want it to be like that . . . I would always make him see that his future depends on it so that he doesn't make the mistake I did. That's what I want for him.

I have a lot of friends, well, acquaintances really, because I stopped seeing them a long time ago. I knew them when I was at school. Some went on to university and they are now in jail. Others were in jail and they are now out. Look, I've a neighbour who's the one I most know. When he finished junior cycle secondary he began the senior cycle course. I don't know why he left it. I think he met up with young people like himself who acted outside the law. They didn't study, they didn't work, they didn't do anything. The only thing they did was loaf about. They started stealing cars and they were caught. He got six months. And there are lots like him . . . Many are in the same situation as myself. They got married young. They have children. Now they can't be independent. They have to live off their husbands. Some have managed to get work like me. Others turn to X . . .* because I know them. It isn't through necessity. Not like in the old days when it was almost essential. But you still don't get much of it here. Young girls, and I'm not saying it's for lack of money, but perhaps it's for want of a change, they go with one guy today and another tomorrow. They break away from their home life. There's a lot of instability among young people. I don't know how to explain it really. I don't know. The parents . . . a lack of pressure in the home. That's where it all starts. In the home. Young people in Cuba today . . . a large number are serious students but I would say that almost 50 per cent of young people are just wasters . . .

And that's going on down the country too, because I lived in Oriente for a while. It's the same down there. The big thing there is to hang out in the parks. Young people gather in the park causing more problems perhaps even than here. Because here people have more facilities. It's different down there. Young people take drugs, they drink rum. Young kids of fourteen and fifteen, not nineteen-or twenty-year-olds. Smoking marijuana. Adults sell it to them. I've seen it. Just as they do here in Havana as well.

I think what's wrong is their environment . . . beginning with the family. From the home to the environment in which we live. Sometimes, I sit down and I think there are things I see and hear, and I know people are doing them out of habit. It's all habit. Nobody does anything because they feel like it, because they want people to learn, so that they might know what reality is. No. Everybody does things out of habit. I give you a biology class because I know in the work programme I have to teach you that this animal is like this, and that's it. Nothing else. It's not because I am really into my profession or because I like teaching. So, the few remaining who do like it, who haven't lost their love for the job, do lose interest in it. Because there is no incentive . . . Even on television, even in what they broadcast to teach us, you can see the lies. You see the fiction of it and the mockery . . . You

* i.e. prostitution.

142

get it on a programme called 'Quick Meals with Nitza Villapol', an older woman who makes barbecued chicken, which I cannot do because if I do that with the chicken I get every fifteen days, I end up with no chicken for fourteen days. And lots of things like that. You see a kid saying to a policeman, 'Policeman, policeman, you're my friend,' and yet our youth, our children, our people do not look up to the police. Every Cuban knows that. This is hypocrisy. It's all a lack of sincerity. You can't honestly say what you feel, say how things are. Because people don't dare. Now they are though. Because now there are a lot of people who aren't afraid to speak up. Young people mainly who go around saying what they like, how they see things.

There are no places for youngsters to go. So, if you don't go to a cabaret or to a party at the weekend, you have nowhere else to go. You go along to Coppelia. Where else is there around here? I am talking about myself and the majority is like me – they want to dance. That's the problem. They want to listen to music, but not to go to the pictures or a theatre or a video salon. That's not where they want to go. There are dances like, for instance, La Tropical, where they go. There's a band. They play and the people dance. They don't sell drink there. But in most cases the dances end in fights and brawls and rows. That's Cubans. That's the way we are. That's the Cuban for you.

And the women, the girls, as they don't have any money and they are caught up in the school-home-party-Coppelia ritual, as soon as they are fifteen they are looking for a boy to take them somewhere . . . to take them out, give them drink, take them to a cabaret. They are looking for things that are not appropriate to their age. I have met foreigners and I see their attitude is different. The children are different, they have another mindset. At ten they are still thinking of playing with dolls, with toys and cars. And here our children aren't like that. At ten our children want to be out throwing stones in the park, moving around in droves, jumping on buses. The girls at fifteen are mad to wear make-up. I was like that. I'm quoting from my own experience: make-up, high-heels, hairstyles, fellas older than themselves. That's what our youth is like.

I think it's like a chain, because, for instance, when Fidel is on in the Plaza on 1 May, it's, 'Everyone to the Plaza,' like ants milling on and on and on, as if saving up for winter. Everyone goes. Delinquents go. Young students go. Young people . . . all off, all off to the Plaza just for the sake of it. They don't go for any particular reason. I don't know, conscientiously. They go to the Plaza, and that's what I mean. Fidel says you have to go to the Plaza on 1 May, and everyone goes to the Plaza on 1 May. The day a president from another country arrives you have to be at José Martí airport and lining Boyeros Avenue and all the roads. It's organised through schools, work centres and the CDRs. And you think people go voluntarily because they want to go? No. Don't believe it. Very few go because they want to hear Fidel speak, to find out what's actually happening in the country, to find out how things are going in the country. I hear the comments. I live among these people and I know that nobody goes because they want to. Nobody goes through conviction. Well, there are a lot of people who go because they like it, they like to hear Fidel, they like to see the parades because they are nice. I liked them. But a lot of people go so that the boss will see them. I know that. I have seen it and I know it.

It's possible that Fidel has the wrong person advising him or that he is misinformed about the reality of the young people. I don't think so. That's the way Cubans are. There is a whole sector that is wonderful. The young people who have been to Angola are fine people. You have to be fine to do that. The FAR [Revolutionary Armed Forces] have a fine group of youngsters. You get them in the university too. But there are also the unemployed youngsters in the street. Youngsters stealing, in jail. And there are a lot of young people who speak badly of him. Badly. I know a pair of brothers who are only fourteen or fifteen, and they left me stunned the other day when the eldest of the two says they are both dying to leave the country. Their father is in the States. He left with the scum. Now he's sent them a letter or whatever. And he's just dying, dying for his dad to sponsor him to leave the country because he says this is shite. That it isn't worth a curse. (*Laughs in amazement*) He's doing a middle technician's course in transport and he doesn't like it. He's studying just to be doing something but not because he likes it. He doesn't like mechanics. And there are a few like him who finish school and take up a vocational course which they know nothing about. They don't know who they are or what they are going to study.

The young people don't know what perestroika is. (*Laughs*) Nobody knows what it is and they care less. Those who are more educated are interested in it, but not the young people. All they say is that we export all the good things we have; that we have a load of Soviets here who are eating our food. That's what people say in the street. I wouldn't risk speaking up like they do, but I have had to shut up on a lot of occasions while agreeing with them. Because, in fact, they are right.

14

Damián Martínez

Damián Martínez left Cuba in the Mariel boat lift of 1980. He was repatriated under the Cuba–US Immigration Accord of 1984, which gave rise to jail riots in Atlanta in summer 1987. We meet in his workplace, a factory, where he works as a welder, and I ask him about his experiences.

August 1987

I went on my own. On my own. My family was here and I had a granny in Miami. My mum was here with my daughter. I had been married. My daughter is now eight. She was one on the very day I left, because I left on 26 May, which is her birthday.

They didn't want me to go. They didn't want me to go off there on my own, not knowing anything about the place. But I went. It was the mood of the time. 'No, I'm off, I'm off.' I was seventeen or eighteen. I had ninth grade and I wasn't working because I didn't want to. I got caught up in the whole idea with some friends from my *barrio*. I got caught up and I went.

I arrived at Cayo Hueso, and then I was in a refuge in Pennsylvania called Indian Town. I was there for about two months. It's a base. A military barracks they have there. We all slept together there in dormitories. I got out because I had work in Miami, as my granny had lived there for X number of years. I was living with my granny, no? She works in a women's clothing

146

factory and she got me work in a market selling fruit. Then I left her house. I visited her and all but I hitched up with a Puerto Rican woman with whom I had a son more or less a year after arrival. So all was fine until I had this problem. I got into a street fight with another guy, in a bar which is in Seventh Street and Seventeenth Avenue. He started shooting at me with a revolver because we had an argument. We're having a drink and we start to argue for no reason, and it ended up like that. Then the police arrived and arrested me.

But you didn't have a revolver?

Yes, I did, and I was firing at him, too, because he wanted to kill me.

What were you doing with a revolver?

A friend had it. So when we started to fight I asked him for it and he gave it to me. We started arguing, no? And the guy ran out to his car. And I had to go out because if he turned around . . . So, he got three years the same as me for carrying an illegal weapon. So, I was arrested and at the trial they gave me three years. I was about five months waiting for the trial but that time was counted as part of the three years. In the end I didn't do three years, I did eighteen months because you earn time off [your sentence] if you work. You get remission. I worked in the laundry room. You don't get paid because it's a state prison. There are state prisons and federal ones. So, that's where I did my time.

So, the day I was to be set free, the day they were to give me my freedom, I didn't get out. Some immigration officials arrived and said that I had to accompany them because I had a detention order from immigration. Then they took me to Atlanta. Well, imagine how I felt. The very day I was supposed to be let out they shove me in another jail. For no reason. For no reason, because Atlanta was just for the heck of it. That was in 1984, or thereabouts. It was before the [Immigration Accord] agreements were signed. So I was in Atlanta from 1984 to 1985. I was like everyone else who's there now – I wanted to get out. They wanted to be let out because they are in there, well, for no reason. They didn't do anything. They did their time for whatever crime they committed, and what they want is to get out because they're being held for no reason. So I was kept in there until I came back to Cuba. I got back, I can't remember the exact date, but it was in April 1985.

When did you know you were going to be repatriated?

Well, about a week before they brought me back. When they said they were going to repatriate people to Cuba, there was a riot just like the ones that are happening now. That's when I found out. At that stage I didn't want to come back. (*Pause*) Well, I thought at the time that when I got back here they were going to punish me for having left the country, no? (*Long pause*) I didn't think I'd be accepted back into society like anyone else. (*Long pause*) And then when I arrived back I realised myself that it wasn't going to be like that.

When we left Atlanta in a plane for here we were handcuffed. Hands and feet bound and with a chain around the waist like slaves. They took the handcuffs and manacles off here and then they took us to the Cuban authorities' headquarters. There were about forty-one or forty-two of us. We were put in quarantine in the barracks for medical tests, a check-up and that.

When we arrived they said that we were going to be freed but that it would take a longer time in some cases than in others . . . Then, when the quarantine was over, they let go one group but not another. They said they were investigating, they were continuing their investigations. I was in the group that didn't leave. So I was there a while until they released me, and when they did release me they found me work, the government people from the Ministry of the Interior. They told us not to get into bad company, not to look for trouble. Well, that we should keep cool and that things would be the same for us as they'd be for anyone else, for anyone else here in Cuba; that if we didn't look for trouble we wouldn't get it. I thought I was going to be in jail for years but it wasn't like that. I've been working here ever since.

And do you like it?

148

More or less. It's better than anything else. Besides, I feel good about it. I feel easy. I'm with my family. I have my daughter and I have my mum. My daughter lived with my mum when I left. She's highly intelligent. She knows so much. She's now eight and going to school. I see my going off like that as something I did for adventure. But I'm here now and I feel fine. Cubans who want to go there [the US] have the same idea as I had, because they don't know what it's like there. I liked it. I must say, I liked it. If I had money I would like to go back on a visit to see my son, but as regards living somewhere, I'm really not going to leave here again. I'm never leaving here again. I had a lot of hard times there, including this last business.

There are people there in prison for no good reason. Having completed their sentences they are still in jail. They are rioting because, apart from wanting to be out, they are afraid of coming back here for what might happen to them. But I'd say to them, there's no problem. If you don't get mixed up in anything when you come back, you can live in peace and lead a normal life like any other Cuban. They're not mad. They are saying, 'No. When we go back there *they are going to shoot us.*' To be shot, no. They know that, but they might think that they'd get five or six years more and nobody likes to be in jail.

Do people ask you about your experiences?

Yes. In my *barrio* lots of people know about it. They've asked me, '*Coño*, how did you get on over there?' Same as here in my work – lots of people know that I've come back from there . . . but they all treat me well, normally. There's no, how shall I put it, rejection or that.

15

Raúl Ygarza Bracho

In 1989 I heard a group of youngsters play Cuban music at the Young Artists' Centre in Guantánamo. They were quite amazing, and very talented. They were members of the EJT, the Youth Labour Army, a paramilitary force of civic action and an alternative to military service. As a group they had been co-opted to the Turquino Plan, a wide-ranging programme set up in 1987 to improve physical and cultural conditions in mountainous regions and to contain the migration to urban areas. The Turquino Plan covers forty-six municipalities, amounting to 17 per cent of the area of the country, and affects some 630,000 people. Raúl, the group's twenty-year-old singer, explains their function and conditions.

4 June 1989

Our work is to revive culture in the mountains. It involves providing and developing cultural entertainment in remote villages in the mountains, setting up small theatre groups, musical groups, working with children, adults etcetera.

It's three years' service. Before joining the EJT I studied in the Yarey art school. I was becoming a music teacher, and about two months after graduating I was recruited into the army to form part of an artistic group. And there they explained what we would be doing . . .

Then they brought us to Sabaneta, and that's where we are

working as a group. It's a *son* or *timba** – as it's sometimes called – musical group, which uses various instruments. There's a trumpet, a sax, a trombone; it has a flute, and me, I'm the singer of the group. And, well, in Sabaneta they had groups for us to work with, like a school or a village, to help in this cultural renewal. We were spread out over the area. For instance, I've to work with a secondary school. They send a musician, they send somebody in theatre, and somebody who works in dance. And each one of us has to form a group according to their speciality.

The plan was set up almost two years ago now. Yes, almost two years ago. It's part of the Turquino Plan. First we were in Santiago and then by order of the Minister of the Armed Forces, Raúl Castro, he sent us to Sabaneta because there we are more in contact with the area where we have to work and we've been there for about a year and a half now.

We were recruited from different places and brought to Santiago. We were there for a while and they sent us instruments from Havana, and then they sent us, after a few months, they sent us to Sabaneta.

Our role is music. Art, nothing else. Art. It's like a special unit. It's a sort of experiment. It's the first of its kind in Cuba. They are beginning to do it in each province now, each one with a different group. We go from the city to the mountains because, imagine, all those young people in the mountains have no kind of recreation. I don't know, they've no conditions in which to get any cultural movement going. There was electricity hardly anywhere. So, with the Turquino Plan movement, they started building video salons all over the mountains and they sent us along so that people might feel happy with where they lived. It's a different scene for them coming down from the mountains to the city. There are theatres, cinemas, video salons in the city, and there are parties every weekend. The city offers different possibilities. But with the Turquino Plan development project of building houses, bringing electricity and the possibility of having a video salon . . . it improves their environment. Now they have things to do, to see, to entertain

---

* An Afro-Cuban musical form, the most popular in the country this century.

them, but before, you see, they went to the city because, imagine, their lifestyles were not very developed. It was work to home. The city offered another scene . . .

And they have work. Coffee – in the mountains it's very good – cocoa and all those things. There are only about two or three houses there [in Sabaneta]. Very few houses, and they are all spread out all over the place. And then a bit further back you have the little town of Jaguayón, which is about 3 kilometres away. They have a store there and a fuel factory they built a while ago. There's a cadet school there, which next year will become attached to the university. And then there's our unit, the only one around here. It's right beside the road. Sabaneta is about 30 kilometres from Guantánamo. About thirty or thirty-five people live around there. About twenty people from our group were sent to Santiago to form another group there and within six months or so we will all join forces to become one group. And the people they've sent to Santiago will work in different units of the EJT in different municipalities of the province doing what we're doing in Sabaneta.

So, that's our work, and what we are doing here [in Guantánamo] is another aspect of it. The weekend we've just spent here is an incentive given us by the provincial arts department. The others who stay in the village, like those from the theatre group, go on camping expeditions at weekends, or they go on a long walk, or go exploring or to the beach, to a tourist spot or an historic spot, and so they get to have some leisure time. When we are not actually working we do some voluntary work, maybe decorating the unit. And when we have a spare moment we watch television or study, because we have a study area. We have a few books on theatre and on music.

The secondary school has a spread catchment, it's not all from Sabaneta. We go along on Tuesdays and Fridays in the morning and we're there till the afternoon. But we also have our own rehearsal programme. We rehearse at the unit, we try out our numbers, we work on arrangements and the theatre group has to rehearse, so that's how we divide up the week. On the other days we work for ourselves, individually, studying and that. And on Sundays, every other Sunday or thereabouts, we have a cultural session and we invite people from all over. We have our session playing music and then we sit down and watch some theatre, then some dance, and we have a great time. And the people are delighted with us.

Have you discovered any talent there?

Talent is something they don't have. Imagine, they're children, and you've got to work really hard with them for them to be able to do something because they are not very bright. They haven't got a chance to be creative in class, to have music classes or any speciality. They have no idea of what they can do. You've got to work with them for them to develop. We're going to be there for three years. I've been there two. And after three years they'll recruit other musicians and other people to continue the work we are doing.

I could invoke Order number 18. Order 18 allows for you to go to a cadet school to study after two years. You can take agricultural engineering and different courses, and then after that you go on to university.

Do you miss your family?

Oh yes, of course. But we get a pass every forty days or so. After forty days we get eight or ten days off. Nearly every month we get home. They pay us 75 pesos a month. As we belong to the EJT they pay us according to our work. But as we are an experiment, they're trying something out, we are a kind of back-up operation, and they pay us 75 pesos for that. In the FAR you only get 7 pesos a month.

I noticed you dedicated one of your songs to Pedro Luis Ferrer.*

---

* Following public anti-régime declarations in Peru, the very popular *guaracha* singer Pedro Luis Ferrer was banned from performing and his records were no longer given air-time. He was given a job in a record shop but allegedly proposed instead that he be sent to the mountains to play. This alternative was evidently accepted. Since this interview he has been formally rehabilitated. One of his most famous hits is about a cow complaining that AI is no substitute for the real thing.

Pedro Luis Ferrer, that's right. He was sent from Havana. Pedro Luis asked to spend some time around here in the mountains . . . so, he was with us for a while. He came on a tour we did around the point, by Maisí. He gave us master classes and we performed some numbers he wrote. He went through the different kinds of music you hear now, pentaphone etcetera, which are new and are now being used in arrangements, and that's how we composed that Sabaneta number. It's an arrangement of his. He was with us for two or three months. He would help us rehearse. He would tell us where we were going wrong, the problems we had, how we should play, the emphases we should use, that sort of thing. Small things, but which really count.

He was great with us. It was a perfect human relationship. A lovely relationship with us. We got on really well. He'd joke and laugh with us. He lived there like us without any problem. He even arranged to come back for a while after. We're hoping he might be along one of these days. I don't know when he'll be back, but he'll be back. I don't know. He was delighted with the group and said we had a lot of potential.

16

Juan Carlos Aliaga

Juan Carlos is a character in Guantánamo, a tremendous showman and a snappy dresser. He invariably wears a fedora. A mulatto, he is twenty-four years old. He does mime shows to taped ballads of his own composition. Out on the street he entertained passers-by and police with his interpretation of a hustler living off tourists and changing money as part of a festival at the Young Artists' Centre. He is doing a practical course in tiling which gives him 118 pesos a month. We get to talk about mime, his first love, and about his frustrations.

3 June 1989

It's a criticism; criticism with humour. I criticise the mess we make through our own fault, but I do it with humour. Through pantomime or mime I can do anything. I would like to have worked as an artist but they tell me there are too many. And with all that talent about it seems a shame. There's never enough money to pay people. We worked in a show for three months and then we had to leave it because they didn't want to pay us, and it was the most popular show in the province. Something I liked a lot. We went to another province and they liked us, but as we are amateurs and that, there were other problems. You have to be assessed, you have to have been to a talent school, so you see . . . In another society talent possibly emerges, imposes itself, but here you have to go to a special school and millions of things.

We're revolutionaries. All Cubans are revolutionaries. But

within that there are people, like the young people, who want to have a bit more fun because they work like madmen. They spend the week studying, so then when they come home from boarding school at the weekend, they don't have a club to go to. Because it costs 5 pesos per couple to get into a club and by 8 o'clock they're full and there's no beer left, do you get me? What's the point in having the same artist playing the different clubs when there's so much talent about? Talented, self-taught people, not professionals, who do much better work than the professionals. These are just some of the problems of young people. And, you could almost say, they themselves, those who are in a position of authority but don't have the ability, have created ideological problems. The kids want to wear Ocean Atlantic T-shirts when there are thousands of things from the socialist bloc in the shops and nobody looks at them. They stay there on the shelves. Suits and things, desperately ugly, hick, old-fashioned – green or dirty black or ash brown. Shop windows have lost all sense of taste. You can leave the same things in the windows all year round.

They could have been a bit more liberal with music as well. Because José Feliciano is banned, yet everyone has tapes of him. There's El Puma and Oscar de León. When Oscar de León came to Cuba [in the 1980s], he bowled people over. And we don't have enough money for ourselves [to pay big artists in hard currency] but we saved up to see Oscar de León, and then he performed free. Why is he banned?* El Puma is banned. Everyone you like is banned.

So the general policy is: no entertainment for young people. The little there is is probably in places we can't go. And if we do go, you have to be a guest to get a pass, and pay 25 pesos. For example, a student with 10 pesos on them who wants to have a beer in the Hotel Guantánamo can't go in. Do you see? Because of the set-up, bad administration, bad distribution of products.

If you open your mouth too wide you are labelled a trouble-maker. You don't see any repression as such. But don't give out

---

* When he returned to Miami from Cuba, Oscar de León apparently came under pressure from right-wing Miami Cubans. He subsequently made disparaging remarks about the Revolution and has since been banned.

too much or you'll get it. If, for instance, you say, 'This is awful and that's the other . . .' 'This is a load of rubbish. It's no good . . . I'm not going to study this,' someone will say, 'Over there [in the US] you'd be shining shoes.' I may shine shoes, or I may wash dishes, but I may also have a car . . . People don't know what capitalism is – poverty, hunger and unemployment. We don't have that here but we could do a lot better. Irrespective of what imperialism has done to us, we could do a lot better. We have the human resources to do it and the will, but things are bad. Bad distribution, so much bureaucracy, bosses who don't want to move their asses, cronyism and easy options. If something has to be well done or whatever they will look for the simplest and easiest way out of it. And nothing seems to come from above. The people at the top don't know what's happening in the *barrios* and in the streets. They have a team which gives them reports. But they don't live that situation. They don't know about it.

Many things are left unsaid. There are people who go to UJC meetings who want to raise serious issues openly. But there are others who don't. There are others who talk of cheating at exams and what have you but they don't say that there's a need for a young people's show. There is a need. They are not very demanding when it comes down to it. And yet they've been working and studying and working all week, and when Saturday comes there's no beer. Saturday! You can't have any – either because there isn't any or because it arrived but ran out early. And there's more beer in the storeroom. There's always a reserve. It's distribution, that's the way it is.

There are very few dances. Very few. Do you know why? Largely it's because there is a policy that people have to go home early to get up for work in the morning. On weekdays the clubs stay open until midnight, but you can't go to a club every day. It's not every day you can go to a club. Sure, just to get in costs 5 pesos, minimum consumption. And if you go with the girlfriend you are going to buy a bottle, you are going to buy a packet of cigarettes. Do you see? And you are going to stay there all night. So, you can't go to a club every night.

Look, the Young Artists' Centre took off. It's an offshoot of the Arts Centre, but I think it could do even better because the human resources are there. The human resources are there. A young people's show, a discothèque. There's no discothèque in Guantánamo. People get into fights in discothèques, that's true, but that's what the police are for. To impose order.

I went off to the Faculty of Medicine the other day – I had some clothes there. It's true, I did something I shouldn't have, because I jumped over the fence to get in and out because they wouldn't let me in by the entrance. I had some clothes in the Faculty and I collected them. I went to the bus-stop by the hospital. I got the number 5 and when we came to a street between Eighth and Ninth five patrol cars stopped the bus because someone had said I had stolen stuff and it was in my briefcase. And they treated me like a dog. They quickly got my hands behind my back (*demonstrates the action to illustrate his point*) and a lady was passing by . . . You see, my wife works there and she had my clothes with her. I went to collect them but as they didn't let me in, I got in over the fence and went to the café-cabaret to dance for a bit and then I left. When I jumped over the fence, a busybody saw me and said that there'd been a robbery, and when the police came to get me he didn't want to come and identify me. So the police searched me, found my clothes, found everything in order, but nevertheless brought me along part of the way in handcuffs and then they let me go and said, 'Don't jump over any more fences.'

At least they asked first . . . they weren't going to do like the police in Miami do, shoot – bang! – and ask questions after. No. Here you have to first ask what happened because that's always been the policy of our people.

As regards education, we're revolutionaries, we're good. Right, all right. Let's say we're good. But what happens in practice? Do you get me? We have another problem in the arts. Very few blacks appear on TV. As an article in *Juventud rebelde** recently put it: 'There's no discrimination but there is prejudice.' There are very few blacks on television. They are either sports-persons or singers. The problem is, the Ministry of Culture doesn't have anything to do with it. There's a whole empire set up there.

* National evening newspaper of the Young Communist Union. Cut back to a weekly in late 1990 because of newsprint shortages.

For example, Consuelito Vidal has a nephew. The nephew has no talent whatsoever but he's Consuelito Vidal's nephew. That's nepotism, that's the politics . . . And there are people in important positions who don't know their job. There are people who don't understand statistics, but they are working in that area because they have standing, because they carry a Communist Youth card which means they are honourable people. But a lot of people working in the arts have no sensibility. They don't know what culture is. They don't know what music is. And they care less. What they are interested in is hanging on to their positions and nothing else. I don't think it should be like that. If there are people who have talent, although they may not be graduates with degrees, they should be followed up, because talent isn't dished out every day, talent is what you are born with.

Then they want to sort everything out by talking. Talk, talk, talk. Bla, bla, bla, the same old song all the time, that's the way it is. We say we are democrats, that we are revolutionaries and communists, that we are living a revolutionary process, no? But blacks have to have the same participation as whites. They argue that blacks appear in programmes of the colonial period when they were slaves. But we can make a young people's programme about general problems and put it out on TV with blacks in the main parts. Why do they only have blacks working in folkloric situations in the ICRT? There are thousands of blacks in the ICRT working only in folksy situations. Cuban television is for whites, I'm telling it to you straight, and I'll say it to anyone.

Efficiency is another story. We like nice things like anybody in any country. We like to have a tape-recorder, we like to have a nice settee and we like work that's well done. For instance, you work and you don't see the fruits of your labours because you send your television to be repaired and they stick the wrong bulb in it, and they give it back broken, and you have to take it back the next day to get another one put in, and that sort of thing happens. There are shortages because of our hard currency situation. Fine. We understand that we have to boost tourism so that the country can develop more. We understand that. But you can't look after tourism and leave the people who do the work, who make tourism possible, without any entertainment. We have to work on the two fronts. Camp-sites have been set up, which are great, but they're not enough. Maybe you can't get to a camp-site because it's too far away. People go along at weekends and it's a very good thing. It's somewhere for people to go. If they start making trouble, we can get a policeman to cart them off.

People have to be able to relax and enjoy themselves. So they set up a discothèque. There was a fight. So they close it for repairs. I don't know what happened but there's no discothèque in Guantánamo where young people can go and dance. They opened a cabaret but that's not exactly what young people need. Young people like to shout and jump about and dance.

17

Vilma Garzón

I saw a factory in a village called Jamaica in Guantánamo province, and just dropped in and asked to speak to somebody in the Young Communist Union. It was a shirt factory. Vilma Garzón, twenty-seven, came over to talk to me. She had a scarf tied around her head. I asked her how she came to be a member of the Union and what it meant.

12 June 1989

Six months after I came here they began the process . . . Well, they saw my attitude to work, that I did my duties 100 per cent, I had no problems. They began with what we call the recruitment of new cadres to the Young Communist Union. The organisation here in the workplace began working with me. I became a member. It's a fairly broad process. First you work with the young people, in the fulfilment of targets and a series of things that have to get done. They started working with me after six months and I passed. They went to the CDR, to my block, wherever, to find out about my attitude as a citizen and all the assessments were positive, and that's why they accepted me as a member of the Young Communist Union.

I always wanted to be a member because every human being aspires to something greater, and to be a member of the Young Communists, of the Communist Party, in the society in which we are, is wonderful. It's recognition of the fact that you are an organised person, someone to be respected, to be trusted. Someone who is secure and defined within the process they live in. So, how was I selected? Well, they called a meeting of exemplary young people where I was chosen, and from then on they worked with me until I became a full member.

It involves doing a lot of things. For a start, a member can never say no to anything. To be a member means to be reliable. To be prepared to go off wherever for whatever reason. For instance, at the moment I am doing my duty as a worker here, eight hours a day. I get a call from whatever, whoever, the state, the government, and I have to go somewhere else. Apart from being head of a work brigade here, I have experience in other areas, and if I am needed somewhere else, I have to go. I am a typist apart from this and I was a teacher, but I had trouble with my daughter, a lot of problems, and so I had to give it up. What with my little girl, my husband and my work . . . I couldn't. Now that my daughter is older, I can. She's seven now, and it's easier.

I liked teaching children, I liked that job. I love it because you have to be dedicated to teach, don't you? You have to be especially calm and tactful to deal with children of whatever race, because if you don't you get all that racism. Honestly, I haven't done much about getting back into it. I haven't done anything yet because my daughter had to have an operation and so I haven't got around to it. Perhaps when I get clear of the problems of the operation and that, I'll go back to it. Although I like what I'm doing here. I feel good about it. And besides, I have a group of *compañeras* here who like me and respect me. And now that I'm here – I've been here four years – I have adapted to this kind of work.

You could say we have a lot of work here, and my main job as head of the brigade is to supervise production; make sure that the garments are properly sewn before they are passed on to the next operation, and especially to make sure daily targets are met. As a member of the Young Communists I must push for target fulfilment, work overtime to ensure monthly technical and economic targets are met etcetera, and so meet the year's target.

In our shift the factory is supposed to produce 650 shirts, so our part of the operation should make that possible. As regards the workers, the women are doing their work and output is on target. The shifts are from 7 a.m. to 3 p.m. and 3 p.m. to 11 p.m., but what happens [today]? We're working the 3 p.m. shift. We should have started at 6.50 a.m. but the light went and we couldn't work so we came in on the second shift.

I live in Guantánamo but I work here. I really have to make a huge effort to get here on time. I have to get up at 5 in the morning to get here for 6 or 6.50. But I make it. Whatever it takes. We all have to get up in the dawn to do our working duty.

My father was a peasant. My brothers – I've one in Angola at the moment and one who just got back. He's an officer. The one who's just got back came just before it was agreed that the Cuban internationalists would return to Cuba. So, there's one out there now doing his revolutionary duty. Every time he writes he says, 'No problem. Don't worry' – that he's a man and for his part he's prepared to die. He's fine there. He's fine. He has no problems and no worries.

My mother is from Nicaro, Holguín province. I was born in Nicaro, but I'm here because I married a man from Guantánamo. My dad was a small farmer. The Revolution gave him a farm. He began working the farm and later he was pensioned off from the farm. I was studying then – teacher-training. I graduated there. My brothers also studied. The farm is now a co-operative. That's progress, because all the peasants got together in a co-operative to produce more and to have more.

I came here because my daughter's father works around here. He works in construction. So, we met, fell in love and got married. I was a teacher then. We came here because his mother was here and my mother wasn't there. I didn't have anyone to mind the child and his mother was here to look after her for me.

18

Charlot Mesa

I stopped the car on the outskirts of the village of Palmar in the mountains behind Guantánamo because I spotted a live-in family doctor's surgery, part of the Family Doctor Scheme, which was introduced in 1985 and now forms a nationwide network of general practitioners based on continuous community diagnosis. Each doctor attends to 120 families. The live-in residences for the doctor and a nurse were purpose-built by microbrigades. They include a one-bed surgery for overnight observation. In primary preventive medicine the scheme has been extremely successful.

Charlot, twenty-one, a black nurse, is manning the surgery. With bonuses and allowances of various kinds, she takes home 218 pesos a month. I ask her about her work. She is most enthusiastic and even takes my blood pressure.

5 June 1989

We give primary care to the people and we get an inside knowledge of what the patient might have, because we talk to the patient's family. We know the social problems, the economic problems, and so with all that information we analyse the situation and help the person to improve their lives; to improve the hygiene and conditions in the home. So, we help to improve all these things as much as we can.

It's very sensitive work, though not complicated. Because after we get to know a person's idiosyncrasies – you get people who don't usually wear shoes and that - we get to know them, and we can tell them that wearing shoes prevents you picking up so many diseases and that that's why children have to wear shoes and clothes. Little things like that, that people can assimilate and learn. So in order to make Cuba a world medical power after the Revolution there were polyclinics, and hospitals were built – and now the family doctor will have responsibility for 120 families, to improve the conditions of rural workers, who almost always had difficulty with births. Childbirth took place at home. Pregnant women didn't have that sort of medical attention, all that sort of thing. So, since the Family Doctor Scheme, since the family doctor has come into being, that's the person who deals directly with the family, with the baby, the old people, the youngsters, the young girls – all age groups. So, priority now goes to infants under one, pregnant women, everyone. Your file is here – what's wrong with you, your age, how many children you have, if you smoke – all that's on record.

We deal with all sorts of diseases, they are reported and controlled. Then children's vaccination programmes are carried out; we work to control parasites; we take tests; we look at dental problems in relation to sickness; we do work with women – we have talks on how to avoid teenage pregnancy. We go to the schools and talk to the girls. Wherever you go now there are nurses showing you how to avoid pregnancy and children when the circumstances aren't right. All that comes up – about not having a child if you don't have a house, or you don't know how to breast-feed or wash a nappy. Young girls in secondary . . . or, rather, in primary school are taught all that.

In the hobby groups we have for little girls they find out about nursing; what they're going to be when they grow up; and we teach them as much as they can take in. We have two who are keen on nursing and they know why we do home visits, why we visit all our patients. We visit all our patients. The doctor and the nurse. They work together. We speak to them about the possibilities of tubal ligation. Sometimes we take fluoride and mouthwashes to the schools for the children, to prevent them getting mouth and dental infections. We are working well and we are beginning to see results. Before, you would have children being born and dying and nobody knew why. Because pregnant women didn't get attention, no tests were done. No one knew if the child would have congenital malformations because there was no monitoring of the pregnancy. Now tests are carried out in the first three months of pregnancy, a monitoring programme is drawn up. She gets home visits and she is told what she should do. Infant deaths are avoided. Now we know that child will have no problem. When it's born, it will be monitored and will get home visits until it is a lot older. After it is one, it gets a visit every three months and has an appointment with us every six months. This continues, but priority is given to children under one year, to avoid infant mortality and, of course, maternal death. Our infant mortality rate for the province is nil; in our hospital it's nil. Last year we had nine deaths per 1,000 live births, and so we are trying to keep it to nil. You can see that we are striving to improve and make Cuba a world medical power.

It's supposed to be 120 families, and we do care for 120 families, but they are bigger families than the average. We have nineteen under the age of one; sixty from one to four years; 133 from four to fourteen years; ninety-seven from fifteen to nineteen years; 260 from twenty to forty-five years; eighty-two from forty-five to sixty-four years; and forty-five over sixty-five years. That's a total of 695 people in all.

The doctor lives here. I live in Guantánamo and I don't usually work here, I work in Argeo. My cousin lives here, but she's on maternity leave, and it was proposed that I come as I am from around here and I know the people. I more or less started when the doctor was away on holidays and the nurse, my cousin, was having her child. I thought it would be all right because they more or less know me.

This is a Model Establishment* so we collected some written remarks about the place to see what people thought. Without people's support we couldn't do anything. (*Takes out a file with papers in it and begins to read aloud in a proud, clear voice*)

'Opinions of the FMC: It is held that the workers in this polyclinic of 120 families treat their patients very well, both the

* An honour awarded all public establishments where standards and service are consistently good.

166

doctor and the nurse. It is very clean. Yours in the Revolution, Balbina Humania.'

This is from a patient:

'Our residential surgery is very good with the public. The workers have a very good way with us, the patients who come here. My opinion of the family doctor residential surgery is that it works very well. The doctor works hard and the nurse too. The surgery is always clean and tidy. They treat the patients very well and we feel quite well. I think they are more than Model, they are an example of what it is to be a doctor in our Revolution. Congratulations.'

That was a patient. And here's what another one says:

'She is very polite. She visits patients in their home. She always turns up for work. She's a good doctor, everything is clean and organised. She is affable and polite. She gets on very well with the patients and treats them well. The surgery is very clean and everything in its place. They have a Senior Citizens Group and a hobby group for those interested in nursing. We don't want any doctor other than the one we have.'

We teach the children things that might some day motivate them to become a doctor or a nurse. Our Senior Citizens Group is for people over thirty-five – exercises, you know, arthritis sets in. It's physical fitness, really, so people will feel well . . . Before, grandparents used to look after the children, the grandchildren, and now they are off at the Stone Zoo;* they don't want to be looking after the grandchild, they feel as young as we do, you see? They want to forget about grandchildren, about, 'I'm not going out because I've a pain here.' Now they have no pains and we see the result of our work.

(*She shows me a kind of exercise book where records are kept of illnesses*) Wherever the patient goes, they bring this book. For instance, they go to Santiago de Cuba and they get a headache or their blood pressure drops, then they go with their book to the doctor there and he or she writes down what they think the problem is. So then, when that person comes back to their own area, there's no reason for them to be stammering, 'He gave me

* A park in the village of Yateras where there are animals carved in stone.

something and said . . .' because the doctor will have written it down, what he thought might have been the problem. You write down the treatment here. This is for the home visit.

The home visit is mainly for the doctor and the nurse to establish what the patient's most intimate problems are. Because sometimes a patient has an ulcer here (*pointing to her crotch*) and is too embarrassed to say, that sort of thing. So you go to the house and, 'Hello, Grandad, how are you? How are your bowels? Don't be embarrassed with me, I know all these things.' He feels easier and you get to know the problems. The patient talks of having had something three or four days and it goes from there. The home visit is to check on the general state of health of each person in the home, because while the house might look nice there might be unhygienic conditions, the roof might be leaking, and they're ashamed to say so or the child might not be eating right or have a fever. And either because they are embarrassed or they don't know, because sometimes adolescents don't know, the child has a fever or diarrhoea, and they don't know the risk they are running with just one bout of diarrhoea, because the baby might dehydrate, and they would come here and say that the child didn't have diarrhoea. So you go to their homes. The child does *caca*. 'Let me see the *caca*.' Then you see if it is liquid. You can see for yourself.

You also get an idea as to why this might happen. You write down what you see in the house, the conditions of hygiene. 'Today I told her to clean the house, that the hens couldn't be wandering about the house,' because up in the mountains people keep animals, pigs and that. So, sometimes the pigs wander about like people in the corridors and the children are there too. If you say to them today, 'Look, the hen and the pig can't wander about like that, nor the cat, because its fur might give the baby a chest infection,' all those sort of things. When you go the following week, you don't find the pig . . . you see that the patient has assimilated what you are saying. You see you have made progress. That child no longer walks around barefoot. That's what the home visit is about.

Another objective of the home visit is to follow up a hospitalisation where a child has had acute respiratory diseases – bronchitis, bronco-pneumonia, pneumonia, or acute diarrhoea – that visit is to give the child the green light, that's the methodology. As soon as you find out, you go to see them at the hospital. And when the child comes out, you visit him or her the same day. Then you go the following day . . . Sometimes they leave hospital and they still have diarrhoea, or they leave hospital well but they get it again at home – you have to find out why that should be. If they haven't boiled the water for it, then you have to go to great lengths to explain why the water has to be boiled over a long period. Really frighten them about the water. Then they will make a point of it, and that prevents infant deaths. And from there they get the idea of keeping the child's clothes organised, ironing them, boiling them, boiling the clothes, boiling the bottles. Up in the mountains, animal dung gets washed down from above, and there's no piped water and they get the water from the mountain, and it has to be boiled because you don't know where it comes from. We give public talks about it. We explain it to the people. You'd get a parasite in that water and then everybody gets it. We go to the next village. And we tell them all there is to know, and we explain it to our patients, and then in coordination with the FMC and the CDRs we do good work with the 120 families. We work very well . . . we have health workers and they are monitored. We insist – well, they are volunteers – but we insist that they go before an assessment board. They are assessed in what they are doing and how they express themselves, their suitability. And as most people here didn't get beyond third or fourth grade, they come to realise the importance of the family doctor. And they are proud of her. Now they don't have the hassle of trying to get a taxi to Guantánamo, because they have the doctor in their own house. It wasn't like that before. So the Family Doctor Scheme is very important as far as I'm concerned. And very good.

As far as the people are concerned, the nurse and the doctor are almost family. They almost see us as part of the family, because when they see how concerned we are, as if they were our own . . . because sometimes we might not be related at all and we join in, 'Ah, look at the little fellow! He's gorgeous! Look at the baby! We'll take him to the surgery. We'll do this for him, we'll do that . . .' So they trust us and they respect us above everything. They respect us . . . We explain to the patient, 'You can tell me whenever you have anything, any venereal disease.' They think we are going to get up and announce, 'So-and-so came to the surgery . . .' 'No. We are working with you. We are going to cure you and we are not going to say anything to anyone. Don't be embarrassed.' And so the patient speaks frankly, leaves nothing out. Because if they start thinking that the doctor or the nurse will go around publicising what they have, they are never going to say what they have. We deposit our trust in them. 'You can tell me anything. When you have a problem, when you feel . . . Don't be embarrassed, I'm like your mother.' Then the patient feels more confident.

19

Alfonso López

Alfonso López is twenty-seven. He tells me about the difficulties of being black and gay in Cuba today.

10 November 1988

I was a musician with a Cuban music group and things were going very well for me until I had an accident and injured my hand. That really changed things a lot. It made things quite difficult for me, because to be black and to be gay is a bit of a contradiction, because of certain established concepts here about blacks as strong, tough guys. Anyway, it's something I still don't understand, because if that's the way I was born, I assume that's the way I'll die, and so it was very difficult for me to be in the firing line [of prejudice], as they say.

My mum was a great friend to me, because she said, 'Well, lad, that's over for reasons beyond your control. What's happened has happened and you have to get on with your life in a different way.' And I started to look for work. Very difficult. Firstly, for the simple reason that there are a lot of graduates about who can't get jobs because there aren't any, and the population of Havana has grown enormously. And then, not that I behave in a camp way, because, really, I have learned how to change that image a little to avoid rejection. Because if I go around acting gay, really, I'd never get work for the simple reason that there is quite a lot of discrimination against gays, mainly in higher education. So, if

I were to start studying medicine, engineering, things which to a certain extent have to do with the state, and it was found out I was gay, the situation would change radically and I wouldn't be able to finish. You couldn't finish because they think that to be gay means you've no reason to study, you should be content to take up hairdressing or do make-up work. So, they think that to be a gay doctor is something scandalous. They have a fairly dodgy image of you attending a young boy or a man, and that's embarrassing. But actually there are gay doctors.

Teachers can't be gay. A resolution was passed there recently that there could be no gay teachers in the schools because in a certain way they distorted the public image of a socialist society. So, there's been a strong campaign, strong but veiled, against gays, but publicly you don't see it. I don't know – gays are fine, they've no problems, but you'd really have to see gay life in Havana. It's sort of in a state of waiting, waiting to see if what happened in 1980 recurs, which I don't believe it will, and that was the Mariel exodus when all the gays said, 'Well, this is the moment to say goodbye to Havana, although we really like it, and to live abroad, because here we can't exercise our professions because we can't be as we are.'

We have been repudiated in many areas and it has been very difficult for gays these days. A lot left in 1980, but since then new gays with new ideas have grown up with different ways of seeing the world, and really society has, once again, squashed them. It has rejected them and has seen them as undesirables. Not just undesirables, they are seen as the plague, and now with AIDS the situation has become even more difficult. When AIDS first appeared they tried to make it a gay disease, something propagated by gays. Gay was synonymous with AIDS. Cubans are like that. They'd see a gay guy sitting in the street and say, 'There's AIDS, get him,' and that sort of situation which has frightened gays. So there were almost stampedes to be AIDS-tested, because the word was only gays carried the virus. But so far it has been established that it's not only gays get AIDS but normal people too get it through promiscuity, through contact with different partners. So to a certain extent that has eased the situation here.

I am speaking up for gays because they don't have a chance of analysing for themselves what it is that's happening to them; why their work isn't going well; why they feel unstable; why they have to change work; why in most cases they end up arrested and become socially unacceptable. It's not because they are really to blame, it's because gay life is very difficult . . . in no country in the world are gays accepted as normal, but they have their world, their places where they can go and say, 'Well, I'm gay and I am going to live my life, I am going to do my work, I'm going to have a life as such.'

There are increasing numbers of gays here and the average age is . . . well, I'm a relatively old gay at twenty-seven, but they begin to emerge here at thirteen or fourteen or eighteen. And they don't know why, because a lot are not born gay. They were born men but then, for some reason, I wouldn't say from boredom but through having nowhere to go to have fun, to have a good time, they have found a form of escape in the gay world. I don't know. Many gays are imaginative, very nice people, so, they have seen in this a way of making life more worthwhile, more bearable, which is a very big mistake, because really when they are gay they see the problems. They realise that the gay way of life is very hard. It's harder than any other. (*Laughs*) But that bridge does exist. And the bridge is that – young people feeling lost; not lost but confused. There are very few places to go . . . I don't know – Twenty-third and L Streets, Coppelia in Havana, around the García Lorca Theatre. They're the places most of them meet, because that's where the best cabarets are, the big ice-cream parlour, the best cinema, the best hotels, and then around that people create a world of going off with gays. To hang out with a gay is great. And then it's like a wave getting bigger and bigger and it's a tangible reality now. There's a fairly big gay population in Havana at the moment, fairly big, and with no outlet. No outlet, because a lot of gays don't want to live in Havana. Many of them want to live abroad, mainly in the United States with their family and with their things. So it's like a bottle-neck situation: the police after them for being gay; work; the bosses; it's like running around in a vicious circle waiting to see what happens.

Of course, things haven't gone well. We have a fairly big foreign debt. We have stopped repayments and we are in a fairly difficult economic situation. People feel a bit lost. Lost because, well, it's December, Christmas-time, and really if you go to the markets or the shops there's a general air of depression because you see people wandering about in the street, and you see their faces, they are tired. They're not tired working but from not eating properly. In Cuba everything is 'coming'. I am not saying that there are hungry people here, but there should be more variety. It's like it was in 1970 or 1969, when things were rough, and Fidel promised that by 1980 there would be no more ration card; there would be a free and equitable distribution of things where, if you wanted to buy five pounds of sugar, you could; when you wanted to buy ten pounds of rice, you could; at a stable price. And there would be more variety and things would be better designed. It's now 1988, nearly 1989, and soon it'll be 1990 and things-have-gone-back-wards (*he stresses each syllable equally*).

There's a complete change in the story, which has been difficult, because people now don't believe in what Fidel says, and that's very sad, because they realise he is telling lies. And he tells lies and contradicts himself in many things – with the foreign debt of Latin American countries he has said things that don't work, so things rebounded negatively on him. Things have changed in Havana. Graffiti has appeared in the streets. Now, after almost thirty years, people have realised that things should not continue as they are. People are now tired, for the simple reason that they have waited long enough; they have waited thirty years.

So the situation in the street is difficult. People have caused crises in People's Power meetings. They have caused crises around the CDRs. They have dared – and I would call it daring, because after the Revolution was won they stopped being daring, but they have become so again – and they have painted graffiti against Fidel proclaiming this Revolution a dictatorship. Before they were afraid to say, 'This is bad,' or 'There isn't any of the other,' 'Havana has problems,' or 'The whole island has problems,' and now they speak up in the streets without fear of the policeman on the corner. They say it in a shop, they say it in a market, they say it in a restaurant and they say it very clearly: 'This is shit!' Excuse the expression. I'm quoting. But do you see, they are saying it very clearly, in a very Cuban way. Because Cubans are . . . how would I describe

174

it? We are tropical people, but really when we don't like things and they are coming to a head, well, that's when you'd better be wary of Cubans.

We progressed from 1975 to 1978. Then there was the problem of the Cuban community abroad. That's when Cubans realised and said, 'These people left before 1959,' and they could see that Cubans coming back again had a new style, a new look, a new image; they had a new way of perceiving things through money, through dollars, and that is now one way of getting a lot of things here. So those people who live in the United States, who are workers, who belong to the middle class, came back, and I don't think the authorities anticipated the reaction here. But to get dollars in, because of the need to pay off foreign debts, they opened the doors to those people and they came. They met up with their families. Then what happened to Cubans when these people left? It was obvious. The following year, 1980, in April, June, July, it began . . . It began in the embassy. But why did it happen after twenty years of revolution? Because the people realised, 'Right, I might be poor in a capitalist country, but if they, in 1959, went off with the same ideas as we have, within five or eight years I can have a fairly decent living.' Up to that time Cubans were happy enough with their *modus vivendi* in Havana. They didn't perceive lifestyle as an option, they saw it as something remote and not accessible to them. When those people arrived it really stirred things up. I don't know . . . to see shops filled with articles not available in the street . . . That's given rise to more prostitution in Havana, to more robberies in Havana, to more hustlers dealing in money, selling drugs to foreigners and living very well.

The hustler gets up at midday, has a cigarette, probably American because they have more style. He wears a European hairstyle like this (*moves his hands back over his hair and down his neck*) to present a different image to the public, and in that way – you'll find him in hotels because his theatre of operations is hotels and dollar restaurants, and, incidentally, many of them are very handsome because they have sought an image that's acceptable to Westerners. So that has given rise to a large network of hustlers in Havana, of prostitutes, of homosexuals who only go with foreigners. They certainly don't work. They do exercises, weight-lifting;

they sunbathe like professional models from the fashion world, or real gigolos. And so that's their life, that's what they do to survive, because there are people who have not been able to cope with society and have not known how to work in a normal way for a salary. They are layabouts.

I have a friend who is a hustler. He says to me, 'Alfonso, what are you?' Me with my 105, 120 pesos a month. 'Can you feed my brother, my sister, my mother and me? You can't, because prices have gone up. Yet I, in one day, doing a deal on the street, can earn 200 or 400 pesos. Not every day, but three or four days a week.' And he goes on, 'Look, Alfonso, I may be arrested tomorrow, and I am sure that one day I will end up in jail, but when I do, I will feel sure of myself. I will feel sure of myself because I will know I have lived. Living is the issue, believe me, Alfonso. I know that there's a policeman on the corner trying to get me, and I'm trying to make sure he doesn't. It's a game of cat and mouse. But meantime, I'm living. It's difficult to say this to you because you are a good friend and I don't like to be harsh. But that's life and you have to see it that way. You've got to open yourself up to the circumstances. Ah, they don't want me to go to a hotel. I'm going to go. How? With a foreigner. So, I'm going to have access to a hotel, to a restaurant where the food is delicious and where there's a lot of variety. You can go with a foreign man or woman. And though you might be black, ugly and Cuban, they can't say no to me because she's paying for my meal anyway and it's in dollars. You ought to live. Life is quite hard at the moment, Alfonso, and things have got worse in the street, but you must admit the percentage of people living like this is ever increasing . . .'

He's a fairly interesting person, because he's not gay and when he was a student he was never gay . . . He has taken up a gay/not gay life because he says to me, 'Alfonso, work is work and whatever turns up you take it on. It's sad but that's the way it is. It's not just me, I've friends doing the same thing because they've had to live somehow . . .' He's been driven to that difficult world. And he says to me, 'Alfonso, pardon me, but you know that I'm not gay, but if a gay appears I have to show him around Havana, the museums, and if he asks me to sleep with him, I have to. What am I to live on?' Then he says to me, 'Alfonso, I'm sorry, but you must never speak to my mother or my brothers and sisters about this, because they think that I work as a translator-interpreter in a French company and that that's how I can buy them a video, a colour TV; I bought a fridge; I have bought essential things for the house.'

I chose a different path. It's not that I think I wouldn't have had success as a male prostitute, but that would have been handing it to the police and the Revolution on a plate – black, homosexual and a prostitute to boot. They might get away with black and homosexual, but also a highly intelligent person who we can't manipulate, someone we know would give us trouble if he were caught, because he's someone who knows how to defend himself; someone who has his own clear view of things – because I have. I know how to argue with anyone, nobody can use me as bait. No one can use me to work for state security, though they might say, 'You're a prostitute, you're going to work for us.' I wouldn't have that. A lot of prostitutes work for state security in this country, it's a cover and an 'in'. I wouldn't be any good as a prostitute. At the end of the day I feel a nostalgia. I prefer to see love between people, which is lovely, and you have to know, I don't know, you have to know how to weigh things up and not to work like a machine, only thinking of money, and knowing that what you do with your body is going to make money. It's better to have a job, however difficult, wretched, easy it may be, and the contribution you make to society I'm sure makes you feel better, because to be gay and not to work and to live like that is terrible.

We don't live in New York, we don't live in London, we don't live in Paris, we live in Havana, where people are rather macho. Some are super-macho, in quotes, and it isn't easy. It isn't easy, because there are super-macho policemen. Perhaps it's because they are not really, but their image, how they project themselves towards people, is fairly difficult. So, I think to work like that is just awful.

I would say that if Cuba really had been a black country the incidence of homosexuality would have been much lower. There's been a fairly big Spanish influence here, and the last to arrive were the blacks. So the legacy of European culture, to a certain degree, then, I don't know, the influence of the Americans here, created a distorted image, and so culture seems to have come from the bottom up. Before the triumph of the Revolution Cuba was normal . . . it had its machos, groups of machos, but it wasn't generalised. After the Revolution, and with Fidel Castro's patterns of militarism, there were a lot of soldiers and a macho image, which meant you had to be macho or very macho to make it in this country. The idea of winning the Revolution was macho. So in this way machos felt even more macho, and over the years Cuba has maintained a very macho attitude. Very, very macho [socially] as regards women as well, because women here have been fairly liberated. She has her problems with her husband because there are thousands of machos who say, 'No, no, no, but I don't want you to dress like that, I don't like it.' So women don't really have what you could call independence. Cuban men like to keep things for themselves. The macho likes to say, 'This is my wife,' and that's it. This is a growing problem.

So, many gays have been able to hide themselves behind machismo. Because many, obviously, who present themselves as machos, are deep inside 'ladies'. They are the most depressing sight. Because you see a normal gay and you say, right, OK, I know how it is with him. I know what parties we could go to, what ones we couldn't go to. OK. No problems there. But you see a macho. You say, 'Oh, he's nice.' A girl would say, 'I'm going to marry him. He's going to be the father of my children. He'll be the love of my life.' Nobody could imagine he's gay. Then one day he starts slipping out at night. 'No, I had a meeting today.' 'No, I have a study group tomorrow . . .'

What is the situation? *'Coño, compadre!'* that's a very macho and very Cuban thing to say. *'Coño, compadre!'* But I really thought you were a *pelotero* and it turns out you're a *canchinflo*. In today's slang that means homosexual, passive gay. Because for macho people or anyone, active gays are macho. They say passive gays are the homosexuals, and they don't understand that active gays are also homosexuals. But as it's seen from a macho standpoint, they think it's a small problem. And when they see him with a 'lady' at his side, the 'queen' at his side, they say, 'What's up?' so the macho image is ever more evident; gays are becoming more macho in order to survive.

I know Cuban writers very well and some have been people I considered very close. It's very hard but they have made concessions. And really they are fabulous people, as writers, fabulous, but they were of the generation of gays around at the time of the Revolution. During those famous purges* they went along and pointed the finger. They had to say a lot, I don't know. There are millions now living abroad who had to leave their country, who still love and adore their country, who speak with fervour of Cuba when they see anyone abroad. Now they are officials of the Ministry of Culture, those people who made concessions. Everything has its price. But it has its price in the measure to which your response is one of dignity, for your own sake not for anyone else's. Because in the end, when you are no longer who you were, when you go to bed and put your head on the pillow, it's difficult. It's difficult because you feel alone, you feel nobody can trust you because you know who you are . . . You were famous in terms of what you published, your writings, but as a person you never became anybody.

When did you realise you were gay?

I realised it when I was at primary school, when I was eleven, and it was rather funny because I was helping a neighbour, a fairly young neighbour, he must have been about thirty-two, I was helping him put in some wiring. I was down below and he says to me, 'Do

---

* Here Alfonso is referring to the 'Padilla Affair'. In 1971 the poet Heberto Padilla was held in custody for thirty-eight days and released after he signed and publicly delivered a statement of self-criticism at a meeting of UNEAC. He condemned several fellow writers present for the alleged offences of 'egoism' and 'vanity', to which he himself had just confessed. Padilla's problem stemmed from having favoured the work of Guillermo Cabrera Infante (who had subsequently attacked the Revolution and taken up residence in London) over that of a high-ranking cultural official. There was a strong international outcry and the Stalinist overtones to the affair were denounced. A new hardline approach followed when, among other things, homosexuals were barred from artistic institutions, the mass media and the universities. For many years certain writers found they could not get published. Padilla himself was reduced to translation work. He was finally allowed to leave in 1981. He went to the US.

you know you're very beautiful?' And I said nothing, and I was thinking 'beautiful'. I said, 'Am I?' Then he came down the ladder slowly. I'll never forget how I felt . . . At first I felt afraid. Afraid because I had never done anything and then I sort of felt a desire, a desire to make love with someone I liked, I don't know. Well, it was terrible. It was just terrible. But as the first time in anything, in love, for a man and a woman, or a man and a man, or a woman and a woman . . . and anyway I thought he was my prince and that he would always be mine. But Cubans are very randy and very promiscuous. That happens with people from the Caribbean or from Africa, they are so randy things don't work out. And I thought he was going to be mine alone. Then one day he arrived at my house and said, 'The problem is, this has got to stop. I'm a married man.' It was such a disillusion. It was the first time I felt sad in my life. Sad because I thought he was for me and nobody else, something one thinks at that age when one is starting out. When he told me I wanted to die.

At the time I was living at home with my mother and father. My father is a big shot in this country. In front of him I maintained a macho image. 'Oh, Dad, the girlfriends,' and all that. I played baseball because that's what macho men do. I played baseball . . . Then, one day, my mother – mothers are so perceptive, as far as I'm concerned, mothers are friends – says to me, 'Tell me the truth. Are you a homosexual?' I was in an awful predicament, because to tell my mother, now, at nearly twelve years of age, that I was a homosexual, that I had had sex and all that, was a little difficult for me, because when I was about six or seven a friend of hers had said, 'Bring Alfonsito to the doctor because, I don't know, but I have lived a lot, I have homosexual friends, and I think . . .' And you can imagine my mother's reaction. I was seven years old. And so my mother said, 'Are you . . . ?' I said, 'Look, Mum . . .' I tried to get round the situation because it was so awkward. She says to me, 'Look. I never wanted to have a gay son, but if you are gay I'm going to help you because I don't want you to feel either sad or depressed. Let's go to a psychologist anyway to see if there's anything to be done. It's going to be a tough life for you . . .' So we went, and he said, 'Look, I'm afraid it's true. Your son was born gay. I can recommend a plan, but the problem is if he hadn't had a first contact it might have been possible to do something.'

So, we went home very sad. And I said to myself, 'Why?' because I still couldn't get it into my head that to be gay was such a painful thing for a mother.

My father is an official in a ministry, and one day his boss called him and said, '*Compañero*, we'd like a word with you.' They said, 'A fairly embarrassing situation has arisen. We have to tell you that your son is homosexual.' And my father says, 'What!' (*Shouts it out*) So that's how he found out. Imagine it. Imagine when he got home.

I lived in Miramar, in a fabulous house. A beautiful house with a beautiful garden. It was a pretty good life. We used to shop at the *diplomercado*;* everything was just fine for me. I saw other people's problems as remote. I never had to catch a bus. I lived very well. We had the food situation organised and we had staff. My mother was a scientist.

Well, when that man arrived home . . . I noticed something strange, because usually when he came in it was, '*Coño, negro*, what news? How many girls . . .?' You know how macho people go on. So, he sat down. He was destroyed. Like someone who dies overnight. My mother sat down. He sat down and just looked at me as if he'd been hit over the head; he was like a skull. He had a liqueur – because he lives very well: his liqueur, his American cigarettes, his cigars. At first he used to say it was his reward for having suffered so much, for having struggled so much for the Revolution. All that sort of thing.

So. I went into the library to read on my own. I put on some music. (*Hums a little*) I said to myself, it seems like he doesn't want to have anything to do with me today; must've had a bad day – *I thought*. Next thing, he bangs on the door like something wild coming to wreak havoc. I said, 'Yes. Yes, who is it?' He came in and he says to me, 'So, I have a poofter son in my house. So, you are a poofter, Alfonso, is that it? Explain it to me.' You're white, but the colour drained from me. I said, 'Look, Dad . . .' 'Shut

---

* A well-stocked supermarket where diplomats, top officials and foreigners may purchase goods in dollars or with special certificates.

up. Do you know my boss called me in this morning? Why did you fool me, lad?' I was sixteen. I was at the stage when gayness is most pronounced. 'Why didn't you tell me before? We could have sorted it out another way.' He just stared at me with a fierce loathing which I will never forget. He got up. 'Get out. I can't have poofters in my house. Pansy. Get out.' Well, I was completely . . . like someone lost in the desert who doesn't know what they are going to do. I said, 'Dad . . .' 'Don't call me Dad. I'm not your father. I am nothing to you,' he says, crying. (*Alfonso is now crying*) It was hard for him. I can't say it wasn't because I had some lovely times with him. (*Sobbing*)

So, I left. But my mum said – this was the worst situation I ever remember – 'Alfonso, wait.' I gathered up whatever I could. I had my wardrobe with my clothes, with all my shoes, my perfumes, my books, my paintings, everything. I had my room lovely. I was going to my grandmother's, whom I never visited up to that point – my mother's mother. And my mum said to my father, 'Are you adamant that Alfonso has to go? Have you decided he has to leave this house? Well, you know, he's as much your son as mine. If he goes, I go with him . . . You never bothered with him, and now you are because your boss called you in and that's when you found out what was happening. But you never asked him if he felt good or bad. Life isn't all about luxury and good living, it's about looking into yourself and seeing what's happening. We're talking about your son. Speak to him . . . Not just about tennis or basketball. Don't bother, you're too cold. I'm leaving as well.' 'No.' 'He stays or we're both leaving.' 'What's that? No. I don't want a pansy here.' 'Well, I'm his mother. I carried him for nine months in my belly and I suffered the birth pangs. Do you understand? Pansy or not, he's my son and yours. At least, up to a day ago he was your son. I'm leaving.' So she broke with all that world of friends that she had had for years, friends of ministers and vice-ministers.

When I got to my grandmother's house, which is where I still live, it seemed like a dream to me. I arrived and I said, 'I want to go back home,' because I lived so well there. Then I realised how Cuba lived; how Cuba lives. The shortages. We didn't have a ration card in my house. The first times I got the bus I got into terrible rows. I wasn't used to it and I saw everyone as inferior. I had lived well; I had had no problems. Then I realised that this is a class-ridden society as well. It was tough.

When I see my father now, we greet each other. Civility always. He found out that I wanted to go abroad for a time and he rang the house. 'I want to speak to you.' 'Fine.' I go there, very masculine in a *guayabera* – I looked like a ministry official myself. Horrible. I was wearing a pair of blue trousers, a dreadful pair of shoes, and I'm very serious. 'Hello, how are you?' as if we were two friends. No, two people with a mutual interest. He says, 'I heard you want to go away. If I so choose, you can't leave this country.' 'I know that. If you don't want me to, I won't get out. I know that. I have to say this although I don't like to, but, Dad, you have to be intelligent about these things; you have to adopt another attitude. You'll see. If I spend some time abroad, I think you'll have time to reflect on what I say. This is our first meeting and that's always difficult, especially when there has been such a distancing. But I think you can understand.' He says to me, 'I'm going to try to understand.' So he didn't give me a straight answer.

So then, one day – very intelligently on my part, because that's true: when I want something, I go after it – I phoned him and said, 'Are you free? Can I drop by?' He said, 'Well, you caught me in a good mood, come on around.' I said, 'Right. Have my lunch ready because I'm starving. I don't think you'll deny me that.' He was in good form that day. Well, I arrived. I said, 'For starters, let's have some Vivaldi. May I use the tape deck?' He said, 'Yes, yes, fire ahead.' A gin and tonic. He has everything there. Anyway. The situation was a little tricky and I wanted it to be easy. I was the interested party. I had to be very diplomatic so he would see that it wasn't really a question of leaving the country; that I needed to rediscover myself. So he sat down at one side of the table and I sat at the other, at the corner. We were like two leaders about to declare war or peace. So I began.

I said, 'Dad, you don't know how much I always needed you. This isn't a prepared speech, it's straight from the heart, and you, as a father, must understand that. A father is important in the rearing of a son, whatever his job, his ideological position, his place in society. It's important that he looks after his son because whether or not I was born gay, one of the determining factors in my becoming so was not biological but social. It was you. You set much more store by your work as such. You gave it much more and you relegated me to second place when I lived here. I need to live abroad not for material reasons, not for a better lifestyle, but because I need to find out in what way I can contribute to my country, even while abroad. I need to see different things; to see human life in other societies, something every human being is entitled to.' I kept saying 'Dad' so that he would feel more familiar with me, more paternal; so that he would see I wasn't bitter, and I'm not. Because I also put myself in his position as a father. 'But, Dad, you've got to understand me and it seems you only hurt me. I want to sort my life out now. It's difficult for me to speak to you about this situation because when you suffer, truly suffer, as I have – with my family, with my work – When I tried to play again and my fingers wouldn't respond, you can't imagine how I felt . . . Do you really think I wanted to be gay? Do you believe that? No. I have suffered enough. But I think I must be one of those unfortunates who has more downs than ups . . . I don't want to involve my mother in this. She has already made enough decisions on my behalf by breaking with you. Up to now she has been a fabulous mother, a perfect wife. She always waited for you though you were off at functions.

'So, Dad, I hope your new son doesn't turn out like me, he's lovely.' Then he got very embarrassed. Because it wasn't easy with me talking and crying. (*He is crying now again*)

'In the first place, I don't have a father. I feel as if I have lost my father and I would like to have one. If he dies, that's one thing. That's life. (*Weeping openly*) And it has to go on. But when you see he's there but that he's always against you and doesn't accept you, that's hard. It makes you feel like a nobody. And it's sad because you have to have self-confidence, and in some measure it's the parents who give that. I can't say my adolescence was good. It was sad, awful, difficult.'

I didn't touch the food. You can imagine. I ended up crying and for the first time in ages my father embraced me. Imagine. He embraced me, but I felt he did so sincerely.

I got into the car and he took me home. He wanted to come in and see my mother, and I said no. It was even more difficult for my mum. 'Mum has spoken to you on the phone, and that was fine. But I don't think she could stand meeting you. So, drop me off here and thanks for everything . . . for lunch . . . it was important to me.'

And four days later he rang. He said, 'I have thought about it. I spoke to two friends at the ministry and they said it would be better if I didn't prevent you going.' I said, 'Dad, thanks. I'm really sorry I can't live with you, because if I did maybe I would have made other decisions. (*Breaks down again*) I have been fairly good in my life, and life has given me a kick in the teeth.'

God, I don't know. Sometimes I think that I owe him something, that I haven't been fair with him, but I still don't think I deserved all this. Sometimes I just can't understand it. Why me? Why? It's not easy, it's not easy being a homosexual. And black at the same time with a father who's a ministry official. That's the only reason I want to leave. Because I'm not against Fidel. There are some very good things about here, some very good things, very human things. I do it for spiritual peace.

IN THE US

20

Carlos García

Carlos García emigrated to the United States before the Revolution. We meet in his comfortable apartment in Queens, New York. Family photos decorate walls and surfaces. At sixty-one, Carlos is philosophical about life. He tells me, in English, about living and working in the United States and how he has no difficulty sharing his loyalties equally between his native and adoptive countries.

13 May 1989

I came to this country in 1946 like many Cubans, illegal. I came for thirty days and I stayed. I stayed here because the economic situation in Cuba was awful, and then it was not communist. We have so many little dictators that this country has conveniently set up for years and years in Latin America, as the Anglo-Saxons consider it to be their back yard. And everybody knows that the back yard in this country is the dirty part of your house. The front yard is the beautiful part of your house. But even in that they don't call us the front yard. We are the back yard. (*Laughs*) For many years they have been throwing garbage in the back yard.

So, I came here looking for a better way of living, an economical way of living. I worked almost immediately at what almost every immigrant works at in this country – washing dishes. I washed dishes, I washed plates and I was a busboy and a waiter and in 1948 I met my wife and we married in 1949.

I was eighteen, just, when I first came, so I grew up here in

189

New York. The paradoxical situation is that this country was composed of all kinds of immigrants. All of a sudden the only immigrants that really count in this country are the Anglo-Saxons. No one can deny that. For a person that lives here for forty years and reads and knows what's going on, we know we have proof after proof that if your name happens to be of Italian ancestry you don't have a Chinaman's chance. The favourite sons of America are the Germans and German descendants. They are the elite of the United States. Against any odds: they have fought two wars with Germany, and instead of being bitter enemies, the Germans control this nation. The Latin Americans, which belong to this country – no? – they are nothing. So, then I started to detect that my dreams of coming to a democrat country, the United States of Franklin Delano Roosevelt, was nothing but a dream; that when you came here as an immigrant of Latin ancestry, you will face some kind of odds. No question about that.

Nevertheless, I worked hard, and I made some money, and materially speaking I live good. Perhaps much better than some who have been born here.

When 1959 came and for the first time I saw this new Revolution in my country, I got great hopes. I got great hopes. I have met Fidel here on his way to Mexico when he was a very young student with no beard. Last time I saw Fidel and I talked to him, he had no beard at all. I have never met Fidel personally after he became Fidel. I met him when he was here raising money, funds. We had a few rallies. We had meetings and we collect money and we were selling bonds, 26 July bonds, raising money to help Fidel.* He stopped here on his way to Mexico and that's the last time I talked to Fidel.

But we had hopes. Cuba has a history of being one of the most rebel countries in Latin America. We don't think we're better than anybody but definitely we're not worse than anybody. We demand equality with anybody. In any way and in every respect. That's why we do the sacrifices. It takes an effort. It

* A fund-raising system whereby people who donated money to the movement got a receipt in the form of a 26 July bond. Castro was in New York in October 1955.

takes a lot of work. Every country has what every country works for. We've been working hard and we're going to work harder. A small nation and a Caribbean island, I must respect them. But I happen to be born there. I say 'happen to be born there' because my mother was Mexican and my father was born in Madrid. So, I myself am an immigrant in Cuba. I am not a Cuban for two generations and I have absolutely no family in Cuba besides my brothers and sisters. But nevertheless, I grew up there until I was eighteen years old. I love Cuba and I love Cubans. I have brothers and sisters Mexicans and brothers and sisters Cubans. I happen to have been born in Havana and it gives me a great, great happiness to know that we have a leader that won equal respect. This is all Cuba wants: to live like anybody else; to fight for a better living; and to make justice equal to all – which doesn't exist in this nation [the United States] and anybody who lives here for a year can see it easily. You don't have to put a pair of glasses (*laughs*), you see it without glasses. There is no equality whatsoever. There is none.

Then the worst part is, by nature, the Cubans are not enemies of the American people. On the contrary, we feel great admiration for the Americans. They are hard-working people, very modest, very honest, they work like nobody works. It's very possible that if the Latin Americans start to work just half of what the United States people work, we will be better off. There's no question about that and anybody that denies that is lying or is an idiot. I take my hat off for the American people. They have welcomed me here. The American people have welcomed me here. I like them very much. They are always enthusiastic about life. They can be seventy or eighty years old and they think they are sixteen. It's great.

The other part is the so-called ugly American where these big monopolies control the economies of the world [and] think that they have the right to intervene in every situation in the world, especially Latin America, using the resources of every other land for their own benefit. They definitely don't have any respect for the poor of this nation. I live here in New York and they build condominiums every day. Mr [Donald] Trump builds buildings every single day in Madison and Park Avenues.* I haven't seen one building being made for poor people here. It's unbelievable. The compassion is very little. They want to live in a world that they create in Hollywood – unrealistic. The world shows always, realistically speaking, that human beings of every nationality, of every race, of every religion, have a percentage of people that are unproductive. They just don't produce. They are either sick physically or mentally or whatever. This country even more because of the mixture of nationalities and races and religions. But, by all means, we should have compassion for those that can't for whatever reason. I grant you that in many cases, in most of the cases, these people are lazy, they don't want to work. It's true that if you want to work, especially here in New York, you can find something. You can always do something. Maybe not what you want to do, maybe not the wage you want, but you do then carry your weight most of the time. But there are some sick people that we have to have compassion with them. And we have to start to try to really live to the democratic foundation of this nation that's going right out of the window.

And right now, as I am talking to you, there's the Panamanian situation. In this moment you have this problem with Noriega. Anybody who knows how to read knows that Noriega has been a very good friend of this country. He was the busboy for these people. He knows Mr Bush very well. They have been many times together. So, when along the line things get sour, Mr Noriega becomes the bad boy. But this is not the issue. No one has any admiration for Mr Noriega: not the left, not the right, not the centre. But the United States [comes along] with the flag of the invaders and the marines. I mean, nobody has made these people the vigilantes of the world. Nobody that I know told these people to tell the Panamanians if Noriega is good or bad. It's none of their damn business. If Noriega is good or bad it's up to the Panamanians. How can they come with a bare face and telling you that they are going to invade

* The New York based multi-millionaire renowned for his extravagant buildings and casinos. His fortunes took a downturn in 1990 when the empire he had built ran into cashflow difficulties.

another nation with the old Monroe Doctrine* of 200 years ago to protect the American lives? These people don't realise that the world has changed and they do a lot of harm to themself and to others. This only can create a lot of death, a lot of destruction, a lot of suffering. For everybody, including the United States of America.

Five months ago there was a fraudulent election in Mexico, a country of eighty million people, next door to the United States of America. The whole world knows that those were fixed elections, but they were fixed in their favour so nothing happens. And this is the issue.

The issue is how these people think that they can govern so-called free countries regardless of their size – whether it's half a million or two million or five million or ten million. Either we respect the freedom and sovereignty of nations equally, regardless of whether they are from the left or from the right, or we don't. The superiority, the mistakes that have been made over and over by the governors of these nations, continues to be so.

My country, Cuba – all Cuba wants is the right to be considered free and sovereign like any other nation; to have the right to choose their system of government; to have the right to have commercial and diplomatic relations with whoever they choose. If this happens to go against the interests of the big monopolies of the United States, that's a problem that they have to solve themselves. After all, this country is constantly bragging about how it is based on moral reasons. My God, they seem to forget the moral reasons every two minutes when it's convenient to the hierarchy.

Well, there were always Cubans coming to this country, a lot of Cubans who were political people. Many of the guys that were here in those years were unhappy. Before the *Granma* we sent a

---

* In 1823 President Monroe declared the western hemisphere to be within the US sphere of influence and stated that any interference in the affairs of the region's newly emerging nations by European powers would be deemed an unfriendly act towards the US itself. It became the 'manifest destiny' of the US to bring 'civilisation' to the area and to do what might be necessary to protect its interests therein.

boat that was called the *Corinthia*.* The *Corinthia* sailed from
Mexico to Cuba and I'm not sure but I think it was something
like twenty *compañeros* and only one lived. Everything was wiped
out on the shores. The *Corinthia*. I was going to go on that boat.
But life has its ways and I guess what happened was that waiting
for the order for us to go to Mexico I met my wife. And like
many other stories in this world, love is very powerful. I had just
met my wife. I fell in love with her and I really felt awful and I said
to these friends, one of my very good friends that died, 'Pepe, let
me stay two or three weeks more because I'm in love. And this
could turn sour and you know nothing happens and I will meet
you in Mexico straight away.' But it didn't happen that way. I
fell in love more and more and I marry a year later. Probably
that was on the cards because only one man survived that. So, it
wasn't my time to die, I guess. But we wanted to go then, and
a year or two later you have the *Granma* landing. It's the same
people. The *Corinthia* was just ahead of the *Granma*. When Fidel
came here we detected that he was going to be our leader. We
all had hopes.

How did you meet up with other Cubans?

Well, we always have contacts in restaurants and barbers' shops
and places. Cubans went to this place called La Salle. La Salle was
a cafeteria in Seventh Avenue and Fifty-first Street. Very famous.
A lot of musicians went there, Cuban musicians including Desi
Arnaz used to be there. I knew him very well, I have a hat that
he gave me. And all the Cubans, musicians and show-business
people, they were always here from Cuba. In fact, two blocks
down, in the Brass Rail restaurant, Camilo Cienfuegos was a
busboy there – the guy who cleans the tables and puts out the
bread and butter. Camilo was twenty-eight, maybe thirty. Tall
guy. Very, very happy guy, always laughing, very optimistic.
Very optimistic, Camilo.

A lot of Cubans really disengaged themselves from what was

---

* Carlos is historically inaccurate here. The *Granma* landing took place on 2
December 1956 and the *Corinthia* landed on 23 May 1957.

happening in Cuba. They were here dedicated to make money. But some of the Cubans then were very close to what was happening in our nation, political and otherwise. And when he came here, Fidel, and he got a rally in the Palm Garden – I'm talking about [October] 1955, on his way to Mexico – we were selling bonds, selling [26 July] bonds. We held a big rally and Fidel spoke. And all of us who were against Batista, of different beliefs, we were there helping Fidel, this young man with a hope to get rid of the dictator. That was the feeling in those years. And we all got these great hopes that Fidel will be what he will be.

Naturally, as things start to fall this way and that way and Fidel starts to show his tendencies to the left, many Cubans that were not really to the left start to fall off, as Fidel starts to show his real true nationalistic feelings. Because his feelings at the beginning were nationalistic. Like all of us – the love for the motherland, the desire to be recognised as a free and sovereign nation, the great desire to be respected, whether from the left or the right, including the ones in Miami, the avowed *anti-fidelistas* – we all have one thing in common. We all want to be recognised and respected. Cubans on that side and this side don't like to be looked down at. We are born that way. We are as good as anybody and we are going to die for that. So, at the beginning there was this tremendous feeling of *nacionalismo. La Patria.* And at the same time we recognised the horror that was Batista's government.

Anyway, the year Fidel came here, we helped. We helped. We gave money constantly and some arms were sent to the *sierra* – all the help that we could give Fidel, we gave.

We started a place called Casa Cuba, in 1957 or 1958. We collected money, helping the rebels, and when the revolutionaries triumphed in 1959, imagine, we are very happy and some of us go back to Cuba, and some of those who went back to Cuba come back to the United States because they laid around with the years, they had no socialist ideals. They were nationalists, they were pro-Prío, there were all kinds of Cubans at that time that united in order to get Batista out. And as things started to develop, many, many Cubans jumped to the other side.

We remained in Casa Cuba. We had ups and downs. More

members, less members, and we stick it, we stick it. We went to a lot of demonstrations in Washington and New York, in the UN, through the very bad years when you were harassed here by the FBI – they went to your job, they went to your house, they tried to persuade you in any way and form and manner not to support that cause. Some of us got fed up with it, didn't join up any more and disappeared. The ones that are now here in Casa de las Américas [formerly Casa Cuba], we are all from those times. We keep it up and we keep on fighting . . .

Well, there were always Cubans coming to this country. I came through Miami. I flew over to Miami and I stayed in Miami two days. Don't forget, when I came, Miami was not today's Miami. Everything was in New York, so I came to New York. I love New York. I've become a New Yorker. If they send me back to Cuba I'm gonna miss New York. Regardless of even if I have nothing after so many years, I'm used to it, I guess. Here there were a lot of Cubans who were political people. People from [the time of] Prío, a lot of people that were unhappy . . . And for years we went through all kinds of demonstrations, all kinds of sacrifices – if you call it sacrifices. I don't think anybody who loves their motherland considers that a sacrifice. But we did go through bitter times here and still, today, we have Casa de las Américas where we have dances and cultural things and movies and things from Cuba. We show Cuban films and we keep very close with our country, our government, our system. Very proud. I am very proud of Cuba and Fidel as leader.

My people have gone through hell. I don't know how many people know how many things they have endured: hurricanes, boycotts, you name it. But I know as a Cuban that if necessary it will be a hundred years like this. Two hundred or three hundred. We hope that some day soon the American people will realise that you just don't harass a country like this for ever for the simple reason they want their freedom and the right to choose their system of government regardless of a system. The American people are a very fair people, and some day I know, and I hope some day soon, they [will] realise that the Cubans are entitled to choose their system of government for good or for bad. If they don't want to help us, they don't have to help us. That's something that is up to the government and the people. But they don't have to hurt us either. Just let Cuba choose the path.

I am an American citizen, and if I have to fight for this country against any other type of system I will do it very gladly. If I have to fight against the Nazis or invaders, even if they were communists and they invade this country. No doubt about it. I am a man of convictions. With the same fervour that I defend the right of Cuba to be what they want to be, I defend the right of *these* people to be what *they* want to be. Sometimes it's difficult to explain this to some people that don't have this deepness in ideals.

The FBI came to my house two or three times. They once came to talk to me, another time they came to talk to my wife. And I remember the day they came to talk to my wife. They said, 'No, we don't want to talk to you, Carlos, we want to talk to Rosita.' I am one of the few Cubans that admit the FBI into my house. I open my doors, they talk to me for hours – two or three hours – they have lunch with me. I make lunch for them. They were telling me that the Revolution in Cuba was communist, enemies of this country; that I was an American citizen and that I have the duty and obligation of supporting the conditions of this nation; that if I don't do that, they could revise my citizenship and perhaps send me to Cuba. I said, 'Well, if that's what happens it's fine with me.' I have nothing against the United States then, now or never. On the contrary, I am grateful to this country because I came illegally and then I legalised myself. I pay my taxes, suffer with the Americans, live with the Americans and, like I say, I love the American people. This system of government has made itself the big monopolies and they disregard the rights of others. This isn't acceptable to anybody with dignity.

I guess that the main thing of their visits was to size you up, as they say here in English, which is their right. That's why I opened my doors because I consider they have the right to protect their country whether they are right or wrong. These people are government officials doing a job, which is to know who they consider an enemy of this nation. That's fine with me. I admitted that I was a political liability, which is true. Violence is not in me and was never in me and I don't think that's the way to fight. If I have to fight, I like to fight like a man. They know that and I told them what was in my mind and in my heart. By this time I have two daughters here, I have a job. I'm just another American working and struggling with a firm political conviction that my country has to be left alone. Period.

At the time I was living in a very nice neighbourhood and one of the guys says to me, 'Look how nice this country is to you, Carlos. I don't have a house like this.' And I say, 'Well, I have a house like this because I work eighteen hours a day. Nobody gave it to me. I guess you don't like to be a servant. I serve people and that pays more than your job, obviously. But nobody's handed it to me on a silver plate.'

And then I went to the headquarters of the FBI on Third Avenue and Sixty-seventh Street. I am one of the few Cubans that voluntarily told them I will go there and I will tell you whatever you want to know. This was a month later. They wanted to continue talking to me. I said, 'No. I'll go down there. And you can put your tape-recorder on top of the desk' – because they keep a tape-recorder in a drawer – 'I have nothing to hide.' I am one of the few Cubans they recorded with my permission. And like I'm telling it now, I told them. I haven't changed my position at all. I remember one phrase they used, 'Well, you cannot be there and here.' And I remember I put the example, 'Yes. You can love your mother and your wife at the same time. And to me, Cuba is my mother and this country is my wife.' They were trying to say there was conflict of interests but there is not a conflict of interests at all. As far as I know this is a country of immigrants and I know that millions of Italians here love Italy. That doesn't mean they don't love the States. So they tried to confuse me but it's not easy to confuse me.

Well, this thing stopped for a while, and then one good day they come to see my wife. 'Hello, how are you? We've come to talk everything over. No, no, Carlos. We want to talk to your wife' – because in those years I didn't go very much to Casa Cuba, Casa de las Américas, because I was a banquet captain and most of the parties were at night. So we went to Casa de las Américas once a month. But my wife was going on a regular basis. So, they wanted to talk to her and I told them, 'Yes, she is a sympathiser of the Cuban government, of the Revolution' – on her own, not through me like some wives join their husbands. 'She goes there on her own and if you want to talk to her, you have to talk to her. She's a free woman and she has her own ideas and I'm sure she would talk to you people.' And they did come once or twice to the house to talk to her, and the situation remained like that.

My wife was a citizen also. She was not born here, she was born in Cuba. She came when she was nine years old. Three months ago I lost my dear wife and we would have been forty years married tomorrow. Breast cancer. She was very Cuban. She loved Cuba and she loved the Revolution immensely and she wanted very much to have her ashes buried in Cuba. And I did. *Compañero* Alarcón,* magnificent *compañero*, helped me a lot, and also many other Cuban officials and Cuban people and my family in Cuba. Everybody helped me. In a matter of days I was able to take my wife's ashes to Cuba and bury them in Cuba, in Havana. She asked me that as her last wish.

How did you first get going when you got here?

Like everybody else, I spoke very little English, but I always have been a very ambitious man. Hard-working, but ambitious. I think the world, in any kind of political system, needs ambitious people. In any kind of system, if you don't work you don't have. This we have to learn, especially in socialist countries. You must work and work hard and be productive and work good or you're not going to get nothing. So, I worked hard. Then I became a busboy because there was always the tips, you know, and then I became a waiter. And I was room-service waiter and I was a cocktail waiter – all kinds of waiters I have been. I tumbled around for the first couple of years but then I settled in the Sherry Netherlands Hotel on Fifth Avenue and Fifty-Ninth Street. On that corner you have the most exclusive jewellery business in the world – The Belle Russe. You can only go into that store with an appointment. I started to work in the Sherry Netherlands in 1948 as a busboy and on room service and I met the most exciting people in the

---

* Ricardo Alarcón, Cuba's Deputy Foreign Minister and permanent representative at the UN.

world: Ernest Hemingway, Mickey Rooney, Cary Grant, Gary Cooper – everybody in the movies, in business.

To tell you the truth I got along very well with these rich people. They are as human as you and I. I started to work as a waiter on breakfasts because you have to know less than for dinner, which is more complicated. In the morning the food is very straightforward and limited. You can have eggs and eggs, a cereal and eggs, and coffee and English muffins and whatever, so it was easier. And I used to go there with the breakfast, to all these people which I meet, and, as I say, many of them very human, highly human people. I will go into their room in the morning and it could be John Wayne, it could be Gary Cooper, it could be the president of Bloomingdales, the owner of the store, people like that.

In fact, a very curious thing happened to me. Working in room service in the Sherry Netherlands I was deported by Immigration. And it had nothing to do with Fidel or nothing because this was in 1956. I am jumping now, I just don't want to forget this part of my life. In 1954 or 1956, I don't really know. I know I was pregnant with my first daughter, Linda. And, well, the Immigration came and got me. I was illegal. I told you I came here for twenty-nine days. And they took me to the Immigration Centre in Columbus Circle and I filled in the papers and this and that, and they were going to send me to Ellis Island where they send the illegal immigrants. But they didn't, somehow. My wife was already a citizen. I was married to her in 1949. And somehow they let me come back to work and it was very nice, they didn't have to, and they set a day for me to go back to Cuba and come back legally.

And I remember I used to be friendly with Mrs Joseph Davis. Mrs Joseph Davis is the wife of Joseph Davis who wrote that book *Mission to Moscow*. He was the first American ambassador to the Soviet Union. His wife was Mary Weatherpost, the magnate from the cereals here, Post Cereals. Multi-millionaire this lady and a very, very good lady. Really a magnificent person. They became the owners of General Foods, but to me she was a blonde American Anglo-Saxon woman. Beautiful woman physically and in every other respect, and I used to serve her breakfasts and dinners, just a waiter. I look at these people like human beings and they always treated me like a human being. I used to talk to them all kinds of things. 'How's the weather?' 'It's cold, Carlos.' 'It's not too cold.' 'It's raining.' 'It's not raining.' And about baseball and many other things.

I used to go quite often to Mrs Davis's apartment – she had a whole floor in the tower of the Sherry Netherlands – and when they sent me to Cuba she knew it through a telephone operator of the room service [who] told Mrs Davis of my problem. 'You know, Mrs Davis, they are going to send Carlos to Cuba because he came here illegal.' And Mrs Davis took part in that and helped me to come back to the States.

She gave me a letter for the American ambassador in Havana. I have my papers already in order, my wife was claiming me as her husband. Legally, I was going to come back and I did. But she helped me to make this quicker. Because it happened to be around Christmas. And she gave me this letter and she said, 'Carlos, why didn't you tell me of your problems? You know I could help.' I said, 'I didn't feel like I should bother you, Mrs Davis. It's not [part of] my work. You learned about it and now I am grateful to you.' And she did give me this letter and I took it to the ambassador in Havana. And sure enough he helped me. So, this is one of the things in my life.

I knew Khrushchev when he came here. I volunteered to serve Khrushchev because it's dangerous, and I served Khrushchev. I served Fidel in the Astor when he was Fidel. My God, and I served Howard and Lyndon Johnson.

But I thought you never saw Fidel again?

I saw him in the Astor, but as a waiter. You know, I just saw him, I didn't even talk to him. It's not polite. Besides, you couldn't, with so many guards and security. You know, he came here once or twice. But when he came for the first time in the Astor – I went to serve him in the Astor because in the union they asked for people that wanted to volunteer. It was dangerous. They were talking about bombs and things already. Two Mexicans volunteered and me, and there was a long table in the Astor Hotel, the old Astor.

Anyway, I'm jumping as things come to my mind. Yes, we served Fidel, Khrushchev, Eisenhower, Nixon.

I met Dr Richard Nixon many times on the street. This is an old thing of my life. When Nixon was down and kicked by everybody after Watergate, he was living on Fifth Avenue in Rockefeller's building. Nelson used to own this building and Nixon was living in it. And these were the years when Nixon would walk around Fifth Avenue and everybody would run away from him like he has measles or something. And I used to see him on the streets sometimes, especially in the spring and July, and I talked to him two or three times. I will approach him. 'Mr Nixon, how are you?' 'You know me?' 'No, I don't know you, I'm just a captain in the Pierre [Hotel].' 'Oh, yes.' Because when he was elected he got his headquarters in the Pierre for two months between the election and the takeover, which is usually November to January. He kept his headquarters in the Pierre and we saw him almost every day. Also very humble, very human. Intelligent man with his ideals and his beliefs, which I respect, but we talked about the weather and this and how the Pierre was going and, you know, plain things.

I also knew Nelson Rockefeller very well. He used to come to the Pierre and go with me to a corner to talk to me. Believe it or not. He used to put his arm around me and talk to me about things. This is when he was governor. 'How are things, Carlos? Busy?' This and that. Also a very plain man. He speaks Spanish quite fluently. All that money, all that name, all that fame – he was a very plain individual. He remembered me distinctly because the first time he ran for governor he got a small party of eight or ten people, very close, political advisers and this and that, and I was a captain at that little party. There were two waiters. And when the party was over I told him, 'You're going to win.' And he says to me, 'How do you know?' I say, 'I know. I'm Cuban and we're born politicians. You're going to beat this guy.' I said, 'Don't worry, you're going to win.' And suddenly he smiles, like saying, 'What does this guy know?' But when he came back a month later to the Pierre he remembered that. (*Laughs*) And he asked me, 'What made you think that?' And I said, 'I told you that we Cubans are born politicians. I saw that you had much more personality than this man.' And people tend to vote first for the guy that they like personally, you know, like a friend or whatever. And then comes the issues. Issues are second, not first.

I became a captain at the banquets and then I became assistant head waiter. That's when I retired. I was just one stop from being in the banquet department. It's a very lucrative job, very lucrative, because the prices are very high and we work on percentage, so, if they charge you $100 for a dinner, and I'm entitled to 12 per cent of that, it's a lot of money. Very lucrative. I made a lot of money, good money. But I was paying sometimes 50–55 per cent taxes. A lot of taxes. You have to work Saturdays and Sundays and holidays, but you make money. I raised my family, two daughters, five grandchildren, and like I say, before I die I would like to see better relations with Cuba.

One would like to get up in the morning and find out that this thing is going away like rain. You know, that relations are re-established and that we can go to Cuba like we did before and, finally, that these people accept Cuba and their government and their system of government. That will be the last thing that I hope in my life to see.

21

María Cristina Herrera

María Cristina Herrera is executive director of the Institute of Cuban Studies, Inc., Miami. An extremely busy and energetic woman – despite severe physical disability – she gave me an hour of her time at her home, which had recently been bombed. We speak in English.

25 April 1989

I was born in Santiago de Cuba, 1934, the year of the abolition of the Platt Amendment,* which I find significant. I belong to an upper middle-class *santiaguera* [from Santiago de Cuba] family. I was educated by the ladies of the Sacred Heart, where I went through high school. Then I attended Oriente University, now the University of Santiago de Cuba, where I graduated from philosophy in 1955. Then I went to New York for graduate studies at Columbia University in the school of philosophy and then I went back to my native land in early January 1959 to join, you know, the new process as a young professor at the university, where I taught through August of 1961, when I left and went to Mexico where my only brother was residing. I came to Miami in September of 1961 thoroughly committed to the overthrow of the Cuban government as a

* In 1934 the Platt Amendment, granting the United States the right to intervene militarily in Cuba, 'for the preservation of Cuban independence', was abrogated following major political turmoil and in return for a trade agreement.

militant member of the underground which I had been for a year before.

We struggled here for the better part of two years, and in the summer of 1963 I came to the realisation that militant counter-revolutionary activity was going nowhere and had no future. And being pragmatic as I am, and a survivor as I am, I decided that I would stop that and begin to do my thing here as an individual, who was previously a college professor back home, and this is what I could do also here.

I have not mentioned that I am a premature baby – a pound-and-a-half, cerebral palsy, and I have visible locomotive impairment – and I was very lucky because I could also have been severely retarded according to the doctors, which I am not. So, I am very grateful to God and to life, to my family and my doctors. For having helped me to survive, number one; to rehabilitate me, number two; and to live a very productive and enjoyable life, as I do.

Back then in the middle of the 1960s, my nostalgia for my homeland made me start weekly gatherings at home on Monday nights to discuss what had happened in our island in a very informal way with friends, fellow university people and other friends. A lot of those informal gatherings on Monday nights gave me the idea to call for a larger conference of all kinds of Cubans coming from different professional backgrounds, which finally took place in April of 1969 in Washington, DC. And that was called '*La primera reunión de estudios cubanos*' [The First Cuban Studies Meeting].

And that was the immediate forerunner of the Instituto that we have been working at for twenty years, the Instituto de Estudios Cubanos.

Initially, nobody knew what would become of that effort, but we liked it so much that we continued to gather regularly until we decided, after the second meeting, that we wanted to incorporate and to do a systematic job of analysing continuously and seriously the Cuban reality both in the island and in *exilio*; to understand what was happening and why it happened, mainly from the social science perspective. But we are now developing the humanities and the literary part etcetera.

Our strength, however, has been in the social sciences, and we have gathered the cream of the crop of Cuban-born scholars on Cuba in the US and elsewhere with such relevant names as Professor Domínguez from Harvard, Professor Carmelo Mesa-Lago from Pittsburg, the late Lourdes Casal who died in Cuba, Professor Nelson Valdés from Albuquerque and a whole bunch of other people that are very dedicated students of the Cuban process. Ever since 1969 we have been meeting on a yearly basis for one or another thing. We either have seminars with in-depth treatment and analysis of a topic and with guests and participants who contribute to the theme in a professional way, or we have open-ended activities which we call *reuniones de estudios cubanos* which are prescribed by our by-laws every two years, and members come, and then we have elections for the board. What we have is like *una cafetería temática*, wide open, whatever people are working on in their research projects, and they report and it's not one topic but many topics. We incorporated fully in 1973 in Washington, a tax-exempt, non-profit organisation. And we have done a modest but valuable job. We have never had enough money but we have had talent and commitment.

One of the things that I think the group has done, initially not by design but later by design, is to provide a hub for dialogue between Cubans – without fear of labelling – initially, dialogue among Cubans here. Then we have also promoted dialogue among all Cubans – here and there – and for so doing we have been vilified and we have been attacked, not only verbally but also physically. As you probably know, my house was bombed a year ago in May because we were sponsoring a local debate on US–Cuban relations with the co-sponsorship of Wayne Smith and SAIS, the School of Advanced Internationl Studies, in Washington. Wayne was the first American chief of the Interests Section in Havana, with the Carter presidency, and he has become one of our few non-Cuban members of the Instituto, and a personal friend. And we thought, a year ago, before the presidential elections, that it was opportune and proper and necessary to discuss the topic because we knew there were a number of contacts and meetings between Cuban and American officials that were taking place, and we thought that the Cuban community should participate in them in some way if only to discuss the possibility as Cubans. And we invited Monsignor Walsh, and we also had Jorge Vals, a very well-known ex-political prisoner and poet. After twenty years in prison, or twenty-two, nobody would doubt that he is not pro-Castro. We also had Carlos Alberto Montaner, who is a foremost journalist against Castro.* And on the conservative side we also had Professor Baloyra from the University of Miami, and so we gathered five people that were beyond question, in terms of their responsibility and their, *eh*, moderation, although they may be perceived otherwise by sections of the community. But the fact that Wayne was the co-sponsor, and the fact that I was also part of it, and the fact that we labelled that debate 'US–Cuba: Another Perestroika?' really exacerbated – together with other things that were happening at the time locally – and I never thought I would be bombed, but I was.

The authorities continue the investigation. They already told me they know who they are but they are gathering the necessary evidence to bring them to trial and to convict them. *Locos* [madmen]. Yes, my assumption is that those who placed the bomb – which by the way was a very professional job of a high explosive that was detonated long distance through an electronic device – my assumption is that the people who placed the bombs were under the guidance of intellectual masterminds . . . I have an idea who they work for, but in terms of, you know, the legal process, I had better not say anything until they get caught.

I have always been a college professor back home and here in the States, though I had a brief interval at high-school teaching at the beginning of my arrival here in Miami. But I have been in Miami Dade Community College South Campus for the past twenty years. I teach there in the social science department. I am a full professor with tenure. There was a time, ten years ago, in which [Cuban] community members here at Miami pressured my bosses at the college to see if I would be fired. But the college was really very supportive and very professional. So, I am grateful to my colleagues and to my bosses because they did not bow to

---

* See pp.334–4 (Wayne Smith), 225–38 (Monsignor Walsh) and 258–65 (Carlos Alberto Montaner) for interviews with some of these figures.

the pressure, and this is an advantage that I have because, as you know, academia is perhaps the freest of environments to do what I do. I think if I would have been working otherwise, I would have probably been a victim and I would have been fired, locally. I don't want to leave Miami, this is my turf, and I think one of my responsibilities with my group and with my activity is to help to educate the community and to move them ahead into the future.

We have been stalemated for thirty years from frozen positions that don't pay off. It is not that I am a communist or that I support Castro or the government. But I am very interested in my people and in my nation's future with the present perspective. I don't want to go to the past but I don't want to remain in the present. And the only way that you can build the future is with different attitudes. And I am very convinced that there are lots of people on the island who are looking forward to some kind of change for a more humane, more tolerable type of system within the framework of socialism, probably. But as we all know, socialism in the whole world under any label is undergoing a lot of change. In the People's Republic of China, in Eastern Europe, in the Soviet Union itself. We also know that the official position of the Cuban government is against perestroika.

I personally feel that – and this is a shared view by some of my colleagues – Castro has the excuse of opposing perestroika and glasnost as long as the US maintains a hostile position [towards Cuba]. Because internally, members of the Party and other elements who want change are afraid that that type of change will weaken the survival of the Revolution, and they know that, to this date, only Fidel can mobilise the population. So, when they weigh survival *vis-à-vis* perestroika, they go on the side of survival, and I don't blame them. This is my understanding. I don't know if this is correct. But, therefore, if the US would change, then he would have no excuse and perestroika will take place and change will come. But as long as the US maintains an official position of hostility, this is not going to happen.

So, in my view, the burden of possible change in the future

resides in the US more so then on Cubans. That's how some of us understand what's going on. In recent times, some of the US pre-conditions have been met. Cuban troops are leaving Angola. Except for El Salvador and Guatemala, Cuba is not supporting guerrillas in Central America. They have expressed a willingness to have a negotiated solution for Nicaragua. So the only explanation that I have for this is that the US resents the Cuban international role and refuses to deal with Cuba as a – well, an equal in terms of negotiations. They want to deal with Cuba as a, you know, a Soviet surrogate, which in many ways Cuba is not, as you know. By the way, I do not deny the complexities of the Cuban–Soviet relation. That's another chapter.

So we are solo in a kind of stalemate at this time. But I am hopeful that President Bush will be a more pragmatic guy than Reagan was, although Reagan in the last year or so drastically changed *vis-à-vis* the Soviet Union. So we have to be patient and we have to do our thing modestly but firmly and be hopeful that eventually there will be a breakthrough. And that's in a nutshell what I'm at.

Twenty-one years ago, when I was working on my doctoral programme at Catholic University in Washington, I wrote a paper which I entitled 'The Reluctant Parent and the Unruly Child'. And the label of that paper and some of its content is applicable to this date. I mean, the relationship between the USSR and Cuba is a very complex one, with ups and downs due to a number of factors, not the least of which is Castro's personality. On the other hand, one qualitative and quantitative change has taken place since 1959: [up until 1959] the Cuban process as a nation and as a society was dominated by the priority of economics for better and for worse. For instance, Cuba was not properly colonised and [was] neglected for a long, long time by Spain because it had no gold and silver. And then Cuba was reappraised in the seventeenth century because of its geographic strategic position and because in the Caribbean you had naval battles reflecting the conflicts on the continent in Europe. And then Cuba was fortified in the ports to preserve the island as a service station for the fleets that were coming loaded with gold and silver from Mexico and Peru, etcetera, etcetera.

So, [Cuba] never had economic significance as such, although internally the economic thing always had priority. For instance, after independence from Spain and the big discussion in the 1902 assembly about the Platt Amendment, the final conclusion of the delegates was that *sin Enmienda no hay República* ['there's no Republic without the Amendment'], and what they wanted to do, most of them, was to rebuild the nation economically with the help of the neighbour to the north. And that took priority over political considerations.

Now, beginning in 1959, almost systematically, with very brief exceptions and periods, the Cuban revolutionary leadership has prioritised political goals over economic goals, and that has really been a turnabout of perspectives . . . [and] you know, everybody agrees that the greatest asset of the Cuban process from 1959 to date is the fact that it has been able to survive under the very noses of the US, in spite of all kinds of US projects to overthrow and even to kill. And the US has had to reluctantly accept the survival of the process and the leadership. But it has not liked that because it had a very paternalistic relationship with the island ever since 1898. And it's like, you know, the resentment of a grandfather who does not forgive the unruly grandchild. And it has never wanted to acknowledge that Cuba has a very definite international role.

But one of the stumbling blocks in normalisation from the US side is that the US has never wanted to acknowledge Cuba as a legitimate spokesman for its own cause. It has always wanted to deal with Cuba as a lackey of the Soviet Union, which it is not, totally. (*Laughs*) Granted that it's fully dependent on Soviet aid for survival, and everybody agrees to that, but you also know that Cubans don't like the Soviets, they call them *bolos* [thickheads] (*chuckles*), and there's put-downs by the people. However, in recent times, because of perestroika and glasnost, that has begun to change. And it's very interesting. Rafael Hernández was saying at the conference, which is true, 'Before we were told that we were lackeys of the Soviet Union and that was a problem. Now we are criticised by the US because we don't follow the

Soviet lead . . .'* But if you take a look at the Cuban process in Africa, although it coincided with Soviet goals, it was not totally for the Soviet purpose. In my view, Cuba has always had a tremendous international impact beyond its size, beyond its wealth. That little island has had a tremendous role, which has been enhanced by the Revolution. Some people say properly, which I think is true, that Castro put Cuba on the world map and it's going to stay there whether we like it or not. And this is what the US as a superpower does not want to deal with out of – out of what I would call *una pataleta*, a temper tantrum, as a superpower that wants to push aside the significance of this little island that has been so annoying (*chuckles*) to US pride and to US power and to US dominance in the Caribbean.

You see, this community has never been monolithic – that is a myth. Cuba in the island is not monolithic, much to the chagrin of the leadership there, and Cubans in diaspora are not monolithic equally much to the chagrin of the leaders here – the so-called leaders. So, it is to the interest of both communities that those elements that are diverse in there and in here make themselves known (*pause*) and organise in a non-threatening way. And as long as we keep having 20,000 coming in every year,† it's going to keep on changing.

. . . One other notion that I have been toying with for some time is the parallel between Cuba and Israel. I call Cubans abroad the Jews of the Caribbean, including myself. We have shown tremendous survival skills and a lot of similarities with the Jewish community in diaspora, and the only thing is what to do in order to get this community to look at the motherland in a different way. Not necessarily to be opponents of communism, but to look into the future as really labouring to find ways of doing things that are good for both, above and beyond ideology.

My personal commitment is both to my nation, and to the people in my nation, and to the Church in Cuba. One of the things my detractors find very difficult to deal with is that they have not been able to either erase or weaken my Catholic identity.

---

* See pp.319–33 for an interview with Rafael Hernández.
† The number specified under the 1984 Immigration Accord.

And they really climb up a wall because of my personal relations, relationships with the Cuban hierarchy, with the laymen people in Cuba, with priests in Cuba, and also with distinguished members of the American hierarchy outside Miami . . .

Because of the hard, and I would even say irrational, attitude of the Cuban community in Miami, what should have taken place locally with the leadership of Cubans is taking place in the north-east triangle – New York, Washington, Boston – *vis-à-vis* the Cuban Church. There's a very noble and productive, mutually productive relationship between the Church in Cuba and the Church in the US, and this is by design from the Vatican, as I see it. And you already know that the Pope's visit has been announced for 1991.* And that's going to be important. And the role that the Church is now attempting to carve into the Cuban process for now and for the future is also very interesting and very challenging. It's very challenging because, as an institution, the Cuban Church was never a strong institution *vis-à-vis* other national churches in Latin America. It was never strong financially, it was never strong pastorally and this is why I find it so fascinating, because it has really risen from weakness slowly. And in my view this is because the Church has, for the first time, historically recognised and respected popular religiosity through all the myriad of syncretic cults and the other cults which are not syncretic. And that's a change. [Previously] they had a condescending and negative [attitude] – either indifference or hostility – and now it's respect and they had to, both the Party and the Church, had to take into account, for different reasons, this reality. And both are being challenged in different ways, and this is why, I guess, President Castro has already publicly acknowledged that the notion of *el opio de las masas*, you know, religion as the opiate of the people, is a foreign element, that we don't have to take into account – which is totally new.

As you probably know, initially, both the government and some Church officials that were not Cuban anticipated that the Church in Cuba would be totally evaporated in twenty years, and this has not happened. On the contrary, it has risen with a new kind of strength

---

* No date has as yet been finalised.

from its weakness, which is kind of dialectical and paradoxical, but that's the way the spirit functions, you know. And one of the common views of the Church in diaspora, even those who are positively positioned *vis-à-vis* the Church in Cuba, is a doubt that the Church would have the know-how and the resources to really assume the role that it wants to assume. I know how poor and weak the Church has been, but the difference between me and these elements is that I trust that the spirit will do the work and that people will rise to the occasion. So we are now engaged, some of us, in building the hope of national reconciliation, which is very new among Cubans. It is not new in the world, because there's already national processes in Afghanistan, in Eastern Europe, in Nicaragua, so Cuba will not be new, but it's new in the Cuban community.

Well, we are, for the first time, going to break ground on the topic at our June gathering, and the Cuban Church has officially accepted an invitation that we extended and they are sending the vicar of the Camagüey diocese, Monsignor José Sarduy Marrero, representing the Cuban Bishops' Conference, to this gathering.

Would you go back?

I would go back but I doubt that the Cubans would let me. I was back [during] the Dialogue.* I was back in the latter part of 1978, 1979 and the first part of 1980 through August of 1980. Then, after Mariel, I haven't been back since then. They don't let me in. I guess 1980 was the year of the Reagan election, and together with that you had the Solidarity problems in Poland, so because of my linkage, which they are fully aware of, with the Cuban Church, I guess they didn't want me there. Many of my colleagues do go frequently and I am hoping to go eventually . . .

I never thought, personally, that I would be pro-Soviet in anything related to Cuba, and now I am, in a qualified manner, because I have tremendous admiration for Gorbachev. And I don't

---

* In 1978 a group of Cuban Americans founded the Committee of 75 with the aim of establishing a dialogue between the exile community and the island authorities.

know if he's going to be allowed to do what he wants to do. I think ethnic unrest is perhaps his greatest threat. But I pray for him every day because I have read *Perestroika*,* first in English, then in Spanish, and I find it very refreshing reading.

And I think, this is an opinion, Fidel Castro, psychologically, resents that he is no longer the youngest, one of the most attractive among communist leaders in the world. And although he will never acknowledge this, I think, deep down, internally, he wants Gorbachev to fail so he can emerge, you know, as the correct one, in opposing perestroika. Because perestroika, if allowed, would mean one thing – sharing power. He doesn't like that. Those that expected Gorbachev's visit to force Castro [to accept perestroika] didn't know the reality.

But anyway, I am very hopeful. Jokingly, in my process, I have always said that in the island, in order for anything to happen, you have to have the agreement of the two Ps, the Party and the Paraclete, the Holy Spirit. And this priest [I know] says you also need a third P, which is *el Pueblo* [the People]. So, yes, I agree, something is cooking and something will continue to evolve even if slow, and I don't have to necessarily witness it, but I will do my very best to contribute to it happening.

I have a feeling that there is a future, of course, and that how that future is going to be depends in great measure on the awakening of a new consciousness among Cubans here and there; that we are one people above and beyond processes and regimes and ideological labels; and that it's up to us to find ways of building that future together because I think this community here has a tremendous potential – not only financial, which it has, but cultural.

If you ask me what is it the community abroad has done best, it's the preservation of the culture against all the odds. And although you find second-generation Cubans here that speak English better than Spanish, they continue to have mental structures that are Cuban, and they continue to hold important values that are very Cuban, such as family. They are very American in how they dress, in the cars they ride, in the way they conduct business, but they are very Cuban in what they eat, in the music they dance and in their

* President Gorbachev's book, published in London in 1988.

mental structures, culturally speaking. Much more so than other communities, and I think that is because of the development of the enclave, the Cuban enclave.

Sociologist Alejandro Portes is perhaps the creator of the concept, and one of the reasons why the Cuban migration has fared differently and better than other Hispanics is because of the creation of this thing called the enclave, which I understand to be a self-sustaining, complete community within the American society. In Miami, for instance, Cubans have created a complete community where other Cubans that come in are totally upheld. They find jobs, they find housing, schools, churches, businesses, services, all by Cubans, and they are sustained until they are ready to do their thing in and out of that enclave precisely because of the strong family ties. But the existence of the enclave has made this possible. You see, in areas in Miami you don't need to speak English at all.

This has to do with the fact that the first wave [of immigration] after the *batistianos* – there are several waves – was not so much moneyed as entrepreneurial. I came with no money. In fact, I went through the experience at the airport in Miami that I had to ask one immigration official to give me a dime to make a phone-call. It's [this] second wave to which I belong, the professional, entrepreneurial, managerial middle class. Jews of the Caribbean.

One of the things that allowed the massive immigration in the early 1960s is the US Department of State policy: to use that as a political tool; to demonstrate to the world the failure of communism. Now, although the Cuban refugee programme allocated millions of dollars to initially help the Cubans, the Cubans have more than repaid those millions through taxes and through the development of the area, which was a sleepy winter tourist place. So greater Miami has become, primarily because of the Cubans, the centre of international finance and tourism and trade of the southern part of the US. And how do we measure that for a fact? Eleven out of fourteen exchange banks of the whole country are based here for Latin American business. Most of the major multinationals that dealt with the Caribbean and South America are based here now. This has happened in the past fifteen to twenty years, and that is primarily all due to the impact of the Cuban thing. This is why we are very arrogant, and we share that with the natives on the island, including 'Comandante en Jefe'. We are very arrogant, so we don't take any BS [bullshit] from anybody, and although most of us have become bilingual or were bilingual before we got here, like me, I speak Spanish any opportunity that I have. In spite of the backlash, we continue to do it, and the hell with it. And we will do it to the day we die. And what I tell the uptight monolingual Anglos: 'It's to your disadvantage, because we are bilingual, we speak English. You are the ones who don't speak Spanish. So that's your problem, not mine.'

22

César Luaices

César Luaices took part in the Bay of Pigs invasion in 1961 as a pilot member of the 2506 Brigade. He lives in Miami. This interview takes place at the Brigade headquarters the day after their annual commemoration of the defeat.

18 April 1989

I compare the problem of Cuba to an incident in the Bible. God comes to this planet, he creates a man in his image and then he gives him a *compañera*. When he finished his work he said to those people, 'Right. The only thing I want is that you don't do this' – an obstacle which some say is an apple but I say it could have been a banana, or they ate God's melon and what he wanted was for them not to touch it because when he came on his holidays he wanted to eat it. Anyway, the first thing those two people do is disobey what he had said to them.

Not content with that they had two sons, number three gave him a belt and number four killed him. So it was all wrong from the word go.

In 1902 Cuba got its independence as a nation. And at that time, I would say it without fear of being mistaken, God came to Cuba again and said, 'Look. Remember Christopher Columbus said this was the most beautiful land in the world, so behave yourselves and follow the teachings I sent with my Son down here to earth when

217

he said, "Love one another." Do just that and you will see that you will be happy.'

We Cubans are a fighting people. We like to work hard to improve ourselves but politically we haven't a clue. Consequently we worked, and we weren't concerned that others had the ability to practically take over the republic. That happened with the first president, the second, the third. In 1917 there was a revolution in Russia which removed the Romanovs from power after 300 years of rule over that country. At that time it created the impression, I'd say it was a mirage, that every country in the world, including the United States, wanted to have a tsar just to cut off his head. In Cuba it was the students, the university students, the workers who at that time made President Sayas's life impossible, and he a decent person who loved the people of Cuba – it's always the young people, like during the Vietnam War here, the hippies didn't want to go and fight. And so those who had a modicum of intelligence in Cuba in 1928 designated as president a gentleman who had been a veteran of the War of Independence, Head of Police at Santa Clara, General Gerardo Machado, and that man imposed tremendous order on Cuba to prevent that sort of problem continuing. For the first four years Machado was an excellent president. Order reigned. But in 1929, at the time of the Great Depression in the United States, [when] people were dying here in the US, oh yes, indeed, it was the same problem in Cuba. So we had, well, in my own case, I only had a milky coffee at night. I'm sixty-nine now.

So this meant that the revolutionary seed from Russia began to flourish again. With the education of some of Machado's government and others with their revolutionary ideas, a whole series of problems arose. Personal problems, massacres and things like that, which meant Machado had to get out in 1933. The revolutionary groupings which had flourished and were headed by intellectuals (*contempt in his voice*), students, etcetera, got rid of Machado's officers from the army and then, imagining that they were going to have a puppet in their hands, supported the army sergeant, Fulgencio Batista, and made him head of the army. Fortunately for Cuba, Mr Batista realised what had happened and he did a complete U-turn, which in a certain way and to a certain extent brought peace to the people of Cuba.

Recently a lady told me that the worst problem Cuba had was the 10 March coup by Batista. And then I said to her that the 10 March coup happened because a group of people wanted to take over the republic, a perfectly germinated seed that had been planted in perfectly fertilised soil by the two previous governments.

Our poor political training made us support a university gangster. We gave moral and economic support to a university gangster. I am going to cite a detail I recently read. In 1947, elections were held at Havana University in which one of the aspiring groups spoke to the communists on the campus, and in the midst of the other group, the right-wingers, as it were, appeared various gentleman, among them a friend of mine and Fidel Castro.

The book entitled *History of the Communist Party of Cuba* says that the communists won and that within two months of taking power Fidel Castro joined their ranks. The communists accepted Fidel Castro into their ranks. Then I asked my friend what he thought of it. And he said to me, 'Well, people write what they want.' But what actually happened? Fidel Castro took part [in the assassination], even if he didn't kill [him], of Manolo Castro who was a student leader. Mr Fidel Castro took part, he was involved in an uprising in Cayo Confite. Mr Fidel Castro fooled a friend of mine who lives in West Palm Beach. He [Castro] took him to Santiago de Cuba at the time of the Moncada; he stayed two blocks away from the Barracks while those he ordered to attack the Moncada Barracks died in the attempt. He hid and later gave himself up.*

It's amazing the sort of things history throws up. Fidel Castro

---

* These are all old arguments. (1) There were allegations that Fidel Castro was involved in the killing of the student leader Manolo Castro (no relative). Although no warrant was ever made for Fidel Castro's arrest he went to the police of his own accord and, in the absence of any evidence, was released. (2) Castro was among those Cubans who with Dominican Republic exiles had planned to invade the Dominican Republic and topple the dictator Rafael Trujillo in the summer of 1947. The invasion was to be launched from Cayo Confite, off Cuba's north-eastern coast. The Cuban navy was sent in to arrest those involved. Castro escaped. (3) Here Castro is being made out to be a coward at the Moncada Barracks attack.

was married to the daughter of one of Batista's ministers.* I often asked myself how many times that gentleman must have said to President Batista, 'That boy is mad. Let's leave him alone, he doesn't know what he's up to.' I would almost say that that's why we are here today. Because if [Castro] had fallen into the hands of someone with a strong character, like you got in every Latin American country, he wouldn't have come out of that situation with his life. So, what happens? Some of Batista's officers didn't carry out orders as members of the armed forces. Not all, some of them didn't. Batista was burnt out at the time and the Cuban people were undisciplined. He hadn't told them to behave themselves. So then he [Castro] started to play at revolution too, and ultimately that gentleman installed communism in Cuba.

In a population of ten million there are men of all kinds. So, some people, a fairly small percentage of them, realised that he was a communist. They came to the United States and they signed up for the Bay of Pigs invasion.

I remember an incident at a meeting I was invited to just recently. There were about 200 people at it and I arrived before it started, and I asked if it was about liberating Cuba. Such was the shock that they nearly wanted to beat me with sticks. They threw me out. They said, 'Get out. We can see that you're no Cuban.' But when the meeting got started the husband of a lady who was there who had said I wasn't a Cuban proposed that I should address the meeting. So in the end, I began to speak and I said, 'On 10 June 1960 I left Cuba, the place I love the most. I left nineteen years of work in Cubana de Aviación which was my club. It was my club, my church, my home, it was my life. I left my mother and my father whom I never saw again and after two months in the United States I went to Guatemala with the 2506 Brigade. The most significant and painful thing about it was that I witnessed the sad spectacle of having to wait eight months to recruit 1,500 men to fight for Cuba and rid it of communism . . .

'That's what has us where we are now; why Cuba has been in

---

* Mirta Díaz-Balart. Her father was a wealthy land-owner with strong political connections. Her brother was Deputy Minister of the Interior during the Batista regime and a one-time university friend of Fidel Castro.

the hands of communists for thirty years. And time, I'm not going to see it, time is the greatest enemy we have because our children don't care a damn about Cuba, and over thirty years Fidel Castro has created a much more confrontational mentality than the one we had to face before.'

I was born in Havana and I was raised in Cuba, and perhaps that was the problem, that we had to get on with work to get by. I was a child in 1929, 1930, when everyone was dying of hunger, and I had to work like a slave. For five years I worked in the telegraph office in Havana as an honorary telegraphist without earning a cent. I was on guard duty for eight hours, for which I got a dollar. But there is no country that has the climate of Cuba. Havana is a beautiful city, and when I was able to say at last I've got a salary, I have a livelihood, which was with Pan American Airways, in those days I was the happiest man in the world. I danced the legs off myself (*laughs*). Then I had the privilege of flying around Cuba. I thought the island was so lovely, so blue, really, people who had the privilege I had of flying around the island felt as if they were the children of Jesus Christ or something like that. (*Chuckles*)

Originally I was a radio operator-telegraphist and then I became a pilot. I studied to become a pilot and then they accepted me as such. But, for instance, when Fidel Castro came to power, I, in particular, could have stayed on there in the top ranks because besides being a pilot I was also a member of the Professional Pilots' Association. They relied on that sort of person and I was even a navigation instructor there. But fifteen days after Fidel Castro came to power I arrived [home] – I lived in Vedado – and on the corner by my house there were six or seven militias standing on the corner with sideburns down to their navals, rosaries hanging out of their necks – I mean, what necessity was there for that? You knew what that meant. Anyone who had a brain cell at all realised that no good could come of it.

When I looked out my window I saw that they were shooting people; I saw that there was no freedom. A journalist might publish something and then they labelled him a counter-revolutionary. They arrested people for whatever reason. For example, I carried the owner of *Avance* newspaper from Havana to Miami and I said to myself, 'Why is this man leaving Cuba?' I arrived at the conclusion that you couldn't live with these people, although they treated me very well. And a lot of people felt the same. That's why we left.

On my flights to Miami I noticed something was happening. I noticed that it was the [US] authorities who were handling the Cuban question. They regularly waited for us off the Havana–Miami run, and when we arrived and went through customs they brought us into an offfice where there were one or two gentlemen. 'How are you?' 'Are you going to stay here? Because we are organising this and that and the other.' That is, the government of the United States. Not a bother on them. Only people with authority could do that, of course. (*Chuckles*) No doubt about it.

I didn't have anyone here. When I left [Miami] for the camps [in Guatemala], I left my wife and six-month-old daughter here in Miami and off I went to the training camps, flying on missions to Cuba to drop arms to the people who were rising up [against Castro]. I arrived there [Guatemala] around 30 August 1960, and in September they planned a mission to the Escambray, and of course, perhaps through lack of co-ordination, the weapons didn't fall into the hands of the rebels and Fidel exhibited them in Havana and caused a great furore.

They always told the pilots that we'd have aerial support, and we think we are going to get the support they promised, and when we get there we don't get any, and in present-day wars, whoever commands the air wins. For example, there was a bombardment [of Havana] on 15 April, and when the planes get back from the bombardment they tell them there aren't going to be any more. That is exactly where they lost the battle of the Bay of Pigs. Because if you stop the bombing, he, Fidel – his most powerful weapon is the microphone, his most powerful weapon is the microphone – but if you keep up the bombing, you stop him from getting to the microphone. (*Laughs*) You don't have to be a military man to know that. So they stop the bombings and in two days he is ready and waiting and we are at his mercy. We didn't stand a chance.

I believe, I believe there is a God. I'm not a religious fanatic but I do believe there is a God who rules over everything. So when I knew I was on my way to Cuba I spoke to him in the middle of the street. There in the street I spoke to him and I said, 'Look, I'm a terrible sinner. I love all the women who come my way and all that and you know I have been a right devil, but let's do something. I am going to place my life in your hands, in your service, so that the people of Cuba get back their freedom and can keep their faith and go where you are freely. So, now you know. If when I go up there you want to condemn me to hell, it'll be because I deserve it, but I'm doing something for you so that you give me a small credit. Let it be purgatory instead of hell.' (*Chuckles heartily*)

So I was never afraid that anything would happen to me. I was perfectly calm about it. If they killed me it would have been while I was completely in His service.

When did you know the battle was lost?

After the landing, on the 17th. Two days went by and Fidel, who had been preparing from before, began to send in a vast number of soldiers to surround the area, encircling it, and then on the 19th it was completely besieged, there was nothing more doing. *Eh . . .* they died, they died on the 19th.

Four planes went out that day. They went with volunteer pilots, which was very honourable on their part. I personally feel extremely honoured to have known them. Three planes with American crews. In two of the planes there were two people each; in the third plane, which wasn't brought down at the Bay of Pigs, went a man by the name of Simpson who was like an angel in our camps, one of those pilots you don't come across nowadays. He was a Second World War veteran and he could fly whatever . . . if you gave him a broomstick he'd fly it. A tremendous man. He went alone. That's the three planes and one Cuban, a friend of mine from Cubana de Aviación who also went as a volunteer, because the game was up and nobody wanted to go there and get shot down. That pilot, Captain Gonzalo Herrera, also flew alone, and he was so courageous that, to end the story, he came back without a single section of his aircraft free of holes. I said it recently on television, and now I remember there was a terrible fuss about it all. By that I don't want to discredit it, because there were pilots who lost their lives and there are others alive who behaved very well. But those people of the 19th were extraordinary people, and the bodies from the other two planes shot down have only recently been returned to the US.

I tried to get back into aviation. I was forty at the time. Then there was a job offer. As I had a sound foundation in electrics I became an electrician and then, in 1966, when I had a good job here in an industry belonging to a former mayor of Miami, Mauricio Ferrer, they came to ask me to fly to Vietnam. I spent a year flying to Vietnam. We'd as easily have been carrying games and entertainment for the troops as explosives (*chuckles*) or weapons – whatever they wanted out there. When we carried arms we were protected by certain life assurances in case anything happened. My son signed up with the Marines. He's very proud of that. He was brought up here since the age of five. He's from my first marriage. He is proud . . . I am too, because he's more American than Washington. (*Laughs*) I speak to him by phone and he doesn't know how to speak proper Spanish. He can't speak Spanish and he's a Vietnam veteran. He lives there in Connecticut and he's a supervisor in an aviation company. He's very proper.

And then I remember, about a year and a bit after flying the Vietnam missions, they sent me to Seattle to collect an award. And there were rows of commandants and colonels from the American armed forces. And when they were giving out the awards they said, 'César Luaices, 100 points,' and those Americans began messing. Funny stuff, joking with me, 'Look at the Cuban, he comes here and picks up 100 points.' When I got back to the hotel I felt as if I'd won the $23 million lottery. I got a telegram to return to Miami. We are in Seattle in Washington. So I get back here and I'm laid off because the United States had cancelled all its military contracts for propulsion aircraft. They didn't want any more propulsion aircraft in the Pacific. So I had to go back to electricity. Then I began working in the Miami Dade Water & Sewer [Department]. I was there for thirteen years and I retired. In the final years I was a supervisor; for three or four years I was a supervisor there. Really, they treated me very well. Everyone liked me a lot. I have a Florida State pension and social security. I have two – two pensions.

23

Monsignor Brian Walsh

Born in Portarlington, Co. Laois, in Ireland, Monsignor Walsh emigrated, while studying for the priesthood, to the United States. In 1955 he became director of Catholic Charities in Miami, a position he has held ever since. Here he relates how he became caught up in Cuban affairs.

19 April 1989

We are Castle Catholics – you know what that means. We are very loyal servants of the Crown (*chuckles*) . . . I carry three passports. I've a British, an Irish and a US one. Which one disappears under the seat if I'm hijacked? (*Chuckles*) It's going to be the US one.

My father had been British Army. We'd been British Army for generations and my [maternal] grandfather was clerk of the courts; clerk of the petty sessions and before that RIC [Royal Irish Constabulary], and so we, you know, were not really part of the independence movement. Although funny thing was my grandfather, when the government changed in 1922, was immediately given another government job by the Free State. So, we were, you know, very neutral.

I grew up in Limerick where I went to the Jesuits – Crescent College and later to Mungret – and then I came to the United States when I was twenty, as a student, and I was ordained a priest here in Florida in 1954, and a year later, after a year in a parish, I was appointed to Catholic Social Services or Catholic Charities here in Miami, and I've been here ever since.

So, I've been part of the Miami scene since 1955 and I've been through all the changes.

My first work with refugees was with Hungarian freedom fighters in 1956–7. And then the diocese of Miami was formed, in October 1958, and three months later Fidel Castro took over in Cuba, and life in Miami has been dominated by the Cuban connection since that time. And so I've been through all the refugee movements and the rest of it ever since.

In December 1960, we got involved in taking care of unaccompanied Cuban children here in Miami and then, for about twenty months, involved with an organised system of helping parents in Cuba send their teenagers to the United States.

And basically, 14,000 teenagers left Cuba under my signature. (*Sighs*) There were a few younger children but they were mostly teenagers. Between December 1960 and the October Missile Crisis. And we figured that of the one million Cubans who have come through Miami in the last thirty years, about 25 per cent of them came as a result of the door that was opened by the Cuban Children's Programme. I could bring any child into the United States between the ages of six and sixteen without a visa. I was given a *carte blanche* by the State Department. The airlines accepted my signature and a letter saying that so-and-so had a visa waiver, and they were not fined for bringing in an undocumented alien. And that operated up until October 1962 when the flights from Cuba stopped.

In Cuba, obviously, an awful lot of people worked to take advantage of this. There were many, many different networks. And basically it involved getting the children the documentation together, making sure they could get a $25 US money order to purchase their round-trip ticket. The principal organiser in Cuba, but by no means the only one, was Ramón Grau, [known as] Monguito – nephew of Grau Alsino* – Ramón Grau Alsino, and his sister, Paula, Paulita. Of course, they were many years in prison, partially because of the Cuban Children's Programme, partially because of (*inhales deeply*) em, other activities. Mongo was involved in supposedly two or three attempts on Castro's

---

* President of Cuba for less than a year in 1934.

life. And in 1978, when the famous Dialogue started between the Cubans in exile, which was very controversial in this community, I worked with those Cubans who wanted to do something with the Cuban situation, particularly the release of political prisoners – Bernardo Benes and the others who went down [to Havana]. Bernardo was a Jewish Cuban who was one of the principal instruments of bringing the Dialogue about. He asked me before one trip to Cuba with a delegation if there was anybody I wanted to get out of prison in Cuba. And I said, 'Yeah, there are two names at the top of the list, of my list: Paulita and Mongo Grau, niece and nephew of the old president.'

So, he went to Cuba and in a moment with Fidel he said, 'I have a special request about two prisoners.' And he says Fidel asked him who was making the request. And he says, '*Eh*, Monsignor Brian Walsh.' And Bernardo, basically I think he's joking, but it's a good story, [Fidel said], 'Oh, that's the priest who did such a good job with the Cuban children.' (*Hoots. Helpless with laughter*) I don't believe it, but it's a good story. So anyway, Fidel knew who it was. He said things about me on television in the 1960s – that I am taking the Cuban children out of Cuba so that they could be hungry in Miami and all kinds of things like that – so the G-2* had looked for me in Cuba for nearly a year. The fact was, I was safe in Miami all of the time . . .

But the funny part about it was Fidel's reaction. He said, 'Who does he want?' And Bernardo said, 'Mongo and Paulita Grau.' And Fidel's answer immediately was, '*Con Paulita no hay problema. Mañana.*' And within two days Paulita was in Miami. '*Mongo es otra cosa. Es más complicado.*' [Mongo is another story. That's more complicated.] That's all Fidel would say. They were arrested, I think, in 1965. It took from 1978 until two years ago, when the US bishops got a whole group out and Mongo was one of those.

Mongo had told me that the night they were being processed they were wakened up in the middle of the night and told they had to pack whatever they had. They were given clean clothes and showers and all the rest of it and one of the G-2 majors,

* State Security. The name is a legacy from US Army Intelligence.

when he was being processed, said, 'Grau, we should have shot you years ago for what you did to the Cuban children.' And so apparently it rankles them.

And Mongo arrives in Miami, walks off the plane, and the first person he asks for after twenty-four years in prison is me. So it was a very emotional reunion and, of course, television and everything else and it was the first time we met. But he told me an interesting thing. 'You know,' he said, 'it's the first time you have seen me, but,' he says, 'I saw you before and I touched you.' I said, 'Where?' 'At the funeral of Cardinal Arteaga Betancourt,' he says, 'in March of 1963' – the old Archbishop of Havana, he'd been senile for years and years, maybe ten years. But he died and the Archbishop and I from here went to Cuba in five hours, between 5 p.m. when I got the news that the Cardinal had died and 10 p.m. that night. Everything was arranged. And we got special permission from the US government, a plane from Pan American.

Next morning at 7 o'clock we got permission from Cuba. Celia Sánchez gave special permission at the request of the Swiss ambassador. And we were met at the airport by the Swiss ambassador and taken straight to the cathedral. It was a fantastic experience (laughs), and Mongo Grau was present at the Mass, he says, and he came up and he didn't want to speak to me, he didn't want to create any problems. He says, 'I just touched you in the crowd.' Now that same day, they announced on the radio in Miami at noon that the Archbishop and I were in Havana. It was the big news of the day. And that afternoon, when we went back for the final entombment of the Cardinal, a great number of people whose children were in the United States came to the cathedral looking for me. And we had to be very careful what we were carrying with us. But people would come up and shake hands and slip pieces of paper with names and birthdays and all the rest of it: 'Please, I want to send my children . . . Here are the details,' and they'd squeeze it into your hand. We had been instructed by the State Department – Don't take any papers. Don't carry anything that's incriminating. And don't accept anything. So, I never looked at the papers. I would just squeeze them into a little ball and drop 'em. And it was, you know, very, you know, it was very emotional, of course.

You see, Celia Sánchez just knew the Archbishop of Miami, and Fidel Castro and Raúl were out of town. Raúl Roa was Foreign Minister at the time and he didn't want to touch it. It was a hot potato. He left it to Celia Sánchez and she okayed it. You know, she was Castro's eh . . . girlfriend, I guess, and secretary of the cabinet at the time. She's since dead. So that was the story of my trip to Cuba.

But during the rest of the time, you know, those twenty months between December of 1960 and October of 1962, 14,000 unaccompanied minors entered the United States.

We received them at the airport here. About half of them had a destination to go to. They had family relatives or very close friends. But the other half we put into care and put them into foster homes and schools and boarding schools all over the country. And from the beginning we were able to get some parents out afterwards, but it wasn't until 1965 that the big bulk of the parents came, and they were reunited here after the 'freedom flights' from Varadero had started. In December of 1965 . . . even though, you know, five years into the programme we had 5,000 kids still in care. By June of 1966 we had 500, the rest had been reunited with their families with the 'freedom flights'. And, of course, they claimed more people, and more people came. (*Laughs*) Y'see, there was never an open-door policy in the United States for Cuban refugees. This has always been one of the misunderstood points – except for the Unaccompanied Children's Programme. Everyone else, well, we had an example of two brothers. A woman got fake visa waivers. They were not officially signed by me but they resembled it. But she brought her two eleven- and twelve-year-old boys to the airport. She was divorced. She came with them and she had a visa waiver in her own name. The officials at the airport let the boys go to the United States but said, 'No, you can't go, you're not on the list.' And she let the boys go and she stayed. The whole lot of it was fake. But it worked for the kids. And one of the interesting parts of the whole thing was what the people did in Cuba who were working in a network, like Grau, [and that] was simply to help people get all of the pieces together: the visa waiver, the $15 [*sic*] money order which we used to smuggle down through the diplomatic pouches (*chuckles*) and things like that.

And the Cubans didn't know that this was happening?

We asked that question, and I was asked that question hundreds of times. And the conclusion I have to come to is we latched on to what may be a weakness in communist society or in communist organisation, and that is that nobody questions. You know, if you got to the airport, like the two kids with their mother, and all your papers were in order, nobody questioned, because you are taught not to question in Cuban society.

The exit permits, that was a little more complicated. What happened with the exit documents from Cuba [was], we were supplied with the paper. And we had enough people working within the system who would type it up correctly, insert the paper in the right file, and when somebody went to look at it, '*Está aquí, puede ir ya*' (Here it is, he can go). It was getting all of the little details in order so that you could go. And nobody questioned. And, you see, that is in a sense the weakness of a completely rigid society. I mean, for me Cuba is not Poland, not even Hungary or Czechoslovakia. The regime is probably the most rigid Marxist-Leninist regime in the world possible outside of . . . even more so than Russia. As a regime. I'm not saying that the people are all, you know, because (*laughs*) – I've always said this – if the communists could make sense out of the Cuban people, good luck! (*Hoots*) Eventually, the Cubans will defeat communism by their own way of doing things. You know, the *cubaniche* sort of thing. (*Shaking with hilarity*)

But in that regard, as I say, it worked. And the kids came, 14,000 of them, and, well, we had to learn fast here too because nobody knew what Cuban kids were like (*laughs*), and it was quite an experience . . . So I organised what we call a group home here in Miami and I took initially twenty and later it became eighty Cuban teenage boys to live with me down off Biscayne Boulevard, and one way or another, later on it was smaller, for twenty years I lived with Cuban teenage boys . . . I took twelve kids or fifteen kids from Mariel for one year, the last year of the programme, and then in 1981 we closed it down.

But we raised these kids here and in doing so we got to know Cuban teenagers. These are the kids who – many of them have made a great name for themselves here in Miami – the vast majority of them are kids who went on to university and (*sighs*) one of them is the US commercial attaché in Ecuador right now. They're all over town and all over the country too. I was walking through the Hilton Hotel one day in Washington and this man came up to me and he says, 'You're Father Walsh from Miami.' I said, yeah. He says, 'I thought so. I was at Camp Matacumbe in 1962 when I came from Cuba.' This was twenty years later and he recognised me.

Why did this operation happen?

Well, the very first connection was in October of 1960, and we were a small agency, we had a child-welfare programme, adoptions, we were taking care of family counselling, unwed mothers and this sort of thing. And foster care. And a man walked into the office, a Cuban man walked into the office, and he brought in a fifteen-year-old kid. He says, 'Father, is there anything you can do for this kid? He's been here in Miami for a month and he has practically slept in a different house every night. He was sent to an uncle but the uncle can't take care of him and he's been passed around and, you know, it's a pretty bad situation.' His name was Pedro. So I said, 'Yeah, we'll take care of him.' And I started making enquiries, and I found out that there was a small number of unaccompanied minors being sent into Miami. And we had dealt with unaccompanied minors with the Hungarian freedom fighters who were very tough kids, you know, and had come out of that experience, not many but some.

And so, at the time, Eisenhower had sent down to Miami a lawyer, named T. S. Voorhees, to investigate the needs of Cuban refugees in Miami. I called his attention to the fact that they were unaccompanied minors, and so, after he'd made a report to the President, he came back and said, 'You know, we'll give you some money if you take care of these kids.' So, that's when we were assured of financing. Then as word spread that we could take care of kids, then the people who began organising this contacted me and one thing led to another (*laughs*) and there were kind of amusing incidents at Christmas. Christmas Eve, 1960, I think it was, I got a telephone call from the State Department head of the Visa Section, Frank Auerbach. He said, 'Father, we understand you are taking care of some Cuban kids in Miami.' And I said, yeah. He said, 'Well, maybe we got some more for you.' I said, oh. He says, 'In the embassy in Havana we have 200 names of kids whose parents would like to send their kids to the United States and we're in favour of them coming here.' I found out later they were active leaders in the underground [counter-revolution]. The parents were. And this was a condition, that the kids be safe. 'So,' he said, 'we can't officially, you know, accept these kids, but we'll give you every facility and, you know, you'll get some money to take care of them, but,' he said, 'I need an OK from you to say you will be responsible for them.'

Well, you know, Christmas Eve, who can you get to consult? I couldn't find the Archbishop or anybody. So, I said, well, for 200 kids it's worth my total career in the Church – save 200 kids from communism. (*Laughs*) So, I said OK. So, he says, 'Would you put it in writing and send it to the State Department by special delivery but also send a copy signed on affidavit to my home and we'll know that if I have that it's OK to send the kids over.' I said, 'When do they come?' And he said, 'Maybe tomorrow.' (*Howls with laughter*) So, that was Christmas Day. So, anyway, I drew up the papers and sent them off. And so a social worker and I went to the airport on Christmas Day. No kids. Next day the social worker went and the first five kids arrived, and so we then started scurrying around wondering where we were going to put the kids. We hadn't the foggiest idea.

I had about ten beds available in Miami at the most, and here I had agreed to take 200 kids. I said, 'Walsh, you're crazy, you know. Your father always said you were crazy.' So . . . I was going down Brickell Avenue and I saw – the school is no longer there – there was a boarding school for girls called the Assumption Academy and I thought, 'They're on holidays, there's nobody there.' So I turned around and went in and saw old Mother Elizabeth, an English woman who was the superior. It was a private boarding school for girls, mostly from Cuba and Latin America. And I said, 'Mother, I got problems . . . I need beds for 200 Cuban refugee children.' She said, 'What!' I said, 'Yeah. I won't need them for long, but a few days, and your kids are on holidays.' 'Yeah, but they have to be out of here by 6 January.' I said, 'That's all right. We'll take care. We'll be fully responsible. How many dormitories do you have?' 'Well,' she said, 'we have two.' I said, 'That's good. One for the boys and one for . . .' 'Boys!' she said. 'You can't have boys in here.' (*Howls with laughter*) I said, 'Listen, Mother, this is a crisis. We're saving them from communism, you see . . .' (*Msgr Walsh has to blow his nose, he is laughing so much*) But anyway, she agreed. But it turned out we never did have to. I got a house across the street from Maurice Ferrer, who was Mayor of Miami.

Things moved fairly slow, and we got about twenty kids that first week and were able to take care of them. But during the course of the week, by Thursday, I got a telephone call from the Archbishop, whom I hadn't seen or hadn't told about what I'd done, you see. And he called and he says, 'Someone has been from the State Department and has been looking for you all day.' And I said, 'Oh. Who is it?' He says, 'Someone named Auerbach.' I said, 'Oh, yeah. I know who it is.' 'Yeah, he said something about you taking care of 200 kids.' I said, 'Well, yes, Archbishop. We are making arrangements, you know.' And he says, 'I hope you didn't put that limit on them.' I said, 'Oh, no, Archbishop. There's no limit on the numbers, it's just 200 on the first list,' which was perfectly true. 'Yeah,' he says, 'you know,' he says, 'I don't want you stopping anybody coming from Cuba. Take care of everybody that wants to come.' I said, 'Yes, Archbishop.' (*Laughs*) And that was how the whole thing got started. So, I was about $100,000 in debt before the federal money started flowing, but we survived and we kept going.

The embassy shut down on 3 January after Fidel made his speech limiting the number of Americans who could be in the embassy to the same number of Cubans that were in Washington – ten people or something like that in the Cuban embassy in Washington –

and Eisenhower shut it down. Well, I figured that was the end of kids coming from Cuba until the next day I got a call from Frank Auerbach again and he says, 'We'd like to talk to you.' 'Yeah,' I said, 'I guess it's all over.' He says, 'No, we don't think so.' I said, 'What do you mean? How can you give them visas?' 'Well,' he says, 'we got a few other things.' He says, 'Can you come to Washington?' I said, 'Well, sure.' 'All right, come up to Washington and we'll have a chat.'

So I went up to Washington on a Sunday. And Sunday afternoon went into the State Department. Monday afternoon they came up with a plan by which we would bring the kids out by way of Jamaica . . . We went down to Jamaica and made all these arrangements and the Bishop there helped us; put the kids up overnight; even kept them in his own house. For a couple of months we brought the kids out by way of Jamaica, and then the people like Grau in Cuba began testing the waters and sending a few kids directly to the United States. Of course, it was much cheaper and easier and the visa waiver was kind of recognised by all as valid, and that's the way they all came. We were interrupted at the Bay of Pigs for about five days. And it continued on until October without interruption. And it kept out of the papers here. The reporters, of course, would catch on. They'd come round looking for the story and I'd tell them the story and I'd say, 'Listen, we don't know what the effect of publicity is, but we are asking you to keep quiet. We don't want to run the risk.'

And so they were the ones who christened it Operation Pedro Pan. The newspaper reporters really sat on the story for a year and a half in Miami. And then one day I got a call from our agency in Cleveland. And they said, 'We got a problem. This reporter wants to know all about the Cuban Children's Programme.' And I said, 'Well, refer him to me in Miami.' So he called me and I said, 'How did you know about the Cuban Children's Programme?' 'Well,' he said, 'my next-door neighbour is a foster home for Catholic Charities and these Cuban kids show up so I'm interested.' So, I said, 'Well, this is the story, and all of the international press and the national press and the local press in Miami know about it and have known about it for a year and a half, and so I'm telling you the story and asking you to maintain confidence for the sake of the children and their families in Cuba.' But he said, 'I'll have to take it up with my editors.' I said, 'I understand that, but I'm telling you what we are asking.' The editor said no, that the American people have a right to know, even if it sacrifices the kids or their families.

So, I called Senator Ribicoff, and of course he was the one we were dealing with on the care of children, and so we decided that we weren't going to let [the newspaper] have its scoop. So, he held a press conference in Washington and I held one in Miami and we released the story ourselves. No change in Cuba. The kids continued to come out for about four months more until the Missile Crisis. That was when the news got out . . . We had the nephew of President Dorticós among our kids.* We had the children of the Cuban ambassador in the Netherlands. He made sure his kids were in Miami through Pedro Pan before he and his wife defected in the Netherlands. There are many stories like that.

Of course, the story of the Cuban Revolution is the story of divided families, you know, divided loyalties. It was true then just as it's true today.

But, you know, it was very clearly a phenomenon of the times . . . Probably it would never be repeatable in quite the same circumstances. I mean, my real admiration always was for the parents who remained in Cuba when they sent their kids here. Because in those days in Cuba sending your kids to the United States was just the same as nailing an American flag to your front door. And you certainly invited the hostility of many of the neighbours, Committees for the Defence of the Revolution, you know, all this sort of thing. I heard many stories about that. And they knew it when they were doing it.

I baptised the child of one of the boys who lived with me down in Twenty-first Street in the 1960s, Eugenio Gayol, and he was looking at his kids and he says, 'I don't know how our parents were able to send us here. I'm glad they did but,' he says, 'I don't think I could do it with my kid.' And I said, 'I don't think you can do it because you don't know. You're not living in the

---

* Osvaldo Dorticós was President of Cuba from 1959 to 1976.

circumstances they were living in. You're not living with your fears, real or imagined.' And I said, 'They had known want.'

Because Cuba was very close to Spain. During the Spanish Civil War a lot of kids were sent to Russia. And that was a great fear in Cuba – kids being sent to Russia. And when Fidel sent Fidelito to Russia in 1960*, that sent waves of fear through families in Cuba. It may not have had a basis in reality, but the fear was real and as a result people were suffering. And they were willing to make extraordinary sacrifices. And we simply were a means to help them. But a great many people would not have gotten out of Cuba because they would never have anybody to claim them in the United States if the children hadn't come. Because, you see, in 1961 and 1962, after the embassy closed, the United States continued to recognise an old visa. Say you had a visa from 1958, that you came to Miami on your honeymoon and the visa was still in the passport, even though it was no longer valid the United States told the airlines they'd accept it.

Visa waivers were given for people, you know, who were in the underground, those sort of people. But the average Cuban, who had never been in the United States, had no hopes of getting out of Cuba, no matter how anti-Castro he was, except in a small boat.

And that's why, for the first twenty years, a very limited section of the Cuban population was able to exercise the choice of going to the US – namely, those who had previously visited the United States on a visa, or people who could be claimed by relatives in the United States when the 'freedom flights' started. So, what opened up on a general scale, relatively small compared to the whole Cuban population, but nevertheless . . . were the children coming. This government said, 'Well, the children are here, we'll give priority to their parents.' And, of course, they came and were a major part of the first six months of the airlift. The 'freedom flights' got under way from 1965 to 1972 because a Cuban in the United States could claim their relatives. So, you had a Cuban boy in the United

---

* Biographies of Fidel Castro do not support this. Fidelito was eleven at the time. He went to school and university in Cuba and then to the Soviet Union to study nuclear physics.

States, fourteen years old, and he claims his parents, his brothers and sisters. Sometimes his grandparents. As soon as his parents got here, they claimed their brothers and sisters and that's the way we estimate possibly as much as 250,000 came out of those.

Now in Mariel it was different. Mariel, of course, was a free-for-all, although 50 per cent of Mariel were relatives of people that were already here. It was the first time that there really was a free-for-all . . .

So, when Cubans get emotional about Pedro Pan and the rest of it, this is part of the reason: many of them know that they're here indirectly because of Pedro Pan. And that's been the story.

And did any of the Pedro Pan children resent what happened?

We got one kid whose family here, his brothers, are very anti-Castro and have always been. His parents were. But this kid was the youngest of three boys, I think. He was raised by an uncle who was a communist. You know, the extended Cuban family. So, the three boys were sent here and this kid came with them. He ended up living with me on Twenty-first Street and he was a nice kid, I always liked him very much, though you try not to have favourites among the kids. His parents came out [to the US] and he left and went with his parents. He used to come around to see me constantly, constantly. And, you know, from the day he arrived in the house, the house parents said, 'He's a communist. He's been indoctrinated.' He would call them reactionaries (*laughs*) when the house parents would tell him what to do, this sort of thing. He had all the slogans and everything else. He was about twelve when he came to us. And his parents came when he was about fourteen or fifteen. He dropped out of high school, spent all his time in the library reading. And one night he was in my room and I was working and he was looking at some of my books and papers, you know, and he picked up a copy of *Granma*,* you know . . . 'Monsignor, you get this?' I said, 'Sure. I gotta know what's going on.' A friend of mine at one of the embassies used to send it to me every week. His eyes were popping, you know,

---

* The daily organ of the Communist Party of Cuba.

the Monsignor was reading this communist newspaper from Cuba. So, one night he came in to see me and he says, 'I've got news for you.' He was twenty-one. 'What is it?' 'I'm going back to Cuba.' I said, 'Well, I'm not surprised.' And he says, 'I feel I belong in Cuba.' 'How do your mother and father feel about it?' 'Well,' he says, 'they're not happy.' I said, 'Well, you know what you want.' And (*sighs*) he says, 'You know,' he says, 'I'm a member of the Communist Party of the USA.' So, I said, 'I'm not surprised.' He said, 'You knew that?' I said, 'I've been listening to you talk.' So anyway, he was very affectionate when he said goodbye. And he went back to Cuba. His family were very upset. He was given quite a welcome as you can imagine. He married. He lives in his family's old house. He went to university for a while and I forget what job he has now. But he calls his mother. His father is dead now. He calls his mother about every two weeks. And I advised the family, 'Keep contact. You haven't heard the end of this. But, you know, he made his choice and I think, you know, we just have to live with it.'

So, when his father was old and very ill, one of his brothers came to me and said, 'My father would like to see our brother in Cuba but he can't get permission to come to the United States.' 'Well,' I said, 'I can understand why. You know, Uncle Sam has a long memory.' So anyway, I made a few contacts in Washington and succeeded in getting him special permission to come here for ten days to see his father.

So, he came. His wife and kids remained in Cuba. But he came about three years ago, four years ago, and he saw his father before he died. And we had a couple of long chats.

You know, he was no longer twenty-one years old. He was the father of two or three kids and, you know, this sort of thing. And he didn't express any regrets – he wasn't bubbling over with enthusiasm, but he was ready to continue to live with his decision. You know, he felt that work was to be done in Cuba, the Cuban people had to be helped and he was doing his part. I respected that. And, of course, he went back. So, through his family I still hear from him, he still calls his mother. He's, what? He was twelve in 1962, so he was born about 1950, that leaves, eh . . . thirty-nine now. And that's one of a thousand and one stories.

24

Andrés Gómez

Andrés Gómez is the editor of Areíto *magazine, so named after the epic oral tradition, which also involved dance, of the indigenous peoples of Cuba. The magazine covers topics about, or of interest to, the Cuban community in the US. It also features articles on Cuba, Latin America and minorities in the US. Andrés is advisor to the National Committee of the Antonio Maceo Brigade, which organises visits to Cuba for the (now adult) children of early exiles. He left Cuba as a child and now lives in Miami. He explains how he came to support the Cuban Revolution and speaks of his political involvement in the country now. He is forty-one.*

20 April 1989

We were a middle-class family as it is understood in Cuba. My family had a business. My father and my grandfather had a car-sales business although most of the family income was from rent. They owned buildings and they lived off the rent from those apartment buildings. That was the family's main source of income.

There were three of us children. I'm the eldest and I have two sisters; my father, mother, grandfather – that was the family. I went to the De Salle schools of the bourgeoisie and then to a military academy because I needed more discipline (*laughs*) – they always said I was a very undisciplined child and that I disrupted classes and never paid attention. So in this military

239

academy, which was the Havana Military Academy, they had smaller classes and more discipline and this would supposedly discipline me.

My parents weren't political people, neither were my grandparents, but I did have an uncle by marriage to whom I was close from an early age, and he was always involved in politics and had fought in the underground in Havana against Batista. He had been imprisoned. He had been arrested on two occasions, but he was a conservative type and when young was more a member of the Auténtico Party.* He was a lawyer.

That's how I spent my childhood over there. The Revolution came in 1959 and that, of course, affected the economic interests of a whole class, a class to which my family belonged. Immediately – because it happened right at the beginning, in February 1959, when the first laws of urban reform were introduced, which reduced rents by 50 per cent – my family began to suffer all the consequences of the Revolution's economic reforms. So, understandably, from that time on, the sympathy felt for the Revolution in the first six weeks (*laughs*) disappeared almost completely. (*Hoots*) And then, a few months later, comes another law which strictly regulates loans, and that again affects them because the loans granted for car purchases were then also hit, and so their second source of income was affected. So all their sources of income began to dry up.

. . . My uncle was already plotting against the revolutionary government by the middle of 1959. My parents never took part in that, and neither did my grandparents, but as they helped my uncle in certain ways, to hide certain things in the house, there was an atmosphere of . . . resistance. There was a huge sense of opposition to this unimaginable situation, because in 1958 in Cuba nobody could have imagined that Cuba would fall victim, from the point of view of the bourgeois class, to a communist revolution. That was completely inconceivable. And when it began to happen

---

* It took its roots from José Martí's Cuban Revolutionary Party and was founded in 1933 by Ramón Grau San Martín. The Auténtico Party was in theory a populist party along liberal–democratic lines. In practice, those values were forgotten in a move to the right and through flagrant corruption.

it was like hell for them. I imagine in the beginning they thought the government would be brought down, that they always had enough power to impose their position and that the United States would never allow it to happen. But the more time passed, the more the revolutionary government could do and the less they could, and that's when panic set in. Panic.

I imagine that at the beginning of 1960 the bourgeois class realised they had lost power and that's what caused the great panic. And one of its consequences was the decision to leave the country. This left the responsibility for bringing down the Revolution in the hands of a foreign government, the government of the United States. As for their capacity or potential to resist, at that stage it was almost non-existent although there were a lot of counter-revolutionary groups being set up. These in fact did do a lot of damage to the Revolution, they did cause trouble, but from their own point of view they knew they had lost that war. To protect themselves they had to organise everything for the fight, and part of that organisation included protecting the family. And this they could no longer do in Cuba; they had to get the family out.

They never thought they were going to be more than a few months out of the country. They actually thought we would be back in Cuba by the summer of 1961. And we were gravely mistaken, because in April of 1961, exactly twenty-eight years ago yesterday, the Bay of Pigs invasion was defeated, and if plans had actually been carried out there would have been a direct North American military intervention, and under those circumstances it would have been very difficult for the Revolution to survive as it has.

My aunts and uncles left first. My grandparents left and then we left. Without our parents. My mother came a month later and my father came after the failure of the Bay of Pigs invasion. My father came in May 1961 via Jamaica. He didn't want to leave while he still had something in the country. My father was very bourgeois, the sort who enjoyed the wealth of the bourgeoisie, not someone who created that wealth. He was the last of the family to leave. The last. Because he wanted to hold on to the house, at least. He didn't want to give up all that because he couldn't cope with the

241

idea of having to work in an ordinary job. And it caused him a lot of psychological problems, to the extent that he died in 1964 in Miami at the age of thirty-eight. He died of a heart attack. Three years after getting here, he died. My mother and father had married very young. He was nineteen and my mother was seventeen when they married. And that's the way my father was, quite the opposite, in fact, to my grandfather, who was always a very active man – trying to set up a business, hard-working, a man who worked very hard. When my grandfather came here he first tried to set up a second-hand car dealers' business with the money he'd brought. That worked for a while but it didn't really bring in that much money. Then, with my older uncle-by-marriage, a man his own age, he began decorating houses. So they painted houses and then, for many years, he was a gardener. And he never had any complexes about the fact that he was now a gardener and once had been a rich man. He saw it as part of life, and while he could look after the children, and while his family was happy and everyone healthy, that was the main thing.

My family was always very protective. Education was a priority. They always put themselves out, every one of them, so that the situation would least affect us. And what they did, they did thinking they were doing the right thing; that they were protecting us. And when the time eventually came, when I grew up and changed and began thinking the way I do now, there was opposition on their part and there was a problem about it, but it never got to the stage where I broke with them. The bond has remained. There were tensions, there was a time when I just didn't want to see them, but that's also part of being young. That just increased the strain, but the family bond was never broken. They never denied me help when I asked for it and I never denied them help when they asked me. All that madness of that time – the end of the 1960s, beginning of the 1970s – I don't blame my family for any of that. On the contrary, the poor devils, they went through a lot. They went through a lot and they are still suffering a lot.

It's a pretty terrible experience because in most cases, those who emigrate for economic reasons – unless they have some intolerable situation but don't actually want to leave the country – are forced to go, but they really love the country. However, in the case of

Cuba, most of the people were the sort who aspired to something else in life which the country could not give them. They aspired to material wealth, nothing else. That was their purpose, that was the reason for their decision. Even if it meant living in the North Pole. But in the case of people who didn't leave the country for those reasons, but because there was a radical revolutionary process in progress, as was the case in Cuba, and they were the opposition, they really didn't want to leave the country. They miss Cuba. They miss it, of course, for class reasons as well; for the way they lived there. It was an uprooting, a profound uprooting of a whole way of life, and the loss of it in a very sudden, quick and absolute way. A whole world fell apart completely. It was a total destruction, and that affects people in a fundamental way and causes enormous sadness. A sadness which time has helped to dissipate, but the first fifteen years were terribly painful. Terribly painful.

And my family suffered this. And they also suffered because they found themselves in dreadful economic straits. My mother, who had never worked – she was only thirty-odd, a young woman – she had to begin working the early-morning shift in a bakery earning $45 a week, when the small house we had with two bedrooms cost $80 or $90. So you couldn't live on her wages. My father had to leave Miami to work up north because it paid better. In New Jersey. On top of it all my father and mother separated. Really the change was (*laughs*) . . . my mother saw her opportunity and said, I'm off, I'm off (*hoots*). So for my father it was . . . well, he lost everything, the poor devil. They never actually got divorced, which meant my mother didn't remarry until 1971 or 1972, when we were all adults. (*Hoots*) She didn't dare marry when we were still adolescents because I think we wouldn't have allowed her. (*Hoots*) The poor thing. Through machismo. On my part and on the part of my sisters as well.

I went to school here. I remember it all perfectly. Then I went on to high school near Coral Gables and after that I went to university. I don't think I was a good student but I got good marks. I went to Miami Dade to a junior college and then I went on to the University of Miami. Because my old lady worked in the university it was free, through some arrangement they had:

the children of the workers could study there and, depending on years of service, they reduced the fees by 50, 75 or 100 per cent. So with that and the loan the North American government gave Cuban students, they didn't have to work and could be full-time students.

I studied history. I specialised in Cuban history, that was my specialisation. I got my BA in 1969. Then in subsequent years I studied for a doctorate in the same subject, but in the end I had to leave, in 1979, ten years ago, for security reasons. Because I studied at the Higher Institute of International Studies of the University of Miami, and as you know all those institutes are information centres. They are research and information centres. There were information, security and intelligence officials of the army, even of the Pentagon and NASA at that institute, because they gave a lot of money to those organisations for the intelligence services they can provide. That's not new, and even people connected to the extreme right went there, and they knew me. My views were known and that was around the time they murdered Carlitos Muñiz in Puerto Rico.★ So, what happens? Well, time passed, I graduated and all that and I went to Spain because I became radical around 1969–70.

How was that?

I imagine it's because I've been crazy since I was born. (*Hoots*) No? I think a lot has to do with an individual's personal circumstances and their ability to see things, and how they process that information. I have an uncle whom I mentioned before, an uncle-by-marriage whom I always loved, and who was like a second father to me. My father figure is in three parts – my father, my grandfather and my uncle. And [my uncle] was very interested in history. With time he became a fascist. A real fascist. I mean along European lines. But my uncle was very anti-Yankee. In his family his father had fought in the War of Independence, although

★ Carlos Muñiz set up in Puerto Rico the first travel agency taking Cubans to Cuba. He was on the Antonio Máceo Brigade National Committee and was an active supporter of Puerto Rican independence. He was murdered on 28 April 1979. See p.249.

he had been a Liberal Party MP and a follower of Machado at one point. An important *machadista*, his father. And so in terms of class position he was completely bourgeois . . . he believed in the inalienable rights of the bourgeoisie, but as a Cuban he was extremely anti-Yankee. And that's what he inculcated in me, too. Respect for the needs of one's country. What changed was that he interpreted those needs in one way and I, with time, interpreted them in another way. The explanations they gave me about why what happened in Cuba happened didn't satisfy me. They didn't satisfy me intellectually or emotionally. So then I began to think for myself and go beyond what they had inculcated. And part of that process was developing a whole understanding of what Cuba was and why what had happened did so, and what my response should be to this situation as I understood it.

And I also lived in this country in the 1960s. That's to say, I wasn't living in a capsule. I was living in Miami but also in the United States. I knew what was going on in Latin America and afterwards in Vietnam; what was happening here with North American blacks – all that began shaping my ideas, which in the beginning were liberal, that was the first change, and then with the assassination of the first Kennedy, the second Kennedy, the liberal option, well . . . the shock of Vietnam, coming up against the realities of the country, the needs of the world, there seemed to be no real alternative. I got over that and became more radical politically.

Here in Miami very few of us thought like that. I always had a lot of Cuban friends. Really, we were very lucky in that . . . we never lost our language, we never lost the relationships we had. My friends in Cuba are still my friends here because a whole sector moved *en masse*. So the friends that met up at the beginning of November in Havana were meeting up here in Miami in February of 1961. The only thing was, we went to different schools because we now lived in different parts of the city. But we met up every weekend. And that went on for years. Years. Until we started making other friends.

Then comes 1972, which was an important year, the 1972 elections when the political conventions are held here in Miami. This is where Richard Nixon was nominated President. So there was a plan to hold demonstrations against the war. So what was then the high command of the American left was mobilised to Miami. Abbie Hoffman,* who died two days ago, came. He spoke at the University of Miami, and we went along. I went with two other friends, and as he was speaking about poverty a Cuban got up, an architectural student, and asked what was for them the burning question of the day, about supporting the Vietcong if the Vietcong and North Vietnam received aid from the Soviet Union and from the Chinese when the US was opening up to China as well. So then Abbie Hoffman tried to give a more or less logical answer and the Cuban, of course, didn't understand the logical reply, and then Abbie Hoffman says, 'Well, what are they supposed to do? Who can they seek help from?' No? If the United States is bombing them and the only ones willing to help them are the Soviets and the Chinese, let them get their aid from the Soviets and the Chinese. So then [the Cuban] says, 'No. You say that because you don't know what communism is.' And then [Hoffman] says, 'How do you mean we don't know . . .?' And then [the Cuban] says, 'I do know what communism is like because I'm Cuban.' That was the end of the discussion. Normally everybody kept their trap shut, but that day I got up. I said to him, 'You don't know what you are talking about because if I were a Vietnamese I would get help from the devil. What would I care where it came from?' Then he says, 'You don't know either,' because he thought I was a North American. So then I says, 'I'm Cuban too, lad, and I don't see things the way you do.' So we went for each other. (*Laughs*) We didn't kill ourselves that day because some Americans (*helpless with laughter*) intervened. They held the others back. They didn't have to hold us back, but they thought we wanted a fight. You'd want to be mad, suicidal, to start that up.

So after that meeting we decided to collaborate with the groups who organised demonstrations here in a park at Miami Beach, and that's when we really got going. A group of us Cuban

* Radical US activist and spokesperson for the counter-culture of the 1960s. He participated in the civil rights movement of the time and staged absurdist antics to demonstrate the evils of the Vietnam War. In 1968 he founded the anarchist Youth International Party aka the Yippies.

friends organised the first showing of Cuban films in Miami. And they were screened in that park with all the demonstrators. They slept there and everything. We also had an exhibition of Cuban posters, and in the evening we screened the first Cuban documentaries seen in Miami. That was in the summer of 1972. The first film we showed in Miami was *79th Spring*, about Ho Chi Minh. And we set up a group. We called ourselves something but I don't remember the name we chose, and from then on we took a public position in support of the Revolution. We went on marches with the Cuban flag with 'UP THE CUBAN REVOLUTION' on it, [and] there was an incident with some old Cubans, but when they saw the number of people there were, they withdrew. They shouted things at us and we shouted back. That was in summer 1972, in July and August.

From there, in the same year, a group of us went to Puerto Rico. What we thought was that Puerto Rico would be more suited to us and that we could also help out in the independence movement there. I went to Puerto Rico in November 1972, and there was already a group of ten or twelve of us out there. I stayed in Puerto Rico until 1976. In 1974, the idea for *Areíto* magazine arose out of that group and another group of people in New York, and so we set up a management committee and the magazine began publication. In the beginning it was published in Miami, the first two issues I think, and then afterwards, for security reasons, we had to go up north, and it was published in New York from 1974 to 1985.

I didn't contribute to the magazine in that first phase while I was in Puerto Rico. I was in touch with all those involved and helped out in what way I could, but I didn't write in the magazine. I honestly thought that I couldn't write and so I didn't. Never.

Then I came back to Miami. The idea for the Brigade came in 1977, the first contingent of the Antonio Maceo Brigade, in December 1977. It was the first time I was able to get back to Cuba since leaving in 1960. The idea for the Brigade arose out of the same group involved in *Areíto* magazine, and many of us were in contact with Cuban officials and diplomats in the United States and other countries, telling them that we wanted to go back to Cuba at least for a visit. Then the Cuban government considered the matter for a good while and from that some of us, I was not among them, went back on a personal visit before the first visit by the contingent, but not as a group. So the idea was accepted by the Cuban government in 1977, and they asked us how we thought it could be organised. So we thought the best way would be to organise a group and from that group idea emerged the need to set up an organisation, and we chose the name the Antonio Maceo Brigade. And the people who comprised that first group were people who had kept in constant touch from the word go, as I told you earlier, and who were living in different parts of the country. Some had worked on the magazine, contributing or getting it out, others had simply been in contact; they had been involved as friends, as *compañeros*. And out of that group of people came the fifty-five who were chosen to go on that first contingent.

The organisation took shape in Cuba, during the trip, really. We chose a director on the trip and most people committed themselves to following the work through when they got back to the United States or to Puerto Rico. When we got back, I was a member of the executive of the group here in Miami, and there were about twelve of us at the time here in Miami. So we began to do work for the Revolution, for Cuba. We gave interviews about the trip, we gave talks about it, we gave slide-shows to interested youngsters, we gave talks in the university and contributed in whatever way possible at the time for the normalisation of relations between Cuba and the United States. A year later, as a result of this, the talks which led to some agreement between representatives of the community took place in Havana. Among the accords reached is the freeing of political prisoners and permission for them and their families to leave the country if they wished. They began leaving in 1979.

It was a productive time in relations between both countries. It was the Carter administration. We in the Brigade and in *Areíto*, the most radical sector of the movement in favour of normalisation, were the ones who got the necessary funds – through organisations in the United States – to get the planes which took the prisoners and their families out of Cuba. After the November and December meetings in Havana a committee was set up called the Committee of 75, which was charged with promoting the Dialogue and implementing the agreements reached in Havana. It was directed at the time by Albor Ruiz, who played a very important part over all those years on the magazine and later on the Committee of 75. He was executive director of the Committee. The president was a Protestant minister by the name of Reyes, a Cuban.

And then that was a difficult time after 1978. In 1979 the problems begin, and in April comes the murder of Carlos Muñiz. Carlos Muñiz was a member of the national committee of the Antonio Maceo Brigade, a very valuable member for us, a young man. He was twenty-six when it happened. He opened the first travel agency taking Cubans to Cuba in San Juan, Puerto Rico. The first Cubans who left the country after 1959, who went back thanks to the Dialogue – thanks to the opening which came with the Dialogue – were Cubans from Puerto Rico which Carlos's agency carried. Carlitos was in a very public and vulnerable situation and, besides, in Puerto Rico he had been a militant supporter of independence – he joined us through the Puerto Rican trade-union movement and the Puerto Rican independence process, despite his youth.

He was from Matanzas, from Colón, and he left the country at the same time I did, but his family went to live in Puerto Rico. He was younger than I was. But he was very mature politically. And very active. He was involved in everything and he was very effective politically. And that was the part he played in the Brigade at that time. I imagine . . . the right in Puerto Rico targeted him. The Cuban right in Puerto Rico. And we now know, the authorities have this information, that a right-wing Cuban . . . who is later involved in other political murders [was responsible]. A lot of money was paid out for the assassination of Carlos, and on 28 April 1979, as he was going to his mother's there in Puerto Rico – he was married but separated at the time – he was going to his old lady's to fetch the kids and they killed him. They shot him from car to car. He was alone and they fired three shots, one of them to the head, and they killed him instantly. Then they shot him again. They were such cowards that after they killed him they got out of their car and shot him again on the spot. The authorities have never yet accused anybody of Carlos's murder. That's ten years ago. And that strengthened our resolve in the work we had to do.

So, at the beginning of 1979, I began co-ordinating the Brigade here in Miami. And we had a big group, a good group, for a long time. Then came the Mariel boat lift, and that together with the murder of Carlos began to have repercussions on the number of people who wanted to take part in the process of dialogue. This coincided with a cooling of relations between the governments of North America and Cuba, and in March 1979 comes the revolution in Grenada and in July of the same year the revolution in Nicaragua. The problem of Angola is brewing and the problem of Ethiopia is on the go. This causes a cooling of relations between Washington and Havana, it affects the climate in Miami. The murder triggers a series of terrorist attacks and threats, and people begin to stop getting involved, and the only ones really left were those of us who started it up and a few others. And then in February 1980 the Reverend Manuel Espinosa, who had promoted the Dialogue for a long time, does an about-face and denounces the Dialogue and denounces those involved in the Dialogue as agents of the Cuban government, and that went out all over the world. (*Laughs*) His involvement proved disastrous. He ended up publicly accusing everyone of being agents. Everyone. And for those of us who were used to being accused of being agents it went in here and out there (*pointing to his ears*), but those who weren't used to it, who were suddenly accused of being Cuban intelligence agents, and who were afraid for their jobs – well, you can imagine. Imagine Miami at that moment.

And then in April, to put the tin hat on it, came the Mariel boat lift. That was like the hurricane of 1926. It left us (*shaking with mirth*) with nothing left standing. That was the lowest point . . . well, the lowest point was in May 1985, when the trips were cancelled.* Because everything hadn't collapsed here yet. There were still the trips and the exchanges and it could tick over. But Radio Martí finished everything off and we had to start from scratch.

* These events were severe ideological blows to the Brigade's efforts and the fostering of good relations between Cuba and the US.

So, I have to get out of Miami in 1981 for security reasons and I lived in New York for four years from 1981 to 1985. The Brigade continued on here and I maintained contact and was a member of the national committee anyhow, although I wasn't the Miami area co-ordinator.

Then in 1985 I came back to Miami in March and there was a debate with Felipe Rivero. Felipe Rivero was the head of the Cuban Nationalist Movement, a fascist group. My uncle was the number two in that group, the uncle I have spoken about. And that was a terrorist organisation which had the idea of mounting a campaign against the Cuban government called 'La Guerra por los Caminos del Mundo'. Really 'La Guerra por los Caminos del Mundo' was a terrorist campaign against Cuban officials outside Cuba or against Cuban targets outside Cuba. Since they could no longer wage war in Cuba they had to do so throughout the world, outside Cuba. But it wasn't an indiscriminate terrorist campaign. It was a terrorist campaign which had very defined and very limited targets. So they never got around to killing anyone, they remained more or less symbolic. They planted bombs all right, but it was really more a question of promoting a whole ideological campaign through terrorism. And these people sold themselves to the Americans for many years. When they announced in 1967 that they were going to bomb the Cuban pavilion at Montreal during Expo 67, the Canadian government put pressure on the North American government to arrest the leaders of the group. (*Laughs*) So they arrested Felipe Rivero and held him for six months. Here, without charging him. As a result of their imprisoning Felipe Rivero a strike was called, and it was the only time – note – May 1967 was the only time there was a large collective action on the part of the exiled community. They went on a one-day strike. Cubans didn't turn up for work for a day and Miami ground to a halt. The Americans went hysterical. They couldn't believe what was happening and they attacked with all they had. Many Cuban workers lost their jobs because they couldn't take the day off. Many took the day off sick and others let it go. But a lot of people lost their jobs and afterwards there were committees set up to find work for all those people. There were hundreds of them without work. It was very interesting that they managed to mobilise that number of people in Miami. Afterwards [members of] that group became the basis for Omega 7.*

Omega 7 and Alpha 66 were all Cubans?

Cubans. Alpha 66 is really a phantom organisation. Alpha 66 comprises four mummies and that's it.† And Alpha 66 engaged in paramilitary activities in Cuba, while the Nationalist Movement worked outside the United States and outside Cuba. Later [the Nationalist Movement] degenerated into Omega 7 and Bosch's people, who are called Poder Cubano, began to operate within the United States.‡ There was a group in the early 1970s who said that before waging war on Fidel Castro they had to clean up the exile community. Imagine it. Everyone got an awful fright. (*Laughs*)

(*Speaks in English for a while*) OK, in April 1985 I came back to Miami and it was possible to arrange a radio debate between Felipe Rivero and myself. It was the first time there was a debate with any of us from the Brigade or *Areíto* in Miami on radio or on TV. And Felipe had the guts to come forward and say that he would do it. Anybody else really would have been accused of collaborating with the Cuban government for allowing us to participate in a radio programme. And it was on two different days – one on the Monday, one on the Wednesday. And the first day we caught everybody by surprise. And although the *Herald* was there, there were few other news media. But the second day everybody was there, including the national press. And it was a big deal and the most listened-to radio programme that year in Miami. (*Switches back to Spanish*) It was in Eighth Street and Twenty-second Avenue right in the centre. And it was interesting because really it demonstrated that the public was very interested in hearing views different from those discussed in the community

---

* A Cuban-exile terrorist organisation working inside and outside the US.
† In April 1990 Alpha 66 began training again.
‡ Orlando Bosch was behind the 1976 Cubana airline bomb over Barbados which killed seventy-three people, including the Cuban Junior National fencing team.

up to then. There is still very tight control of the mass media by the right, and they do not allow discussion. The best you'll get in that context are liberals. But they won't give us any access to discussion programmes. Either the advertisers are pressured or it's the owners, because they are people who are members of the Foundation.* Because economic interests and political interests are intertwined. In fact, the political function of the Foundation is the control of Miami. That's their main task.

So this debate was very important. There have been very few. For instance, I have debated with the Mayor of Hialeah, who is an important political figure in Cuban politics because he's the only member of the Democratic Party who is still voted in, and Hialeah is the second largest city of the county, and 85 per cent of Hialeah is Cuban. So those debates with Felipe made us realise that I should return to Miami and that we should have more follow-up to our political work in Miami. So I come back to Miami in the summer of 1985 and I've been here ever since.

In 1985 it was decided to take another look at *Areíto*. Publication was suspended. Really, there was a reassessment of the objectives of the magazine. At the very beginning the magazine was directed towards all the community. Afterwards, due to resources, it was decided that it was better to limit the direction of the magazine to influencing academic sectors, because those were the sectors that were going to have most influence in terms of North American policy towards Cuba. But in the long run it meant that the magazine had an ever-diminishing circulation and that the people on the team producing the magazine over all that time got burnt out. So we were looking at that problem and reached the conclusion that it should be brought out in Miami. That was a year later in 1986. We spent a year trying to get funds and seeing how we could do it, and then in the summer of 1987 the magazine came out for the first time in its second phase and we decided that the work of the magazine should be a work of political debate covering the most interesting topics, the subjects that would most interest, and treating them in a way that people would understand. We decided,

* The Cuban American National Foundation is a right-wing lobby of wealthy businessmen headed by Jorge Mas Canosa. See pp.272–5.

with the money we had, that we should publish four times a year – something we have yet to do – and distribute it. They prevent us from selling it in Miami. Well, no one will distribute it and no shop will sell it. They are afraid. So we distribute it free, house to house, or we give it out in shopping centres on Saturdays and Sundays. So, economically, it's money we have to get together which will not return any profit. But that's the way it is, you know, it's a political project and that's the object of the magazine. And there is interest in the magazine and it annoys people. It annoys them to an extraordinary degree. They are always asking where the money comes from. The only one who works at it full time is me; the others who help out have their work and I don't take a salary at the moment. There are several friends who donate sufficient money to cover my expenses. (*Laughs*)

There has been a change in these years . . .

There has been a change, and really the press has managed to stifle it. There has been a change on the part of the people in the Cuban community in Miami *vis-à-vis* Cuba and travel to Cuba. For some months now it is clear that people are losing their fear of speaking up about travel to Cuba. For a long time there was a lot of fear. The year 1985 was very bad, when travel was suspended and everything was set at nought. The trips were reinstated in 1986 and the whole migration policy was restructured by the Cuban government. And I think that was very salutary, because they had to get away from a lot of the crap that existed before. And there's still a lot of crap, and that has negative repercussions for people wanting to meet up because it limits . . . who they can meet. Like, they can meet people from the left, which is ourselves, who are not corrupt; or they can meet people who are nothing politically but who are corrupt. Really, there is still no middle ground which consistently and publicly favours relations. Which is what we have tried to create, because we see ourselves as having to create the conditions for this to happen. We are establishing bases so that the people lose their fear of participation and dare to speak out. Now there is a families' committee which is in favour of relations. This committee held a breakfast a few months ago in a central city hotel. A thousand-odd people attended and they had money to boot. I think Marazul was sponsoring it.* So [Msgr Brian] Walsh went along, he was for relations and trips; he spoke at the breakfast, and within the community there was a division between the more moderate sectors and the more intransigent positions on matters which affected them here. For example, there's a huge problem with the Cuban Museum of Art and Culture, which is a very small museum. [There is a] wrangle over the pictures by painters who live in Cuba, which the museum wanted to exhibit.† What happened was the right wanted to create a scandal about it, but the result was a rupture between the moderates and the intransigents. It's for that sort of thing: the right proclaims itself dictator of what can and what cannot be done. And there are other people, also people with a lot of money now, who are not prepared to be ordered about and told what to think. That wouldn't have been possible five years ago because that moderate sector would have kept its mouth shut and would have accepted it. The fact that they have dared to speak up and oppose intransigent positions is a good indication of the change.

Now, this moderate sector is anti-communist. It is also counter-revolutionary. It might be for better relations with Cuba. It might also be that they are under pressure in the present political climate and have to say things which actually do not accurately reflect moderate positions, but they have to resort to anti-communism to protect themselves. But they are still counter-revolutionaries. They may be all for better relations, for travel, but they are nevertheless counter-revolutionaries.

Then there is that very important element – the people who came with the Mariel boat lift. The people who left via Mariel, which is

---

* Marazul Charters Inc. is the agency which runs flights to Cuba.
† A picture by one of Cuba's foremost living artists, Manuel Mendive, had been bought by a right-winger who immediately destroyed it by setting it alight. The museum has also been bombed. The right objects to it promoting in any way works by artists living in Cuba, even when they are by dissidents. Mendive is not a dissident.

a huge number, some 120,000 on top of those who have since left, which is another few thousand, they are mainly in Miami. If they went north, they came back. And these people do want to go back to visit Cuba because they have family there who matter to them. The right, those in control here, who came over thirty years ago, don't have family in Cuba. And if they do they couldn't care less about them. That's why they can now adopt these positions of distancing themselves from Cuba. But those who have family there – they don't want anything bad to happen to Cuba. It's a human question, a personal issue. And up to now they have been afraid to speak out because they have always been treated here like second-class citizens. They have always been discriminated against. But now they have their residency or their American citizenship. They have a fair amount of economic security and after nine years they are fed up with being told how to think and what to do and with being abused when spoken to. They are contesting all that now, and in the lastest Gallup polls for Johns Hopkins, and also other surveys conducted here in Miami for the *Herald* by Florida International University, it showed that around 60 per cent of the community favours travel to Cuba. Around 40 per cent was in favour of establishing relations. Almost half. The two surveys coincide in that. Of course, this is not reflected in the Cuban cummunity media. Here the *Nuevo Herald*★ is completely controlled by the right. Completely. It's an autonomous paper which makes its own decisions as to what goes in and what line it takes. Neither the opinion page nor the editorial reflects the editorial line of the English edition. They have the economic power to force the paper to do what they want, or they will simply open another paper. And *El Herald* bowed. We have another newspaper, the *Diario de las Américas*, which is something from beyond the grave, it goes beyond reaction. It's a madness. And then you have all the radio stations controlled by the extreme right, and you have two television channels in Spanish, 23 and 51, whose local news

---

★ The *Miami Herald* and *El Nuevo Herald* are sister papers, produced in English and Spanish respectively. They have very independent editorial lines, with the Spanish edition almost exclusively concerned with Cuban exile affairs and controlled by Cuban exiles.

is controlled by the right. The news is completely against Cuba, against relations, against normalisation, and they are constantly bombarding people with it . . . and the mass media in English simply try to ignore the existence of Cuba and of Cubans and all that. And they reflect nothing about it.

25

Carlos Alberto Montaner

Born in Havana in 1943, Carlos Alberto Montaner is director of Firmas, a press agency based in Madrid, which services the entire Spanish-speaking world. He also has a small publishing company in Madrid, Playor, which publishes the works of dissident Cuban writers. He has written several books on Cuba and two novels, Perromundo *and* Trama.

2 November 1989

My family was middle class. My mother was a teacher and my father a well-known journalist who nevertheless had a low income. So we were a middle, middle-class family.

The interesting thing about us is that Castro was a very good friend of the family. He was a great friend of my father and I met Castro when I was a small boy when he used to come to our house. He once stayed the night. He was with his first wife and with Fidelito, who was a baby at the time. I was always hearing about him because on some occasion he hid in my father's house, because my father belonged to a group called the Revolutionary Insurrectional Union, and the head of action of the group was an uncle of mine called José Jesús Jimjaume Montaner.

So, whenever any of those people committed a political crime – we are talking here about the end of the 1940s, [and] sometimes those political crimes were murders of opposition leaders – they had to go into hiding. And on one occasion Castro had to hide for the attempted assassination of Lionel Gómez, a student leader at the University of Havana. Fortunately, Lionel Gómez didn't die but he was shot. He got one bullet in the stomach and another in the leg. So my family hid him. They hid Castro because he was being hunted. When that business was over my father, my uncle and Castro remained very good friends and I used to see him from time to time. Then I didn't see him again until 1955.

At that stage my parents were separated and my father lived in a Havana hotel. Fidel Castro, who had been in jail for the attack on the Moncada Barracks, got out. He had spent two years in jail and, on getting out, one of the people to hide him, because there was a certain danger, was my father, and so he stayed the night in the Central Hotel in Old Havana. I don't know if that hotel is still there. Anyway, it was in front of the Cinecito in Zulucta Street or thereabouts. I don't remember Havana too well.

Well, my memory in this instance is of having gone into the room looking for my father and of finding Fidel there waiting for a woman, who was his lover at the time. I was struck. I had gone to see my father and I find this man whom I much admired, because he was the idol of all young people after the Moncada attack, and he was a great hero for me. He wasn't in the least interested in talking to me. He just wanted me out fast because this woman was about to arrive. Naturally, she was his lover.

When my brother and I were very young we had to leave Cuba because we got involved in political activities. We were fourteen or fifteen around the time of Batista. Then we came back, and when the Revolution was won we were sympathisers, of course. But we belonged to that Havana middle class and in our case were well informed, thanks to my father being a journalist. I grew up among intellectuals, writers and journalists and both my brother and I were fairly well educated.

I was fifteen at the time of the Revolution and a lot of things happened in 1959. I finished my Baccalaureate at sixteen and I married my wife, Linda. She had been my girlfriend since we were thirteen. We married when we were sixteen and at seventeen we had a daughter. Naturally, I worked. I had begun to work at fourteen. Of course I studied at night. I had finished school and in 1960 I started studying at the university.

By this time there had been a total break with the government. My father had left Cuba in 1959 because somehow he realised that his former friend – they had even met up and embraced – he realised that this was definitive, and he said to me . . . he realised that Cuba was going down the wrong road. So I started up in the university. That's when we began. I began to demonstrate against the government, to protest against it. We began to organise a student strike and we all ended up in jail. I got twenty years. They sentenced a friend of mine, Wilfredo Garrión, to thirty years and then later murdered him in prison. And all we were doing was organising a kids' strike. I was very lucky because as I wasn't yet eighteen they put me in a less rigorous prison and I escaped. I cut through a bar one night. My wife had been able to get out with the child and ten of her brothers and sisters and go to the United States. It was easy at that stage. My mother stayed behind to try and get me asylum in an embassy. Once again age was in my favour. The ambassador took pity when my mother explained that she had a child who wasn't a child but a rather large, very old and very long-haired seventeen-year-old who looked even older. Of course she gave him a line about a young child who was in hiding in Havana and who needed asylum. So the Honduran embassy gave me protection.

When Honduras broke relations in 1961 I went, *eh*, Venezuela put up its flag and I left [Cuba] under Venezuelan protection. In September 1961, the United States broke relations. I spent six or seven months in the [Venezuelan] embassy. And then in the United States we began life by working where everyone else begins – as a waiter, selling encyclopedias, all those small things, but imagining that we would be going back to Cuba very soon. Because the way my group saw it, my generational group, was that the government was very weak and that it was going to fall or there would be a huge conspiracy. That's what we all thought in 1961.

It didn't happen. I began to study at the university. I finished an M.Litt. and I wanted to write. It had been my vocation since I was a child. So then I went to Puerto Rico, where I thought there would be a certain – in 1966 – a certain chance of developing my career as a writer. In Puerto Rico I realised that there was practically only one newspaper, no publishing houses, little interest in literature, and I got very bored teaching medieval literature, one of the things I taught.

So in 1970 – we now had another child who had been born in Puerto Rico – my wife and I decided that the best thing to do was to go to Spain and begin again, because in Spain there were publishers, newspapers, there was a richer intellectual life. We sold the few bits we had and we began again in 1970. I wanted to do a doctorate in philosophy, specialising in literature at Madrid University, and I set up a small publishing company producing text-books to live on while I wrote articles and began to write for the press and to make contacts in the world of journalism. And I began to write another book. And, fortunately, this all turned out well. The publishing company turned into a nice little business – it brings out language text-books, 95 per cent of it is text-books, that's what Playor publishes. We have a small collection of Cuban books which don't sell. I do it out of a personal interest with that part of Cuban history, based a little on the experience of Ruedo Iberico, the publishing company of Spanish exiles in Paris, which didn't sell anything but which was worth the effort because some things had to be published. That was our idea.

There was controversy over a book published by Playor . . .

I received two identical manuscripts; one from Bofill's wife and the other was given me by the Pen Club.* An important figure in the Pen Club [wrote] saying he had received this manuscript from Cuba and was I interested in publishing it. Then Bofill's

---

* Ricardo Bofill now lives in Miami, where he receives a stipend from the Cuban American National Foundation. A founder of the Cuban Committee for Human Rights (CCPDH) within Cuba, he was ultimately exposed as a self-appointed double agent. The plagiarism case is still not resolved. Gabriel García Márquez claims that another writer, José Lorenzo Fuentes, gave him a manuscript of his novel *Brígida pudo soñar*, which he read. Fuentes claims he also gave a copy to Bofill, who then said he lost it. The characters in the book appear in previous works by Fuentes. Playor published the identical manuscript under the title *El tiempo es el diablo*. Fuentes is still working and living in Cuba.

wife told me her husband had written this book . . . I don't have any reason to doubt what she told me and she signed a contract saying that the book was her husband's, and the book was published. When Bofill got out of Cuba I asked him if he had written the book and he said that if it wasn't him, and I have no cause to doubt his word, let the other man who says he wrote it prove it in court. That's all I can say about it.

Well, in Ecuador there's a publisher's called Conejo who published the same novel by another author, José Lorenzo Fuentes. Well, I don't sell books in Ecuador. If Bofill doesn't accept it, let him take an action against Conejo. I'm not going to. I couldn't care less about it. And I have already said the same to the Cubans who wrote to me through a Spanish lawyer. But they never replied . . . I would willingly pay for Mr José Lorenzo Fuentes and his wife to come to Spain and sort out the problem, because that poor devil, José Lorenzo Fuentes, has suffered a lot in Cuba. He's been imprisoned, he has lived in fear for a long time . . . But the Cubans never replied. I was prepared to put up the price of the passage so that they both, not one, not just him, but him and his wife, and if he had children I would pay for them too, so that they could all get out and discuss it with Bofill. And, in passing, if they wanted to stay in Spain, they could.

Anyway. In 1971 I published my first novel, *Perromundo*, in which I recount my experiences in jail and I deal with the phenomenon of political prisoners who are put in the predicament of having to choose between accepting the truth and bounty of the regime in return for getting out, or simply taking refuge in their own stance and never getting out, even dying in jail – becoming a *plantado*.* That seemed like a very interesting dilemma to me ever since I began to see it in jail, although I was there for a very short time. I have written twelve books, novels, two of short stories and the rest essays, and a syndicated column which appears in a series of Spanish, Latin American and American newspapers. It appears in the *Miami Herald* in English and in

---

* The name for those prisoners who, instead of death sentences, received long-term jail sentences at the beginning of the Revolution and who refused to comply with prison regulations. There are two remaining.

Spanish in *El neuvo herald*. In Spain it comes out in *ABC*. I have published in all the Spanish newspapers, but I mostly write for *ABC*.

So, in some way, everything we set out to do, except returning to Cuba, which is something I have also determined to do and which some day I think I will, we have achieved. Really, the only thing we can complain about is the political aspect, which, in our case, well, it will take some time for that government to collapse and for things to change in Cuba. I think it may take a good few years, but I am – at least, I think I am sure that it's a question of time. Because, among other reasons, Cuba can't remain isolated from what is happening in the rest of the socialist world.

For all Castro's shouts of 'Marxism-Leninism or Death', whoever runs a country that is so dependent on the socialist world cannot defy what appears to be a sort of political rule that's in operation, and that is change: change in Hungary, change in Poland, in the Soviet Union, and he cannot control that.

I think that, fortunately, Cuba is heading for a conflict with the Soviet Union. I think one way or the other, the Soviet Union is going to greatly reduce its economic aid to Cuba, its subsidy, which could amount to 30 per cent of the country's gross national product. That is, Castro is going to have to make one of two decisions: either he squeezes tighter and represses more, or he loosens his grip. Common-sense and experience dictates that, when there is no way of solving the critical situation with economic resources, he should loosen his grip and permit open discussion and the search for other solutions. That's what Castro will have to do if he wants to stay on or if he wants Castroism to survive his death. I don't think he's going to do that because he's a very stubborn sort. So, I imagine that he will copy the North Korean model. But that has a limit. The moment of crisis will come. It's inevitable. When the number of unemployed in Cuba, because of the lack of supplies to factories, becomes huge; when the economic squeeze is such that there isn't even enough to cover what's on the ration card; when he dies. He's sixty-three. It's a matter of, I don't know, five years, ten years. In the end all these battles are biological. Franco didn't win the Civil War,

Santiago Carrillo won it.* After they buried Franco he arrived and became part of the power structure and participated in the complete change. That's to say . . . these wars are never over, they are replaced and they change. The possibility of a civil war in Cuba is taking shape. That could also happen. The army could split in the face of a crisis and there'd be a civil war. [And] with the fire power of the Cuban army what might happen could be fairly huge.

What about Miami?

In Miami, as in all exile communities, there's a great diversity of opinion about relations with Cuba. Those who have a lot of links with Cuba, who have family in Cuba, naturally have a very different opinion from those who have nothing there, no friends or family, because they left a long time ago and because all their family is out, and those people can permit themselves the luxury of holding more extreme views. Those who have more connections with Cuba, however anti-Castro they might be, have to see it differently. There's a sort of . . . I wouldn't exactly call it permanent friction there, but there is certainly a diversity of opinion. What seems to be the case, when it boils down to it, is that most Cubans are interested in visiting Cuba, and I think it's a good thing that they should. There's a kind of universal law which indicates that dictatorships soften with information. It happened in Franco's Spain with tourism, the millions of tourists who went there and brought information about what was happening elsewhere, all that contributed to weakening Francoism.

Sometimes I get worked up in the defence of things in which I believe. But the problem is, in my case, I don't see myself as some analyst, as remote from the political process. I can discuss the Mexican Revolution perfectly calmly, the Soviet Revolution, but I am part of the Cuban Revolution, and that part has a right to be passionate. And you can't ask the adversary and the victim to

* Santiago Carrillo is a former General Secretary of the Communist Party of Spain.

264

be impartial in their judgment. When it comes to my friends, my dead friends . . . I left recently married lads in jail, and when they emerged twenty years later, their families were destroyed. Others died in jail, and others were abused in prison for thirty years, and really I have every right in the world to feel passionate about it. As Unamuno said, the last thing a person, a decent person, can lose, is their capacity for indignation. I want to keep that capacity, keep it alive, and ultimately, every analysis of a political process can only lead us to one point – a kind of ethical balance. Because what's the point of talking about health-care in Cuba, about education or about the political process, if in the final analysis we don't say, 'All right, gentlemen, but has this been good or bad for the society that has had to put up with it?' And the definitive ethical judgment requires a scale of values. That scale of values is regulated and governed by passions and emotions and by no means do I wish, nor am I able, to renounce that.

26

René José Silva

René José Silva is area director of the Cuban American National Foundation in Miami. We meet in his office, where he speaks, in English, about being a Cuban in Miami and about the Foundation. René is thirty-four.

24 April 1989

I came to the United States when I was six years old, the day after Christmas 1960, 26 December. I'll never forget it because two things stand out in my mind. One is that we came with more toys than personal belongings because my parents did not want to create the impression that we were actually leaving. And I don't actually think they thought that they were leaving permanently, because they were coming for six months.

And the other thing I remember is coming to Miami. When I got to Miami the first question I asked my mother was, 'Why don't the people at customs here have machine-guns?' which gives you a clear situation of what Cuba was like at the time and still is.

But I came here in 1960. We lived in Miami for six weeks like all Cuban exiles who eventually start through here, and then we went to a town called Levitown, Pennsylvania. We lived there for a year and a half; moved to Philadelphia; lived there for about five years; and then we lived in about four or five different places in New York, in New Jersey, up until 1980 when I actually moved down to Miami.

So, for me living in Miami as a Cuban is very comfortable. It's very important to me to live here. I felt like a fish out of water for many years up in the north. There are some concentrations of Cubans up north – there's west New York, New Jersey, there's a town in New Jersey, Union City, [where] almost the entire population is Cuban. You know, we're talking about 100,000 to 200,000 people, a concentration that's really big. But I didn't grow up there. I lived in an area which was all non-Cuban and I was one of three or four families in that area that were Cuban. And I didn't enjoy that that much. You know, I got along and everything was fine, but in 1980 I made a conscious decision to come here because Cubans lived here.

I feel at home here. This is the second largest Cuban city in the world after Havana and you can literally live here and not speak English if you like. So, you know, it's a very comfortable situation for me. I've been here now almost nine years and I wouldn't want to live anywhere except in a free Cuba, anywhere else, so. I think that kinda says it all about what Miami is for me.

My father was a chemical engineer and he always had an engineering job. He didn't do any manual work or anything like that stuff that some people had to do when they came here. Many doctors worked sweeping floors at the airport and that sort of thing. My father found the job in Pennsylvania, like I mentioned before, so he was an engineer right from day one. But I would say my father didn't speak good English until about twenty years later when he had a situation where he had to go to Oklahoma for an extended period of time to work and he was the only one who spoke Spanish there, so he had no choice but to learn English at that time.

My mother went to high school here in the United States, the Sacred Heart Academy in New York, so she spoke perfect English. Of course, we all grew up speaking Spanish at home and speaking English outside the home, my brothers and sisters. I've two brothers and a sister.

I guess in the sense of my parents demanding we spoke Spanish at home, that they always had a great deal of respect for Cuban culture and so on – in that sense they inculcated me. But I don't think my parents made any special effort beyond what was normal among Cuban families up there.

They made some effort in the beginning, for instance, first to make sure we continued to read in Spanish and write in Spanish. But you know, the people who were teaching us were friends and they didn't have the time to keep it up. They tried to teach us Cuban history in the same way, and they couldn't keep it up. You know, it was a volunteer type of a situation and so we just kind of grew up. I always had an interest in history and politics *per se*, not necessarily with Cuba. Just history and politics in general. In that, when you start studying World War One and World War Two and the development of humanity and the history of civilisation and so on, eventually you ask yourself the question, why have things happened in Cuba like they have? And when you ask yourself that question it becomes a very intriguing study.

And so, almost every young Cuban that I know, both in and out of Miami, who has any sense of history or political understanding, has gone through that process. Not everyone has come to the same conclusions.

That I'm working with the Foundation also is just an extension of that. You know, we have a tyranny in Cuba, we have a dictatorship. We have a situation that is totalitarian in its very nature. And you know the people who control Cuba after Castro are the state security and secret police. And you know that is an intolerable situation for me.

I don't know if I'll go back to live in Cuba some day. I've thought about it often. But even if I don't, I think I would like to have contributed something to the eventual democratisation of Cuba, and that is why I'm doing what I'm doing. Because I could very easily do what most Cubans do in Miami – start a business. (*Laughs*) And I've had many offers to do that. And without sounding overly conceited, I know I could succeed. But I see this almost in a sense as a military service. And until the job gets done and after the job gets done, we'll decide what else we'll do with our lives.

I see a change coming within the next few years. And I think that the people in Miami, the Cuban people in Miami and in the United States in general, the Cuban people in the United States and the United States government have a very important role to play in the reconstruction of the island. Bringing democracy and bringing a degree of pluralism and freedom and rebuilding it economically. That's the role I see in the future.

The change will come from within. Inevitably, regardless of what propaganda from there tells you. The change will come because there's general disaffection within the higher ranks, for the first time within the higher ranks of the Communist Party itself. And we've seen that through all the defections – of General del Pino in Washington and Gustavo Pérez Corto, who used to be in the politburo economic advisory council; Manuel Sánchez Pérez, ex-Vice Minister of Economics; Florentino Azpillaga, ex-security agent in Czechoslovakia in Eastern Europe for the Cuban government.* And it just goes on and on.

We've seen major defections at the highest levels. We've seen the Cuban people vote with their feet since the beginning of the Revolution. I mean, there's over a million Cuban exiles that would represent about 10 per cent of the population of Cuba. If you put it in terms of the United States you would have to exile almost 25 million people to get the same percentage. So it's been a massive exodus. But in the last few years we've begun to see, for the first time, major disaffection at the highest levels since the beginning of the Revolution. So, that plus a whole series of other factors – you know, the fact that Castro has to withdraw from Angola, and he has a stagnant economy. Where's he going to put all those soldiers?

Most of those people know how to fight and have carried arms, and most of them didn't like being in Angola and have felt they have been betrayed by being sent there. They were told they were going to fight white South Africans and they wind up fighting black Angolans. So there's a tremendous amount of disaffection there.

---

* General del Pino, former hero of the Bay of Pigs invasion, defected to the United States in May 1987. Florentino Azpillaga's defection to the States in June 1987 forced Cuba to bring in twenty-seven long-term double agents from the cold. He was at the centre of a shooting incident in London in September 1988, when he was injured and rapidly spirited away from the scene. The Cuban ambassador to Britain was consequently expelled.

You have an economic situation that is more severe than ever before. You have pressure from the Soviet Union for perestroika and glasnost and Castro has rejected that as a possibility. The Soviet Union can't afford a subsidy of the size it's been giving and will probably demand more from Castro economically.

The young people in Cuba have been brought up within the Revolution and despise it. We get that from people who come over all the time. That's just standard now, and then the Communist Party of Cuba has admitted that their most flagrant enemies are the young people who were brought up within the Revolution. Raúl Castro himself has said that not even with a hundred thousand policemen could you control the young people in Cuba.

The situation you have with Radio Martí and now TV Martí* has ended the monopoly of the Castro government on information in Cuba and has made the people wake up. The fact that the Cuban people had their relatives visit them is what caused the Mariel exodus in 1980. The government told them for years that everybody here lives miserably and yet everybody went back with a lot of money and a lot of goods and were able to purchase things for their family in Cuba in the foreign stores that the Cuban people couldn't even go to. You know, all these things combine. Kind of a situation where people just don't believe in the Cuban Revolution within Cuba any more. So, you know, I could go on for ever, but the point being that that's why I see a change coming.

Along the lines of what country?

The only good Latin American country in my opinion that presents any degree of a model is Costa Rica. It's the only country. Venezuela may present some degree of democracy but Costa Rica is probably the closest model that we would like to strive for.

That had a particular basis in history.

---

* With the inauguration of TV Martí in 1990, Cuba jammed both the television and the radio signals. The latter had been received more or less clearly for five years.

270

Yes, there were particular circumstances, obviously. I think we will be different from Costa Rica in some ways. I think, number one, is that having had so much state control for so many years, which people basically repudiate, I think what you'll see in Cuba is a lot more free enterprise than exists in Costa Rica. And, of course, the nature of the Cuban exile community being able to do business within Cuba, maybe even live there and vice-versa, will create a situation where you have a lot more entrepreneurial activity. There seems to be something in the Cuban nature that creates entrepreneurs. I don't know why that is. We've been called the Jews of the Caribbean by other Latin American countries. It's funny and it's amazing but it's true.

You know, the dream of every Cuban is to have a business; have his own business and have his own destiny in his own hands. So I think we'll see a lot more activity than exists in Costa Rica and less state control down the road. I think we will see for the first time in a long time a country that will be genuinely in arms with the United States. I think there's a desperation in Cuba for wanting things American. The most popular music in Cuba is rock music from the United States.* Of course, that's no different from anywhere else in the communist bloc within the young people. But I think that it's an irony and a paradox that Castro comes to power on a wave that he creates of anti-American sentiment and a need to isolate Cuba from the United States. And the long-term historical consequence of that will be [that Cuba will be] more American than it ever would have been if Castro had not come. Because when he leaves and the government changes you have a million Cubans in the United States who have a tremendous interest in Cuba, and you have 10 million people in Cuba who have a tremendous interest in the United States. So you'll see a country, hopefully, and I say hopefully because I think that's good – I think that every country that has got into the economic sphere of the United States and Western Europe has succeeded, and you see that in South Korea, you see it in Japan, you see it in Singapore, you see it in Taiwan and you see it in countries

---

* Rock is very popular in certain sectors but Cuban music is by far the most popular and is going through an immensely creative phase.

that are generally pro-West even though they are not Western in their own traditions. Of course, I consider Cuba part of Western tradition. I don't see Cuba as a Third World country. I mean, it's been created into a Third World country, but Cuba, in 1959, based on UN statistics and the World Bank and so on, was the second most advanced country economically in Latin America after Venezuela. And Venezuela had petroleum and we didn't, so . . . that was a pretty decent situation. The problem in Cuba in 1959 was that we had a dictator.

It's interesting that most of the Foundation people that I work with who were students or young people at the time, almost to a person fought against Batista in the 1950s. They were not necessarily in Castro's movement, because there were many movements, but they fought against Batista and now they're fighting against another dictator, so it's really a continuation of the same struggle.

I used to work for the University of Miami here, which was a job I had for eight years before I came to the Foundation, and while I was there I met Mr Jorge Mas Canosa, who's the chairman of the Foundation.* And he was looking for someone at the time to begin to build bridges with the next generation of Cubans that had grown up in this country. So they gave me the task of creating a young professionals' organisation. You know, an organisation of young people who still felt something for Cuba and its future and who would be willing to co-operate, in fact, to work at the Foundation. And we formed an organisation of more than fifty young professionals here in Miami, and I was co-ordinator of the group for two years. And I guess, without sounding overly conceited, I did a good job, and when a possibility opened up in the office here of hiring someone [as area director], they offered me the position. And I've been here since September of 1988. So about eight months now.

Honestly, for the first time in my life, I get up now to go to

---

* Mas Canosa is the brains behind Radio and TV Martí and a very powerful lobbyist for the right wing of the Cuban community. He has set himself up as president-in-exile of Cuba.

272

work and I feel great about going to work. (*Laughs*) You don't find many people with that situation. Not that I don't get tired, because there's a lot of work here. Sometimes it overwhelms you, but it's a great place to be. It's an interesting moment in history, you know, within Cuban history, and I think we're going to see some more interesting moments coming in the near future, and I, you know, if God wills it, I will play a small role. So, that's where we're at. The young professional group has continued and we have over seventy-five members now.

The Foundation was founded in 1981. It was founded by Jorge Mas Canosa and three other directors. To be a director or trustee you have to make a substantial economic contribution to the Foundation. In other words, you give, you don't take.

Basically it was founded with the idea of just giving out objective information on Cuba. The idea comes from the realisation that there was a need to change tactics within the struggle against the Castro tyranny. Basically the struggle before had been from 1959 to 1961 or 1962. It was an organised armed struggle with the help of the United States. After that what happened was that many people got involved in a lot of these commando raids to Cuba, and so on and so forth. They were minor operations and, you know, we could have a twenty-year debate on whether or not they were effective. But the bottom line is by the late 1970s certain sectors of the community begin to realise that there are other ways to struggle against Castro, and the realisation comes that perhaps, you know, we live in the world's largest and longest-lasting democracy. It's probably militarily and economically and so on the strongest country in the world. That could be debated.

But what we have been doing traditionally is standing down here in Miami kind of discussing with each other among ourselves what we should do. And this message of what has happened within Cuba – human rights things and so on – has never gotten outside of Miami really. So the decision was made to try to work within the American system to try to bring about changes that would affect in a positive way the future of Cuba. And the Foundation is founded in Washington precisely because of that.

And over the years we have obtained a large degree of respect within the Congress and the Senate and have a lot of close friends within the US Congress and within the executive branch, who understand the situation in Cuba now, who we co-operate with in trying to do things like implement the economic embargo that hasn't existed for many years towards Cuba, and pass laws that will make the struggle more effective, like Radio Martí, TV Martí etcetera. So, things have changed dramatically.

Castro's government used to basically lobby in Washington. I mean they were doing it before we were. They would lobby in Washington and basically get whatever they wanted during the 1970s, and we have displaced them in Washington. Most people go to the Foundation first for information on Cuba now, which is what our function is – an information service. So, we're very pleased with what's happened.

The Foundation receives no US government money at all, or any other government [money].* We get money from the contributions of the directors and trustees and from the Cuban people, who give their $5 or $10 or whatever. Never in the history of the Cuban exile community has there ever been an organisation who even gets close to having the amount of contributors we have. You know, because of the fact that many of the directors and trustees are entrepreneurs who have made a lot of money, our enemies accuse us of being elitist and, you know, just a bunch of rich people who don't care about the rest of the people, but, you know, the numbers don't show that. The numbers show that the Foundation is backed by popular demand – I mean, there has not been an organisation in the history of Cuban exile, and there has been a lot of them, that have ever had these kind of numbers. If you measure the fact that there are only 400,000 Cuban families in exile, and only one member of each family who probably makes a contribution, we've basically contributions of about 10 per cent of the entire Cuban exiled population. So that's pretty substantial.

Maybe I'm a bit of an idealist, you know, but I firmly believe this organisation represents the ideals of democracy and freedom. And if given the chance will implement those ideas in Cuba. You know, we're not backers of any one person or institution, we're

* The Cuban American National Foundation receives money in the form of grants from the National Endowment for Democracy.

backing a series of principles. You know, human rights within Cuba, and freedom and democracy, and if those things can be brought to Cuba, then we hope to be able to play a role in bringing those things to Cuba.

This is almost a religious commitment in a sense. Because, you know, I don't make a lot of money here. I have a good salary but I don't make a lot of money here, and, as I said before, most young Cubans are people looking to get ahead professionally and so on. Sometimes I look around and I say, you know, I could be doing a lot more, money-wise. I could be doing a lot better for my family. But the compensation I get back in personal rewards from being able to play a role historically with what I consider the men and women who are forging the nation from outside, and the compensation you get in personal satisfaction in being able to just play a role is way beyond anything you could pay.

I think you won't find a lot of young Cubans like me. Most young Cubans work within the structure of the American traditional parties – Democratic and Republican – and some are very involved with the Foundation also, but it's interesting to see how people react to the issue of Cuba politically as they grow older and have grown up here.

For instance, for me, I find a greater affinity to people who have left Cuba recently. When I first moved to Miami the friends I made here, before being involved with the Foundation and so on, were people who had either grown up outside of Miami or people who had recently come from Cuba. Those were the two groups that I got along with. I had a hard time adapting to the young Cubans who had grown up in Miami because I saw them as very apathetic. They really did not seem to care about Cuba. Since then I have met quite a few Cubans who grew up in Miami who have the same interests that I do. But at the time I didn't and I just saw everybody with an interest in making money and having a large car or something, and I thought that was quite irrelevant. (*Laughs*) But since then I've had to change my opinion, because many of the people who are involved in our group grew up in Miami, so.

I think what happens when you grow up outside Miami [is] you don't take Cuban culture for granted, which you do here.

You can take it for granted because it's all over. But when you grow up outside of Miami it becomes either something you long for or forget about. I think in most cases you forget about it. The young Cubans who I came to the States with, who settled in the north, they probably don't even know who's in power in Cuba. (*Laughs*) But then the ones who grow up here, it's amazing. They think this is typical of the rest of the United States, and they don't realise that this is totally, totally unlike anything else in this country.

I'm married to an Italian–American who has learnt Spanish. We have one son and he speaks Spanish and English. We speak Spanish at home. Italian, no. She doesn't speak Italian that well. She's a second generation. Her experience is exactly what I don't want to happen to my son. In other words, her parents stopped speaking Italian, her grandmother spoke Italian. The grandmother did not pass it on to the parents, which is very common among the old immigrant families to this country. As a result they've lost that touch with Italy and I don't want that to happen whether I go back to Cuba or not. My experience has been, so far, that that's not going to happen. The intensity of the Cuban exile community here in proportion to what surrounds it is much different to, say, the Italians in New York. Without sounding overly trite, there's a majority of Cubans in this community. We're the majority, not the minority, so, for good or for bad. And that means we'll be able to maintain our culture and our language and so on.

None of us have any interest – and when I say none of us, I can speak for 95 per cent of the Cuban community in exile – in dealing with Castro or a communist state without Castro. The mythology of the Castro regime is that the people in Cuba fought for a communist revolution in Cuba. That is blatantly false. There was a communist party in Cuba, the Popular Socialist Party, pro-Soviet line, who in the late 1950s – well, they'd been around for years – condemned Castro's revolt, and you know it's a very complex situation . . . but Castro was fighting for a democracy in Cuba. He was fighting to take out a right-wing authoritarian dictator who should have been taken out – there's no question about that. Castro was one of the many leaders, certainly, and when the Revolution triumphed what people expected was a bringing about of a cleaning of government and a democracy in Cuba; a return to democracy, because there had been a democracy before Batista's coup in 1952. So, it's important to understand that what people struggled for was democracy.

Most of the people who live in Miami today [are] people who fought against Batista, with few exceptions. I would say that over 90 per cent of the people who are in exile today fought against Batista, and many of them fought for Castro, within Castro's own movement. And what Castro did was basically, after triumphing in 1959 when Batista left the country, was to take a situation where he allied himself with the Communist Party as a way of perpetuating his stay in power. But that is not what people fought for. They did not fight for communism. So, the people who fought with Castro and who allied with Castro in other organisations, turned against Castro when they realised what he was doing, and that's where you have all the political prisoners. That's where you have a lot of executions. That's where you have a lot of the exiles. I mean, when you turn against a totalitarian government you only have three choices: you either win the struggle; you get shot or go to jail; or you leave. And those are the things that have happened.

What about the distribution of wealth?

Well, you've got to start with scraping away the communist mythology. I mean, ABC News stated that Cuba had a 67 per cent illiteracy rate, you know, prior to the Revolution, and those facts were given to him by the communist government in Cuba during the Gorbachev visit.* That's totally ludicrous. In 1959, Cuba had a 76 per cent literacy rate, which is one of the highest in Latin America, and the intense campaign for literacy at the beginning of the Revolution was with the remaining 24 per cent

---

* This statement is at odds with the official Cuban literature on the subject. It suggests an error of interpretation on the part of the Cuban official or of the journalist. René Silva's figures are correct. In parts of rural Cuba illiteracy would have been as high as 60 per cent plus but the overall statistic was around 24 per cent.

or so of the population, which were mostly the people living in the mountains and so on. But the mythology has turned it around and falsified the statistics and it looks ridiculous. Cuba was basically a country with a higher standard of living than Spain in 1959, and some of the other countries in Europe. There were segments of the population that were impoverished, which you could find in the United States too if you looked hard enough, although it was a little more blatant in Cuba. I mean, you could go to rural Mississippi and you're gonna find yourself a heck of a situation in the United States today. None of that justifies the crimes that have been committed in the name of social justice, which has not been implemented by the way in Cuba.

But wealth distribution, it depends on how you look at it. My personal opinion is that the highest standard of living exists within those countries that work within the framework of democratic capitalism. I think even the communists have realised that, because they're making their own changes now, and you see that everywhere the model of Western Europe and the United States has been undertaken, that's where you have seen the growth.

The bottom line with all this is that the Cuban people today, as a whole, are poorer than they were twenty years ago. All across the board. Probably the only things that exist where Castro has made an impact socially was taking medical clinics to the rural countryside. That's about the only area I can think of.

If you could measure it, I would consider myself a liberal Republican in the traditional sense. In US terms. In traditional Latin American terms I would consider myself a liberal. The traditional Latin American liberal is what is probably called the neo-conservative here. You know, I believe in capitalism in the non-exploitative sense. I believe in the values of the West, even democracy *per se*, which comes out of those values as a political system.

You know, what happens is a lot of people outside, and certainly the propaganda machine of the communist government in Cuba, tries to create a vision of us in exile as being these radical right-wing bomb throwers who spend all our lives screaming at each other. We have vampire teeth and wear Dracula uniforms all day long. It's totally ludicrous. You know, the typical Cuban here is no less than the typical American. You want my personal opinion? This is not the Foundation speaking. My personal opinion is that the Cuban agents in Miami, Cuban communist agents, are putting the bombs in town to create a situation whereby you can point fingers and say, the Cuban exile community is a bunch of reactionary slobs, right-wing bomb throwers and so on and so forth. And the reason I come to this conclusion is because I ask the question, who benefits from this? The only people who benefit from the bombs being put in town are the communists themselves. So, I have to come to that conclusion. One thing Cuban exiles are not, and that is stupid, and it is counter-productive and stupid to do that. That is why I come to that conclusion. You know, I don't have proof, and you know there could be factions on the right who could do that. But my personal guess is that that is the Cuban government itself doing it. And I think you have to be very careful. And, *eh*, I almost hesitate to give you that opinion because most of the time when I give that opinion, people think I'm nuts. But if I had to place money – a fella's up against a wall facing a firing squad, and they said, if you guess right you'll go free, I would play the Cuba communist card . . . I don't have the exact proof, but if that was the card I had to play, that's the one I'd play.

27

Elba and Jorge

Elba and Jorge are in their sixties. She is from Sancti Spíritus and he is from Santa Clara. They live in a small, depressing mobile home parked off a main road in Miami. Jorge washes cars and Elba mends clothes for a living. They came to the United States in the Mariel boat lift and regretted the move from the outset. Listening to Elba is like trying to follow several radio stations at once. She is all energy and tangents. She speaks excitedly and in that particularly sharp, rasping voice Spanish speakers often have. Jorge loves her dearly and indulges her. Why did they leave Cuba?

22 April 1989

Then things get going, there's excitement, 'We're going to the States.' And I said, 'Ay, let's go to the States.' I saw that people were going over. I dressed better and ate better in Cuba than . . . yes, sincerely, I'm speaking from the heart. I'm not being hypocritical because I want to go back to Cuba. I say it even if I have to die here, I'll die here. But I don't want my children and my family here.

I lived better and I ate better. We used to go to the beach. We used to go to the cinema, we used to go everywhere, I'm telling you how I lived in Cuba, what it was like for us in Cuba. But it was to hell with everyone, let's go to the States. And I said, 'Ay, Jorge, let's go.' And Jorge said, 'We're too old to be going there.' Can you get over the madness of it? We women put the devil into

men, don't we? That's what I think, I do, because he didn't want
to come and I was like a madwoman, me a Christian woman. He
didn't want to come. That's the way I am. I would speak to Fidel
Castro, and if he was here I would say to him, 'Look, Dr Fidel
Castro, Comandante, it was madness on my part that got us
here. I wanted to come here. Why? How would I know? How
would I know, didn't I tell you I dressed better and ate better
in Cuba! I didn't know what this was like. And I come over.
Right. Just wait now and I'll tell you. Well, we got caught up
in the excitement.'

My husband is a political prisoner. Let's start there because it's
worth it. Political prisoner. He was in jail for ten years. You see
that there are human rights there. Well, he sent a cable to Cuba
about human rights and they have a copy of it up North [in
Washington]. You don't have torture like they say here, like
they say on the radio. But my husband is a poor man and
we can't go anywhere to speak up. He sent a telegram from
here. 'I, so-and-so, spent ten years in prison in Cuba. There's
no torture in Cuba. In Cuba they do not commit the crimes they
say they do here.' Right. He sent off the telegram and the copy is
in Washington in the Cuban Interests Section in the Czechoslovak
embassy.

(*Jorge gets a word in edgeways*) I'm going to tell her about that.
I was the one in jail.

Fine. He lived through that experience. But shut up. Let me,
the little I know. Over in Cuba they treat prisoners well. They
pay them. They study. Because I saw that, I don't need my
husband to tell me about it. I saw that. In the evening they
have study groups and all. But now you know there are some
Cubans and we aren't all right in the head. I shouldn't be here
myself. What am I doing here? What did I come here for? 'So the
political prisoner,' said Fidel Castro, Comandante Fidel Castro at
a meeting in Cuba, 'can leave.' He used to work on the buses.
He earned 180 pesos. My house didn't cost much. Didn't I tell
you, I had everything. Imagine, I didn't work in Cuba. I did my
guard duty, I did my duties, we used to go and cut cane, I was a
member of the FMC [Federation of Cuban Women], all that sort
of thing that we have in Cuba I was involved in. And what do

you know but the devil gets into me to come here and leave all my family behind.

When did you get this idea?

Cursed idea, how would I know? Isn't that what I'm saying, it was a bad idea? I say, if only that boat could have turned around, if only I'd broken my leg. I say it in all sincerity. So then, what do you know, but Fidel says, the Comandante says, 'Prisoners here work,' and that's the truth, they do. That is the greatest man the world has ever known. That man. He says, 'I think our prisoners here don't want to go because they're working, they're educating their children.' He [Jorge] has two children. They were internationalists. You see. And it's true what Fidel said. I think the prisoners don't want to go because they have their families there, they have their children who have studied under the Revolution. But we get this devil of an idea of, 'Let's go to the States.'

So we came, I tell you, not knowing a thing. So we came. So we came. Well, we start to get our passports and the children, 'Ay, but you are out of your minds.' 'We'll be back, kids. We're going over to see what it's like. You're not going but we are.' The youngsters, I didn't want them coming over, I just thought of seeing what it was like.

You thought you could go back?

Of course, love. Upon my children I swear it. I thought I'd come over here and return immediately. If it isn't true what I say . . . sure, this man (*pointing to Jorge*) didn't come here for political reasons or fleeing from communism as they say, not at all. I swear it upon my children. Let us never return to Cuba alive if we are lying. I say, 'Come on, let's go.' 'But we're very old now.' 'Don't you see how everyone is coming here? We'll go and if we can't come back in a month, we'll come back in two months.' We couldn't tell anyone or say a word to anyone about it. And the kids, 'Why are you going over? What are you looking for over there?'

It was a cousin of his who wrote. 'Listen, here you earn so much. It's wonderful here,' and it's not as if I needed that money.

I didn't need anything. Because I had clothes, I had shoes like everyone else in Cuba. There are shortages, no?, on account of the terrible blockade imposed by imperialism on the revolutionary government. And Jorge says, 'But we're too old now.' And me, 'What do you mean, old?' So he says to me, 'Right. We'll go and see. We'll start organising passports.' So we start getting the passports, giving our names and addresses and all, paying for those passports . . . What do you know, but didn't the authorities arrive at the house: 'Are you going to the United States?' 'Yes.' 'Look, tomorrow get some money and go and pick up your passports.' That's what we did. We arrived in Cayo Hueso. We arrived there like sheep. Like sheeep, I say. Do you know how sheep are, one behind the other? We left Cuba on 18 May. What a lousy date.

(*Her husband tries unsuccessfully to say something*)

I say, 'Ay, I'm going back. I don't want this.' And he says, 'What are you on about? How are we going to go back?' That sea and everything, dreadful, I vomited. We were as sick as be damned. So then we get on a plane and I go to phone my children to tell them that I want to go back. The very day we set foot in that place Cayo Hueso. Wait. Oh, what a mistake! We arrived. They put us on a plane at about two in the morning. We got into that plane without knowing where we were going, believe me.

(*Jorge*) Three and a half hours.

They put us in a place in Wisconsin where there were soldiers. It was all army stuff, everywhere closed off, military service barracks. They put us in there. The only thing you could see was the sky and the ground and not knowing how the children were getting on; not being able to phone because that was really something.

Well, we were stuck there – how did it all happen, ay! – one month. One month.

(*Jorge*) One month.

No contact with the family. Stuck there with soldiers everywhere and BANG! shots and planes and all. Ay, it was . . .

How did they treat you?

No. They took the soldiers out. Afterwards they took all the soldiers out.

(*Jorge*) Behind a fence as if we were the military.

Like prisoners, like being in prison for a month. Then someone came looking for you and says, 'Look, there's a telephone . . .' and I don't know who the guide was, someone from a church, someone like that, I don't remember now, nor do I want to, and he said [to contact] this cousin who wrote to you about this being wonderful . . .

(*Jorge*) You had to have someone to sponsor you.

Yes, otherwise we'd still be stuck there prisoner. So we get in touch with the cousin in Tarrytown, Tarrytown, New York. 'This is New York,' says he, instead of saying Tarrytown. So Jorge says to him, 'Look, this is your cousin, the one you wrote to in Cuba telling us to come and we're stuck here in Wisconsin. We've been here a month already.' He says '*Ave Maria!*' so they talk to the people here. The cousin. 'So, you'll accept responsibility for them?' And he says yes. So the cousin gave all the details and that. Right. And one of those Christian churches, what was it . . . ?

(*Jorge*) Methodist . . .

Methodist, got us out. Listen. On 7 July we arrived in Tarrytown, in New York. I went mad immediately. I said, 'Ay, no,' and sent a telegram to my daughter in Santa Clara. Well, my daughter said, 'I thought the sea had swallowed you up.' Madness. Everyone, imagine. So, I sent a telegram to my daughter to phone me at my husband's cousin's. Orlando Rodríguez is his name. So then my daughter phoned me at that number but when I hear her voice . . . (*Elba starts crying now in distress*)

(*Jorge*) Come on, calm down. You're here now, what are we to do about it? The milk is spilt.

(*Sobbing*) I said to her, 'Ay, child, get us out of this hell. Get us out.' Ay. I beg your pardon. Then Jorge says, 'Give it to me, let me speak to her,' because I couldn't. 'Ay, get us out of here, I don't like it.' Then my daughter sends us a telegram (*still in tears*) saying, 'Mummy, go . . .' because the poor thing hadn't a clue either, because we have always lived in Cuba, it's the first time we got caught up in such madness. She says, 'Go to the offices of the Czechoslovakian embassy* in New York.' And they went wild where we were staying, which was at his cousin's . . .

I want to tell you about the good side and the bad side of it all. The good part is that we are now with the Antonio Maceo Brigade† and with the Party, and we are with people we can talk to.

(*Jorge*) They're the only people we meet up with here. I don't leave this house except to work. Here, behind. I wash and polish cars. That's what I do here. I don't have any other job.

Wait, let me finish the story. So when my daughter sends us the telegram with the address, we go to New York and we haven't a clue. We got a train in Tarrytown and went to New York asking along the way where the Czechoslovakian embassy was.

(*Jorge*) We get to New York and we thought that that was where all the embassies were and where we could see the people who would sort our problems out. When we get to New York we discover that that's not where it is. It was in Washington, DC.

Wait. Shut up. Look, when we arrive there was a man at the office they have for Czecholovakian journalists. A lad who spoke a little Spanish, fortunately. Wait till you hear the luck of it. We get there and I am beside myself, crazy. There was a security man on duty at the door, they have them everywhere. So I say to him, 'We're loooking for the Cuban Interests Section at the Czechoslovak embassy.' And the man says, 'No. This isn't it. There is a Czech office but it's for journalists.' I say, 'Well, I want to go in, I want to go up.' 'But you can't just go in there,' says the security man. So he goes up and the Czech journalist comes down. He shakes our hand, says hello, and takes us upstairs. So we tell him the story and he says, 'Wait, I have the phone number for Washington.' He phones Washington. A girl comes on the line who must have been . . . I don't know what her name

---

* The United States and Cuba do not have full diplomatic relations but have reciprocal unofficial embassies called Interests Sections. Both countries arrange representation through a third country, which in Cuba's case was Czechoslovakia. Switzerland now represents the US in Cuba and Cuba in the US.

† See pp.286–8.

is. And then he says, 'Look' – he spoke in English: that there was a Cuban couple who had arrived in the Mariel boat lift and who wanted to go back to Cuba; that all their family was in Cuba and they wanted to go back. Then the girl says to him, the *compañera* who was there in Czechoslovakia in the Cuban Interests section, said, 'Put them on the line.' And I say, 'You take it because I'm only going to weep and bawl.' Imagine, I couldn't even tell her what I wanted and longed for. So then Jorge says, 'Look, we're an elderly couple. We came over in the Mariel boat lift but we want to go back to Cuba. We don't like it here and we don't want to be here.' Then she says, 'Right. Look, write a letter explaining your reasons for wanting to return and why you came.'

So . . . you couldn't say a word with the cousin about. So we'd lock ourselves in the room. So then we secretly sent off the letter (*conspiratorial voice*), but then a letter arrives in Jorge's name with the Czech address on the back, in an embassy envelope. And he [the cousin] says, 'Ay, what's this? Why are you getting this letter? These people are communists.' I say, 'No. It's for the passports, we haven't got any.' So, what do you know (*low voice*) they write to say we can't go back to Cuba. 'The people who left . . .' as they say, but very proper, I don't have any complaint about those people. 'Ay, but write another letter,' because I don't write very well. So he writes another letter. And then I tried, I tried writing. I phoned. Bawling, crying. Then I ask who it is and she says Barbarita. I say, 'Ay, Barbarita,' and she says, 'No, if you keep crying on me I can't deal with the case, I can't speak. Calm yourself down.' Those people, those *compañeros* never – neither the newest nor the oldest there, because I don't know any of them, or the Cuban consuls who are from Cuba – have never sent us back a nasty reply. Never.

And then we moved down here to be nearer Cuba, and I'm in hell here too. Those Cuban reactionaries you get here. Miami is pretty bad.

Then my daughter wrote to me from Cuba. 'Look, see if you can link up with the Antonio Maceo Brigade.' And I said to myself, right, but who can you ask here about the Antonio Maceo Brigade with all those bastards, those Cuban reactionaries around who were the very ones you got politicking around Cuba before, when the country was dying of hunger, dying of poverty – why would I speak to them? Because I am sixty you know. Who is going to tell us about Cuba, about what happened before? No one. About what happened in Cuba before and how it is now? Imagine.

It has its shortages and its needs. But why? Because of the tremendous blockade this imperialist state has imposed on Cuba. And it's now it dawns on us.

So then I say to myself, ay, where will I find out about the Antonio Maceo Brigade? Where? Where? Where? Who? We went out. We went to the immigration services to get deported. We went four times. Then, what do you know, one day I put on the radio. I put on Cuba, the station here, to see what they say. And says El Fuste, a fellow they call Fuste, La Cubanísima station here, he says, 'Tonight the communists of the Antonio Maceo Brigade,' just like that, 'are holding a meeting in number 28, Fifty-fourth Street.' They gave all the details. I was like a madwoman. I know how to write a little, but very badly. Imagine, and them shouting about communism and going at it. Now I have the address. We whizzed off.

And that reactionary neighbour of ours, I had a fight with him. I most certainly did. I paid him $250 for a tiny room this size, look (*indicating the dimensions with her hands*), a tiny bathroom, that's how we lived until we got this place here. And he saying things about Fidel to me, he wanted to demolish him, and denouncing Cuba and communism. And I said, right, we're going to have to get out of here because they are going to bomb us, they are going to make bits of us. Because you can't say a bad word about the Revolution or about Fidel Castro to me. I want you to know that. I want you to know that.

Jorge gets in from work. And, 'Jorge, look at what I have here.' 'What?' he says. 'No, I'll read it to you,' because nobody can read my writing because it's half-spidery, half-illegible, and he writes a bit better than me. So then I, 'Look, tonight there's going to be a meeting in Fifty-fourth of the Antonio Maceo Brigade.' He says, 'You're not serious.' He has a quick shower, snatches a bite to eat and we're into the car and away. My dear, we almost didn't find it. We didn't know the area and it was at night. Up the street, down the other side, up again and around and about. We couldn't see number 28, the one we had to look for there in Little Haiti. So then we go in by the laundry where they used to have their meetings before. We knock, and as luck would have it a man who knew me from the ATC, a workers' organisation here, opened up. And I say, 'Ay, Pelier.' His name is Pelier. I embrace him immediately, anything that night, I embrace him. And so there we were talking to them, dancing, drinking, and I say, 'Ay, now I'm among my own.'

And Elba, are you working?

Yes, mending clothes in a laundry. Where they wash clothes. And I'm sewing, repairing clothes, but what awful people and you have to work so hard! You have to do 200 items in the eight hours. You get ten minutes, then half an hour, then at it, at it, at it, because if you don't do your quota they throw you out. If you don't maintain production, you're in trouble.

Look we went to the immigration services four times. We don't have residency and we don't want it, we want to go back to Cuba for good. We didn't speak English and there was a girl there and she said, 'Do you speak English?' and I said no. Then an American lady said, 'Tell me and I'll translate for you.' I said, 'Look, we came here to get deported to Cuba. We got here in the Mariel boat lift. We don't like this country and we don't want to be here. All our family are over there.' Then she said nothing could be done. And I said I didn't want residency, that I didn't have residency. Then she said to the girl that we should write to Washington. And then next thing I was doing the paperwork, that isn't easy either. That was in 1984, and the Cuban authorities went to my daughter's to see if they were agreed that we should return, and she says, 'Of course.' My daughter's house is small, and then they say, 'Where are they going to live?' She says, 'Here with us. I'll take responsibility for them.' And so on it goes. We'll be at them all the time until we get there because it all takes time and nobody sent us here. We're to blame for leaving our country.

There's something else. Ourselves and two or three others – one of them died, he was a great person as well, like ourselves he didn't want to be here – we bought a boat with the little money we earn. (*Laughs*) I don't want luxury, I don't want anything. All I want to do is go. I'm not interested in money. That's why I don't decorate the place. That car there is an old car we bought second-hand. So we bought a boat between us all and we set off for Cuba. That was in the same year of 1984.

(*Jorge*) All this was a result of our going to the immigration services to get deported. And as that didn't work out, we decided we had to do something . . .

So we get organised and I phone work and say, 'Look, I'm going to be away for about a week because my cousin is very sick and we have phoned everybody to come to the vigil . . .' and what have you. And so Jorge got off work, and what do you know, we buy the boat and in the early hours putt-putt-putt-putt, oh, I was so happy to be going back to my Cuba. I didn't care about the vomiting or anything. I was going to Cuba, but when we got out into the middle of the sea a large boat . . . what do you call those boats?

(*Jorge*) A coastguard boat.

A coastguard boat, one of those huge ones, stops. So he only spoke a little English, I mean Spanish. He says, 'Where are you going?' So the man driving the boat . . .

(*Jorge*) He asked, 'Who is captain of this boat?'

Aha! And it was Ernesto, Ernesto is the one who died, the poor man. He died wanting to go to Cuba. A good man, too. But the worst was coming here to this shit. And then, what do you know, Ernesto says, 'I am.' 'Let's see the boat's papers.' 'Here you are.' 'And where are you going? To Cuba?' (*In English*) To Cuba? To Cuba? as they say. And Ernesto says, 'No, no, no.' You couldn't say you were in case they'd kill you there and then and we'd drown. And then – click – they take a picture of us. Imagine. They took our picture to make us afraid because we hadn't done anything. And then Ernesto says, 'Look at my papers, look. I am the captain, look.' The poor old devil. Poor fellow.

(*Jorge*) The problem was, the captain of the coastguard boat didn't swallow the story because how were we lost? We were going fishing. How come we had so much petrol in the tank? And the two tanks full of petrol for the journey.

No, no, no. It was terrible, my dear. So they make us turn back and he says, 'You are not lost. You were heading for Cuba.' And we said, 'No, no.' I hated him so much I wanted to say, 'Yes, I'm going to Cuba. I don't want to stay here.' Then he says, 'Go that way, because you know very well that Miami is there behind. But the next time we meet here, we'll kill you. We'll sink that boat.' That's the way they go on, and then all this talk of human rights. Where is the kindness here? Where? I want to see it and I can't.

(*Jorge*) After that all fell through, there was a woman here who had a travel agency, here in Eighth Street. So we got in touch through a person and she said to go along. And she asked us, 'What do you want?' 'Well, we want to return to Cuba for good.' And she said, 'Right. I can fix that up for you.' I said, 'Is it possible?' And she said yes. She said she had a . . . what do you call these things? . . . a telex. She says, 'I'm going to send a telex immediately . . . If you are prepared to pay $3,000 I will get you to Cuba.

(*Elba*) Robber!

I said OK. We go back the next day. We gave her the 3,000 pesos [sic]. I had got paid that afternoon and the next day we went and gave her the money. She says, 'OK. Come back in fifteen days.'

(*Elba, imitating the travel agent's voice*) 'Who are your children in Cuba? Orquídea and . . . ?'

(*Jorge*) All the details. All the details. Then she gave us a piece of paper, which is over there, a receipt for the $3,000, because she had her agency and her husband had another one and the two of them were robbing everyone. Fifteen days went by, a month, a year, three years went by and four years, and we don't know where she went, where she is. She stole the money. But not just ours. She has robbed about two or three hundred people from our group. Then later she told us by phone that they stole the money in Cuba. That was her statement. That Cuba stole the money. We told her that there was no chance of them stealing the money in Cuba, that the robber and the liar was herself. Because I had a row with her in the office. Then . . . they closed down, they disappeared, and to date we don't know where she is.

(*Elba interrupts*) Shut up. Then later we heard there was a man here in Coral Way who did trips to Cuba. It was on television. Because those brazen-faces even appear on television – the way they let those people rob! He has his agency, he has his documents. That was around 1985. A year after the other problem. So we go along. He sells us a full ticket. Departure gate, ticket, the time – $2,600 each. The photograph he asked us for, all the data, absolutely everything, we brought it all along. The 23rd passed, so did the 50th and the 1,000th, up to now we still haven't been able to find him or his office. He got lost. Those are the two times they robbed us here.

Jorge tells his story.

We got married in 1970 and the Mariel business was in 1980. She got me involved and I did it to please her. I spent ten years in prison in Cuba. I was in Batista's army. I was a soldier. It was the only thing I could do in Cuba, there wasn't anything else. When I was the right age I went into the army, which was the only thing that would give me a wage. I had no other trade. I was illiterate. I had no other trade and no other option than to go into the army. I was in the army. I was eighteen years in the army. Then when the Revolution came many of us were taken prisoner. I was one. I did ten years. And I never fought once. I never had to fight in my life. They say it was for ill-treatment.

(*Elba*) That's it. Ill-treatment.

Some civilian accused us. I didn't know anything about it, but anyhow. That was at the beginning of the Revolution. The government didn't want to . . .

(*Elba*) It had to act.

It had to act on whatever someone said. But it's over. I did my ten years. I rehabilitated myself. I was rehabilitated. That means you weren't a *plantado*. A *plantado* is someone who doesn't agree with the Revolution, who doesn't comply with the prison regulations of the time. They refused to work. They went on strike, hunger strike, didn't eat. I never went along with any of that. I ate. I went to work. They paid us to go to work. They gave us a percentage to buy things within the prison because they sold us different things like, for instance, razor blades, things to eat and so on. And the rest of the money, I think we got 25 per cent, and the rest of the money was sent by the prison authorities to the family. You designated who you wanted the money given to – your wife, your children, your mother. I had it sent to my mother. I was divorced at the time I went to jail. I got married again after I got out. So I got out. No, before that they called us to say that the 10 million tonne sugar harvest had to be done, and I volunteered. Nobody was obliged to go to the harvest, we went voluntarily. They were going to let us out immediately after it was over. We committed ourselves to doing that harvest and they'd let us go. That was it.

If you did the harvest you were given your freedom?

No, no, no, no, no. We were already free. We went to the harvest dressed in civvies, not in prison gear. Earning money. This time we got the money directly into our hands.

And you had completed your sentence?

The prison was shut and we were in the street. The sentence was done. The only thing they wanted . . . they wanted us to experience how the Revolution worked, how things were done, such as voluntary work, so I did my harvest voluntarily.

And if you didn't do it?

Nothing. Nothing happened. The only things is, the process of being released might get held up by three, four or five months.

So there was a good reason to do the harvest.

No, no, no, no, no. The issue was that you should start adapting to the new way of life. Rehabilitation was about your always being willing to, for example, 'Let's go to work,' and you went to work. They didn't expect an extraordinary effort on our part. That wasn't it. We had study groups every day. It mainly consisted of getting grades because a lot of us were illiterate. So they got us teachers according to our groupings. That was then. I'm talking about

1959 on. I knew how to write, but barely. So when I left there I had a secondary education, I had fifth grade of secondary school. And we got diplomas. We got diplomas for every grade. When we got out we had all our diplomas. We had the last grade we attained so that if we wanted to continue studying we could.

So as soon as the harvest was over we were given our liberty. We earned our money and they gave us our money. You'd begin in the morning. We'd start cutting cane at about 7 in the morning. There was an hour's break for lunch. We had lunch. We'd take the hour. Then we'd go back to cutting the cane and we'd be at it till 4 in the evening. At 4 p.m. we'd wash and eat. Then there was a half-hour break. We were some distance away from the village where we were. We were in the country. They didn't have us there because they wanted to keep us from the town. No. We were there because that's precisely where we were cutting the cane. So after our evening meal we'd have classes there in the country as well. We had classes there every night except when the circus might come, and they took us to the circus. Took us, no. They'd let us go to the circus. Because we were dressed as civilians and we could wander around there freely wherever we wanted.

(*Elba*) And still prisoners.

We were prisoners but free. I was even in charge of food stocks. I was responsible for the personnel at the time. I kept count of the cane, I was responsible for food supplies. Of course, we had our boss to whom I gave the number of *arrobas** of cane cut. They gave me all the money in cash and I went off to buy supplies in a lorry. I went to the village and I bought the produce we cane-cutters ate.

Then I came to Santa Clara. I presented myself in the police station and immediately they asked me what my skill was. You go there to hand in your freedom papers and you leave with your freedom papers. So I told him I was a tractor driver; I was a driver. So then they send me . . . I don't remember what you call that place where they give you work. Anyway, I got there. And he says, 'Right. We have a job for you but not in Santa Clara at the moment. You have to go to Santo Domingo.' Santo Domingo

---

* One *arroba* equals 25 pounds or 11.5 kilograms.

is a town in Santa Clara. So I get to Santo Domingo and they set me to work on a tractor drawing cane. And I hauled cane. I hauled so much that they made me head of the squad. After that they made me head of personnel. I was in charge of the payroll, I paid out the wages. I went to the bank in Santo Domingo to pay the personnel, thanks to my boss who was responsible for the hostel where we stayed. Then I could go wherever I wanted and I also worked hauling cane. I continued hauling my cane. During the day I got on with my personnel business but at night I began at about 9 o'clock and went on till 5 in the morning hauling cane. I kept it up until the harvest was over. When it was over I came back to Santa Clara.

When I arrived in Santa Clara I went back to the place where they had given me the job in Santo Domingo. So there they asked me if I knew how to drive. I said I did. 'What kind of machine?' 'Whatever you like.' I could drive anything. So then they sent me to Omnibus Locales in Santa Clara. I was practising for a week. After two weeks the man in charge of the station told me I could go out on the road if I wanted to, because really I am pretty good at driving buses. I went out. I had an exam. I passed and I got my bus immediately and went out to work. I was a bus driver for ten years and then we came over here. Well, we met and got married.

(*Elba*) A friend of mine introduced me to him, and she says to me, 'Look, you're . . . he's divorced' – he was never married before. He married me as a bachelor but he had a woman and two children, but I was the divorced one. I didn't have any great expenses or needs, because my children were at boarding school. It was all different by then, the government was bringing them up, Fidel Castro's government. And I did sewing and I managed, and with the maintenance I got from their dad for my two younger children, and then the government gave my son a supplement every month,* I didn't need to get married, but you know how things are. We got married and here we are.

And Jorge, do you not feel bitter about those ten years you spent in prison?

* A grant worth 15 pesos a month.

No. Honestly, I don't. I don't, because I think it's right, and I think there was a reason for doing those ten years. Because we made a lot of mistakes in the past. We were no saints. We didn't do what we were supposed to. We should have done what we were supposed to.

And do you personally feel responsible for something?

Well, I think . . . I'm not going to say I didn't. I did. Because if I didn't they wouldn't punish me. That's the fact of the matter. For shoving or . . . whatever you did. For detaining someone, some small thing like that . . . and there was the atmosphere of 1959, which wasn't exactly the Revolution but the people who were revolting in the streets. It was they who condemned you; it was they who punished you; it was they who accused you. It wasn't the Revolution. The Revolution has its form of government, because who exactly was it who brought the Revolution to its triumph? It was those same people. So the Revolution had to allow what the people said. Naturally. (*Pause*) I think it's right and I think it's fine. The sentence I got was right. I have nothing against the revolutionary government, not the slightest thing. On the contrary. In all the time that I was inside, they never tried it on. They never tried to annoy me. Even when I was leaving via Mariel, nobody tried to get at me. Nobody said a word to me. I left quite peacefully like you and I are sitting here now.

(*Elba*) We got away without any problems. The CDR person on duty never did anything. No eggs thrown at us, no stones, no dogs.

(*Jorge*) We had absolutely no hassle. Now, honestly, having been here, our idea is to GET OUT of here. We don't adapt and we don't like it and we don't want wealth. Look at where we're living. I don't want a house here. I don't want a fancy car. I don't want any kind of luxury. I have worked all my life and I spend my leisure time with the Brigade, as I told you before, and with the ATC. With the Party. And we have gone on all sorts of demonstrations, and this is the worst place in the United States, where you get the worst and most degenerate Cuban counter-revolutionaries around. I'm not at all afraid. We went and placed pickets on Radio Mambi.* We picketed there. That appeared in the press. It appeared in the paper, it appeared on television, it appeared everywhere. Almost two hundred of us went along that day. It was set up by the ATC, a workers' organisation called the ATC. That's where we're going today. Asociación de Trabajadores Cubanos.

(*Finally, Elba and Jorge play me a recorded pro-Cuba radio programme put out by Marazul Charters on Tuesdays and Thursdays*)

* An anti-Castro radio station in Miami.

28

Mirta Ojito

Mirta Ojito meets me at the offices of El nuevo herald, *the Spanish edition of the* Miami Herald, *where she is a reporter. She was born in Havana in 1964 and left Cuba in the Mariel boat lift, 1980. We go out to a café and I ask her about her life now in America and why she left Cuba. Her English is near perfect.*

23 April 1989

Being a *marielita* specifically is different to being a Cuban in Miami. I feel first of all Cuban, not particularly *marielita*, but I can't deny that I left Cuba in 1980, and that sets me apart from other people that came here at the beginning of the Revolution, because I lived the Revolution, therefore I think I can talk about it with a bit more authority than other people, who never lived it. They might have studied the Revolution in books, but they've never lived there.

Being a *marielita* was hard at the beginning. A lot of people didn't understand us, didn't care for us, we were different. We were darker. Some of us were black, poorer people, working class.

The people that left in 1959 or immediately after were in a better economic situation in Cuba. So, of course, they tended to be white and better educated and they didn't quite understand who were these people who were coming here. They didn't understand how the language had changed. Everything had changed about us. We use different words. It's easy to recognise a *marielito* if you just let him talk. I guess it's only normal after twenty years, language is a living thing. It changes, it grows, it adds new words. And it adds words that have to do with a particular economic and social situation in the country at the time. And, of course, as they didn't live it, it was hard for them to relate to that. But once you've been here for a few years and they realise you're just like them, you are assimilated . . . it hasn't been, *eh*, it's an asset, if anything, because people are really surprised I'm a *marielita* and yet I look like them. And I went to school and I had a career and I'm so successful, I'm normal. So that hasn't been bad.

And being a Cuban in Miami hasn't been difficult either because everybody here is Cuban. I mean, I have a hard time finding someone who's not Cuban. I think something like 42 per cent of the population in Dade County is Hispanic, and most of them are Cubans. I have a hard time finding a place where I can go to a restaurant and speak English. It is amazing. So, I don't particularly feel out of place. I miss Cuba, of course, in fact – well, it's my country, so I'm always going to miss it. I miss my relatives and I miss, well, a bit of the solidarity that people have there.

This is a different system, and even though the Cubans say they have changed Miami, you know, they have made Miami home and everything, this is part of the United States. And it's a different frame of mind, a different concept of friendship and family than in Cuba, not only because of the Spanish culture but also because we had to survive somehow. We shared a lot of things and there was more solidarity among friends and neighbours. It was the type of thing where you would go to your neighbour's house to get a cup of milk or a bit of sugar. And that type of thing tends to create very strong bonds. And I miss that. Days go by and I don't see my neighbours. I don't talk to them. I don't know who they are. I took the precaution of taking their phone number just in case something happened to me, [so] I had someone to call. I live alone. But I'm not really sure that I could count on them. Do you know what I mean? So, it's, *eh* . . . a difficult thing. And I miss that about Cuba. And, of course, I miss the country. Even if there are beaches, Miami Beach is not the same thing. But other than that I feel comfortable here.

At the same time, I know I'm Cuban, I'm not Cuban–American. I resist that title. I resist that hyphen. I'm Cuban. I'm only here because of the political situation of Cuba right now, and I will go back. As soon as there is a political space for me to go back, I will go back and live there. This is only for the time being, temporary. That doesn't mean that I don't try to be part of this. I just became an American citizen last week, because I don't know how long this is going to take. And I'm not going to say like the early Cubans did: 'We're not going to adapt, we're going back to Cuba next year.' I don't know how long this is going to take. And I'm young and I have to adapt and I have to vote and I have to have a say in this country. But as soon as I can go back to mine, I will.

I was sixteen at the time I left. And I always knew that my parents wanted to leave. As a matter of fact, my parents got married in 1962 so they could leave together. My father was twenty-two, I think, at the time. And he knew he wanted to leave Cuba but he didn't want to do it without my mother. So they got married. But they got married in October 1962, in the [Missile] Crisis, and after that everything shut up so they couldn't leave. So, I was born in 1964 and I don't remember a moment in my household when I did not know that we were leaving at some point.

However, I managed to have a normal childhood and adolescence. My parents wanted to make sure, at all costs, that I was a normal student, that I was a Pioneer,* that I participated, that I didn't get a view at home so totally opposite to what they were telling me at school that my life would be totally chaos.

So, I believed in the Revolution. I was like any other Pioneer. I belonged to organisations. I was active. I got good grades. I was president of this, president of that, and I was always one of the top students and involved in everything possible. But in the back of my mind I knew they wanted to leave.

My father wanted to leave first of all. He felt he couldn't talk in Cuba. He felt totally oppressed. He's a self-educated person, went to school only up to sixth grade, and he had small dreams, but nevertheless he had some dreams. He wanted to be a buyer, I think, for stores and that, and he worked in a store in Havana, downtown Havana, where he was working up to that. When the

---

* Pioneer is the youngest level of the communist structure, starting at primary school. All children are automatically Pioneers.

Revolution came and they confiscated everything, the store went down and my father's dream went down the drain too. And they gave him a truck and they said, 'Now you have to drive this truck.' He had never driven a truck in his life. So, he had to do that, and in a way his dreams were shattered. He had lived in Cuba for twenty years and he felt he didn't have anything. And from the beginning he didn't like the Revolution. He knew it was communism and he knew where it would lead to, and he knew that he would never be free in that kind of a system.

My mother worked in a factory until my sister was born, and then she stayed at home and worked in the house, sewing things. She was a dressmaker until we left. So, I knew we were leaving. My father constantly complained about everything. He complained about having to be a member of the CDR. He complained about *las guardias* from 11 p.m. to 2 o'clock in the morning. And I did, too. It was a totally ridiculous concept. He complained about the neighbours interfering in everybody else's affairs; the constant surveillance; the constant warped mentality there is in Cuba; *la mobilizacion*; Red Sundays, everything. He hated all that and he wanted to leave.

But then, you know, I was a teenager, and he didn't know if at that point it would be all right leaving Cuba, because I already had a boyfriend and I had my friends, everything. And then my boyfriend got sent to Angola, so things sort of cooled off. I was very young, too, only sixteen. And I talked to my father the year before, and I said, 'Listen. If you really want to . . .' He was complaining because I had been sent one more year to the *escuela al campo* [school in the country] and it was very difficult for him to get a bus or truck to get to see me there on Sundays. And I said, 'You've been complaining for the past twenty years, if you really want to leave, let's do something about it. Let's do it.' So then he said, 'Are you sure?' You see, he had never touched the subject with me, and I said, 'Fine, let's go.' So then we tried to leave through Spain like a lot of Cubans do, and then the Mariel thing came up. And my uncle [from Miami] who always knew that my father wanted to leave Cuba at the first opportunity, didn't wait to call us, he just got a boat – paid for a boat, I guess – and went down to get us. And by the time the news came on the paper that there were boats in Mariel, my uncle was already there. And then on 7 May we finally left. It would never have occurred to me to say, 'No, I'm not leaving.' I could have, I guess. But it would never have occurred to me. We're a very tight family. Plus, at the time, I already had a political consciousness. I had already changed my mind about Cuba and there were several things that bothered me tremendously.

First, one thing that changed me radically was, I think, in 1978, when the Cubans who lived in the United States were allowed to go back for the first time for many years – to go back to visit. For many, many years we had been told that those people were bad; that they were traitors; that they were *gusanos*. And my uncle and aunts were part of that, among them. And then all of a sudden Castro says . . . well, there was a joke, a running joke in Cuba, where they said, 'They're not *gusanos* any more, they're *mariposas'* – they're not worms any more, now they're butterflies, you know.* Because all of a sudden it wasn't important whether they had left Cuba or they were pro-capitalism. All of a sudden the only thing that was important was that they had money; that they had dollars to spend. And it occurred to me that, really, it didn't have to do with ideology, it had to do with money. It was all about money. I was very disappointed, because I was very much into the ideology of the Revolution, into bettering the world, into that sort of thing – bread for everyone, let's be equal. I believed all that. And I felt . . . God, I felt betrayed. That's what it was.

My uncle and my aunts went, of course. I was very happy to see them, because I have always been very close to my family. I don't know how they feel politically, I was always very close to them. I was interested in learning more about the United States and what their life was like, and I realised that they had left, my uncle had only left ten years before, not even ten years before, I think seven years before, and he already had a home and a car and nice things. And he wasn't exploiting blacks, and he wasn't stealing, and he wasn't into prostitution or drugs, he wasn't doing

* The pun is on the word *gusano*, which means worm, maggot, grub or caterpillar.

anything illegal. He was working as an accountant in a firm. So, I realised: Wait a minute. What they are telling me about the United States is not all true. It might be partially true, but it's not all true. There are people who basically work hard, make a living and lead normal lives.

So, that was a big disappointment. And then right before Mariel, with the Peruvian embassy events in 1980,★ there was a situation in Cuba close to civil war. People turned against people, friends against friends, relatives against relatives, and there were the so-called *actos de repudio* [public repudiation], where people got killed. Some of the people committed suicide. People got dragged for blocks and blocks. They were bitten; they were spit on. I mean, it was horrible. It was a really bad situation. And I realised: Wait a minute. What kind of country is this? We turn against each other like vicious animals, repeating the slogans, and we don't really know what we are doing. And the saddest part is that some of the people who are doing this, they're doing it because they are envious. As a matter of fact, I have seen some of those people who repeated those slogans here in Miami. So, I know what I am talking about.

And at that point I was really sure that I had to leave Cuba. I was so disappointed that I couldn't continue living in the same block with the same people, that I had seen turning against people, that I had considered friends before. So, there were a lot of reasons why I wanted to leave – my parents, my disappointments and the events of 1980 in particular.

I hope things will change and that I will be able to go back. I'm not looking for economic change right now. I don't particularly care whether my towels match the tiles in the bathroom or whether I have shampoo or not. I just want to be able to read the books I want . . . Y'see, one thing that I don't forgive the Revolution for is not letting me read; not letting me know there was another world out there. I love to read and I love to be informed. And since I've been here I have realised, my gosh, there are so many things I don't know about. And I know sort

---

★ On 1 April 1980 twelve people seeking asylum crashed a minibus through the gates of the Peruvian embassy.

of the same thing happens in the United States – kids don't read in high school – but if you're motivated, you go to a bookstore and you buy a book. Anything you want to read in the world is there: Marxism, Nazism, anything. And in Cuba I couldn't find that. I have books written by Marx in the house right now. Yet I couldn't have books in my house in Cuba written about anybody that had any kind of Western ideology, Western thought. When I came here I realised how ignorant I was. And I hated that. I still resent that. And every time I hear a new name and the people that are fifty years old and they know, 'Oh, of course. That's the well-known Soviet dissident.' Well, I don't know. I didn't know who Cabrera Infante was. How can that be? One of Cuba's best writers. I didn't know who Reinaldo Arenas was, and he lived in Cuba at the same time.* So I resent that. I would only go back if I am allowed to speak, to think – because that's the thing in Cuba, you're not even allowed to think.

Now things have changed. I'm not going to generalise. I'm sure people are obviously daring to think. People are obviously getting more information. Their minds are more open. They travel outside and go back, like in the case of Sánchez.† But when I was there it was a closed, totally, totally, closed totalitarian society. And there was no room for any type of growth outside the things imposed by the Revolution. So, I will go back if I am allowed to do those things. If I have freedom, basically. That's the bottom line. To live.

* Guillermo Cabrera Infante is now living in London. Reinaldo Arenas took his own life in Mallorca on 7 December 1990.
† Elizardo Sánchez, founder and president of the Cuban Commission for Human Rights and National Reconciliation, who at the time of this interview had been allowed to travel abroad. Sánchez has been imprisoned on several occasions, and later, in 1989, was given a two-year suspended sentence for telling the foreign press that the key figure in that year's drug scandal, General Arnaldo Ochoa Sánchez, was drugged during his trial. Fourteen senior army and Interior Ministry (MININT) officials, including General Ochoa Sánchez, were found guilty by a special court-martial of hostile acts against foreign states and of drug-trafficking. General Ochoa Sánchez and three others were executed. The remaining ten received long-term prison sentences. Later, the Minister of the Interior, General José Abrantes, was imprisoned for twenty years on related charges including corruption and abuse of power. Abrantes died in January 1991.

I would go to visit any time. I want to go now. Legally I could, it's just a matter of whether they give me the visa or not. Writing for the *Miami Herald* is not one of the best tickets to Cuba, especially writing for *El nuevo herald*, because we have written some things against the regime and they just don't tolerate that. If I go I would go not as a reporter. I mean I would love to go as a reporter, because aside from everything else, it's a wonderful place for news. But I don't think they'll let me.

I've covered the Human Rights Commission in Geneva for two years now. This year [Cuban diplomats] didn't, but last year [Cuban personnel at the Interests Section] told me they didn't like the articles I wrote out of Geneva. Well, I didn't like them either. I had only been a reporter for two months. I mean, it wasn't particularly good stuff. But that's not what they meant. What they meant is that they thought they were biased. I don't think they were biased. They weren't particularly well written, but they weren't biased. This year they haven't complained, so they must have liked them.

So, I'm hoping that they consider my application as strictly a family affair. I'm just going there as anybody . . . anybody has the right to their country. I think about it every day of my life. Well, it's just a very personal thing, because I have my mother's sister there and her children. And we were very, very close. So, I love my aunt. She's also my godmother.

I could be driving, and if it's a long drive I start my fantasy from the moment I get the telegram saying: You can go to Cuba. And then I go on from there: what I'm going to take to them; the nice things I'm going to buy for them; the magazines that I will be allowed to bring in – I don't know – the records; all kinds of things. When I get there; the arrival at the airport; the view of the island from the aeroplane. I've seen the island from the aeroplane, so I can nicely fit that in, and just all the time I'm going to spend in Cuba. Where I'm going to go. You know, it's just . . . and then by the time I get to where I'm going, driving in my car, I'm already in tears. (*They well up in her eyes now*) And that happens practically every day of my life. It *is* an obsession. It's an obsession. But I'm sure that I'm going to go this year. I mean, I've asked for it. I've asked blowing out the candles on my birthday, on Christmas Eve, on New Year's Eve, every time I've seen a falling star. I mean, I've asked in every single way possible that you can. Now it's just a matter of filling out the papers and seeing what they do . . .

They are allowing people to go back, but in such small numbers that if I'm not lucky I might wait twenty years. I'm hoping not. But it could. I mean, it's just ridiculous that we have to beg and plead so much just to go back, see your people and come back. A basic human right. It's in the Declaration of Human Rights, and Cuba signed the Declaration of Human Rights. It's just elementary.

The biggest thing that's happened in Cuba since 1959 is the human rights movement. They didn't start on the outside, that started on the inside. And if anything changes it will come from the inside. And I don't think it will need a lot of help from the outside. I think it will work itself out. And I'm hoping that some of the groups that are here in Miami – I mean the radio people, the bomb threats, their organisations – will not have a lot of influence once we all go back to Cuba. If we all do. As a matter of fact, most of the people I talked to will not go back to Cuba. They will go back to visit, perhaps to open businesses, to rent a house, to buy a place in Varadero. But they will not live there [or] help put the country back together. My parents, for example, wouldn't go back.

My father continues to be a truck driver. He never learnt to do anything else. My mother works in a factory, same thing. My sister goes to college and is about to be married in July. My father just had an accident at work so he's disabled now. So, it's not great times. But as long as he has his Buick in the garage and a house where he can have a barbecue and sit with his family, he's happy. He wants to have his family and not be afraid if he brings home a chicken at night; not be afraid that the CDR is looking over his shoulder to see what food, what strange food he's bringing into the house. That is a problem. If you happen to bring home in Cuba anything that is not part of the rationing book, *la libreta*, they know you got it on the black market. And anything you buy on the black market is illegal. I understand now the government has its own black market, so I guess it wouldn't make any difference. But before if you brought home a chicken, for which my father had to pay 15 pesos, which is big money, it was a problem. He had to hide it. He had to put it inside a box, make sure the box wasn't bleeding – all kinds of arrangements – because you could get detained for that. If you had more milk in the house than you were supposed to, you could go to jail for something they call *acaparamiento* [hoarding], which was bad. That's punishable, because you have more than what other people need at the same time. So, I imagine living in that kind of system so long, and having to worry about the food you're going to put on the table for your children, being here for him is a breeze. All he has to do is work, go to the supermarket, consume it. I mean, it's not a big deal. And even if one is not so worried about material things, it's nice to know that if you want something – I'm not going to say that if I want something all I have to do is work and I'll have it, because it doesn't matter how much I work, I probably will never have the things that [Donald] Trump has. But I don't care for that.

I was thinking about that last night, because last night – I was at home yesterday – and there were two things that I really wanted. I wanted a pair of Reeboks, because I want to start doing exercises, and I wanted a [specific] book. I got in my car, went to the mall, and came back half an hour later with both. And I've been here for nine years and I still don't get used to it. It still amazes me that I'm able to do that; that I can go to a mall and just come back with the book, and it's just a wonderful feeling, even if shampoo is not important to you. And that's the kind of thing that people like my parents value. And I don't know how things are in Cuba right now, but there was a time there when I had to eat a lot of eggs. I mean, it was eggs for lunch, eggs for dinner, eggs all the time. And it was a miracle if we had a steak in the house.

It's still better than in other places, where a lot of people have all the steaks and some children don't have anything. But still I think it's possible to combine both in a nicer way. Perhaps not as well as in the United States, it's a bigger country. It's a totally different thing. We can't compare it. But I think it's possible for a small country to combine some sort of social justice with freedom. Maybe I'm just a dreamer, but . . .

29

Andrés Santana

Andrés and I talk in a video salon of the Museum of Modern Art in New York where he works in the cloakroom. He is thirty and he left Cuba in the Mariel boat lift of 1980.

16 May 1989

I had put my name down to leave four days before, and a soldier came for me and said, 'You've got to get over there right away.' I put my name down because they were saying, 'They're letting people who put their names down leave.' And at the time so many people I knew were going, and I was dying to go, because I wanted to find something, I wanted to travel, I wanted to have things, so I said to myself I'm going to put my name down because this might be the opportunity . . . I thought that, although a lot of people said that this was going to be some sort of survey to find out who wanted to leave the country. I didn't think so. They couldn't do that. I put my name down and four days later this guy comes to get me at four in the morning. He said to me, 'You've got to get over there right away. Get dressed and get to the Cuatro Ruedas.'

I got to the Cuatro Ruedas at about 5.30 in the morning. It was still dark. You know that dawn in Cuba is at about 7 a.m. So everything was dark, and there I began to realise what I was doing, I saw the reality of it, saying goodbye to my parents, which was very sad, especially my mother. My dad, well, it's sadder now because at that time I didn't know I'd never see him again. But it was a very emotional parting with my mother, not for the tears but for what she said to me.

I went to the Cuatro Ruedas. I was there till about 7 a.m. At 7 a.m. they called me. They asked me for my identity card, put me on a bus and took me to Mariel. I got to Mariel at about 9 or 9.30 a.m. They gave us breakfast and dinner and that. So, I was in Mariel for a few hours. The tension was huge. On both sides. We were laughing nervously, not knowing what was happening, because when you take such a step you don't realise what it's about when you're planning it. But once you've taken it you become aware of the magnitude of what you've done, of everything. And at that time everybody realised and there were a lot – I witnessed it – there were a lot of flare-ups. You know how Cubans are explosive, and there were incidents. Painful incidents between the Cuban soldiers and the group of us who were there. But as I say, at that stage I didn't understand it at all, and I felt that everything they did was wrong. Now I realise that it was understandable that it should have happened, because tempers were frayed, everyone was very tense. There was like a feeling of enmity between us and them. You didn't feel hatred or contempt, but there was like a social tension. And everyone exploded and there were, as I said, lamentable incidents. They let some dogs loose. You know, those dogs are trained, and when you let them go they are uncontrollable. They can do anything. So, of course, when they let the dogs loose . . . I can't honestly say I actually saw them letting them go, all I can say is that when I looked the dogs were already attacking the people. But I honestly don't know if it was an accident that they let them loose, because I can't believe that anyone would let a dog loose on another person knowing that it could tear them to pieces.

There I was until 7 at night, which was when they called out my name. At 7 p.m. they put us on to a shrimp boat and made us head out to sea, and afterwards they made us come back, and we didn't finally get away from Havana till 10 that night, and the *práctico* – the boat that patrols the bay to ensure everything's in order – followed us as far as international waters.

That's when everyone, I think everyone felt a sort of great

sadness, because the only thing that united us symbolically, like an umbilical cord, was the *práctico*, because it was Cuban. It wasn't right up against the shrimp boat, of course, it was a certain way back behind us. And then suddenly, on reaching the territorial boundary, it turned around and went back. And I believe I watched it until it disappeared on the horizon. And that was the last link between Cuba, our families, and the rest broken.

And almost as the *práctico* disappeared on the horizon, such a storm blew up that I don't know how I survived. Not just me, everyone. There were twenty-eight of us altogether. There were two families, because there were two families who lived in Miami who had clubbed together to hire the shrimp boat. And there were a lot of children. I met them in Mariel and they were really lovely. Crying, mainly. They were all crying when they met up, and they didn't stop, especially a fat lady, she didn't stop crying. They spent almost the entire journey crying. They didn't get seasick (*laughs*), but they got sick from crying.

The journey was appalling. Thanks be to God I didn't get sick or anything and I fell asleep. I don't know how I managed it. I don't know. I must have been so tired. We got to Miami, to Cayo Hueso, at 7.30 in the morning on 1 May 1980. What a date to arrive! As we were coming into Cayo Hueso a coastguard approached and escorted us to the bay. But before landing, the Cubans who were there – they were euphoric, blowing their horns – welcomed us like heroes and that . . . I was moved, because these were my people, too. They were living here, and I was moved because I understood what I was leaving behind. At that point I felt well. I think it was the only time, perhaps it was the only time, since I've been in this country, that I honestly felt happy and contented; that I felt accepted by the people, even though it wasn't specifically directed towards me, it was directed towards everyone.

We arrived and they took us to different places for a medical check-up. They were surprised that we were all in such good health. They were also surprised that none of us had tuberculosis. They couldn't believe it. And that's where they began to ask me a series of such stupid questions about what was happening in Cuba, and it was so twisted, not only questions that made no sense, but ones that were not even true – it just seemed silly to me that they could think such things could be happening in Cuba. Like they didn't know Cuba had television. They didn't know that there was a whole load of things that we were at that stage fed up with having. It was ridiculous. They were on the point of asking me if it was true they killed people in the streets. (*Hoots*) The rubbish they asked.

But of course some people used that, the people who had got bitten by the dogs – which were one or two, no more, because they immediately caught the dogs. They threw themselves at the journalists – 'Look, look, what they did to me,' and they showed the reporters everything. I wasn't in fit condition to speak, because I was thinking about my family. 'I don't want to talk, I don't want anything. I have nothing to say.' But they were really on top of us. I think if you'd said you'd say something but that it'd be a lie, they'd have said fine, because they were desperate to get us to say anything. Sometimes they spoke to me and I didn't know how to answer. Though they addressed me in Spanish. It was like as if my mind was elsewhere. I realised, I don't know how, that everything that's happening to me now – the distance separating my mother and I, the death of my father, not having seen him again – was somehow being foretold – my economic situation, everything, everything, everything, as if it were foretold, as if I were visualising it. For that reason alone I didn't want to speak, I wanted to be in my own world at that moment. But there were a lot of people who spoke up, who exaggerated, and many people even lied for the sake of saying something. And there were shouts of 'Down with Fidel', anything that struck them, and the soldiers, they encouraged them to shout louder because they were recording it and filming it and what have you.

The soldiers, there were lots of soldiers, I do remember that. Especially the North American soliders, you noticed that you weren't accepted by them, that there was a kind of rejection . . . And from then on I began to suffer, not as a Cuban but as a human being. I see everyone as they are – human beings. I don't care where they are born, or about their race, and I owe a lot of that to my education in Cuba. So, I began to see that hatred they have of Hispanics, that lack of acceptance of Hispanics or blacks or poor people. I began to assimilate that. I picked up on it. And I said to myself, 'Right, now you've got to live with it. Now you're here, you're stuck with it.'

When I arrived I asked to make a phone-call, they'd laid on a free line, and I rang here, I rang my sister in New York, and I told her that I had arrived, and she couldn't believe it. Then she said, 'By coincidence, Santiago' – my brother-in-law – 'has gone to Miami to try and find his parents, and when he phones me I'll tell him you're there.' So my brother-in-law looks for me all over the place, but they changed me twice, until finally he finds me and brings me here to New York, and that was nine years ago now on 1 May.

Everything I remember about my life in Cuba was, as Guillén says, 'All time past was better', and I can't complain about my past life, and although I had tough times like everyone else, it was all beautiful.

I can't say the same for now. (*Wry laugh*) It's not so beautiful. Everything is so much more different: more difficult, more harsh, more spare, let's say. My life now is much more tense by comparison. In Cuba, although there were bad moments, it was much different, and more beautiful in the end. I used to write. I felt well. I had my family, no? My sister was already here since 1971, but . . . it wasn't the desire to see my sister, it was the desire . . . you know how it is when you're younger, you want to change the world and you dream of all sorts of things. You dream of having it all, and you think that this is a wonder, that this is the promised land, that everything will be fine.

So, as you're young you get caught up in all that talk, and when you get here you see the reality. I knew a bit about the reality of it before I came, but I didn't think it would be quite so hard.

It's also leaving a whole series of things which is what living in Cuba is all about. That way of life is lovely. That *joie de vivre* that we have in Cuba . . . all that I miss very much, because I am losing it, because you get so bound up in working, in paying the rent, you forget you're a human being and you become more and more like a machine, like a robot, and less like the human being with feelings that you are. When I was in Cuba I used to write.

Anything would inspire me to write a poem or a play or would give me an idea. Here I have so little time I can't even think. Nor get an idea about what I might write next. And everything I feel now – because I am extremely left-wing, extremely, I believe, humanist – I owe to having lived in Cuba and to having steeped myself in all that, and I didn't realise how lovely everything around me was. I didn't realise it.

One of the things that has happened to me since I got here is not just the time factor, but a sort of culture shock – I can't write. On many occasions I have wanted to, I'm trying to make a superhuman effort . . . and that was something I undervalued as well: my father's love, what he felt for me – I didn't know how to appreciate that, I didn't know how to understand him. Now, with separation, incredibly, I realise everything.

My father also wrote and he admired me a lot as a writer. For a time I thought he admired me more as a writer than as a person. (*Laughs*)

My father worked in an office . . . I'm forgetting things in Spanish, he was an 'accountant' (*in English*). I worked with him for a while in the same department of the Ministry of Construction. My mother didn't, she was always a housewife. She's working now, especially since my father died. She needs a little extra and so she has to work. But she was always a housewife. All her life. She's working in a factory, cleaning the kitchen or something like that. And my youngest sister lives there, and my older sister now lives in Miami. But she's old-guard, like most of the Cubans who live in Miami. I don't like speaking to her much because she has a rather backward mentality.

Friends, that's another thing. It's very difficult to have friends here. It was different in Cuba. In Cuba I had, God, an incredible number of friends. Of acquaintances. You know how we are. We make friends very easily and we are very given to helping people. I had a lot of friends. And I miss that a lot, too. Without that you're almost nothing.

My finances at the present . . . I don't know what to think. I've gone over it so often I don't know what to think now, because I'm in a difficult situation. And despite the fact that I'm working here in the museum, which gives me a good wage looking at it in one way, I now have . . . on top of my rent and the rest of it, I am paying what they call here 'bankruptcy' (*in English*) so as not to lose my apartment. I was on the point of losing it in 1987. My life had become hopeless. Never, not even in the time of Batista, was anybody thrown on to the street. And I was terrified that would happen to me. And I had to file for bankruptcy, which cost me enormous sums . . . vast sums, because I lost my job overnight. A job I had before, working in a restaurant, earning a lot of money. But fool that I was, I never saved a penny. They sold the restaurant and the new owner threw us all out. He wanted new people. I was in the street. No money. No work. And I said to myself, I have always had luck in that respect – I had always had luck since I'd arrived – I'll find something tomorrow.

I spent nearly six months without a job. I was starving, and I never wish what I went through on anyone. Then the landlord took me to court because I couldn't pay. I got a letter from a firm of lawyers saying, 'Don't lose your apartment, come and see us.' That they'd help me. The help was, I had to pay up a huge sum of money so as not to get thrown out. At that stage I was working here in the museum. I tried to come to some arrangement with the landlord but he wasn't having any of it. He wanted the money up front and I owed him a lot. I couldn't pay it all. I could, as I did, pay the lawyers, but I couldn't pay the landlord all I owed because it was a horrible figure. I finally made an arrangement to pay it over a time and I'm still paying it. You feel (*deep breath*) as if you are drowning. And I try, I do all the overtime I can, but on the other hand it doesn't work out . . . when you look at it from another angle, because then you have to pay more tax. You get out of the problems for a moment, but then you realise when you pay your taxes (*laughs*) what cruel things they are. (*Laughs*)

I found the museum because when I was unemployed during those six months I tried everywhere. And I remember in one place I almost went down on my knees. I went to employment agencies, to restaurants, I tried everything. Then I saw this ad in the *Village Voice*, that they were taking on staff to work in the Metropolitan Museum. So, I went along. They were acoustic guides which are like cassette recorders. You put them in one ear and they tell you where to go, what galleries and so on. I had to explain to people how to work the recorders, how to use the fast-forward, the rewind, and how to fit the earphone. And give them other sort of information they might want on the exhibitions. That was my work. Then they put me here because I sold more of those tapes than anyone. And sales had been low. So then I overheard one of the security guards talking to one of the girls who works with me and saying how well things were going for him, the good money he was earning. And I said to him, 'Where's that? Here?' And he says, 'Yes, yes. You fill in an application form on the sixth floor and if they call you well and good.' I did that, and within a week they called me and they said, 'When do you want to start work?'

But, even though I had found work, my financial situation remained difficult, very hard, and I couldn't keep on paying so much rent, and that's why all that happened to me, the business of the rent, the credit cards. I'll be three years working here come November.

You have to put up with a lot from people, especially people with money. (*Sighs*) They're horrible. Every time you have to deal with them . . . On Christmas Eve last year I had a serious run in with one of them, one of the millionaires who donates a lot of money to the museum, because I said we could not accept responsibility for fur coats in the cloakroom. And he had a girl with a fur coat. I just said no. It was a regulation of the museum that we could not take fur coats. He slowly began to sort of insult me. Then in the end he was extremely rude. He said, 'Fuck you.' So then it transpired that I, who did nothing, didn't say a word, ended up with a final warning letter, and the boss himself said it was because he was a trustee, a millionaire who donated a lot of money. He didn't want to tell me the whole story, but they used me as a scapegoat. Because [the millionaire] had said, 'I'm going to do everything in my power to get you fired.' And I didn't say a word, because I have witnesses. And then, in order to accuse me of something or have some grounds, the boss said that I had responded by saying the same to him, 'Fuck you'. (*Lowers voice*) Which is not true, because everyone you just saw here was around me. They heard everything. They saw everything and they said I never said anything. Then our boss said to me, 'Right. If you

314

get me a letter from each of them saying that you said nothing insulting, that you said nothing to him, everything will be sorted out.' I got three letters from the girls who were around. 'No, he never said a word at any time. We were present.' And about four days later I get the final warning letter. And when you get a final warning it means if you get one more, or there's another incident, they fire you.

I'm still in that situation. I'm in the process of fighting it through the union, since we pay for it. So I'm working at trying to get the notice rescinded through the union. It's not that you just have the final warning, but if at some future date I try to get another job, that will go against me. When you are working at what you are supposed to, and on top of that you're not saying a word and they are insulting you and you are trying to tolerate it, to hold on, and finally it turns out you're to blame, that's very sad. And paying the union and all. So, that's what I'm more or less trying to do with the union now, because it's not fair. It is most unfair. Everyone here has said the same. 'They've been very unfair to you because you're an excellent employee.' And I'm never absent. I never phone in sick. Nothing, in three years. I don't annoy anyone and I work like an animal. That's what everyone says. That's why I'm telling you so many things have happened to me that I can't feel too happy at all. And I want to feel well. I try to adapt to everything, to get accustomed to everything, to be like everyone else because I'm here now, and yet I don't get the chance. It's very hard.

Would you like to go back for good?

I don't know. I say that not for me, but I don't know how people would accept me if I went back for good. I feel as if I have committed a crime, having gone and left my family, my friends, the places I love so much. My country. I think I would always feel as if I had committed a crime, as if I had been in jail, and although I would have repaid my crime there'd always be the feeling that I had committed it.

As I was saying, I've been a writer for a long time. One of the things I'd like to do is write about all this. About the part in Cuba before I left, the journey, what's happened since I've been here. Because the Americans always talk a lot about the American Dream, and I want to do a kind of story or article called My Not So American Dream. Because it's really just arrive, work, live, let live, but at the same time it's got nothing to do with that dream about the house and the car, which all seems so strange to me, so hard to swallow. It's like a pill that, I don't know . . . It all seems so absurd – the house, then the couple with the two children, the boy and the girl. The children always seem to be a boy and a girl, the dog, the car in the garage and the big house and the big job. I don't know. I think life is something bigger, something more beautiful.

THE ACADEMICS

30

Rafael Hernández

Rafael Hernández is deputy director of the Centre for Studies on America (CEA) in Havana and director of the department that deals with North America.

13 June 1990

How will Cuba be affected by changes taking place in the Soviet Union and the events of Eastern Europe?

In the short term I think Cuba will suffer economic consequences, as certain products coming from the USSR, such as oil, might be affected not by a change of policy on the part of the Soviets towards Cuba, but by a new and unforeseeable situation within the Soviet Union at a future date. By that, I mean that economic difficulties may develop in the Soviet Union as has happened in the countries of Eastern Europe. In fact, they already have economic difficulties in the Soviet Union, and all that could contribute to – although such might not be their aim – an adjustment in policy towards Cuba, a major adjustment.

In any event, the supply of certain products would be affected, and already there are delays in supplies of certain goods coming from the socialist camp which have affected the Cuban economy.

This does not necessarily mean that relations between Cuba and the Soviet Union are doomed to deteriorate. I believe a myth has grown up around relations between Cuba and the Soviet Union. People say that Cuba receives oil from, and sells sugar to, the Soviet Union at preferential prices, but, in fact, trade relations between Cuba and the USSR are mutually beneficial. It is cheaper for the USSR to buy Cuban sugar than to produce it domestically; it is cheaper for the USSR to buy Cuban citrus fruit than to buy it at home; and Cuba is a market for Soviet products which are not necessarily marketable in other countries. So, I think both parts have to make the market more efficient and make the quality of trade and products more efficient.

So, in that regard, I don't anticipate a fall-off in trade relations. What has happened in the last two years is that after Gorbachev's visit – and Abalkin, Deputy President of the Council of Ministers, has just been here – these visits have contributed to reformulating our collaboration and trade relationship and the general economic ties between Cuba and the Soviet Union.

There has been too much speculation, probably wishful thinking on the part of Cuba's enemies, about a dramatic reduction in this relationship.

And then Cuba has a policy of economic expansion towards the countries of Western Europe – Spain, Italy – [and] towards Japan and China, and they all have trade relations with Cuba. Cuba has also expanded its economic relations with Latin America in the last few years. Fidel's visit to Brazil helped to broaden horizons in that sense.*

Therefore, I would say that the changes in Eastern Europe have to be taken in context and not simply seen from one perspective, because it is a more complex relationship, in which both parts, I repeat, mutually benefit. And then I would also say that the USSR, as a superpower, cannot not have a policy towards the Third World. Nor can it not have an international alliance policy. It is one thing for the USSR to have revised its foreign policy, and another for it to leave a vacuum in its alliance policy. I think Cuba, more than an economic ally, has been an important political ally of the USSR. It has been a sort of problematic alliance model – I mean, it has not always been harmonious, but it has been

---

* Fidel Castro visited Brazil in March 1990.

a model for acceptable relations between a large country and a small country, especially if you look at the type of relationship the United States has with most of its allies, or even the Soviet relationship with its East European allies. I think it is in the Soviet Union's interests, politically speaking, to maintain good relations with Cuba for its international standing, in the Third World, in the international community and as a matter of credibility. If the Soviet Union were to abandon Cuba, what credibility would it have for Third World countries given a choice? So I think the whole subject must be seen in that more complex context. Nor do I believe that Soviet policy can be reduced to a single variable. Of course, that is not to say that there are not trends within the USSR shouting for the need to reduce aid to Cuba, about the need for a less committed policy towards the Third World etcetera. But I think they are very short-sighted attitudes which will with difficulty find currency, because they are not in the interests of the Soviet Union as a superpower.

What direction will Cuba take in this new phase of political isolation?

I don't think we are suffering political isolation. I think there is ideological isolation, which is a different thing. Cuba has more political relations internationally than ever before. What is happening is that our ideological terminology, a certain form of our ideological rhetoric, got imprisoned in many patterns or formulae of a dogmatic or traditional kind, and these forms of ideological discourse curiously existed side by side with very creative changes. The paradox started when a revolution like ours – which didn't follow established doctrine and was at variance with the patterns of the traditional Marxist-Leninist-Stalinist vision in the 1950s, which did not allow for the possibility of a socialist revolution in Cuba – actually happened. And this revolution was, besides, capable of finding its own road and of creating new forms of development, of exercising revolutionary power and of mass mobilisation etcetera.

In other words, a feature of this revolution was its creative forms of participation and international influence, yet with time it adopted a very orthodox, very classical form of ideological speech, especially from the 1970s on, so I think what you hear is that same old rhetoric stamped with the most orthodox Marxist-Leninist phrases and terms, but what is actually happening in Cuba now has nothing to do with orthodoxy.

It is our fault that we have not been able to convey, or find appropriate terms to convey, that new reality. So, while there are very important changes taking place in Cuba, while debate is being made openly accessible to a new generation of people – people who think, who are a product of the Revolution – there is a growing awareness in Cuba of problems which we have had for many years and which need to be resolved. We don't have a solution to them all, but there is an awareness of them and [of] the need for a solution in the immediate term, as they are problems which involve the fate of the Revolution and the fate of socialism in Cuba.

So, I think there's a sort of schizophrenia developing around international change and the vocabulary being used which still doesn't express it well or cogently. In any case, the content of public debate has changed substantially in Cuba in roughly the last two years, and I believe certain things contributed to that. One of those things is the need for us to revise our relations and our vision of socialism in Cuba and in the world. But another matter of major importance is the need to make our society develop and operate on the basis of ever more dynamic, participative and creative patterns, and all these things are on the agenda for internal discussion. The discussion document for the Fourth Party Congress* is exceptional in its call for open debate of all problems.

What has given rise to this new culture, this new moment in internal political debate, is a tremendous blossoming of thought and ideas. Of course, this doesn't take the sometimes violent form it has taken in Eastern Europe or the Soviet Union; this is something more measured in its responsibility and awareness of the problems we have, because we are still only 90 miles from the United States, and that's the way it will remain until they wipe us from the map. That presence is always there, so we cannot just throw ourselves into – and it wouldn't be advisable even if

* Scheduled for 1991. As yet no date has been set.

we were at the other end of the world – a cultural revolution. The price of the cultural revolutions that have taken place in the socialist countries has been too high, and I think it's better to take it step by step, and by this I do not mean to justify conservatism or immobility. Changes have to be made and they have to be made day by day. At the same time, there's no need to be constantly waving the flag of the besieged fortress . . . that the Americans are there and they are going to invade us. What I do believe is that there must be an awareness of the responsibility we have in this country regarding the gradual development of a process of change, not of violent change or difficult change, because those prices have always been paid, and we too, at times when we have wanted to have violent and very fast changes, have paid for it later.

Personally, I am all for the idea of moderation, that the spaces for discussion open up more and more, and what we have witnessed here in Cuba in the last two years has been the opening up of space for discussion. Whoever doesn't see that is blind. Whoever comes here to Cuba [will hear that it] is being discussed on the radio, and [in] the papers – of course, not just one paper, you have to read them all, *Trabajadores, Juventud rebelde*. You have to read *Tribuna de la economía*. You have to read from different sources of information, and you have to speak to people and go to workers' meetings where they discuss problems, and you will not yet get the broadest and most open and profound participation, but nevertheless there is a wide space for discussion. I mean, there's still a long way to go before that collective participation becomes participation in decision-making and the control of policy. But that participation in discussion is an increasing sign of change and development, of a new political stage of socialism in Cuba.

Up to now that space has been circumscribed by the definition 'Within the Revolution, everything. Against the Revolution, nothing.' How do people know where the dividing line now stands?

Well, there isn't a perfectly defined line in many areas, so it is the debate among revolutionaries that has to widen the democratic space. Democracy has to come from revolutionaries, not from the enemies of socialism. I don't think, along with most people in Cuba, I'm sure, that the Cuban community in the United States, a fine example of intolerance and ideological inflexibility, is going to give us democracy. Nor are the North Americans who oppressed this country for 150 years. We have got to give ourselves democracy.

Take those Christians who for thirty years have been fighting for this country, for the homeland, to develop the nation and to advance the goals of social justice, of equality, of the redistribution of income, of improving the living conditions of the people, of national independence – those Christians have won the space they have after putting up with years of discrimination here, political discrimination, and they have now won that space, fighting. This must be recognised, and they must have a space, and they must be – not only from the point of view of their civil rights, but of their political rights in Cuba – considered among the finest revolutionaries of the land, vanguard revolutionaries. They have earned that.

I think that in the measure the democratic participation of revolutionaries is guaranteed, democracy will expand, and this must be done in a rational, intelligent, measured and balanced way. At the same time, there must be a policy not just for revolutionaries, because the people, the nation, is not composed entirely of revolutionaries, of people in the vanguard, of communists. So, in the measure that revolutionaries can take greater part in the decision-making process and in the control of decisions, to the same degree, I believe, we will be laying more solid foundations for a broadening of democracy and political participation in Cuba. What will political participation and the possibility to dissent in Cuba be like in ten years' time? That depends on us – that is, on what we revolutionaries do in this country to extend democracy.

I think there is already a push for change from below. The issue is that politicians everywhere have responsibilities, and part of their responsibilities is to respond to those pressures from below. Another part is to make people aware of the real difficulties facing the country, and I think that the more this dialogue between politicians and the people is co-ordinated and made effective, the more we can move ahead in a balanced and rational manner. Because at a certain point, when the temperature rises to 35 degrees in the shade, what people in Cuba feel like doing is screaming because they can't get a cold beer on the corner. So the issue is to try and harmonise the social objectives of long- and medium-range policies with the short-term needs of the people. Of course, that all sounds very nice in a sentence; the question is to reconcile these issues in a country which is not rich. We are not Sweden. We cannot debate the issues like the Swedes because this is not a rich country. This is a country which has scant resources, and that implies the need to develop ever more creative and practical ways of developing our economy. To what extent we can develop these new forms of economic organisation, of administration, of control over the economy, of initiative and of decentralisation – to what extent we can combine centralisation and decentralisation and what weight is given to that – will depend to a large degree on the immediate situation we have to face.

The fact of the matter is, in my view, that bad times often make for more effective and more politically astute decisions. I think the bad times are going to make us abandon some Byzantine discussions and bring us into a phase of realism without, of course, ever discarding the idea that a socialist society has to have values. A socialist society cannot permit itself the luxury of forgetting that it is based on values, not just on the growth of the economy, and those values are social justice, equality, participation, freedom – the exercising of a socially aware and responsible freedom – responsibility towards the social order. Let's say, to a large extent, a socialist regime is based on a political culture, it is not solely based on a political regime. And what happened in socialist Europe is that there was no socialist culture, only political regimes, a political power, historically a product of the Second World War, as everyone knows, and of Soviet tanks; to a large extent, an organic culture of a socialist society and of socialist values never developed there. Cubans who went to the Soviet Union and especially to Eastern Europe as of the 1960s always felt that the values which we aspired to create here didn't exist in those countries. And in the 1960s, when we were going through a phase of revolutionary idealism, we felt that more keenly in countries like Hungary and Poland, when you might walk around the streets talking to people, and see that there wasn't the slightest thought for their neighbour, not the slightest concern for what was happening in the world, nor the struggles that were taking place in other parts of the world. And when we stopped being idealists, Cuban society nevertheless retained a set of values which, I believe, are inseparable from socialism, inseparable from ethics or morality, from a set of *human* aspirations. And I think that that socialist content is not at odds with criticism, nor with freedom of participation, nor with public debate, nor with economic efficiency. I think that's what we have learned and what we are learning, especially in these last few years.

Do you think these values have caught on among the youth of Cuba?

Look, one of the things most criticised by young people is the double standard – the preaching of values and then the practising of the opposite. I think young people in general are not disillusioned or opportunist. That's not to say that there aren't opportunists and disillusioned people among them who simply want to adapt to the rules of the game of society. I think the vast majority of Cuban youngsters, or an important and very active part of them, have a spirit of rebellion, of criticism, and are not afraid, and I think these are the essential ingredients of a revolutionary change. I think it is good that it should be so. And while I may agree or disagree with some of the things they have to say, I always find them totally honest. This honesty is particularly aimed at criticising the double standard, the pretence you get in older generations, all of which at bottom means a reclaiming of socialist values, since they are criticising behaviour which is not consistent with those values, which is all show and no substance, and it is against this show, this *teque*, as we call it, against this pretence and false unanimity that young people direct their criticism.

*How do you think something like the drug scandal of last summer could have occurred in this country?**

* A scandal involving General Arnaldo Ochoa Sánchez. See p.303.

Well, there's no easy answer to that one. I think it happened for various reasons, but especially because at institutional level there is not enough control by the people. That was one of the great lessons, and I think that is one of the subjects for debate on the current agenda: the need for the people to have more control over government. In my view this showed that even people who had demonstrated loyalty to the Revolution, who had shown themselves capable of sacrifice for the Revolution, who had undoubtedly been key figures at certain times and in certain tasks and had served the Revolution, were susceptible to corruption, and, evidently, they weren't the only ones – there are other people too who have given in to corruption. So, in the measure in which we open up participation, not only to debate, but to decision-making and control – that is, political control from the bottom – I believe we will be able to deal much more adequately, in a much less tragic and sorrowful way, with situations such as this, as we will be able to foresee when these things might happen or when they begin to happen, and not when they have already exploded. In that respect, I think the Ochoa and Abrantes trials revitalised the morale of the Revolution, as it was something which was discussed publicly; there was the political clarity to decide that this should be publicly discussed. And everybody took part in those public discussions. I think, in that regard, there was a collective examination of conscience. It was an exercise in self-criticism and deep reflection on our faults and on our problems – not those caused by the enemy, by imperialism, which is right there besieging us etcetera – but on our own problems, the problems which we ourselves have created. From that point of view I believe the affair, however tragic and sorrowful it was, represented an important moment in all this critical review of our situation. I still don't think we have got all there is to get out of this process yet, nor that we have learned all the lessons. But I think what is happening now is proof that we are heading in that direction.

Is Cuba going to be the last socialist state?

I wouldn't be so quick as to say that socialism is going to disappear everywhere except in Cuba. I think this is an evolving story. I would like to know what will happen in Eastern Europe when the working masses can't get by on a daily basis, when the socialist state isn't there to solve social security problems and other issues. I think that the aspirations towards a more just, more egalitarian society, where people can have freedom and equality at the same time, will go on, because it is part of humanity's aspirations towards social justice. I don't see why we have to think that that will be swept away by the worldwide triumph of capitalism. Because in the United States – which is supposedly the opulent society, the wealthiest society in the West – you find serious problems still exist: the difficulties faced by a considerable part of the population; the situation of thousands of people who have nowhere to live; or the situation of thousands of people who live in conditions of poverty or have problems with the health service or with access to education. I think these are examples of how capitalist society does not solve the problems despite the fact that it is prosperous.

Now, let's imagine socialism in a small country, a poor country which has economic problems, or a country which has limited possibilities of launching itself on the international market. In that respect, I don't think socialism will disappear as an option or as an historic programme. But what type of socialism are we going to have? I think that's the question for Cuba. Are we going to continue with the socialism we had in the 1970s or 1980s? We have to have a different socialism; political rectification in Cuba is about that – it's about having to change the socialism we have, to be able to continue being socialist. It is not a vindication of what we have up to now, it's the need to change what we have had up to now, and in that sense I think there is a crisis of that kind of socialism: of the authoritarian kind, of the vertical kind, of the kind of socialism that is not linked to the masses, that is built on bureaucracy and not on the values of socialist culture. I think for the moment there's no way out, but we are only half-way through the story, perhaps we are only at the beginning of the story of all those changes in Eastern Europe and the Soviet Union, and we are still not sure of what's going to happen. So far, most of the signs we are getting from Eastern Europe and the USSR are signs which say that they have still not found working formulae. So, they have abandoned a Stalinist socialism, they have abandoned a socialism that was still prisoner of a host of problems which gave rise to the Stalinist regime and its later expansion through Europe after the Second World War. But they still haven't found a suitable form. Perestroika, glasnost, the New Thinking and all that has still not produced an efficient political formula. Not that there aren't good and positive aspects to those changes, but they still haven't found a formula which guarantees a minimum of political stability. If every day there is less butter in Moscow and more unemployment in Warsaw, whatever they are doing isn't working. That doesn't mean that it might not start working next week, but up till now it hasn't worked.

I would say that even though many changes had to be made in Eastern Europe, those societies, before the changes, were much more stable economically than they are now – the GDR, Czechoslovakia, Hungary, Romania – and, obviously, the Soviet economy under Brezhnev was in better shape than it is now as regards solving the people's immediate needs. By that I do not mean to defend the methods of economic organisation of the USSR as being the most adequate. I think we ourselves copied a system of Soviet economic management which had many flaws. We achieved a growth in the economy, but after a certain point this tended to produce stagnation, and it also left aside many very important social considerations in the economy. I'm not going to defend that. But, objectively, there was butter in Moscow, and now there isn't. So that could undermine the positive values in the spirit of perestroika, as in every revolution there are positive and negative aspects to it. One sector of the pro-perestroika faction is all for liberalism. They are more liberal than the North Americans, to the right of J. K. Galbraith. There are ideologues of that rubbishy kind. That doesn't make sense – I don't mean from a classical Marxist-Leninist point of view, but from a classical North American liberal perspective. So, in my opinion, I think the Soviet Union is in a period of confusion or of lack of direction as to the road it's taking. This was a sort of Pandora's box that they opened, and so what was good came out along with a series of evil spirits. The issue is now whether in the competition between the good and the evil spirits, the good ones will win out. And that has created an atmosphere of total instability, because for the people, or for the vast majority of the people, politics goes via the stomach. So, there are economic difficulties . . . they have stopped believing in what until now they said was the best system in the world, that socialism was the marvel of all marvels. That's not the case. And, on top of that, they have nothing to eat, or they don't have what they want to eat.

It's not the first time that there's been a revolution which carries within it a conservative tendency, and that tendency makes the experiment fail. There have been many occasions of social crisis when the left has not been able to articulate a coherent programme and the right has simply taken the lead with popular support. Why was fascism popular in Germany? Why? Because it simply improved the country economically. Then it led it to the Second World War, to the Holocaust. But it got the country going economically. So, the worst is, you now find in Eastern Europe a predominant tendency leading to economic growth but which, from a political angle, could turn into terrible systems with popular backing. It wouldn't be the first time it happened.

I think what has happened in Cuba is that prudence has predominated, because we have been experimenting for thirty years and we have brought those experiments to the whole country. So, at the moment, various experiments are being carried out in the economy. It's wrong to think an orthodox attitude of the period of Soviet stagnation prevails there. We completely rejected Soviet political economy of the 1970s and 1980s. We have to think beyond what the Soviets are now doing in their economy. We have to address our own economic problems and see what is the most efficient system to apply to Cuba, taking what is good from an economy where the state plays a fundamental role and, at the same time, drawing on what is good in management, organisation and efficiency in the capitalist system. And that's what's being done. Now we are not doing it all over the country, or in a whole province, or in a specific sector of the economy, but on the basis of individual enterprises, and we are looking at how these work. There is, for example, a group of military enterprises which produces uniforms, boots and that, not weapons. A group of those military enterprises is working under a capitalist management system, with a market and salaries, and whoever produces more, earns more. They are decentralised and have a budget, because that is one of the problems we have, the excessive centralisation of management.

So, now you ask, are you going to forget about centralisation? Is everything going to be decentralised? You can't do that, because if the country has $600 million to spend on everything, you can't let every enterprise have its own dollar budget, or dollar account, simply because there are certain sectors of the economy that bring in hard currency, and others that spend it and don't bring in any. So, you need to buy medicine, you have a priority project, so how would you work it out if every enterprise takes its own decisions. Those are the two extreme positions, let's say. A middle course has to be found which combines decentralisation, making management more efficient, and which ensures that there is more incentive to work, more efficiency and more productivity, and yet at the same time retains a capacity to identify goals at a national level for which priorities are set out. This would be fine if this was a country with all the financial and economic resources at its disposal, but that's not the case. This is a small economy and we have to work wonders. But again, I feel that our current difficulties will make us more creative and more efficient, because nobody is going to help get us out of this spot. We have to sort this out ourselves.

How do you think relations will develop with the United States?

In the short term, I don't think there will be much change. The main problems between Cuba and the United States in the last few years were international questions: the conflict in Central America, the conflict in Angola, the conflict in the Horn of Africa etcetera. However, in the last eighteen months there has been a dramatic evolution in those international conflicts. The situation in Africa is no longer a problem, because the United States participated in the South-West Africa talks as an active member and intermediary in all the negotiatons. Cuba withdrew its troops from Ethiopia, Cuba withdrew its military advisers from Nicaragua, and now the Sandinistas have lost the elections, so Nicaragua isn't even a subject for discussion between us. The situation in El Salvador is moving towards negotiation. And if in the past the United States accused Cuba of being a Soviet base, now relations between the United States and the Soviet Union are such that the Soviet threat has ceased to exist. It's no longer a credible line; the Soviet presence in Cuba is a metaphor. So, in that sense, the problems that up to now have been on the Cuba–US agenda . . . from the North American perspective there has been huge progress in the last eighteen months, and in some cases both the United States and Cuba have done their bit to achieve this progress, as in the case of South-West Africa.

However, now the United States, on foot of perestroika and the collapse of Eastern Europe, hopes Cuba will collapse. So when one asks people in the United States what has to happen for Cuba and the United States to have better relations, it's no longer that Cuba should stop aiding Nicaragua, or that Cuba should withdraw its troops from Africa. Now it's that Cuba should make changes along the lines of perestroika. That is outrageous for any Cuban, because up to now it was always that we copied the Soviets, and now it's that we're not copying them enough, and that's the reason why the United States won't alter its policy towards Cuba.

I think what will happen is that the United States will wait a year or two to see what happens, and when the regime doesn't collapse they will try and do what they have always tried to do, that is, destabilise socialism in Cuba, only instead of using force they will try to do so by diplomatic means, which is what many people in the United States think should be done.

So, finally a 'Let's sit down and talk with Cuba' line will prevail, because we will achieve more than we have done so far after thirty years of isolation and pressure. Now, I don't think they are going to stop the pressure. I think the negotiating table is also a set for pressure. And if at this stage there is no substantial, significant dialogue, there may be in two years' time, but they will not give up on force. I'm not necessarily thinking here of military force, I'm thinking of force in general, of coercion, and I think that means relations will improve very slowly.

I think that when that decision is reached, the government of the United States won't care about the Cuban community [in the US], or the right wing of the Cuban community, or the Cuban American National Foundation, or any of that. It won't care, because it will feel the need to do so in the national interest. The United States had the national interest in mind when it sat down to negotiate with Cuba and to talk with Cuba in 1974, 1975, 1977, and it did so without reference to the Cuban community. When the United States decided to abandon plans for a direct attack on Cuba in 1962, as a result of the Missile Crisis, they did so in the national interest and they didn't ask permission of the right-wing Cuban community. And when under Reagan they signed the Immigration Agreement, and they sat down to negotiate about South-West Africa, two issues opposed by the right-wing Cuban community, they did so because it was in the national interest of the United States.

Is it in the interest of the United States to sit down and talk with Cuba now? I think so, but they can wait two years to see what happens, and I think that's what they'll do, because they think that within two years, if socialism hasn't collapsed in Cuba, if Fidel Castro isn't gone from the scene – which is what some of them think will happen – if there are going to be more economic difficulties . . . I think, well, they are banking on that, on economic difficulties, and if Cuba is in that situation, they think they will be in a better position to negotiate.

I think that's a mistake. If we sit down feeling more economically insecure, or more militarily insecure, we would not be in the best form for negotiating. Because, historically, we have been more flexible in negotiations when we have felt more secure. If we feel threatened, if we feel under pressure, we are not going to negotiate, we are not going to go about it the best way, in such a way as we would take the most appropriate steps, do our best, or contribute to a spirit of dialogue and negotiation. So, I think that's a mistake. But anyway, I think Cuba will respond to signals of negotiation if they are based on a certain amount of realism and a will to achieve concrete results.

31

Wayne Smith

Dr Wayne S. Smith is Adjunct Professor of Latin American Studies at the School of Advanced Studies (SAIS), Johns Hopkins University, in Washington, DC. He is the author of the book The Closest of Enemies, *which analyses US policy towards Cuba during the early revolutionary period, when he was a junior officer at the US Embassy in Havana (before it was closed). Later, under the Carter administration, Dr Smith was Head of Mission at the US Interests Section in Havana when it opened in 1977. He resigned his position and left the foreign service in 1982 because of Reagan administration policy.*

June 1989

We are all very disappointed in the attitude reflected by the Bush administration recently. It had been hoped that the Bush administration – that is, no one expected that the administration was going to rush to re-establish diplomatic relations; certainly, that would not be at the top of its agenda – but at the very least [that it would] be willing to sit down, negotiate some of the issues between the two countries, and perhaps ease up on visa policies, have some cultural exchanges; that there might be some slight warming of relations.

Well, all these hopes, at least for the moment, have been dashed. Dashed by the Baker Memo of the end of March of this year, which says in effect that the United States is not interested in improving relations with Cuba. I quote: 'because Cuban behaviour hasn't

changed sufficiently to warrant a change in US attitudes'. It goes
on to say that Cuban policies in the hemisphere haven't changed.
It still likes supporting revolution and so forth. I mean, this is
patently absurd, and one really despairs. I recall that when I was
director of Cuban Affairs at the Department of State back in 1977,
we indicated that there were three major fields or issues that had
to be addressed before there could be a substantial improvement
in relations. Number one: Cuban troops had to begin to leave
Africa. Number two: There had to be some improvement in
Cuba's human rights performance, and especially in terms of
releasing political prisoners. And number three: A reduction in
Soviet–Cuban military ties.

Well now, ha-ha, ten years later, troops are coming out of
Angola. They have negotiated seriously in southern Africa in
negotiations brokered last year by the United States. Sensible
negotiations, I might add, which for the first time took into
account the security concerns of all sides. Up until that point,
the United States, without any regard for what was happening
on the ground, would simply demand that Cuban troops leave.
I mean, these demands were being made at a time when South
African troops would be 150 miles deep in Angola. The US
response to that was simply to demand that Cuba get its troops
out of Angola, as though we were trying to clear the way for
South Africa. Finally, in 1988, a sensible Assistant Secretary
of State for African Affairs, Chester Crocker, did broker these
talks. The Cubans negotiated seriously. They obviously wanted a
negotiated solution. They had put forward a negotiating solution
in 1984, which is very similar to what was agreed in 1988. The
difference in 1984 was that South Africa was not interested. What
brought about the change that made the agreement possible in
1988 was not so much a change in Cuba's attitude, as the fact
that Cuba sent in about 15,000–20,000 more troops on a wing
of MiG-23 aircraft that badly bloodied the South Africans at
the battle of Cuito Cuanavale, and it became apparent to the
South Africans that they had better negotiate because they might
lose, and later were going to have to pay an increasing cost to
remain in Namibia and Angola. So the South Africans came
around, negotiated, and now Cuban troops are coming out of

Angola. In other words, one of the terms we made in 1977 is being met.

Human rights? Cuba has released now most of its political prisoners. There are only a handful left, maybe 200 or so, and the Cuban government indicates that most of those will be released very shortly.*

Now, there hasn't been any particular reduction in Soviet–Cuban ties, but then there really cannot be until there is some easing of tensions between the United States and Cuba. But, as both the Cubans and Soviets have privately indicated, they are perfectly willing to reduce the level of Soviet military assistance to Cuba, provided that it is accompanied by, or provided that follows on, an indication from the United States that it wishes an easing of tensions. In other words, if Cuba doesn't feel so threatened by the United States, then there can indeed be a reduction of the Soviet–Cuban military relationship.

But two of the preconditions, if you want to call them that, of 1977 have now been met, and the Bush administration chooses to say there hasn't been any change in Cuban conduct, and therefore we aren't interested in improving relations. I mean, this is patently absurd. And you find people in the US government who refer to Cuba as though its policies hadn't changed since 1961. Again, this is absurd.

During the 1960s, Castro used to say that Cuba would help guerrillas anywhere and everywhere, that the objective of the Cuban government was to turn the Andes into the Sierra Maestra of Latin America. They wanted to bring about many Vietnams. He chided the Soviet Union for thinking it was possible to carry on *détente* with the West. Peaceful co-existence, said Castro, between East and West was impossible. There was only one way to deal with the imperialist and that was through the barrel of a rifle. Not a shred of accommodation in Castro's policies at that time.

And let me add, as a postscript, that I certainly am not at all sure, I have very strong doubts, that we could have come to an accommodation with Castro in those early years. And I thought that the containment policy which we put in place in the early

---

* In July 1990 there were two long-term prisoners left.

1960s made a lot of sense. Though I don't mean the extremes to which we went. The Bay of Pigs, obviously, was [that] rarest of all things, as someone described it – a perfect failure. Ah man! Trying to get the Mafia to assassinate Castro, and some of the raids and all that, were a violation of international law I don't at all condone. I was too junior an officer at that point to have known about them. Had I known about some of the assassination attempts against Castro, and some of the other things, I might have left the foreign service almost as soon as I came in. It might not have taken me until 1982 to leave. But a policy of trying to contain Castro where he was in the process of trying to thrust out in the hemisphere made sense. But that policy on Castro's part of thrusting out into the hemisphere really came to an end, pretty well, by the 1960s, by the end of [that] decade. It hadn't worked, first of all. Nowhere had the guerrillas won. Secondly, the Soviets didn't like it, and they put constant pressure on Castro to swing in behind their gradualist popular front tactics. So, by the end of the 1960s, Castro did begin to swing in behind popular front tactics; to give up by and large on armed struggle and to reach out to re-establish diplomatic relations with the same governments he had once vowed to overthrow.

There was what you might call a bleep on the radar screen in 1979 when the Sandinistas won in Nicaragua, and that caused Soviet and Cuban theorists to ask themselves, for a brief time, if perhaps they had moved away from the armed struggle too quickly. Perhaps, after all, as someone put it, Che Guevara was right. And there were some meetings in Moscow at which Soviet and Cuban theoreticians mulled over the possibility or the desirability of going back to more aggressive tactics in Latin America. But, with the failure of the Salvadorean guerrillas in January of 1981, they decided that, in fact, they had been right in going for popular front tactics, and the Soviets began to put out statements, and articles appeared in Soviet journals, saying that the moral of the Sandinista Revolution, or the lesson to be learnt from it, was not that armed struggle is successful, but that leftist unity is. Since this is simply a variation on popular front tactics, it was a way of saying we are sticking to the old traditional line.

There was a meeting held in Havana in 1982 at which the

Cubans themselves indicated that [in all of Latin America] armed struggle might remain a valid tactic, [that] the proper conditions [for it] existed . . . only . . . in two countries – El Salvador and Guatemala – and after the elections in Guatemala that was removed from the list. So El Salvador remains the single country in Latin America where the Cubans say that armed struggle is an appropriate tactic, and it's quite clear that even there they prefer a negotiated solution. So that the US government, when first the Reagan and then the Bush administrations say – and here I am quoting from the [March] Memo of Secretary of State Baker: 'Cuba continues to engage in military adventurism abroad and to support subversive movements in the western hemisphere to the detriment of peace, stability and democratic processes' – I wonder what he means? The administration charges that the Cubans are supplying the Salvadorian guerrillas with arms and so forth, but they haven't come up with any real evidence of it. I am sure the Cubans are providing medical attention to wounded guerrillas, possibly some training. We seem to think it's OK to continue to provide humanitarian assistance to the Contras, which would be the equivalent, I would say. We don't see anything wrong with that. We have stopped military aid to the Contras, at least for the moment. Cuba says that it isn't providing military assistance to the Salvadorian guerrillas. Now, we may wish to dispute that, but it seems to me that since we haven't been able to come up with much evidence of it, the best way to address the problem, rather than arguing about it, is to have a large UN or OAS verification team on the ground to make certain that no arms are going in to either El Salvador or, for that matter, to the Contras in Nicaragua. Now that's the way to deal with it, not simply to argue. It's a sterile argument when you say the other side is, and they say they aren't, and neither of you produce any evidence. Anyway, the point I am trying to make here is that there isn't really any evidence of this Cuban adventurism in the hemisphere. That simply isn't true. Some question-mark in El Salvador, although even there it is perfectly clear the Cubans do prefer a negotiated solution. But they don't control the FMLN (Farabundo Martí Liberation Front); they can't produce the FMLN at negotiations, for the FMLN doesn't feel that the time has come.

It's apparent to most, I think, that we could productively deal with the Cubans. I mean, after all, if we can have serious negotiations in southern Africa, reach an agreement, and Cuban troops can begin to go home, as they are, why can we not have similar negotiations on Central America? Why can't the United States, Cuba, the Soviet Union, the Central American countries, the other interested parties, the Group of Eight – why can't we all sit down at a table and work out a formula or series of formulae covering military assistance to the area, and perhaps bring about phased reciprocal reductions, hopefully leading to negotiations or agreement or a series of agreements which might even lead, in the future, to a demilitarised zone in Central America. It seems to me that this is eminently do-able. But the United States says that it will not negotiate with Cuba or negotiate with the Soviet Union, or, for that matter, it won't even sit down at the table with the Nicaraguans, because this is our back yard and we are not going to negotiate anything with anyone here, and because we have, as Mr Fitzwater in his inimitable way put it the other day, we have a security interest here and the other side doesn't.

It seems to me a peculiar argument to make at a time when we are fuelling the war in Afghanistan; when we refuse to sit down with the Soviets to work out a formula for ending military assistance both to the government and to the Mujahadeen – we won't do it. What are our security interests there? That's the Soviet back yard, so we want to have it all ways. We won't negotiate Nicaragua, because that's our back yard, but we are going to do what we want to in Afghanistan. It's the kind of argument that might have worked in 1927, but it doesn't work today, and it certainly does not respond to the sort of New Thinking that Mr Gorbachev is putting forward in the world.

I have been working on the Cuban problem for thirty-two years now, and I must say [to] this latest development, [to] the fact that the Bush administration now says that they are not going to improve relations either, and [that] Assistant Secretary for Latin American Affairs, Mr Bernie Aronson (the designated Assistant Secretary, he hasn't been confirmed by the Senate yet), in a briefing ten days ago, was saying that we really were not interested in improving relations with Cuba, they would have to completely change or they would have to change their conduct in a more significant way – [my answer was], 'Well, what is it precisely they have to do?' He said, 'Well, I cannot tell you that. I cannot tell you exactly what the Cubans would have to do, but if they do it, we will recognise it.'

Let's be honest about it. The fact is that Cuban policies have changed; that we could now easily deal with Cuba. Cuba now has relations with about 118 countries, that's full diplomatic and trade relations with about 118 countries, with all of our NATO allies, with the socialist countries, with Japan, with the People's Republic of China, with virtually all the countries of the Third World, with the countries of the Non-Aligned Movement and with the majority of Latin American countries. The United States deals with the Soviet Union, with the People's Republic of China and, for God's sakes, with dozens of other countries around the world with which is has sharp disagreements and of which it does not approve. It deals with them anyway because it understands that normal diplomatic relations, normal engagement, is the best way of achieving its objectives and advancing its interests in these countries. That is also true of Cuba, but Cuba is a peculiarly emotional case with the United States. As I once said in a *New York Times* piece, Cuba has the same effect on American administrations that the full moon used to have on werewolves: they just lose their rationality at the mention of Castro or Cuba. [And] administration after administration – or, should I say, adviser after adviser to various administrations – says to the Secretary of State and the President, 'Look, there isn't really any strong constituency in the United States to improving relations with Cuba. Oh well, yes, there may be Wayne Smith and two or three other guys, but there isn't really any power constituency pushing us in the direction of improving relations. On the other hand, we have a small but very strident vocal opposition to any improvements in the persons of the right-wing group in the Cuban-American community . . .'

Now it's perfectly true that the Cuban-American community is not monolithic. Recent polls indicate that probably the majority of Cuban-Americans would prefer to have some sort of dialogue with the Cuban government. That is, they don't like Castro, they don't like the government, if they did they wouldn't be here rather than in Cuba. But after thirty years they understand that it makes sense to deal with that government, to negotiate with it, and that that would, in fact, advance their interests. They want to travel back and forth in the best conditions possible. They want better mail services. They want their families to be able to come up here. They want to be able to send money to their families. All that sort of thing. And that could only come about through negotiations between the two countries. So they are coming around to favour it. But where the majority may favour negotiations, there's the very small minority, stridently right-wing minority, that screams at suggestions that we might even sit down at the same table to negotiate some issue with the Cubans. And they are the ones that are heard. There are a number of them, not only in the Cuban-American community . . . the right wing of the Republican Party does not want even to contemplate dealing with Cuba. That's like waving a red flag in front of a bull. There have been some signs that the Bush administration would take a new look at Cuba policy, that it might take a somewhat more sensible attitude. But once a compromise had been reached in Congress, very early, back in February, on the matter of military aid to the Contras – a compromise bitterly opposed by the right wing of the Republican Party – then the Bush administration began to worry that if it did anything or even suggested that it might take a more sensible attitude towards our Cuba policy, that that would stir up the right wing of the party, and so Mr Baker issued his memo saying we are not interested in improving relations with Cuba.

Obviously, it was addressed to domestic political circles, not to the diplomatic missions. This was described as a memo to US diplomatic missions, but the memo was handed to the AP [Associated Press] long before it reached any of the missions. Now, as I have often said, I don't have any sympathy for the Castro government. I wish that there was a democratic government in Cuba, but there isn't, and there isn't going to be. Castro has been there thirty years. There is no indication that he won't be there another twenty, and after Castro some other socialist Cuban leader will more than likely take over. So, the time has come for the United States to begin to engage with the Cuban government, simply to try to deal with it in a more sensible way.

If there are problems, disagreements between the two countries, as there certainly are, why should we not sit down at the negotiating table, discuss them, and try to resolve as many as possible? That's all I advocate. That isn't anything very sweeping or dramatic, simply a matter of being willing to talk and being willing to solve problems where they can be solved. Who could possibly be against that? Well, I know that the right wing of the Cuban-American community is against it, but how can anyone sensibly be against talking and resolving problems?

As I say, I really, at this point, almost despair that the United States will in my lifetime be able to bring itself to be able to deal sensibly with Cuba, and I think that is ultimately more harmful to the United States than to Cuba. First of all, the fact that we are so irrational, with respect to Cuba, I think undermines the credibility of our leadership. Well, let's say that it tarnishes our image as a strong, self-confident, pragmatic leader of the Western world. It rather suggests someone who is rather pettish and spiteful and bases policy on emotion rather than on careful calculation, and that's not the sort of image that the United States should give. I guess I feel so strongly about US–Cuban relations and the need for sensible US policy towards Cuba because as a younger officer I helped to put together the containment policy, and that made sense at the time, because, as I say, I don't think we could have reached accommodation with Castro at that point. But that time has long since passed. If I helped to build the wall between the two countries, I now am devoting what I had hoped were a few years of my life to bringing the wall down. But apparently, it will be that I will spend the rest of my life, and then perhaps others can take over, in trying to bring it down.

There's that. That certainly lends to the strength of my feelings about this. But there's also the fact that I saw Cuba as something of a metaphor for the way the United States deals with a lot of Third World countries. I mean, Cuba may be an extreme case, but it is not really isolated. I think we need a whole new approach to our dealings, especially with the Third World. We tend to deal rather seriously with the Soviet Union because they are another superpower and they can shoot back. With Western Europe because they are our traditional allies – or in some cases adversaries, but we spring from Europe and, moreover, if our principal foreign policy priority is the Soviet Union, then, concomitantly, NATO and Western Europe as right behind it, because this, of course, is the principal front against the Soviet Union. We deal seriously with Japan because they are a major economic power. China, because they are huge and useful against the Soviet Union. But when it comes to Third World countries, the US behaves almost as though it doesn't matter what we do, because the power margin is so great on our side that we can make almost any mistake we want. In other words, that our superiority is so great that the margins for error are almost limitless. And we tend to deal with the Third World not on the basis of fairness and international law, but simply on the basis of what we want. Our bumbling into the war in Vietnam because we insisted, by golly, that there wasn't going to be any plebiscite there and we were not going to have Ho Chi Minh ruling Vietnam because we didn't want it that way. But one has to weigh costs and risks against the magnitude of the problem and the possible gains. We simply didn't have interest in Vietnam ever to make it worthwhile to go in there, and by going in we simply made things a lot worse. Had the plebiscite been held in 1954, Ho Chi Minh would have become the ruler of Vietnam. It might not have been ideal. Obviously, I would rather have had a Jeffersonian democracy there really, but the Vietnamese people would have avoided almost twenty years of bloody warfare, at the end of which they were more deeply divided, with a bitterness that couldn't be wiped away, and economically destroyed. So we didn't solve anything.

We have to take a new approach in the Third World, and I think not only in the Third World. I think the United States needs to get back to some of the fundamental principles on which this country was founded. Our foreign policy should be based on international law. We should try to work through multi-lateral organisations whenever possible. The fact that our Central American policy brought us to be condemned by the World Court I regard as humiliating. It never should have happened; that's not a position the United States ever should be in. In other words, I see Cuba as linked to all these things. It seems to me that when we can bring ourselves to deal rationally with Cuba, then that will probably be a sign that we are dealing more rationally on a much broader basis, and that is what I think we should all be working towards.

But to end on a pessimistic note, despite the fact that Mr Bush has said it's going to be a 'gentler, kinder nation', and although there has been some improvement in Central America – I mean, we are now talking about some support for the Esquipulas Plan,* and we have suspended military assistance to the Contras. But I think that's only because the Bush administration knows they couldn't have gotten that aid out of the Congress anyway. Although there has been some improvement, there hasn't been any major change. The Bush administration continues basically to follow the lines of the Reagan administration. In fact, in dealing with the Soviet Union they have been more, well, how should I put it? They have dug in their heels, they are even slower, they are even less forthcoming than the Reagan administration, and, certainly, when it comes to US–Cuban relations, I see really almost no reason to be optimistic.

* A Central American regional peace plan put forward by President Oscar Arias of Costa Rica and signed by Costa Rica, Nicaragua, Honduras, El Salvador and Guatemala at Esquipulas, Guatemala, on 7 August 1987.

32

Jorge Domínguez

Jorge I. Domínguez is Professor of Government at the Center for International Affairs, Harvard University, and author of Cuba: Order and Revolution *(1978). Born in Havana, he came to the United States with his parents when he was a teenager. He is an acknowledged Cuba expert. He spoke, in English, about the future of Cuba just before the momentous events of Eastern Europe took place.*

3 November 1989

I think one of the interesting features about this particular moment is what is happening with younger Cubans. One, there is a sense that life is not very exciting if you are thirteen years old; that there could be other exciting things, and that these other exciting things seem to be associated with a world that Cuba does not encourage, whether it be music or jeans and things of this sort. The second aspect of it is that many of these kids – and this is understandable, I think, in any society – tend not to be very reflective about their life's conditions. They do assume and take for granted many of the things that only the Revolution made possible: that they are in school; that they can probably go to the university; that if they get sick they can have reasonable health-care. So that in many ways what is interesting, I think, is that the alienation of the young is made possible by the successes of the Revolution. Surely, this must drive crazy a Communist Party official in Cuba or a government official who would like the young to appreciate how hard it was to have educational opportunities and health.

So, what I think is interesting as Cuba reaches the end of the 1980s is that it is the very successes of many of the social policies from which youngsters have benefited that enables them to desire other things, because they do not have to worry about other things that young kids elsewhere in the Third World worry about. Nonetheless, once you have alienated kids, you have a serious social problem. Alienated kids can also make for alienated young adults, if you project ten years into the future. The social base of the Revolution to continue to support the themes of sacrifice, hard work, work toward the future, I think have very little support among young Cubans today, and thus the future of societal backing for Fidel's revolutionary project is, I think, weakening markedly after thirty years of being exhorted to be virtuous. Well, you can do that for a while, but after a while you don't want to do it, and for the young, they don't see any reason to do it.

Cuba without Fidel is much more likely to have a leadership that will believe it has to be responsive to the society. Fidel thinks that he can be the master leader, the great teacher, the shaper who can resist these trends in the society. I cannot imagine any successor, including his brother Raúl, who would feel that he can resist the demand of the society for more consumer goods, for better quality products, for a greater role for market forces, under a recognisably socialist framework. The kind of ideological commitment Fidel has, I cannot, frankly, believe will survive him.

What might these socialist options be?

Well, the ones most readily acceptable in Cuba by others in the leadership, the ones that are least radical because Cuba had been experimenting with them. Instead of having former Central Planning Board president Humberto Pérez to be a man in disgrace, he could be recognised as the only person who made the Cuban economy grow at any moment of the past thirty years. I do not want to appear to be defending everything that Humberto Pérez might have done, but only under his tenure has the Cuban economy grown. The Cuban economy did not grow in the 1960s. Humberto Pérez had no role. The Cuban economy has not been growing in the second half of the 1980s. The only time the Cuban economy has grown is when that man was in charge of it. That there were many problems under his economic stewardship, of course. That there were things that were made badly, mistakes in the adoption of policies, to be sure. But in the Cuban context of thirty years, this was the only man who made that economy grow. So a return to the very limited, modified market practices under what was unmistakably a centrally planned socialist economy is something I think Cuban leaders in the 1990s or later, after Fidel in any event, would think is plausible. Now, whether Cuban leaders would go further and adopt the kinds of economic reforms that China adopted over the past ten years, or that are being adopted even more vigorously in Hungary today, or being experimented on in Poland and the Soviet Union, that's a little harder to say. But it would seem to me that at a minimum there would be a return to the modified market principles of the Humberto Pérez period.

How much would change in Cuba depend upon relations with the US?

Well, for any Cuban economic development strategy in the future, there has to be better economic relations with countries other than the Soviet Union and Eastern Europe. In part because just simply the dynamism of the Cuban economy would require those relations. Whether that would require economic relations with the United States . . . I am prepared for the thought that that is not politically feasible. The question is whether the Cuban economy under better management can export more, export better quality products, export things other than sugar-cane, which it could sell to the Netherlands, to Japan, to Sweden, to the United Kingdom, perhaps even to Ireland, in the thought that it would have a more diversified base to earn hard currency. There is no doubt that life in Cuba economically would be much easier if Cuba could have economic relations with the United States, even if the economic relations were relatively modest. But if I were a Cuban Communist

Party member, I would not want to plan for Cuba's future on the premise of significant US–Cuban relations. I think it would be nice, but I don't think it is politically feasible in the foreseeable future. The key, therefore, is to have a Cuba that can earn its way, which it does not do now, and that can earn its way by trading, exporting quality products in the non-sugar sector to other countries of the world that are not the socialist countries and that is not the United States.

They are trying to do that with tourism. That is a good strategy. The development of tourism as a source of hard currency earnings, however – this is not to make a political point – is not possible unless Cuba changes its current political–economic model. You cannot keep tourists bottled up in enclaves. You simply cannot increase the number of tourists – roughly, I think the number now is perhaps 100,000 a year, maybe more, from hard currency countries, and multiply that by five: half a million tourists per year – and think that it will have no effect on the rest of your society. Unless you are prepared to have the rest of your society accept the proposition that it does not make you a bad person to like some high-quality consumer goods, unless that is a politically feasible thing, then the idea of developing the tourist industry at some point would become an enormous source of political, social and ideological conflict.

I happen to think that liking access to high-quality consumer goods does not make me a bad person, and therefore I have no reason to think that it would be so hard for other Cubans. But it is very hard for Fidel. And in a way he thinks about the development of tourism as in enclaves – in Varadero, or on the little islands off Camagüey province where Europeans can go take their clothes off when they lie out in the sun. You cannot insulate all of that for ever, from the rest of Cuba. So that's the problem of the tourist industry. It's not that it's a bad idea, it's a very good idea. It is that it has political consequences that Fidel has not been willing to recognise.

At the moment it is a very corrupting force. But it is a corrupting force in part because they have created norms which no Western tourism of any real magnitude can abide by. I mean Western tourism, by the very nature of what it is, when they go to a place in the Caribbean [they] want to lie in the sun, enjoy themselves, want to be hedonistic for at least one week or two weeks of the year, would like some entertainment other than a heavy political lecture about the meaning of the march of history, and, for heaven's sakes, that's what tourism is about. The people who are doing this may like to go to a museum and they may like, you know, to tour some historical places. They may like to see some of the social and economic and political experiments under way in Cuba, but maybe one day out of a week, and the rest of the week what they want is swimming and sunshine and the like. The norms of austerity are not the norms to which tourists respond. That is not why one becomes a tourist.

I think the Spaniards are betting on the Cuban government backing off from some of the more austere norms; that the rewards to the Cuban national treasury from the development of tourism will be sufficiently high that when it is faced with the conflict between the corrupting effects of tourism – corrupting only because of the way the Cubans have set up their society – and the hard currency earnings, the Cubans will relax some of these constraints. It's a bet, but after all, the investments of any capitalist firms require some risk-taking, and the Spaniards are earning a fair amount of profit in part because the risk is high.

Tourism is corrupting in most Third World contexts.

I agree, I agree. Having been a tourist myself, even trying to be a reasonably well-behaved one, it is at odds in Third World settings with the standard of living of ordinary people. There is simply no way that one can avoid the manifestation of differences in income, the standard of living and the like. There is by nature, in a Third World setting, a sharp contrast between the facilities necessary for tourism to serve an international elite, and the conditions of the poor. But Cuba has very few means, economic means, over the next five or six years to develop its economy, and one of them is tourism. And it probably would be better, healthier, if that were not an industry they would have to develop. But because the Cuban economy is so grossly inefficient across virtually every item except sugar, they have to go for the very few things they can do relatively quickly. And one of them is, they are blessed by sunshine and good beaches. So, it is something that can be developed. If I had the political objectives that Cuban leaders have, tourism would not have been my choice as an engine for economic growth because it has a great many – not just in a socialist Third World country, but in any Third World country – a great many bad effects with inequalities manifested to the worst degree. I don't think they think they have any choice, and I agree. I think that this is the right decision. It is unfortunate that it is the right decision.

Will there be improved political relations with the US?

My sense is that improved political relations, and therefore improved economic relations, with the United States are not something I can foresee, and it could change tomorrow or in a couple of years from now, but I would not want to bet that they would change before the end of the century, just to give you a faraway date.

Why is the US so hostile towards Cuba?

Perhaps the easiest function is that it provides a sturdy and effective tie between the Bush administration and those that it perceives lead the Cuban-American community and deliver significant support in elections in the State of Florida and nationally. I think that's one reason. I think the more interesting reason, and I think it is one that has merit, is that as the Cold War with the Soviet Union recedes there is within the administration and within the Republican Party, I think, a felt ideological need to find a left-over enemy; to find a need to maintain a degree of ideological militance which is a significant feature among conservatives in the United States, and Cuba and Nicaragua are now the only two communist countries that play that role. Not even Vietnam plays that role any longer. And so you witness in the United States that the Republican right has been galvanised by this last, as they put it, bastion of Stalinism, by the one unreconstructed old-style socialist leader who does not believe in perestroika, who does not believe in the market reforms that Deng Xiaoping believes in in China, and you witness in Washington and in the Congress remarkable efforts to reactivate all the hostilities toward Cuba, whether it's through TV Martí or tightening up the embargo, that I think are frankly inexplicable except as a reaction to the reduction of conflict with the Soviet Union.

Some of these things were there before. Just to illustrate – the tightening up of the embargo. Well, what they are trying to reverse is what was adopted in 1975 as the policy of the United States under a good card-carrying Republican administration. Gerry Ford was President, Henry Kissinger was Secretary of State, and they came to the view that to attempt to impose the US embargo on US subsidiaries operating out of Canada, US subsidiaries operating out of Argentina, made no sense. No sense generally for US foreign policy objectives. What they are now trying to do is reverse that. What they are now trying to say is that it will be the policy of the United States to go after what are really Canadian companies, what are Argentinian companies, what are French companies.*

So, sure, there have been these thaws before. This was even once the policy of the United States, but they are trying to reverse the clock to 1975. And that is new. That did not happen under Ronald Reagan. But take something like TV Martí – well, sure, that occurred under Ronald Reagan, but it has been activated as the only, the *only*, underline that word, ideological project of the Bush administration. This administration couldn't care less about much of ideology, except in the extent that it plays a political purpose, and Cuba is one of those. Cuba and Nicaragua are those rare examples where practical politics feed and are fed by ideological politics.

---

* This refers to the Mack Amendment – proposed by congressman Connie Mack (Rep. Fla) – attached to the Omnibus Export Amendments Act of 1990, which would, if it had been passed, effectively block US subsidiaries in third countries from trading with Cuba. Congress passed the Act but President Bush withheld approval on the grounds 'that it would severely constrain presidential authority in carrying out foreign policy'.

What effect will changes in the Soviet Union have on Cuba, and what do you make of the banning of Moscow News *and* Sputnik *by Havana?*

Even if you assume the best of intentions on the part of the Soviet leaders and the most correct and proper behaviour on the part of the Soviet leaders in their dealings with Cuba, purely on the basis of the objective facts of the case, the news for Cuba is awful. The Soviet economy is in deep trouble; the Soviet government is facing an enormous budget deficit; the Soviet Union does not have resources to throw away, or even to give to what has been for many years a favoured ally, namely Cuba. Many of the economic changes and political changes in the Soviet Union, moreover, are creating severe dislocations and are making it difficult for the Soviet Union simply to meet its contract obligations with Cuba. In years past, the Soviets have criticised the Cubans for not meeting their commitments to deliver sugar and other products. It's now the Soviets that cannot meet their commitments. So, you know, even without imagining anything, any ill-will on the part of the Soviets or anyone advocating a cutback, the realities of the Soviet economy, present and foreseeable, make it very difficult even to maintain the existing level of economic support. That is why the circumstances, the international news, for Cuba is so bad, because there is no likely improvement in relations with the United States, and, even under the best conditions, the Soviet Union will need to reduce, in real terms, its assistance to Cuba. I don't expect the Soviets to leave Cuba high and dry. I don't think that the Soviet Union will want to make any drastic cuts. But they have to tell the Cubans that not only can they not continue at the same level, but they will have to reduce. What is at issue is to negotiate the circumstances, the terms, the amounts of the reduction in Soviet assistance.

I think the banning of *Sputnik* and *Moscow News* is one of the worst decisions that I have witnessed in Cuba in recent times. Worst for any number of reasons, all of which are obvious, but let me just mention them. One is, it has to be taken in the Soviet Union as an insult. The Soviets do not like those kinds of decisions, nor should they. Secondly, it suggests inside

Cuba intolerance towards ideas, even ideas expressed inside Cuba's premier ally, the Soviet Union, which does not augur well for the quality of normal political discussion inside Cuba. Thirdly, as much as I think the decision to ban these Soviet publications is a bad one, I would have understood it if it had been coupled with a means of fostering debate among Cubans about the issues raised by *Moscow News*, so that Cubans, among themselves, in their own terms, would be assessing these kinds of issues. It's not that *Moscow News*, after all, is the best publication in the world. It's not that its quality is so spectacular that the mind would be dulled if one could not read it. But the fact is *Moscow News*, and the content of what is carried, speaks to things that matter to socialist countries and that matter to Cuba. But the absence of creating, inside Cuba, magazines, journals, or even newspapers or occasional periodicals that would be legitimate and legal and that would address these issues, again speaks to a degree of intolerance that is extraordinary. Fourthly, another reason why it is a terrible decision: it suggests that the Cuban government thinks that it can block information, which is bizarre. It suggests that someone in the leadership – not excluding Fidel, because he must have participated in this decision – has lost touch with reality. After all, there are thousands of Cubans studying or working in the Soviet Union, in East Germany, in Czechoslovakia, in Hungary. These Cubans are going to come back. They will be infected by the virus that socialism need not be rigid, and they will write letters to their family, and they will eventually talk to their friends. There are tourists who come in, and even if they have limited contact with the Cubans, they will ask. There are even the couple of thousand Cuban-Americans that visit. There is Radio Martí broadcasting regularly about these things. The notion that the Cuban government could think that they could block out, by a crude act of censorship, the entry of this news is crazy. And it suggests that there is a process of thought and decision in the Cuban leadership that simply has lost touch with reality. So, it is a bad decision across the board – from foreign policy to the very nature of the capacity of socialists in Cuba to talk to each other, to what it tells you about a regime that acts in a dumb way.

What are the implications of the Ochoa drug scandal?★

An interesting question that no one will ever solve is, what did
Fidel know, and when did he know it? The same kind of question
that was posed in the Watergate scandal by Senator Howard Baker
with regard to Richard Nixon, and the same kinds of questions that
could be asked of Ronald Reagan about what he knew about the
Iran–Contra scandal and Oliver North. I am prepared to believe
that Fidel Castro did not know about what General Ochoa was
doing. And I confess that one of the reasons I lean to that is
because I think that intellectually and politically that raises the
most interesting issues. It would be easy and, in fact, sort of
boring if Fidel was a drug lord. I don't think there is really very
much chance of that. But if you take the other view, that Fidel is
not a drug lord, that he did not authorise this, that he really was
surprised, what does it say? It says that here is a political leader
who built a career by means of hands-on management, who now
cannot even keep up with the closest associates; that he can no
longer provide the minimal amount of supervision to what the
country's top general is doing and what the Ministry of the Interior
is doing. It tells you something about the malfunctioning of his
leadership and of the country's institutions. And that is the most
severe crisis *in* the regime. It's not a crisis *of* the regime.

The Cuban American National Foundation in Miami is not
about to take over power in Havana. There are not going to
be insurgencies. It's not a crisis *of* the regime. It's a crisis *in* the
regime: that this remarkable man, astute, clever, effective and
charming, lost touch with reality – in banning *Moscow News*, not
knowing what Arnaldo Ochoa was up to and not knowing what
General Abrantes was up to. This is what is worrisome. This is
what is worrisome. What had rescued Cuba over the past thirty
years from disasters of one sort or another is that Fidel was a
magician, he could pull the trick out of the hat. Well, someone
who doesn't even know what his closest associates are doing can't
pull rabbits out of a hat. Or the rabbit that he might pull out of
a hat is not a rabbit I would want to have nearby. It could be

★ See p.303.

some dumb decision like banning *Moscow News*. So, I think that the assumption that he did not know is one that I find credible. Castro has never been motivated by money. If we know anything about him it's that he is a radical in that sense. So, I'm prepared to believe that he did not know and it's for that reason that I find this a trauma.

Further Reading

Medea Benjamin, Joseph Collins and Michael Scott, *No Free Lunch: Food and Revolution in Cuba Today*. San Francisco, Food First, 1984

Frei Betto, *Fidel and Religion*. Sydney, Pathfinder, 1986

Peter Bourne, *Castro, A Biography of Fidel Castro*. Basingstoke, Macmillan, 1987

Philip Brenner, *From Confrontation to Negotiation: US Relations with Cuba*. Boulder, Colorado, PACCA/Westview Press, 1984

Philip Brenner, William M. LeoGrande, Donna Rich, Daniel Siegel, *The Cuba Reader: The Making of a Revolutionary Society*. New York, Grove Press, 1989

Fidel Castro, *Speeches*. 3 vols. New York, Pathfinder, 1981–5

Fidel Castro, *In Defence of Socialism: Four Speeches on the 30th Anniversary of the Revolution*. New York, Pathfinder, 1989

Noam Chomsky, *Turning the Tide: US Intervention in Central America and the Struggle for Peace*. Boston, Pluto Press, 1985

Joan Didion, *Miami*. London, Weidenfeld & Nicolson, 1988

Carlos Franqui, *Family Portrait with Fidel*. 2nd edn. New York, Random House, 1984

Che Guevara and the Cuban Revolution: Writings and Speeches of Ernesto Che Guevara. New York, Pathfinder, 1987

Che Guevara, *Guerrilla Warfare*. Manchester, Manchester University Press, 1986

Hildebrand's Travel Guide, *Cuba*. Frankfurt, K+G, KARTO+GRAFIK, 1985

William M. LeoGrande, *Cuba's Policy in Africa, 1959–1980.*
Berkeley, CA: Institute for International Studies, 1980
Peter Marshall, *Cuba Libre: Breaking the Chains?* London, Victor
Gollancz, 1987
Lionel Martin, *The Early Fidel: Roots of Castro's Communism.*
Secaucus, N.J., Lyle Stuart, 1978
Herbert L. Matthews, *Castro: A Political Biography.* London, Penguin, 1969
Hugh O'Shaughnessy, *Latin Americans.* London, BBC Books, 1988
Jenny Pearce, *Under the Eagle.* London, Latin American Bureau, updated edn. 1982
David Rieff, *Going to Miami.* London, Bloomsbury, 1987
Rius, *Cuba for Beginners.* London, Writers & Readers, 1977
Wayne Smith, *The Closest of Enemies: A Personal and Diplomatic History of the Castro Years.* New York, Norton, 1987
Jean Stubbs, *Cuba: The Test of Time.* London, Latin American Bureau, 1989
Tad Szulc, *Fidel: A Critical Portrait.* New York, William Morrow, 1986
Peter Wyden, *Bay of Pigs.* London, Jonathan Cape, 1979

OTHER PUBLICATIONS
Cuba Business. 287 City Road, London, ECIV 1LA
Granma Weekly Review. Apartado Postal 6260, Havana 6, Cuba, C.P. 10699

A NOTE ON THE AUTHOR

Lynn Geldof was born in Ireland in 1947. She has travelled throughout
Central America working as a journalist, contributing to *The Irish
Times*, the *Guardian* and *Newsweek*, among others. She lived in Cuba
from 1985 to 1989. She now lives in Dublin.